Between One and Many

THE ART AND SCIENCE OF PUBLIC SPEAKING

Fourth Edition

Steven R. Brydon

Michael D. Scott
California State University, Chico

Boston   Burr Ridge, IL   Dubuque, IA   Madison, WI   New York
San Francisco   St. Louis   Bangkok   Bogotá   Caracas   Kuala Lumpur
Lisbon   London   Madrid   Mexico City   Milan   Montreal   New Delhi
Santiago   Seoul   Singapore   Sydney   Taipei   Toronto

McGraw-Hill Higher Education

A Division of The McGraw-Hill Companies

Copyright © 2003 by The McGraw-Hill Companies, Inc. All rights reserved. Printed in the United States of America. Except as permitted under the United States Copyright Act of 1976, no part of this publication may be reproduced or distributed in any form or by any means, or stored in a database or retrieval system, without the prior written permission of the publisher.

1 2 3 4 5 6 7 8 9 0 VNH/VNH 0 9 8 7 6 5 4 3 2

Library of Congress Cataloging-in-Publication Data
Brydon, Steven Robert.
    Between one and many : the art and science of public speaking / Steven R. Brydon,
Michael D. Scott.—4th ed.
        p. cm.
    Includes bibliographical references and index.
    ISBN 0-7674-3015-8
      1. Public speaking. I. Scott, Michael D. II. Title.

PN4129.15 .B79 2002
808.5'1—dc21

2002023083

Publisher, Phillip A. Butcher; sponsoring editor, Nanette Kauffman; developmental editor, Nancy Lubars; production editor, Holly Paulsen; manuscript editor, Judith Brown; design manager, Jeanne M. Schreiber; cover designer, Cassandra Chu; art editor, Emma Ghiselli; text designer, Ellen Pettengell; photo researcher, Brian Pecko; production supervisor, Pam Augspurger; media producer, Jessica Bodie. The text was set in 10.5/12 Goudy by Thompson Type and printed on acid-free 45# Publishers Matte by Von Hoffmann Corporation.

Text credits appear on pages 421–422, which constitutes a continuation of the copyright page.

Cover art © Lauren Uram.

www.mhhe.com

To the memory of Jonathan Studebaker—who showed us that there is no obstacle in life that cannot be overcome with courage and determination.

Brief Contents

Contents

Preface

Public speaking is a dynamic transaction "between one and many"—between the one who is speaking and the many who are listening. The meaning of the message emerges from the relationship between speaker and audience. No speaker can succeed without knowing his or her audience, and no audience member can benefit by just passively receiving a message. Both speaker and audience—and the transaction between them—are essential to the process. As teachers and as authors, we focus on the transactional nature of successful public speaking.

Public speaking is also an art, a science, and a skill—one that can be learned, improved, and polished. We encourage students to think of public speaking as a learning experience—they don't have to be perfect at the outset! We also encourage students to think of their speech transactions as a refined extension of their everyday conversations, and we offer them the tools to become the speakers they want to be. Public speakers can draw on a vast body of information, ranging from classical rhetorical theories to empirical communication research. In this book we include traditional topics, such as logos, ethos, and pathos as the roots of persuasive speaking, and current ones, such as research on cultural diversity and the uses of technology in public speaking.

Today's students of public speaking will face many different speech situations in their lives, and they will face audiences of increasing cultural, demographic, and individual diversity. Throughout this book, we focus on ways to adapt to audiences in order to have the best chance of being heard and understood. We stress the responsibilities and ethical issues involved in being a good public speaker. And we discuss how to be a good audience member: one who knows how to listen, to behave ethically, and to critically evaluate the message being presented. In sum, we attempt to provide students with a broad understanding of the nature of public speaking as well as the specific skills they need to become successful, effective public speakers, both as college students and throughout their lives.

FEATURES OF THE BOOK

Integrated Text and CD-ROM   This is the most interactive edition to date of *Between One and Many*. We provide you with an integrated package of text and CD-ROM for the students. This Speech Coach CD brings to life the theories and skills discussed in the text. Rather than simply reading examples of speeches and perhaps seeing them in class, students can view and study speeches and delivery styles on their own time, at their own pace, and in their own space.

Text and CD are coordinated so that students can see examples of the type of speech they are studying throughout the course. This technique allows us to reinforce our points through modeling, which research has shown to be an excellent way to learn skills like public speaking. Not only does the Speech Coach CD provide several speeches for students to view and analyze, but it also provides a wide range of learning tools, such as Audio Tips and Tactics and Key Terms Flashcards with audio, and supporting software, including Outline Tutor and PowerPoint Tutorial.

The concepts and skills required for effective public speaking are fully described and illustrated in the text. Annotated outlines of student speeches show students how to apply the principles discussed in the book to actual speech situations. The full texts of several speeches, including those by public figures, are also included in the appendices.

Integrated Pedagogy   Throughout the text, boxes are used to focus attention on subjects of special interest. Five different types of boxes appear: Profile boxes offer examples of individuals who have used public speaking in their lives; In Their Own Words boxes provide examples of speeches by students and public figures, including several student speeches in outline form with marginal comments; Self-Assessment boxes allow students to assess their own skills and attributes (such as speech anxiety); Considering Diversity boxes show how the topic of a chapter applies to today's multicultural, multiracial, and multiethnic audiences. They not only add to the discussion of diversity throughout the book, but also challenge students to think about diversity as it specifically applies to the topics covered in a given chapter. Speaking of . . . boxes contain current, topical information that relates to the text discussion. Throughout the book, speechmaking skills are highlighted in special lists labeled "Tips and Tactics." These lists make it easy for students to apply practical suggestions to their own speeches. Speech Coach icons in the margins call attention to corresponding video segments and other CD features.

Help for Speech Anxiety   We recognize that many students come to a public speaking class with some trepidation. As was the case in the earlier editions, we devote a full chapter early in the text to speech anxiety. Speech anxiety and speech anxiety reduction skills are also featured in the CD-ROM. Because research continues to inform us about speech anxiety, we have also updated our treatment of the topic, making sure that speech anxiety is explained as being distinct from stage fright and communication apprehension. Finally, the text and interactive CD-ROM offer many specific, concrete techniques that students can use to productively manage and channel their anxiety.

Emphasis on Adapting to Audience Diversity   We give significant attention to audience diversity based, in part, on Geert Hofstede's work on understanding cultural diversity. Using Hofstede's dimensions of collectivism and individualism, power distance, uncertainty avoidance, masculinity and femininity, and long-term versus short-term orientation, we offer ideas on how to analyze and adapt to audience diversity across cultures. By the same token, diversity encompasses more than culture. Thus, we also offer specific tips and tactics students can use to analyze and adapt to the demographic and individual diversity in their audience.

Full Chapter on Ethics   We feature a full chapter on ethics. Working from classical and contemporary notions about what constitutes ethical behavior, we provide and reinforce ethical guidelines for both public speakers and audience members.

Emphasis on Critical Thinking   Central to effective and ethical communication are the abilities to critically evaluate evidence, to present sound reasoning in speeches, and to detect fallacious reasoning in the speeches of others. *Between One and Many* continues to provide a strong critical thinking component, based on Toulmin's model of argument.

HIGHLIGHTS OF THE FOURTH EDITION

Based on the feedback from many instructors who used the third edition, we have incorporated a number of changes into this edition to strengthen the book. We have tried to make *Between One and Many* even more accessible to the reader, without compromising the intellectual integrity of its content. Throughout the book we have worked to prune jargon, provide specific advice on how to deal with various situations faced by speakers, and to update examples so that they are relevant to students in the 21st century. For example, President Bush's address to the Joint Session of Congress and the American people in the aftermath of September 11, 2001, is included in Appendix B.

Revised Models   We have revised and improved the model of communication in the first chapter so that it better illustrates the public speaking transaction. A new model student speech in Chapter 2 better illustrates the principles of organization used throughout the book. Our discussion of persuasion better connects classical rhetorical principles with contemporary social science research, and we have revised our presentation of the Elaboration Likelihood Model so that it is more readily applied to persuasive speaking.

Updated Discussion of Speech Anxiety   Our treatment of managing speech anxiety has been updated to include the latest research. We clearly distinguish speech anxiety from communication apprehension, and point out how speech anxiety is both more common and more easily managed than communication apprehension. Since so many competent actors and entertainers report that they are speech anxious, moreover, we clearly make speech anxiety distinct from stage fright as well.

Revised Treatment of Audience Adaptation   We have thoroughly revised Chapter 5, to place the emphasis squarely on audience analysis and adaptation to the results of such analysis. Specific recommendations of how to deal with audience diversity are made throughout the chapter. We also have tried to make sure that the emphasis on audience adaptation is reintroduced and reinforced in all subsequent chapters.

Using the Internet for Research   Recognizing that most students already know *how* to use the World Wide Web, we have shifted our concern to *evaluating* what they find there. We offer specific examples of bogus Web sites, and tips on how to avoid them.

PowerPoint Use and Misuse   We have updated and revised our treatment of Microsoft PowerPoint, recognizing its increased prevalence in the workplace, but also recognizing the danger of overuse and misuse. A specific discussion of some of the perils of misusing technology has been added. In addition, the Speech Coach CD contains a PowerPoint tutorial, so that students can learn how to constructively use the software on their own.

More Student Speeches   We have increased the number of student speeches in several chapters, both in the text and on the Speech Coach CD. The CD now includes a speech of introduction and a storytelling speech. We have a new and improved "first speech" in Chapter 2. In the discussion of informative speaking, we offer two student speeches, one dealing with a fairly complex topic and the other a more concrete demonstration. The chapter on critical thinking (Chapter 14) remains a major focus, with updated examples of fallacies of reasoning. We provide a side-by-side comparison of two student speeches taking the opposite position on a controversial issue. The complete video of these speeches is on the Speech Coach CD.

Expanded Tips and Tactics   Students have found the Tips and Tactics sections in each chapter to be particularly useful. We have expanded their use and kept them to half-page sections, which provide ready advice to student speakers on a wide range of topics. There is an audio Tips and Tactics on the Speech Coach CD to further emphasize these important hints.

ORGANIZATION OF THE TEXT

The basic chapter structure of the fourth edition remains unchanged, allowing an easy transition for teachers accustomed to the third edition. *Between One and Many* is organized to allow students to get up and speak early in the semester. As they learn more about the art and science of public speaking, they are also preparing for more demanding speaking assignments. We hope that our organizational scheme will suit the needs of most instructors, but we also know that different instructors have different preferences for how material is sequenced. Therefore, we have designed each chapter to stand alone. Instructors can assign them in the order that best matches their own course plan.

Part One deals with the foundations of the art and science of public speaking. Chapter 1, retitled "Practical Speaking," focuses on the personal, professional, and public reasons for becoming a good public speaker, with specific examples of average people who use public speaking in their daily lives. We also introduce a revised model of public speaking and preview the remainder of the book. Chapter 2 provides an overview of the skills needed by public speakers and allows instructors to assign speeches early without having to assign chapters out of order. Topic selection and writing purpose statements have been incorporated into this chapter to provide an early foundation for students in preparing their first speeches. Chapter 3 provides students with the tools they need to cope with the nearly universal experience of speech anxiety. Chapter 4 presents a thorough treatment of listening, with a focus on listening to public speeches.

Part Two deals directly with adapting to the audience. We make explicit that the key to success in public speaking is focusing on the audience. Chapter 5 provides the tools for analyzing the cultural, demographic, and individual diversity of audience members. In addition, emphasis has been placed on offering practical suggestions for adapting speeches to audiences once the analysis has been completed. Chapter 6 thoroughly discusses ethical communication behavior, both by speakers and by audience members, with a detailed treatment of the problem of plagiarism.

Part Three is about putting theory into practice. Chapter 7 covers researching and supporting the speech. In recognition of the fact that most students already use the Internet, but often without applying critical standards to the information they find, we have emphasized how to distinguish reliable from unreliable Internet sources. Chapter 8 treats organization from an audience-focused perspective. We include a variety of organizational patterns, such as Monroe's motivated sequence, the extended narrative, problem–solution, and stock issues, and discuss nontraditional patterns of organization and delivery such as the star, wave, spiral, and call and response. Material dealing with transitional statements is also located in this chapter. Chapter 9 addresses language use, with particular attention to adapting language to diverse audiences. We suggest ways to choose language that is inclusive rather than exclusive, nonsexist rather than sexist, and thoughtful rather than stereotypic. We have also expanded the discussion of particular techniques for enhancing the effective use of language. Chapter 10 deals with delivery skills, again focusing on audience adaptation. This chapter provides both a strong theoretical foundation based in nonverbal communication research and solid, practical advice for the public speaker. Chapter 11 presents a comprehensive discussion of visual, audio, and audiovisual media that can be adapted to the audience and occasion to enhance most public speeches. Our discussion of PowerPoint has been updated for this edition, with an emphasis on using it to enhance public speaking, *not substitute for it*. The Speech Coach CD has a PowerPoint tutorial that will allow students to learn the mechanics in an interactive fashion.

Part Four addresses the most common contexts for public speaking that students are likely to face in the classroom and in their lives after college. Chapter 12 treats informative speaking. In this chapter we again stress audience adaptation, particularly in terms of diverse learning styles. Practical applications of learning principles are shown for speeches that explain, instruct, demonstrate, and describe. Chapter 13, dealing with persuasive speaking, has been significantly revised. The Elaboration Likelihood Model is made more accessible to students with a revised illustration and an expanded discussion of its application to public speaking. Chapter 14 provides detailed treatment of critical thinking, with a special focus on recognizing and responding to fallacies of reasoning. A side-by-side comparison of arguments taken from student speeches helps students hone their own critical thinking skills. Finally, Chapter 15 provides a discussion of speaking throughout the student's lifetime. It includes helpful guidelines for impromptu speaking; speeches of acceptance, introduction, recognition, and commemoration; speeches to entertain; speaking on television; and speaking in small groups.

TEACHING SUPPORT PACKAGE

The textbook is part of a comprehensive package designed to help you solve teaching problems in your public speaking course.

Instructor's Manual   Written by the authors and updated by Rachel Holloway, Virginia Tech University, the Instructor's Manual includes a variety of useful resources, such as strategies for managing multisection courses, a primer for graduate assistants and first-time teachers, and lists for quick reference of the speechmaking skills highlighted in each chapter. Revision of the manual has included new materials for the sections offering in-class activities, sample semester and quarter syllabi, sample evaluation forms, and transparency masters. The contents of the manual are based on the authors' collective four decades of teaching experience; many of the activities and materials have been class tested with the thousands of students enrolled in the basic public speaking course at California State University, Chico.

Printed and Computerized Test Items   Approximately 1,500 test questions, including multiple choice, true-false, and essay questions, are included in the Instructor's Manual. As with other materials in the instructor's package, many of these test items have been class tested. The complete test bank is also available in computerized format, allowing you to edit the questions from the test bank and to incorporate your own questions. The computerized test bank is available in both Windows and Macintosh formats.

Transparencies   Overhead color transparencies are available free of charge to adopting instructors. The transparencies illustrate and review major concepts from the text.

Web Site   Instructors will have password-protected access to a Web site at www.mhhe.com/brydon, where they will find additional supportive materials. Included in the Web site are a number of useful pedagogical aids for the instructor, including PowerPoint slides, a syllabus generator, the Instructor's Manual, activities, a bulletin board, and guidelines for first-time teachers. Students will have access to a Web site that will offer chapter quizzes, crossword puzzles using key terms, and a number of useful links to other Web sites that can assist students in developing their speeches.

Speech Coach CD   The old two-hour VHS videotape that accompanied the first three editions of *Between One and Many* has been adapted to a new format. It is now contained on a two-CD set that all students will receive with their book. In addition to the many video segments, the CD contains a number of interactive learning features for students. Chapter quizzes, flashcards, speech critique software, outlining assistance, a PowerPoint tutorial, and other materials are either on the CD itself or on the Online Learning Center, which is linked to the CD.

The Speech Coach CD allows us to show what most texts only talk about. It also frees up valuable class time for the instructor and students to use in other ways. Each segment can be viewed independently of the others and is coordinated with a specific chapter in the text. Speech Coach icons in the margins of the book indicate where a particular video segment would be appropriate. The CD not only reinforces the text but also previews material to be covered later in more depth. In addition to the CD, the video segments will be available to instructors on a VHS videotape that can be shown in class.

Small Group Communication Supplement   A 50-page supplement is available for those who wish to add a group presentation assignment to their class.

ACKNOWLEDGMENTS

We gratefully acknowledge the support and assistance of many people at McGraw-Hill who played a role in this book, including Nanette Kauffman, sponsoring editor; Nancy Lubars, developmental editor; Jessica Bodie, media producer; Holly Paulsen, project manager; Jeanne Schreiber, design manager and art director; Emma Ghiselli, art editor; Brian Pecko, photo researcher; Pam Augspurger, production supervisor; Melissa Williams, managing editor; Robin Mouat, art manager; and Judith Brown, manuscript editor.

We are especially grateful to George Rogers, of Chico State, who produced the video segments of the Speech Coach CD that accompanies this text, and to the numerous students who consented to be videotaped for this project. Special thanks go to the speakers who shared their talents in providing sample speeches: Jonathan Studebaker, Kyle Soler, Shelly Lee, Karen Shirk, Miranda Welsh, Evan Mironov, Josette Parker, Lorenmarie Manning, and David A. Sanders. We would also like to thank the individuals profiled in this book for generously consenting to contribute to our effort: Jonathan Studebaker, Keith Hawkins, Enrique "Rick" Rigsby, Tomoko Mukawa, Jeraline Singh, and Russ Woody. They are friends, colleagues, former students, and role models; they have all enriched our book and our lives. We also thank Dr. Nichola Gutgold of Penn State Berks-Lehigh Valley College, Lehigh Valley Campus, for contributing her profile of Elizabeth Dole.

A grateful thank you for the reviews and counsel of our peers in the classroom who graciously prepared careful critiques of our manuscript and videotape in various stages of development:

Sandra L. Alspach, Ferris State University

Carol Bledsoe, University of Central Florida

Jeanette Brossmann, Lakeland Community College

Robert Greenstreet, East Central University (Oklahoma)

Nichola Gutgold, Penn State Lehigh Valley

Pamela Hopkins, East Carolina University

Barbara Ann Mastrolia, Indiana University Northwest

Patricia J. Palm, Minnesota State University

Bruce W. Russell, Slippery Rock University

Jennifer H. Waldeck, University of Kansas

Nancy Wendt, Oregon State University

We appreciate the help of all these individuals in preparing this book, but we are, of course, ultimately responsible for its content. Any errors or omissions are solely our own.

And last, but certainly not least, we wish to thank our families, Pamela, Robert, Julie, Randi, and Colin, who not only showed great patience as we worked on this project but often provided assistance in more ways than we can possibly list.

Between One and Many . . .

About the Authors

Mike Scott and Steve Brydon

STEVEN R. BRYDON
California State University, Chico

Steve Brydon is a professor at California State University, Chico, where he teaches public speaking, argumentation, communication criticism, and political communication. He coached forensics for twelve years and served as department chair for ten years over two separate terms. He has co-authored three books, and has also published in the areas of political communication, and argumentation and debate.

MICHAEL D. SCOTT
California State University, Chico

After receiving his Ph.D. from the University of Southern California, Mike Scott served as a member of the Communication and Educational Psychology department at the University of West Virginia. While at West Virginia, he co-authored two books; the first dealt with interpersonal communication, and the other—a first of its kind—discussed communication in the classroom. In 1977 he was named Outstanding Teacher at the University of West Virginia. For the past 18 years Mike has taught at California State University, Chico. He began in the Center for Information and Communication Studies, where he served as director. Most recently, Mike has been a member of the faculty in the department of Communication Arts and Sciences.

presents public speaking as a **living** and dynamic transaction between the speaker and the listener

Approach

Between One and Many presents public speaking as a living and dynamic transaction in which the meaning of the message emerges from the relationship between the speaker and the audience. The goal is to get students to think critically about their communication as well as to emphasize the importance of considering the audience in speech preparation.

Between One and Many covers both the art and the science of public speaking by integrating classical rhetorical principles, contemporary communication, and social-science research. This balance of the skills derived from theory and research and the actual practice of those skills provides students with the tools necessary to develop and organize their speeches, manage speech anxiety, anticipate and prepare for presenting speeches, and become both competent speakers and skillful listeners.

Between One and Many offers ideas on how to analyze and adapt to audience diversity across cultures, individual diversity, and demographic diversity.

Brydon and Scott write from a contemporary and student-friendly point of view. Their inviting style is clear and concise and stimulates critical thinking by the student. The depth and variety of examples provide a full explanation of often difficult concepts.

What's New

The updated fourth edition of *Between One and Many* includes new student speeches and more of them, expanded treatment of Internet use, and increased coverage of the use and misuse of visual media including PowerPoint.

Between One and Many

demonstrates that public speaking is a refined and extended version of the **conversational skills** we put to use daily

Anxiety

In Chapter 3 an updated treatment of speech anxiety clearly distinguishes speech anxiety from communication apprehension and stage fright and shows students how speech anxiety influences preparation, delivery, and post-speech confidence.

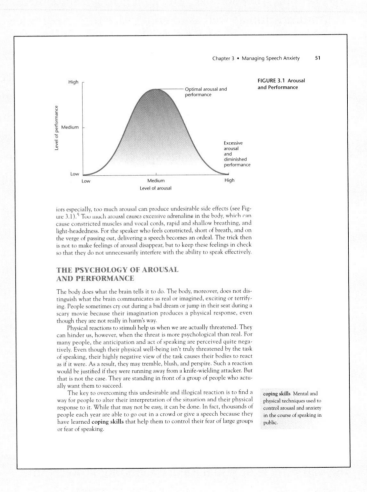

FIGURE 3.1 Arousal and Performance

ors especially, too much arousal can produce undesirable side effects (see Figure 3.1).[5] Too much arousal causes excessive adrenaline in the body, which can cause constricted muscles and vocal cords, rapid and shallow breathing, and light-headedness. For the speaker who feels constricted, short of breath, and on the verge of passing out, delivering a speech becomes an ordeal. The trick then is not to make feelings of arousal disappear, but to keep these feelings in check so that they do not unnecessarily interfere with the ability to speak effectively.

THE PSYCHOLOGY OF AROUSAL AND PERFORMANCE

The body does what the brain tells it to do. The body, moreover, does not distinguish what the brain communicates as real or imagined, exciting or terrifying. People sometimes cry out during a bad dream or jump in their seat during a scary movie because their imagination produces a physical response, even though they are not really in harm's way.

Physical reactions to stimuli help us when we are actually threatened. They can hinder us, however, when the threat is more psychological than real. For many people, the anticipation and act of speaking are perceived quite negatively. Even though their physical well-being isn't truly threatened by the task of speaking, their highly negative view of the task causes their bodies to react as if it were. As a result, they may tremble, blush, and perspire. Such a reaction would be justified if they were running away from a knife-wielding attacker. But that is not the case. They are standing in front of a group of people who actually want them to succeed.

The key to overcoming this undesirable and illogical reaction is to find a way for people to alter their interpretation of the situation and their physical response to it. While that may not be easy, it can be done. In fact, thousands of people each year are able to go out in a crowd or give a speech because they have learned **coping skills** that help them to control their fear of large groups or fear of speaking.

coping skills Mental and physical techniques used to control arousal and anxiety in the course of speaking in public.

New **Tips and Tactics** for managing speech anxiety, two Self-Assessment boxes, and three new tables for constructive self-talk offer concrete techniques that students can use to positively channel their anxiety.

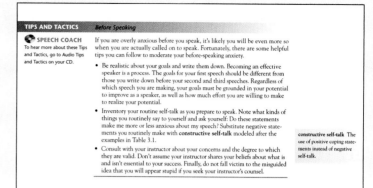

TIPS AND TACTICS *Before Speaking*

SPEECH COACH
To hear more about these Tips and Tactics, go to Audio Tips and Tactics on your CD.

If you are overly anxious before you speak, it's likely you will be even more so when you are actually called on to speak. Fortunately, there are some helpful tips you can follow to moderate your before-speaking anxiety.

- Be realistic about your goals and write them down. Becoming an effective speaker is a process. The goals for your first speech should be different from those you write down before your second and third speeches. Regardless of which speech you are making, your goals must be grounded in your potential to improve as a speaker, as well as how much effort you are willing to make to realize your potential.
- Inventory your routine self-talk as you prepare to speak. Note what kinds of things you routinely say to yourself and ask yourself: Do these statements make me more or less anxious about my speech? Substitute negative statements you routinely make with **constructive self-talk** modeled after the examples in Table 3.1.
- Consult with your instructor about your concerns and the degree to which they are valid. Don't assume your instructor shares your beliefs about what is and isn't essential to your success. Finally, do not fall victim to the misguided idea that you will appear stupid if you seek your instructor's counsel.

constructive self-talk The use of positive coping statements instead of negative self-talk.

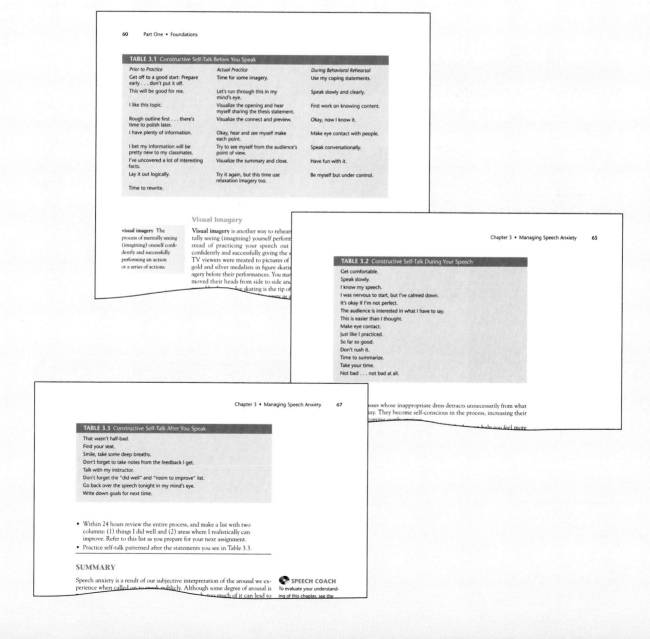

60   Part One • Foundations

TABLE 3.1 Constructive Self-Talk Before You Speak

Prior to Practice	Actual Practice	During Behavioral Rehearsal
Get off to a good start: Prepare early . . . don't put it off.	Time for some imagery.	Use my coping statements.
This will be good for me.	Let's run through this in my mind's eye.	Speak slowly and clearly.
I like this topic.	Visualize the opening and hear myself sharing the thesis statement.	First work on knowing content.
Rough outline first . . . there's time to polish later.	Visualize the connect and preview.	Okay, now I know it.
I have plenty of information.	Okay, hear and see myself make each point.	Make eye contact with people.
I bet my information will be pretty new to my classmates.	Try to see myself from the audience's point of view.	Speak conversationally.
I've uncovered a lot of interesting facts.	Visualize the summary and close.	Have fun with it.
Lay it out logically.	Try it again, but this time use relaxation imagery too.	Be myself but under control.
Time to rewrite.		

Visual Imagery

visual imagery The process of mentally seeing (imagining) oneself confidently and successfully performing an action or a series of actions.

Visual imagery is another way to rehear... tally seeing (imagining) yourself perform... stead of practicing your speech out... confidently and successfully giving the s... TV viewers were treated to pictures of... gold and silver medalists in figure skati... agery before their performances. You ma... moved their heads from side to side and... move their bodies. Ice skating is the tip of... ...very as a...

Chapter 3 • Managing Speech Anxiety   65

TABLE 3.2 Constructive Self-Talk During Your Speech

Get comfortable.
Speak slowly.
I know my speech.
I was nervous to start, but I've calmed down.
It's okay if I'm not perfect.
The audience is interested in what I have to say.
This is easier than I thought.
Make eye contact.
Just like I practiced.
So far so good.
Don't rush it.
Time to summarize.
Take your time.
Not bad . . . not bad at all.

...asses whose inappropriate dress detracts unnecessarily from what ...say. They become self-conscious in the process, increasing their ...coming overly anxious... ...help you feel more

Chapter 3 • Managing Speech Anxiety   67

TABLE 3.3 Constructive Self-Talk After You Speak

That wasn't half-bad.
Find your seat.
Smile, take some deep breaths.
Don't forget to take notes from the feedback I get.
Talk with my instructor.
Don't forget the "did well" and "room to improve" list.
Go back over the speech tonight in my mind's eye.
Write down goals for next time.

- Within 24 hours review the entire process, and make a list with two columns: (1) things I did well and (2) areas where I realistically can improve. Refer to this list as you prepare for your next assignment.
- Practice self-talk patterned after the statements you see in Table 3.3.

SUMMARY

Speech anxiety is a result of our subjective interpretation of the arousal we ex-perience when called on to speak publicly. Although some degree of arousal is ...too much of it can lead to...

SPEECH COACH
To evaluate your understand-ing of this chapter, see the

Between One and Many

provides students with the tools necessary to reach their audiences at **school,** in the **workplace,** and in the **community**

Considering Diversity

Considering Diversity boxes encourage students to understand and explore the effects of all aspects of diversity in order to help them become more competent speakers and listeners. These boxes discuss topics as they apply to today's multicultural, multiracial, multiethnic, and multigenerational audiences.

CONSIDERING DIVERSITY

Between Two Cultures: Tomoko Mukawa

Tomoko Mukawa was born in Japan and lived there until she was 15, when she first came to the United States as a high school exchange student. When she returned to the United States as a college student, Tomoko was struck by the differences in the way students and professors communicate in the two different cultures. Tomoko gives an example of differences between the two cultures:

I wanted to keep my fluency in Japanese, so I took a class from a Japanese professor. Although the American students were allowed to call the professor by his American nickname, I was required to follow the Japanese tradition of always using his title and surname. He stressed that, as a Japanese student, I needed to preserve my cultural heritage.

Tomoko also noticed that the language in which she spoke made a difference in how she was treated. As an English tutor for Japanese students coming to America, Tomoko discovered that when she spoke English she was perceived as more assertive than when she spoke Japanese. "You are like a different person when you speak Japanese," she was told by one of her students.

These experiences illustrate the differences between a large-power-distance culture like Japan and a small-power-distance culture like the United States. In Japan, students would never be familiar with professors, and women are generally not assertive. Simply speaking in her native language

changed the way Tomoko was perceived. Language and culture are closely intertwined, as her experience has shown.

For an example of how one Japanese student reacts to the culture of an American university, see the box "Between Two Cultures: Tomoko Mukawa."

Collectivism Versus Individualism   The second dimension common to all cultures is collectivism versus individualism. "Collectivism stands for a society in which people from birth onwards are integrated into strong, co[...] people's lifetime continue to protect them [...] holistic society on th[...]

CONSIDERING DIVERSITY

Cultures on the Web

One of the great advantages of the Internet is that it is a global phenomenon. You can literally read newspapers from anywhere in the world. You can send e-mail to and receive it from people on the other side of the globe. In fact, Dr. Madeline Keaveney, a professor at our university, established an e-mail pen-pal program with students in Japan for her intercultural communication class. The possibilities of learning about other cultures and sharing information with people from these cultures is endless.

Although there are Web sites that deal with Native American, Latino, Asian, and African American cultures, any list of these sites would be incomplete and

highly selective. Rather, we suggest that you do your own Internet surfing to learn about other cultures and then incorporate that information into your next speech. For starters, we suggest you try Yahoo!, which has numerous links dealing with society and culture (http://www.yahoo.com/Society_and_Culture/). For example, you can learn how different cultures deal with topics such as death and dying, disabilities, families, fashion, food and drink, gender, holidays, mythology and folklore, religion, sexuality, and weddings, just to name a few. So go ahead, reach out globally—from your own computer!

from the Internet because you have no assurance as to its reliability and verifiability. There have been instances of material being altered on the Net. As a speaker you have an ethical responsibility to ensure that such information is accurate, even if this requires tracking down the original source of the information. So, all the tests of supporting materials that apply to published materials apply doubly to sourc[...] Nevertheless, there is the advantage [...] uncensored, you can

In Their Own Words

In Their Own Words boxes provide sample student speech outlines, which serve as models for how to invent, organize, and develop a speech. These samples include marginal notes to help students focus on key elements. These boxes also have excerpts from speeches by prominent public speakers.

IN THEIR OWN WORDS

Sample Speech Outline

Title of speech.

GO SUN SMART
Shelly Lee

Specific purpose is to inform audience how to protect themselves.

General purpose: To inform
Specific purpose: To inform the audience how to protect themselves from deadly skin cancer.

Introduction

Speaker begins with rhetorical question.

I. **Open with impact:** How many of you can remember a sunburn so bad you could barely put your clothes on? How many of you have simply been burned while spending the day at the beach, tubing on the river, water skiing at the lake, or even skiing or riding your board on a fresh powder day at your favorite mountain?

Source is cited in parentheses. Your instructor may prefer a different method of citing sources.

   A. Did you know that there are over 1 million new cases of skin cancer each year in the United States, including over 51,000 cases of melanoma (Kalb, 2001)?

   B. Did you know that many of these cases can be directly linked to the cumulative effects of the sun?

   C. Did you know that there is no such thing as a safe tan, despite what the indoor tanning industry would like you to believe (Young and Walker, 1998)?

Speaker connects topic directly with audience members' experience.

II. **Connect with audience:** Every one of you who raised your hand needs to know that those sunburns you got put you at increased risk for skin cancer. Further, even if you've never burned or you are dark skinned, the information I'll share in a moment is important to you as well.

Thesis statement is clearly labeled.

III. **Thesis:** Skin cancer is not only the fastest growing form of cancer in the United States, it also is one of the easiest forms of cancer to prevent (American Cancer Society, 1996).

Preview of speech is provided.

IV. **Preview:** As a result, I'd like to look at three important things we all need to know to reduce our risk for skin cancer. First, there are three basic forms of skin cancer. Second, skin cancer is all too often a by-product of too much fun in the sun. And third, you can reduce your risk for developing skin cancer by following some easy steps.

Body

Body of speech is labeled.

Main points are indicated by Roman numerals beginning with I.

I. There are three types of skin cancer: basal cell, squamous, and melanoma (Kalb, 2001).

   A. Basal cell is the most common and easily treated and is rarely life threatening.

   B. Squamous cell cancer is the next most common, and it too is easily treated and seldom fatal unless completely unattended.

   C. Melanoma, which is the form of skin cancer Maureen Reagan died from, is increasing at an alarming rate in the United States. It is deadly if not treated early in its growth.

Signposts are transitional statements between main points.

(Signpost: So what causes skin cancer?)

II. Much as we may like the sun, too much of this good thing is bad for us.

   A. The sun's rays contain ultraviolet radiation.

IN THEIR OWN WORDS

"We, the People": Barbara Jordan

The late Congresswoman and scholar Barbara Jordan was one of the most impressive and eloquent speakers of the second half of the 20th century. Not only did she possess a powerful voice and impeccable diction, she used language in a way that few could match. Many compared her speeches to those of Winston Churchill and Franklin Roosevelt. Here is a brief excerpt of her statements during the debate on the impeachment of President Nixon in 1974:

We, the people. It is a very eloquent beginning. But when that document was completed on the 17th of September in 1787, I was not included in that "We, the people." I felt somehow for many years that George Washington and Alexander Hamilton just left me out by mistake. But through the process of amendment, interpretation and court decision I have finally been included in "We, the people."[1]

Two decades later, Jordan was asked to head the United States Commission on Immigration Reform. Testifying before the very congressional committee of which she was once a member, Jordan echoed her words from long ago:

I would be the last person to claim that our nation is perfect. But we have a kind of perfection in us because our founding principle is universal—that we are all created equal regardless of race, religion or national ancestry. When the Declaration of Independence was written, when the Constitution was adopted, when the Bill of Rights was added to it, they all applied almost exclusively to white men of Anglo-Saxon descent who owned property on the East Coast. They did not apply to me. I am female. I am black. But these self-evident principles apply to me now as they apply to everyone in this room.[2]

[1]"Barbara Jordan: A Passionate Voice," *Sacramento Bee*, 18 January 1996, A16.

[2]Jerelyn Eddings, "The Voice of Eloquent Thunder," *U.S. News and World Report*, 29 January 1996, 16.

about inclusive speech. Both facts are featured in her speech, which is printed in the box "We, the People."

Between One and Many . . .

Self-Assessment

Self-Assessment boxes allow students to assess their own skills and attributes, experience key insights, and practice skills to become stronger communicators.

SELF-ASSESSMENT

What Are the Sources of Your Speech Anxiety?

Listed below are common sources of speech anxiety. As you read each item, consider how much it contributes to the anxiety you experience about public speaking. Rate each item on a scale of 1 to 10, from least important to most important.

Sources of Speech Anxiety	Least Important/Most Important
	1 2 3 4 5 6 7 8 9 10
Your attitude toward speaking	— — — — — — — — — —
Lack of preparation and practice	— — — — — — — — — —
Previous experiences with speaking —lack of or bad experiences	— — — — — — — — — —
Unrealistic goals	— — — — — — — — — —
Perception of your audience as hostile or unsympathetic	— — — — — — — — — —
Negative self-talk	— — — — — — — — — —
Misdirected concerns with how you will be evaluated	— — — — — — — — — —

Rearrange the items in order of importance. Use this hierarchy to better understand the sources of your speech anxiety. What steps can you take to address and change your patterns of thought and behavior?

1. _____
2. _____
3. _____
4. _____
5. _____
6. _____
7. _____

those you write down before your second and third speeches. Regardless of which speech you are making, your goals must be grounded in your potential to improve as a speaker, as well as how much effort you are willing to make to realize your potential.
- Inventory your ~~routine~~ ... ~~as you prepare to speak.~~ Note what kinds of ~~yourself:~~ Do these statements

---

SELF-ASSESSMENT

When Is It Acceptable to Lie?

Read the following scenarios carefully. Put a check mark next to the scenarios in which you think it would be acceptable to lie. Be prepared to present your responses in class and to discuss any differences between your responses and those of your classmates.

_____ 1. You know your best friend is cheating on a lover. The lover is suspicious and asks you, "Is Jane/Joe cheating on me?"

_____ 2. The person seated next to you during an exam appears to be copying your answers. As you turn your exam in, the instructor asks, "Was X copying from your exam?"

_____ 3. A casual friend misses several lectures in a class you both attend. He asks to borrow your notes to copy them. You don't want to hand over your hard work, but you also don't want to appear unsympathetic.

_____ 4. A person repeatedly asks you out on a date. You've run out of excuses, but to be honest about it, you find the person completely unattractive.

_____ 5. Your parents have always trusted you. Over a break from school they ask you whether you've experimented with marijuana. Even though you have used marijuana, you are of the opinion that what your parents don't know won't hurt them.

thoroughly prepares students for public speaking by offering **interactive techniques** and **real life** examples

Profiles

Profile boxes offer examples of individuals who have used pubic speaking in their lives

---

PROFILE

"The Dole Stroll": Dr. Nichola D. Gutgold*

Former secretary of labor and transportation, former president of the American Red Cross, and wife of presidential nominee Bob Dole, Elizabeth Dole is one of the most polished and prepared public speakers in America. She made history and captivated the American public when, at the Republican National Convention, she abandoned the podium and walked among the delegates to speak. Mrs. Dole explains why she chose to break with tradition:

I was told by two experts that I could not walk around at the 1996 GOP convention successfully. . . . Walking down 12 steps in heels was something to think about twice before you do it! But I think when the audience saw me come down, they all got quiet. They hadn't seen this before. They all wondered "what is she doing?" And because of that, they were more attentive and cooperative as I walked around the audience. . . . That walking around really works well for me in other speeches as well. I like doing that, and I frequently use that style when I speak for the American Red Cross and I speak to victims and their families. I think that it is a very effective way for me to reach the audience. The audience seems to respond so much better when I move around and I am not behind the podium with bright lights glaring at me. I now feel that the podium is a barrier between the audience and me. What we found during the campaign was that a fascinating thing to do was to interview people—stop them and have them tell their story and then tell them what Bob Dole would do. . . . I found that the reason that I started moving from the podium is about three months before I left for my leave of absence from the Red Cross, when I was trying to get people to give money to the Red Cross, or blood or their time, if I could get close to them—if I could talk to them like it was a conversation, it worked much better.

Source: Elizabeth Dole, interview in Hershey, Pennsylvania, 7 April 1998.

*Dr. Gutgold is an assistant professor of speech communication at Penn State Berks-Lehigh Valley College and is writing a book about the public speaking of Elizabeth Dole.

a manuscript have an artificial quality. Sentences are often too long and complex. The audience often loses track of the point being made. "Oral essays" are not an effective way to communicate with an audience.

If the manuscript pages get out of order or some are missing, you may be ... en your speech altogether. Most teachers have had the ... mble for words as he or she looks

---

SPEAKING OF...

Codes of Conduct for Public Speaking

Although it is not a full-fledged ethical code, such as those found in law and medicine, the National Communication Association's Credo for Free and Responsible Communication in a Democratic Society forms an important touchstone for the ethical public speaker. Other guidelines that may be of help to the public speaker are found in the American Advertising Association's Code of Ethics, the Code of Ethics of the International Association of Business Communicators, and the Public Relations Society of America's Code of Professional Standards for the Practice of Public Relations.[1]

CREDO FOR FREE AND RESPONSIBLE COMMUNICATION IN A DEMOCRATIC SOCIETY[2]

Recognizing the essential place of free and responsible communication in a democratic society, and recognizing the distinction between the freedoms our legal system should respect and the responsibilities our education system should cultivate, we the members of the National Communication Association endorse the following statement of principles:

We believe that freedom of speech and assembly must hold a central position among American constitutional principles, and we express our determined support for the right of peaceful expression by any communicative means available.

We support the proposition that a free society can absorb with equanimity speech which exceeds the boundaries of generally accepted beliefs and mores; that much good and little harm can ensue if we err on the side of freedom, whereas much harm and little good may follow if we err on the side of suppression.

We criticize as misguided those who believe that the justice of their cause confers license to interfere physically and coercively with the speech of others, and we condemn intimidation, whether by powerful majorities or strident minorities, which attempts to restrict free expression.

We accept the responsibility of cultivating by precept and example, in our classrooms and in our communities, enlightened uses of communication; of developing in our students a respect for precision and accuracy in communication, and for reasoning based upon evidence and a judicious discrimination among values.

We encourage our students to accept the role of well-informed and articulate citizens, to defend the communication rights of those with whom they may disagree, and to expose abuses of the communication process.

We dedicate ourselves fully to these principles, confident in the belief that reason will ultimately prevail in a free marketplace of ideas.

[1]Richard L. Johannesen, *Ethics in Human Communication*, 4th ed. (Prospect Heights, Ill.: Waveland Press, 1996), chap. 10.

[2]Used by permission of the National Communication Association.

Speaking Of . . .

Speaking Of . . . boxes contain current, topical information that relates to the text discussion.

Such philosophical relativism ran counter to the philosophy of Socrates, who taught that absolute truth was knowable through a question-and-answer ... as dialectic. Socrates' student Plato wrote two dialogues, the ... expounded this Socratic view of rhetoric. To

Between One and Many

coaches students to become better public speakers in many ways

Tips and Tactics

Throughout the book, these speechmaking skill builders are highlighted in special lists that make it easy for students to apply practical suggestions to their own speeches.

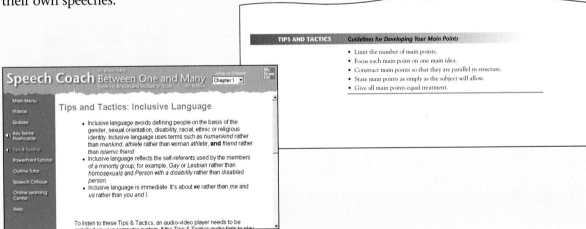

Audio Tips and Tactics are based on the popular text version. This version of useful advice has been recorded by the authors themselves! Audio Tips and Tactics are found on the Speech Coach Student CD.

There are over 40 Tips and Tactics. They include:

- Six Criteria for an Appropriate Speech Topic
- Seven Steps for Organizing Your Speech
- Ways to Open
- Ways to Close
- Ethical Guidelines for Speakers
- Ethical Guidelines for Listeners
- Tips for Preparing PowerPoints
- Inclusive Language
- Speaker Credibility
- The Speaking Environment
- Steps for Library Research

Speech Coach Student CD

The new Speech Coach Student CD-ROM 1.0 is packaged FREE with every textbook and is fully supported by McGraw-Hill Tech Support at 1-800-331-5094. Speech Coach provides a variety of learning tools to help students prepare, organize, and deliver speeches. Speech Coach brings to life the theories and skills discussed in the text. An icon within the text prompts students to use Speech Coach.

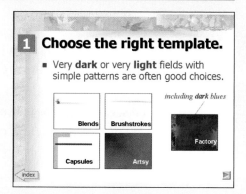

Video Study Guide   Students can view and study student speeches and delivery styles on their own time, at their own pace, and in their own space.

Quizzes   Practice tests with immediate feedback reinforce chapter objectives.

Key Terms Flashcards with Audio
A reinforcement of the key concepts from the text. Both audio and visual for varied learning styles.

Audio Tips & Tactics   Provides students with an opportunity to see and hear some of the most popular Tips and Tactics from the text.

PowerPoint Tutorial   Basic steps in creating and using PowerPoint effectively in a presentation are explained in this vivid tutorial.

Outline Tutor   A computerized template for creating outlines helps students to organize their material by creating, editing, and printing their speech outlines.

Speech Critique   This unique software program enables both students and instructors to evaluate speeches and generate written reports, either on a computer or on a printed evaluation sheet.

Between One and Many . . .

PowerPoint Slides

PowerPoint slides, available at the On-line Learning Center, provide instructors with a visual aid of the key concepts for each chapter.

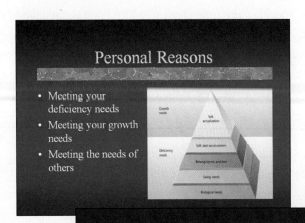

Video Study Guide

A new edition of the popular Video Study Guide is available in VHS format as well as on the Speech Coach Student CD. Each segment can be viewed independently of the others and is coordinated with a specific chapter in the text.

is supported by **supplements** that service the challenges of taking, teaching, and managing a public speaking course

Online Learning Center

The FREE Online Learning Center (OLC) Web site offers students and instructors a variety of resources and activities that support the content of the text. These include interactive chapter quizzes, vocabulary-enhancing crossword puzzles based on chapter key terms, PowerPoint slides, and the Instructor's Manual. Students do not need a password to access the Student Center on the OLC.

PowerWeb

PowerWeb, a password-protected, course-specific Web site is also available. Accessible from a link on the *Between One and Many* Online Learning Center, PowerWeb helps students with online research by directing them to more than 6,000 high-quality academic sources. It also contains materials on how to conduct research on the Web, student study tools, interactive exercises, and more.

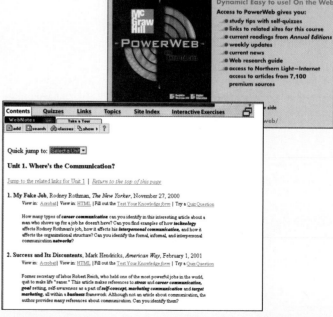

Foundations

PART ONE

Actor and activist
Edward James
Olmos speaks
frequently to high
school students
about issues of
diversity and gang
violence.

Practical Speaking

 OBJECTIVES

After reading this chapter and reviewing the learning resources on your CD-ROM and at the Online Learning Center, you should be able to:

- Describe the relationship between personal needs and the ability to speak publicly.
- Explain the role speaking plays in the professional promotion of self.
- Describe how speaking skills can make people better citizens.
- Demonstrate an understanding of the transactional and symbolic nature of the process of public speaking.

 KEY CONCEPTS

In each chapter we will introduce you to some key terms you need to know. We place these at the beginning of each chapter to alert you to important terms you will encounter. In this chapter look for the following terms:

channel	growth needs	symbol
content (of messages)	interdependence	system
decoding	message	transaction
deficiency needs	perception	
encoding	relational component	
feedback	(of messages)	

> *If all my talents and powers were to be taken from me . . . and I had my choice of keeping but one, I would unhesitatingly ask to be allowed to keep the Power of Speaking, for through it, I would quickly recover all the rest.*
>
> —DANIEL WEBSTER

3

At the start of each new term we ask students two straightforward questions. First, how many of you resent having to take a class in public speaking because you believe you could better spend the time with your major? Second, how many of you fail to see the connection between a class in public speaking and your personal and professional goals?

We ask these questions because we know they are ones students are asking themselves. After all, wouldn't your time be put to better use in a class in your major? And is there truly a connection between a class in public speaking and becoming a computer scientist, information manager, chemist, Web designer, graphic artist, biologist, nurse, exercise physiologist, or writer?

Much as we understand these questions, we are compelled that first day of class to demonstrate to our students that these questions are misplaced and based on too little experience in the so-called real world. Simply put, time spent in this class can have more bearing on your success than some of the courses in your major. The reason is simple. People who are good at what they do get promoted to positions that have less to do with their initial job title and more to do with managing people both internal and external to their profession. With this kind of promotion comes increased responsibility for communicating both interpersonally and in public. That's why communication skills, including public speaking, top the list of qualities that companies which recruit on your campus and throughout the world seek in a prospective employee.[1] Knowledge and skill in public speaking are *that* important. Further, this is true whether we're talking about science and medicine, the law and public service, education and the social sciences, and even the fine arts.

But don't just take our word for it. Consider the people you see on the next page. Cindy Peete returned to college at age 40, following in her two children's footsteps. Although she is a talented potter whose work has been exhibited at juried events throughout the United States, Cindy has always been fascinated with human behavior. Initially she studied sociology, then public health, and finally, demography. She now holds a Ph.D. and is in charge of data collection and analysis for the University of California Chancellor's Office. Lest you think otherwise, data crunching is but one facet of Cindy's job. She is called on frequently to share her data in a variety of public settings including the UC Board of Regents, local and statewide governmental agencies, meetings of professional demographers, and groups of ordinary citizens with little or no background in behavioral science. "Thankfully, I was required to take a public speaking course," Cindy now laughs. "Public speaking may not be my job title, but it's what I do day in and out."

The same could be said for Randy Larsen and Keith Hawkins. Randy Larsen is an environmental educator and environmental talk-show host whose program is carried nationally, including New York City, Los Angeles, and Chicago. Randy, who actually keeps a running record of his presentations, counts them in the hundreds since he graduated. In addition to his public speeches before live audiences, Randy's environmental radio talk show has been aired locally for several years. Now that it is being nationally syndicated, it will undoubtedly reach hundreds of thousands of listeners.

Although Keith Hawkins always wanted to work with people and actually enjoyed speaking in public, he was never certain he could use these two interests to carve out a career. Keith learned in his speech class that some of the highest paid people in the United States are professional public speakers.

Cindy Peete   Randy Larsen   Keith Hawkins

Whether Keith now counts himself in the highest paid group of professional speakers we can't say. But we do know that Keith, who has been featured in articles in *Time* and the *New York Times*, is a paid professional speaker who has even spoken before the General Assembly of the United Nations.

Public speaking is an essential communication skill in today's world. Public speaking also is an extension and refinement of many of the skills you already practice in your one-on-one and group communication encounters. Our goal in this initial chapter is threefold. First, we demonstrate how common it is for people to use their speaking skills to satisfy their personal and professional needs, and to help empower others to satisfy theirs. Second, we make clear the connection between public speaking and the other forms of communicating you routinely practice, and we discuss public speaking as a specific kind of system of communication. Finally, we preview the chapters that follow this one.

PERSONAL REASONS FOR DEVELOPING SPEAKING SKILLS

Although we may not consciously realize it, human communication is a need as basic to our well-being as the food we eat, water we drink, and air we breathe. Both clinical and case studies compellingly show that when we are deprived of this need, we are affected both physically and psychologically.

Satisfying Your Personal Needs

Abraham Maslow wrote that we experience two sets of personal needs: deficiency needs and growth needs.[2] **Deficiency needs** are basic human needs. **Growth needs** are higher-order human needs. Maslow arranged these two sets of needs in the form of a hierarchy to show that our deficiency needs must be satisfied routinely before our growth needs become important to us.

As Figure 1.1 indicates, there are four sets of deficiency needs: (1) *biological needs*, such as for food, water, and air; (2) *safety needs*, such as protection from physical harm; (3) *belongingness and love needs*, such as those experienced

💿 **SPEECH COACH**

Segment one of Speech Coach shows you the role public speaking can play in people's lives. See segment 1.1 on your CD.

deficiency needs Basic human needs, which must be satisfied before higher-order needs can be met. They include needs for food, water, air, physical safety, belongingness and love, and self-esteem and social esteem.

growth needs Higher-order human needs, which can be satisfied only after deficiency needs have been met. They include self-actualization (the process of fully realizing one's potential), knowledge and understanding, and aesthetic needs.

How Much Experience Do You Have Speaking?

Most of us recognize that there is a high degree of correspondence between skill and training. Most of us also will admit that any skill suffers from lack of training and practice, whether it is shooting free throws or solving math problems. With this in mind, answer the following questions:

1. On a scale of 1 to 10, with 1 being little and 10 being considerable, what is your *training* in public speaking?
2. On a scale of 1 to 10, with 1 being little and 10 being considerable, what is your *practice and experience* with public speaking?
3. Given your score for numbers 1 and 2, how would you rate your *effectiveness* as a public speaker on a scale of 1 to 10, with 1 representing ineffective and 10 representing highly effective?
4. How well do you think the three scores you gave yourself correspond? We raise this question because students frequently think they are better speakers than their training and experience would predict.

Using your responses to these four questions as a guide, list 10 public speaking skills you could improve on—for example, listening more attentively, feeling more comfortable speaking, and thinking more critically about speeches you hear from others. Write down those skills or record them in a journal. At the end of the academic term, compare your goals with what you believe you have achieved in the class.

by a child for the love of a parent; and (4) *self- and social-esteem needs*, which involve believing in our self-worth and finding confirmation from others of that belief.

Growth needs are not as straightforward as deficiency needs. They include self-actualization, knowledge and understanding, and aesthetic needs. Self-actualization is the most commonly discussed growth need. According to Maslow, *self-actualization* is the process of fully realizing one's potential. Self-actualized people not only understand themselves but also accept themselves for who they are and what they have achieved.

The ability to skillfully present our thoughts and feelings publicly is increasingly important to the satisfaction of both our deficiency needs and our growth needs. Consider again the case of Randy Larsen. As an environmental educator and advocate, much of Randy Larsen's time is spent speaking to groups of all ages about protecting the air we breathe, water we drink, and food we eat. Randy covers many topics in the process, ranging from the destruction of rain forests to the effects of agricultural pesticides on groundwater. Although Randy's public speaking skills are directly connected to his and others' deficiency needs, they also are connected to Randy's desire to self-actualize his own potential as a human being, a clear growth need. For an example of a person who used public speaking skills to overcome serious physical disabilities, see the box "A Passion for Speaking: Jonathan Studebaker."

As a first- or second-year college student, you may recall giving speeches in high school, whether you gave a class report, participated in a debate, or spoke to an assembly of your fellow students. Even if you have not had high school experience, it is likely you will use public speaking skills in the future. After

SPEECH COACH
To see a speech by Jonathan, view segment 1.2 on your CD.

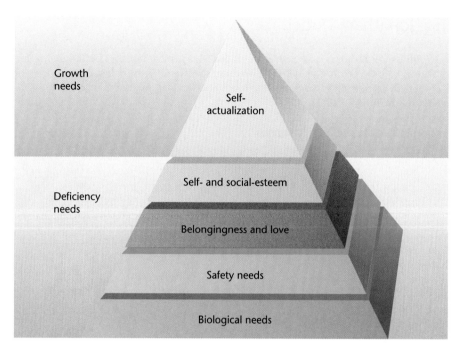

FIGURE 1.1 Maslow's Hierarchy of Needs

college, you may find yourself speaking as a parent at a PTA meeting, a citizen speaking before your local planning agency about a development in your neighborhood, or as part of a nonprofit organization, such as the Red Cross, seeking to raise public awareness.

Meeting the Personal Needs of Others

Public speaking skills also can empower others to satisfy their needs. Often people need someone who can bring their needs into better focus and enable them to act to meet those needs. Actor/activist Edward James Olmos, star of *Stand and Deliver* and *American Me*, spoke at the authors' campus on the topic "We Are All the Same Gang."[3] Having succeeded in meeting his personal and professional needs as a critically acclaimed actor, Olmos is now using his talents to speak out for the needs of others. He targets his message to those who are tempted to join gangs. His speeches promote peace, racial harmony, and the need for children to be vaccinated against violence. As he points out, "No child comes out of his mother's womb with a pistol."[4]

PROFESSIONAL REASONS FOR DEVELOPING SPEAKING SKILLS

Besides satisfying needs, there are many professional reasons for honing your public speaking skills. One major reason is to become an agent of influence in your career. As an agent of influence, you will be in a position to (1) promote your professional self, (2) better present your ideas to decision makers, (3) create positive change in the workplace, (4) become a functioning force in meetings, and (5) develop active listening skills.

A Passion for Speaking: Jonathan Studebaker

His list of accomplishments was impressive: honorary football coach for the East-West Shrine game, kicking coach for the Chico State Wildcat football team, college graduate, television sports commentator, member of the Chico city planning commission, writer, motivational speaker, and founder of "Project Speak Out." In the 35 short years of his life, Jonathan literally and figuratively touched the lives of thousands, including ours when he was our student at Chico State in the 1980s.

Few could have imagined such a life for Jonathan when he was born May 20, 1965, with several broken bones, including both legs. Jonathan had a disease known as *osteogenesis imperfecta,* or brittle bone disease. During his life, he broke bones throughout his body hundreds of times. He explained that his bones were like glass, so "when you carry me, treat me like your best crystal." His life was so fragile that the doctors didn't expect him to live two weeks, let alone 35 years. No one ever expected him to attend a college or university, let alone graduate in four years, but he did. In fact, when he passed away on April 3, 2001, he had lived double the life expectancy of a person with brittle bone disease and accomplished more than many people do in twice that life span.

Speaking was Jonathan's passion. When we interviewed him for the first edition of this book, he put it this way, "Speaking isn't broccoli; it's fun!" He stressed the importance of "feeling passionately" about your topic. His motivational speeches helped his audience understand that people are not their disability. As he said in the speech you can read in Appendix A and view on your CD, "I've been asked: 'Are you a midget?' 'What do you have?' 'What's your disability?' 'Why are you small?' But I'd really like people to ask me: 'What do you like to do?' 'What's your favorite color?'"

We'll miss Jonathan: his infectious laugh, his courage, and his moving speeches. We've dedicated this edition of *Between One and Many* to his memory because he shows us that with determination, we can use the power of speech to reach goals that seem unattainable.

Promoting Your Professional Self

The chance to speak in public frequently presents us with an ideal opportunity to enhance our professional credibility. Some time ago the authors of this text were treated to a presentation by Dr. Bonnie Johnson. She spoke about work she had done for Intel, the world's largest manufacturer of silicon chips. As someone trained in organizational communication, Dr. Johnson was given permission by Intel to study how well personnel were adapting to technological change in the workplace—for example, electronic workstations. When she had concluded her study, Intel offered her a position with the corporation.

Following her presentation, Dr. Johnson welcomed questions from the audience. One undergraduate asked her why she thought Intel had hired her. "Do you want to know candidly?" she asked. "Because initially they were more impressed with the public presentation I made to top management on the results of my study than the study itself. They hired me because I not only knew my subject but could effectively speak about it and its implications for Intel."

As exemplified by Dr. Johnson's anecdote about her experience with Intel, communication skills in general and public speaking skills specifically are both desired and rewarded in the workplace. Surveys of personnel managers at top companies consistently demonstrate that they look for college graduates who not only can communicate interpersonally and in writing but also can deliver a speech well. Ask just about anyone who has climbed the corporate ladder, and you will learn that public speaking skills helped tremendously along the way.

Presenting Ideas to Decision Makers

Another reason organizations put such a high premium on speaking skills concerns the effective communication of ideas. Your success depends not only on your ideas, but also on how well you can present those ideas to people whose decisions will affect your career. When you think about it, every occupation and profession involves selling ideas to other people. For example, the life insurance salesperson who must persuade a client to increase coverage is unlikely to close the deal simply by dropping a brochure in the mail. On a larger scale, most corporations require managers to present reports or briefings describing their accomplishments and future plans and goals. Those individuals who seek to move beyond entry-level positions need to be able to convince others of the wisdom of their ideas. Thus, being able to speak to decision makers with confidence and authority is an indispensable tool for corporate success.

Dave Davies's experience at 3M is a good case in point. Although scientists by training, Davies and the people in his department have to justify resources they believe are necessary to their research. Thus, when Davies needed $20 million to advance his work on laser disks, he was required to publicly present his case to 3M's executive operations council, which included 3M's CEO. This was no sit-down presentation at a conference table. As is usually required in such cases, Davies made a stand-up presentation using both a lectern and visual aids.[5] The fact that Davies was successful in procuring the money reflected not only the promise of the product, but also the skill with which Davies presented its promise to 3M's executive council.

Creating Change in the Workplace

One of the most important tasks for any supervisor or manager is to be able to convince subordinates that proposed changes are desirable. To remain competitive, companies must implement new technologies and procedures. Yet many employees fear change. Often the best way to implement change is to sell employees on new ideas rather than to tell them to simply get used to those ideas. A willing and enthusiastic workforce is far more likely to accept change in the workplace than is a reluctant and suspicious one.

In addition, change need not always be initiated from the top. Many of the best ideas in industry come from employees who convince their managers that change is necessary. Consider the example of America's most successful retail store, Wal-Mart. Founder Sam Walton believed, "Our best ideas come from clerks and stock boys."[6] To prove the point Walton once rode 100 miles in a Wal-Mart truck just to listen and talk to the driver.

Lest you believe that this approach is unique, companies as diverse as Delta Airlines and Hewlett-Packard also listen to their employees. For example, "Delta spends a lot of time and money . . . checking out the employee's side of the story. Often the result is a substantial policy change," according to management consultants Tom Peters and Robert Waterman.[7] They report that senior management at Delta meet in an "open forum" at least once a year. Those in the lowest ranks of the organization have the opportunity to speak directly with those at the highest levels. And Hewlett-Packard has an "open lab stock" policy that allows workers to take equipment home for their personal use, in the hope that they might come up with an innovation.[8] Successful organizations don't just talk to their employees, they listen to them as well.

Becoming a Functioning Force in Meetings

Although small-group communication is not the principal focus of this book, many of the skills we discuss—ranging from active listening to critical thinking to making impromptu presentations—are directly applicable to functioning in group meetings. As communication professor Ronald Adler reports, the average business executive spends about 45 minutes out of every hour communicating, much of this time in meetings.[9] Further, surveys show that executives spend as many as 700 hours per year in meetings.[10] Your ability to speak effectively in meetings will be indispensable to your success in the workplace.

Developing Active Listening Skills

It is not enough to know how to present your ideas to others. You need to listen to the needs of others and to what they say in response to your ideas. On the average we spend up to 55 percent of our day in situations that involve the potential to listen.[11] Seldom, however, do we take full advantage of this potential. Active listening, which we discuss at length in Chapter 4, is essential to your development as a speaker. First, you won't have anything important to say unless you have listened actively to those around you. Second, listening will make you more effective in working with people. Study after study demonstrates that people who actually hear what is being communicated to them are much more responsive to others than those who listen with "only one ear." Responsiveness to one's audience, moreover, is one of the distinguishing characteristics of some of our nation's best public speakers.

Public speaking skills will help your development as a listener in several ways. For example, learning to give an effective speech requires the ability to analyze your audience, including what they think about you as a speaker and about the topic you plan to address. As part of their audience analysis, the best speakers listen to what audience members say well in advance of speaking. These speakers know that what they hear contains clues about what an audience is thinking. These speakers then use these clues in both the preparation and delivery of their speeches.

Learning to speak requires skill in organizing your thoughts and highlighting key points for listeners. As you learn to do this for your speeches, you will also learn how to organize the information you receive from speakers, separating the important ideas from the unimportant. Finally, speakers have to learn how to research and support their ideas. As a listener, you will need to evaluate the research and support other speakers provide to you. In fact, almost every public speaking skill we will discuss has a parallel skill for the listener.

PUBLIC REASONS FOR DEVELOPING SPEAKING SKILLS

Skilled public speakers serve as agents of change not only in the workplace but in the larger world as well. Were it not for those who spoke out publicly, the voting age would still be 21 and only White male property owners would be able to vote. All the progress of the past century has resulted from people coming up with new and sometimes controversial ideas and speaking out to persuade others of the wisdom of adopting them.

Becoming a Critical Thinker

As we discuss at length in Chapter 14, the ability to think critically about your own messages and those of others is essential to reaching sound conclusions about the issues of the day. Not only should speakers strive to base their persuasive efforts on sound reasoning, listeners need to take the responsibility to detect unsound reasoning. Some arguments that seem valid actually contain flaws that render them invalid. Becoming a critical thinker will make you less susceptible to phony arguments and less prone to engage in them yourself.

Functioning as an Informed Citizen

Our nation is a democratic republic based on the premise that for our country to thrive there must be a free exchange of ideas. Thus, it is no accident that the First Amendment to the Constitution guarantees freedom of speech, as well as freedom of the press, religion, and peaceable assembly. The fundamental premise of our Constitution is that the people must have the information necessary to make informed decisions. Even if you don't have an immediate need to speak out on an issue of public policy, you will be the consumer of countless speeches on every issue imaginable—from atmospheric warming to zero-tolerance policies in college dorms for drug possession. The ability to forcefully and publicly present your thoughts to others—whether as a speaker or as an audience member questioning a speaker—is more than a desirable skill. It is also a responsibility you owe to others and yourself.

Preserving Freedom of Speech

For some people, the way to deal with unpopular ideas is to invoke a quick fix: censorship. One of our goals in this book is to give you an appreciation for the importance of free speech in a democratic society. The empowerment of more and more citizens to express their views publicly should lead to vigorous debate about those ideas. Those who have confidence in the truth of their own views should welcome the opportunity to debate, rather than suppress, opposing views. Yet hardly a day goes by when we are not treated to an account of some person or some organization trying to suppress another's right to speak freely.

Raising the Level of Public Discourse

Regrettably, much of the public discourse of recent years in response to controversial issues has degenerated into name-calling and emotional appeals. Daytime TV is overrun with programming on which people verbally assault each other with messages that bear little to no semblance of reason. Geraldo Rivera quit his enormously profitable daytime talk show, for example, because he believed it was contributing to the erosion of reasoned speech in America. Even so-called current events shows such as *Crossfire* on CNN frequently break down into name-calling and emotional screeching.

We believe almost any topic—from abortion to religious zealotry—can be debated without the debaters personally attacking each other's pedigrees. Learning to focus one's public speaking skills on the substance of a controversy rather than the personality of an opponent is an important step in raising the level of public discourse. As more Americans learn how to make their views known rationally, and learn the critical thinking skills necessary to evaluate public discourse, the overall level of debate about issues in contemporary society is likely to improve.

Promoting Ethics

Finally, you cannot become a skilled public speaker without a corresponding commitment to becoming an ethical speaker as well. For example, while running for president, Senator Joseph Biden was caught plagiarizing the speech of a British politician. Biden's presidential campaign came to an abrupt halt. Both Biden and his advisors instinctively knew that his serious breach of ethical behavior was unacceptable to voters. So important is the subject of ethics to public speaking that Chapter 6 is dedicated to the topic. For now, suffice it to say that ethical speech is synonymous with effective speech.

THE PUBLIC SPEAKING TRANSACTION

transaction A simultaneous exchange of verbal and nonverbal messages between two or more people.

system A collection of interdependent parts arranged so that a change in one produces corresponding changes in the remaining parts.

interdependence A relationship in which things have a reciprocal influence on each other.

Although this book deals with public speaking specifically, we recognize that public speaking is but one of many modes of human communication. We communicate one on one, in small groups, and through the mass media, as well as in public. Although each context in which we communicate has its own distinguishing features, certain principles of communication apply to all of them. Whether the focus is an intimate conversation between lovers, an informative speech before your class, or a speech at a political rally, the process of communication is best viewed as a transactional system.

A **transaction** involves a simultaneous exchange of messages between two or more people. A **system** is a collection of interdependent parts, parts arranged so that a change in one produces corresponding changes in the remaining parts. Consider a mechanical system such as a car. Its parts show varying degrees of interdependence. **Interdependence** exists when things have a reciprocal influence on one another. Changes in some of a car's parts will produce subtle changes in others. For example, even minor tire tread wear will affect a car's handling. The change is so subtle, though, most drivers don't notice it. In contrast, changes in other parts of the car can result in dramatic changes drivers cannot help noticing. Engine failure, for example, produces obvious changes

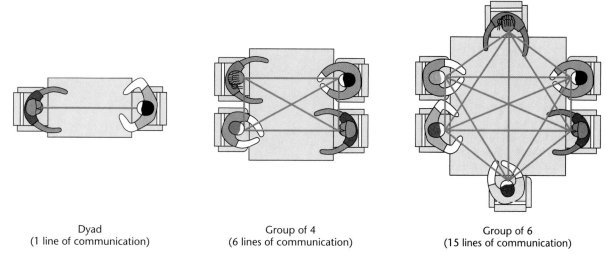

Dyad
(1 line of communication)

Group of 4
(6 lines of communication)

Group of 6
(15 lines of communication)

FIGURE 1.2 Lines of Communication. The lines of communication increase with the number of people. This may be one reason people are fond of the saying "Too many cooks spoil the broth."

throughout the hydraulic system of the car, including failure of the car's power steering and power brakes.

Perhaps this is why the public speaking transaction seems such a significant departure from the more familiar contexts of communication in which we engage. Whereas the changes that occur to the communication system when moving from an interpersonal to a small-group exchange are subtle, the changes that occur to the system when moving to an exchange between one and many can seem rather pronounced. Consider something as simple as the number of people communicating in a system and the number of lines of communication between or among them. As illustrated in Figure 1.2, the lines of communication increase geometrically as the number of communicators increases. Whereas this change isn't especially dramatic as you move from two communicators to three or four, the change is staggering by the time you get to a group of even seven.

Figure 1.3 models the interdependent parts of the public speaking transaction as a system. Consider (1) the situation (context) in which the public speaking transaction takes place, (2) the speaker and the audience, (3) the messages they exchange, (4) the process of constructing and interpreting the symbols they use to convey their messages, (5) the channels through which the messages are sent, and (6) the role perception plays in the process.

The Situation

The situation (or context) in which any communication transaction takes place affects the nature of the transaction. This is especially true of the public speaking transaction. The situation includes the physical environment in which the speech is shared between speaker and listener. For example, is the speech shared in a classroom? An assembly hall? An outdoor amphitheater? It makes a critical difference.

FIGURE 1.3 Public Speaking as a Transaction. In this model of the speech transaction, messages are simultaneously conveyed between speakers and listeners, with both parties functioning simultaneously as sources and receivers of messages. Communication is bound by the situation, and each person's perceptions are significant in interpreting the content and relational components of messages.

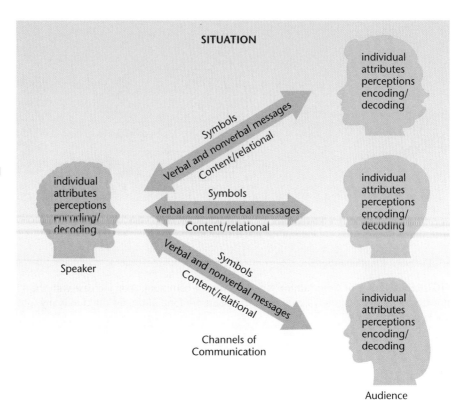

Usually the situation also defines the purpose of the speech transaction. Are the people gathered to hear a speech eulogizing a beloved family member? To learn about a new policy that affects the amount of tuition charged students? Or to listen to a politician announcing her decision to seek higher office? Does the speaker want simply to pass on information to the audience? To motivate the audience to take some action? To persuade the audience to abandon old beliefs in favor of new ones? The purpose of the speech, too, makes a critical difference in the overall transaction.

The Speaker and the Audience Members

In contrast to early models of speaking, which implied the speaker first talks and the audience then responds, the transactional model tells us speaker and audience exchange verbal and nonverbal messages simultaneously. That is, rather than taking discrete turns in this regard, speaker and audience members send and receive messages at the same time. Although the speaker typically is the dominant sender in the transaction, the audience is hardly passive. Even as the speaker talks and gestures, audience members provide **feedback**—they convey information back to the speaker with their eyes, seating posture, and voices. An audience leaning forward and staring intently at the speaker sends a far different message than one that is obviously fighting off sleep.

The sheer number of people in an audience also affects the overall speech transaction. It's one thing to speak with 25 other students in a traditional col-

feedback Audience member responses, both verbal and nonverbal, to a speaker.

lege classroom. It's quite another to speak to an assembly of the entire graduating class at commencement as people shift restlessly in their seats. Thus, you can no more afford to ignore the size of your audience than you can afford to ignore their feedback, the environment in which the transaction takes place, or the purpose for which you have gathered.

Messages: Content and Relational Components

The **message** is the meaning produced by the speaker and the audience members. In the transactional system modeled here, the message and the medium through which it travels are intentionally blurred. This is because the two are *interdependent*—not independent. What we would like to say to our audience is significantly affected by the manner in which we say it, and the way we convey the message is affected by what we want to say. This reciprocal process has a tremendous impact on how our message is perceived by our audience.

> **message** The meaning produced by communicators.

All messages are composed of two parts. The first part of the message is its **content,** the essential meaning, the gist or substance, of what a speaker wants to convey. For example, you might wish to convey your affection for another with the three words "I love you." The second part of a message, called its **relational component,** involves the collective impact of the verbal and nonverbal components of that message as it is conveyed. Consider how you might use your voice, face, and eyes to alter the impact of the words "I love you." You could make these three words an expression of sincere endearment, a plea, or even a statement of wanton desire.

> **content (of messages)** The essential meaning of what a speaker wants to convey.
>
> **relational component (of messages)** The collective impact of the verbal and nonverbal components of a message as it is conveyed.

Meaning is derived from both the content and the relational components of a message. Moreover, neither component is subordinate to the other in its contribution to meaning. What you say and how you say it, in other words, are roughly proportional in this regard.

Constructing and Interpreting Symbols

When we seek to convey our thinking to other people, there is no way to directly communicate our ideas. Our thoughts must be converted into words and gestures whose meaning can be interpreted by those receiving the message. These words and gestures are really **symbols,** things that stand for or suggest other things by reason of relationship or association. This process of converting our thoughts and ideas into meaningful symbols is called **encoding.** These symbols are then interpreted when received by audience members, a process known as **decoding.** This is simpler said than done. Whether an audience decodes a speaker's message as encoded depends on many factors, including but not limited to:

> **symbol** Something that stands for or suggests something else by reason of relationship or association.
>
> **encoding** The process by which ideas are translated into a code that can be understood by the receiver.
>
> **decoding** The process by which a code is translated back into ideas.

- language
- culture
- age
- gender

On occasion, for example, some of our male students have referred to female audience members as "girls." When they used this label, we doubt these men meant adolescent and immature members of the opposite sex. Yet, that's exactly how most women in our classes decode the word. Thus, those males who have used the word *girl* in reference to women have "turned off" many, if not most, of the women in their audience.

Channels

A **channel** is the physical medium through which communication occurs. The transmission of the light and sound waves that make up the picture you see on your TV set requires a channel through which they can be signaled and received. Picture and audio are encoded into electronic impulses, which must be decoded by your television receiver. In human communication, we primarily use our senses as channels for the messages we send and receive. We use our voice, eyes, and body, for example, to channel our speeches, conversations, and group discussions. On occasion, we also use our sense of touch, sense of smell, and even our sense of taste as channels of communication.

In the case of public speaking, we can also use supplementary channels of communication to augment the five senses. We can electronically amplify our voice so that it can be better heard or use visual media such as poster boards, overhead transparencies, and projected images stored in our computer to magnify what we want our audience to see.

Perceptions

The transactional system we've been describing for you demands that we both understand and appreciate the role of perception in public speaking. **Perception** is the process by which we give meaning to our experiences. It also is a highly selective process, as you are about to see.

Take a close look at the lithograph by M. C. Escher on the next page. Though it appears at first glance that the water is running downhill, a more careful examination tells you that this is impossible because the water is flowing continuously. Escher was able to create "impossible illusions" by taking advantage of our perceptual predispositions. We assume that the perspective in this print is an accurate representation of reality, when, of course, it cannot be so. When people look at an ambiguous stimulus such as this picture, they automatically look for something familiar . . . something for which they have pre-existing meaning. This helps fool the eye, in this case, into seeing something that cannot exist.

This tendency to perceive the familiar is both good and bad from the standpoint of public speaking. It is good because it enables us to quickly establish a reference point from which we can plan our own speaking behavior as well as interpret that of others. It's bad, on the other hand, because it can perceptually blind us to other data that may be even more important to how we behave and interpret the messages of others.

Consider a cross-cultural example. Direct eye contact is perceived as a sign of attention and respect in most of North America. Thus, when we give a speech, we use this knowledge to gauge how our audience is reacting to our message and delivery. This North American norm, however, is not universal. Direct eye contact in some cultures, such as certain Asian societies, is perceived as an aggressive sign of disdain and disrespect.

It's common, then, for unaware North Americans who speak in one of these cultures to walk away from the experience with their confidence severely shaken. They mistakenly perceive their audience's lack of eye contact with

This lithograph, *Waterfall* (1961), by M. C. Escher, creates an "impossible illusion" by taking advantage of our perceptual predispositions.

them as a sign of disapproval. This mistaken perception, in turn, usually has a negative influence on their entire speaking performance.

As a public speaker, you can never assume that your perceptions of such things as the context, your audience, or the messages your audience feeds back to you are foolproof. Just because some person, some place, or some circumstance strikes you as familiar, that doesn't necessarily make it so.

Words and Things

Finally, public speaking, like other forms of communication, is symbolic.[12] Words are symbols that we use to describe persons, places, and things. Gestures, too, can be symbols, as is the case when we wave our hand to signal good-bye or shake our fist at someone to signal that we are angry.

Although we deal with the symbolic nature of public speaking at length in Chapters 9 and 10, we mention it here because you need to understand that the meaning you attach to the verbal and nonverbal symbols you use to express yourself may not correspond to the meaning others attach to them. What's more, this may be the case even when you share a common language.

As you prepare for your first speeches, you need to think about the degree to which you and your audience share meaning for symbols you commonly use to express yourself. This means, at a minimum, checking out the degree to which you and your audience share a common language, come from a similar culture, and share a similar socioeconomic background.

PREVIEW

The preceding discussion is a framework for the entire book. In the chapters to follow we flesh this framework out. This means the concepts just introduced will be refined and expanded to fit the primary topic of a specific chapter.

Because public speaking classes typically are taught in a limited period of time, you can expect to be up on your feet and speaking long before you have learned everything you need to know about the subject. We wrote Chapter 2—which overviews the process of developing, organizing, and delivering your first speech—with this fact clearly in mind.

If you are the least bit apprehensive about your first speech, then you can look forward to reading Chapter 3. This chapter clears up confusion about the common fear of speaking in public, explains the origins and consequences of this fear on speech performance, and provides you with easily understood and practiced skills to help you manage your fear. What's more, you will learn from reading Chapter 3 that these same skills can help to improve your performance even if you are completely confident about your speaking ability.

To reiterate, a major reason for learning about public speaking is the development of listening skills. Much as we need to listen, most of us are not as skilled at it as we need to be. Research shows most of us would benefit from listening training. Chapter 4 discusses the relationship between good listening habits and effective public speaking. In the process, it details for you the types of listening involved and suggests practices for improving each of these types.

The best prepared and delivered speeches are those that are developed with the audience in mind. Competent public speakers try to learn as much about their audience and the speaking situation as they possibly can. What they learn assists them in predicting what kind of speech will succeed with their audience. Chapter 5 details the process of analyzing your audience and speaking situation, and the necessity of adapting your speech to both.

Chapter 6 zeroes in on a topic of real significance to today's world: ethics. Reading Chapter 6, you will learn about varying ethical perspectives and their relationship to the speech transaction. You also will be called on to make a commitment to the ethical practices described there in your own speeches.

One of the toughest tasks for many beginning students is getting started. Aristotle called this process of getting started invention. In Chapter 7 you will learn not only about developing your speech, but also about avenues for research you can travel to prepare your speech, including the Internet.

Just as there is more than one way to putt a golf ball, there is more than one way to organize a speech. This is especially true in light of the fact that today's multicultural audience may decode your message using different patterns of organization. You will learn about organizing your message using alternative patterns of speech organization in Chapter 8.

As noted earlier, public speaking is a symbolic transaction. We elaborate on this fact in Chapter 9's treatment of the language of public speaking. You will learn that language is both complex and central to one's cultural heritage. You also will learn how to use this knowledge to your and your audience's advantage in your speeches.

Chapter 10 throws a realistic light on a subject fraught with misinformation: the delivery of your message. How nonverbal communication functions in the delivery of your speech is explained and examples provided. Common misconceptions about this type of communication also are dispelled.

Using media to enhance your speeches seems such a simple thing. Yet, as you will read in Chapter 11, nothing could be further from the truth. Media such as overheads or media projected from a laptop computer in combination with a projection machine require precise care in both their construction and execution. Public speakers routinely abuse these presentational media in the classroom, in business, and in government.

Informative speaking is far and away the most common type of public speaking you are likely to encounter. Informative speeches are an essential component of most college classes, whether or not they are labeled as such. A lecture essentially is an informative speech. So too is a book report or an oral presentation based on a term paper. Chapter 12 outlines and discusses the types of informative speeches common in everyday life and details the elements that combine to make an effective informative speech.

Chapter 13 builds on the discussion about informative speaking. You will learn about the process of persuasion as well as the process of persuasive speaking. You also will be shown the perceptual characteristics that influence judgments about your credibility and will read about message variables that can enhance the persuasive effect of your speeches.

Chapter 14 extends what you learn about persuasion to thinking and speaking critically. You will be treated to information on deceptive communication practices that are commonly used by unscrupulous communicators, and you'll learn how to recognize the fallacies that frequently characterize their messages. In the process, you also will learn how to avoid using such fallacies in your own reasoning and speaking.

Finally, Chapter 15 introduces life circumstances in which you can expect to be called on to speak. Some of these circumstances, such as a wedding toast, are social. Others, such as being asked without warning at school or at work to make a progress report on a project, are task oriented.

All in all, we think these chapters combine to provide you with the introductory knowledge and skills necessary to see you through not only the speeches you will share in your class, but also the lifetime of public speaking all college graduates can expect. Good luck as you proceed.

SUMMARY

There are many good reasons to study and practice public speaking. Among them are:

- Public speaking is an essential skill in the professional world.

 **SPEECH COACH**

To evaluate your understanding of this chapter, see the Quizzes on your CD.

- Communication in general and public speaking specifically help you in satisfying your own needs and the needs of others.
- Public speaking helps you with your other classes, including those in your major.
- Public speaking skills help to make you a more effective force for change.
- Public speaking helps you become a better listener.
- Public speaking is a key to becoming an informed and active citizen.
- Public speaking helps you think more critically about the issues of the day.

Remember too as you move on to the next chapter that:

- Public speaking is a transaction between speaker and audience.
- This transaction is comprised of interdependent rather than independent parts.
- These parts include (1) the situation, (2) speaker and audience, (3) the message, (4) verbal and nonverbal symbols, and (5) perceptions.

CHECK YOUR UNDERSTANDING: EXERCISES AND ACTIVITIES

 **SPEECH COACH**
For a review of key terms in this chapter, see the Key Terms Flashcards on your CD.

1. This chapter introduces you to Maslow's hierarchy of needs. How can public speaking skills help you fulfill each of these needs? Write a short paper or give a brief speech explaining your answer and giving examples.

2. How important are public speaking skills in the profession for which you are preparing by attending college? If possible, interview either a practitioner of the profession or a professor in the appropriate department about the ways public speaking might be applicable in your field. Give a brief (1- to 2-minute) presentation to your classmates, or write a short paper about your findings.

3. Attend a meeting of a local-government agency, such as a city council, planning commission, or board of supervisors, or attend a student government meeting on your campus. Chances are you will see several speakers present their views in a public forum. Write a short paper about one of the speakers. What impressed you most about the speaker, and what impressed you least? How did the ability to speak help this person achieve his or her goals?

NOTES

1. National Association of Colleges and Employers, "New College Grads With Communication, Interpersonal, Teamwork Skills Have the Edge Say Employers," 30 March 2001. [Retrieved from http://www.naceweb.org/press/display.cfm/2001/pr033001.htm, 3 September 2001.]
2. Abraham H. Maslow, *Motivation and Personality*, 2nd ed. (New York: Harper & Row, 1970).
3. Elaine Gray, "Actor/Activist Brings His Message of Peace to a Packed Laxson," *Chico Enterprise Record*, 16 September 1995, A1.
4. Gray, "Actor/Activist Brings His Message," A8.
5. *In Search of Excellence* [video recording]. (Boston: Nathan/Tyler Productions, 1985.)

6. Thomas J. Peters and Robert H. Waterman, Jr., *In Search of Excellence: Lessons From America's Best Run Corporations* (New York: Harper & Row, 1982), 247.
7. Peters and Waterman, *In Search of Excellence*, 253.
8. Peters and Waterman, *In Search of Excellence*, 245.
9. Ronald B. Adler, *Communicating at Work: Principles and Practices for Business and the Professions*, 3rd ed. (New York: Random House, 1989), 4.
10. Adler, *Communicating at Work*, 216.
11. Anthony P. Carnevale, Leila J. Gainer, and Ann S. Meltzer, *Workplace Basics: The Skills Employers Want* (Washington, D.C.: U.S. Government Printing Office, 1988), 11.
12. W. Barnett Pearce and Vernon E. Cronen, *Communication, Action and Meaning: The Creation of Social Realities* (New York: Praeger, 1980).

Your first speeches to your classmates will help you gain experience and confidence.

Your First Speech

 OBJECTIVES

After reading this chapter and reviewing the learning resources on your CD-ROM and at the Online Learning Center, you should be able to:

- Analyze the basic features of the speech situation as it applies to your first speech.
- Identify the general purposes associated with public speaking.
- Select an appropriate topic for your first speech.
- Construct a specific purpose for your first speech.
- Develop a clear thesis statement for your first speech.
- Prepare your first speech, utilizing appropriate sources for information.
- Organize your speech to (1) open with impact, (2) focus on your thesis statement, (3) connect with your audience, (4) preview your main points, (5) organize your ideas with three to five main points, (6) summarize your main points, and (7) close with impact.
- Present your speech in a conversational, extemporaneous manner.

A journey of a thousand miles begins with a first step.

—CHINESE PROVERB

 KEY CONCEPTS

audience	invention	specific purpose
brainstorming	main points	thesis statement
credibility	manuscript delivery	
extemporaneous delivery	memorized delivery	
general purpose	preview	
impromptu delivery	signposts	

23

The wisdom of the proverb "A journey of a thousand miles begins with a first step" rings true for anyone who has ever given a speech. Often the toughest part of a speaking assignment is deciding where to begin. For example, you may have a general idea of what you'd like to speak about but have no clue about where to begin your research. Or you may be like many students, uncertain about a topic that you find interesting. Will your audience also find it interesting? Is it appropriate for the classroom?

This chapter takes a general look at the individual steps you need to master to develop and deliver your first speech. This is not a substitute for the content to follow in later chapters, but a detailed preview of it. It's designed to assist you in developing an overall sense of what effective public speaking involves, starting with choosing the right topic and ending with identifying a style of delivery that best suits the situation. The steps we discuss are (1) analyzing the situation with which you are faced, (2) deciding on a purpose, (3) choosing a topic that is suitable to both the situation and chosen purpose, (4) constructing a specific purpose and developing a clear thesis statement for your speech, (5) preparing the substance of your speech, (6) organizing your speech, and (7) presenting your speech effectively.

FIRST THINGS FIRST

Analyzing the Situation

One of your first speech assignments may be to introduce a classmate or yourself, to share a brief story with the class, to prove a controversial point, or to illustrate your pet peeve. Whatever the assignment, you need to understand completely the situation in which you find yourself and the expectations that come with the situation. This is essential in order to effectively develop a speech that fits the situation and addresses those expectations.

audience The individuals who share and listen to a public speech.

For starters, you need to know who your audience is. **Audience** refers to the individuals who share and listen to a public speech. Typically, you will be speaking to your classmates, some of whom you may already have come to know in the first few days of class. But even if you have not, you can make certain assumptions about them based on their attendance at your university or college. Do you attend a small, rural, liberal arts college or a large, urban university? What are the common majors emphasized at your institution? Beyond knowing these general facts, you can also observe your classmates in the effort to discover things about them. Are most of them the same age as you, older, or younger? People of the same age tend to share many of the same experiences. For example, the authors of this text grew up in the '50s and '60s. For us, the assassination of President John F. Kennedy was a defining experience. Yet for most of today's younger college students, Kennedy is but a distant historical figure. Although Kennedy's death is still important in a historical sense, the deaths at the World Trade Center, in Pennsylvania, and at the Pentagon on September 11, 2001, probably seem like a defining experience for you and your classmates.

Knowing the common experiences you share with your audience allows you to predict what topics are likely to elicit a favorable response. Factors such as the age, sex, and social status of the people with whom you speak may also help you predict audience response. Depending on who they are and what experiences they share, audience members come to any speech situation with a variety of expectations. For example, your classmates probably expect you to speak to them as a peer. If you violate that expectation, taking on an air of su-

Today's public speakers need to adapt to multicultural, multiethnic, and multiracial audiences.

periority, for example, you may not get the response you desire. Regardless, only after you thoroughly understand your speech situation, your audience, and their expectations should you begin to consider the purpose for your speech.

Choosing a Topic

Once you've analyzed your audience and the situation you face, one of the hardest things for many beginning speakers is the selection of a topic. Sometimes your instructor will do this for you, but it's just as likely you'll have to decide on a topic yourself.

In many classes, the first speech you give may not require choosing a complex topic. For example, some instructors ask students to introduce themselves or a classmate. We often ask our students to tell a story about something that has happened to them or to someone they have known. Thus, many of the suggestions in the pages that follow will not become relevant until later in the class. However, even if you are simply introducing yourself or telling a story, you still need to choose what you will say about yourself or what experience you will relate. Many of the same criteria that govern topic choice for research-based topics also apply to these early speeches. They should be interesting, appropriate, and worthwhile, as should any speech topic.

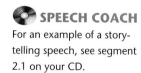

SPEECH COACH

For an example of a story-telling speech, see segment 2.1 on your CD.

An obvious place to begin is with your own interests, experiences, and knowledge. Remember to look for topics as you go through your day. For example, you may see a television program, such as *20/20* or *60 Minutes*, that deals with a topic that interests you. Or a magazine or a newspaper may suggest a topic. For example, an article in *Newsweek* titled "Overexposed" was the source of an excellent speech on skin cancer prevention.[1] Moreover, because the article pointed out that skin cancer is the leading cancer for people aged 25 to 29, the topic proved to be of interest to other students.

Television, newspapers, and magazines are but a few of the places where you might find a topic. Other sources include campus publications, instructors, and fellow students. Computer users who surf the Internet may find ideas there. The number of places to find a good topic, in fact, is limited only by how aware you are of what's going on around you. The following list summarizes a few good places to look for a topic.

TIPS AND TACTICS   *Suggestions for Finding a Topic*

- *Make a personal inventory.* What hobbies, interests, jobs, or experiences have you had that would interest others?

- *Talk to friends.* Perhaps they have ideas to share with you, including topics they would like to know more about.

- *Read.* Newspapers, newsmagazines, and books are filled with ideas. You should commit to reading at least one newspaper a day and one newsmagazine a week while enrolled in this course.

- *Check the Internet.* Many subject areas are discussed on the Internet, and there is a wide range of interest-based chat groups. If you enjoy "surfing the Net," you may well find speech ideas there for the taking.

- *Brainstorm.* **Brainstorming** in a group is a creative process used for generating a large number of ideas. (The activity in the box "Brainstorming for Topics" explains the process in more detail.)

brainstorming A creative process used for generating a large number of ideas.

In addition to knowing *where* to look for a topic, it is important to know *what* to look for. First, the topic should be interesting to you. If you don't care about the topic, how can you expect your audience to care? Second, select a topic that will be interesting to your audience—or at least can be made interesting to them. This is why it is crucial to know as much as possible about your audience. Third, your topic should be appropriate to the situation. If your instructor has asked you to speak on your pet peeve, she or he probably is thinking of topics like dorm food, roommates, or people who blow smoke in your face, not the destruction of the rain forests. Fourth, make sure your topic is appropriate to the time available. One limitation facing all speakers, not just those in a public speaking class, is time. Know what your instructor expects and stick to it. Further, consider the time you have available to prepare. If the speech is due next week, you won't be able to send off for information from your state's senator. Pick a topic that you can research in the time available. Fifth, make sure your topic is manageable. Don't pick a topic that is beyond your abilities or

Brainstorming for Topics

In a group of about three to five people, brainstorm different possible speech topics. During brainstorming the following rules apply:

- The goal is quantity of ideas; even silly ideas should be listed.
- No criticism or evaluation is allowed during the brainstorming process.
- One person is designated to write down every idea. Ideally, write ideas on a chalkboard or an easel so that everyone can see them.
- "Hitchhiking" ideas is encouraged. If you can add to or improve on someone else's idea, do it.

- When you think everyone is out of ideas, try to get at least one more from each group member.
- After all the ideas are listed, go through the list and select the best ones. Look for ideas that fit the assignment, are feasible given the time limits, and would be appropriate for this class. Cross off ideas that don't seem to apply.
- Now rank the remaining ideas in order of value. You may want to modify or combine ideas in this process. Which ones are most promising? How well do these possible topics fit the assignment? Will they be interesting and worthwhile for the members of the class?

---

resources. One of your greatest assets in speaking is your own **credibility,** which is the degree to which your audience trusts and believes in you. Nothing will undermine your credibility faster than speaking on a topic with which you are unfamiliar. Know more than your audience. Why else would you speak to them? Finally, it is crucial that your topic be worthwhile. We treat time in our society as a commodity. We bank time, spend time, and buy time. You are angered if someone wastes your time, so don't waste your audience's time. Pick a topic that will inform, persuade, or entertain the audience by presenting them with ideas or information they haven't already heard. Just as we hate to hear an old joke told over again, we don't like to hear for the umpteenth time that we ought to recycle our aluminum cans, unless the speaker tells us something new and insightful about why we should do just that. If you pick a well-worn topic, then you must give it a different "spin" or focus.

> **credibility** The degree to which an audience trusts and believes in a speaker.

Six Criteria for an Appropriate Speech Topic

1. The topic should be interesting to you.
2. It should be interesting to your audience—or at least be capable of being made interesting to them.
3. It should be appropriate to the situation.
4. It should be appropriate to the time available.
5. It should be manageable.
6. It should be worthwhile.

TIPS AND TACTICS

 SPEECH COACH

To hear more about these Tips and Tactics, go to Audio Tips and Tactics on your CD.

Choosing a General Speech Purpose

One of the first decisions a speaker faces is to decide on the **general purpose**—the primary function—of the speech. The three commonly agreed upon general purposes are to inform, to persuade, and to entertain. The most common types

> **general purpose** The primary function of a speech. The three commonly agreed upon general purposes are to inform, to persuade, and to entertain.

of speeches seek to *inform* others about things they do not already know or to *persuade* others to believe or behave in certain ways. Persuasive speeches not only seek change, they also may seek to reinforce social values, as when someone gives a Fourth of July speech or a sermon. Other speeches seek to *entertain* by sharing an enjoyable experience. Obviously, these general purposes are not mutually exclusive. A persuasive speech will also inform the audience, and an informative speech should be interesting enough that it encourages the audience to listen. Nevertheless, the general purpose you either have been assigned or have decided on yourself should tell you something about the topic you ultimately choose. Simply put, some topics may be inappropriate or only marginally appropriate to your purpose. Though controversial topics, for example, lend themselves to a persuasive speech, they are less well suited to an informative speech.

Writing Your Specific Purpose Statement

specific purpose The goal or objective a speaker hopes to achieve in speaking to a particular audience.

You may be assigned a general purpose—to inform, to persuade, or to entertain—for your early speeches. But you will not be assigned a specific purpose. The **specific purpose** is the goal or objective you hope to achieve in speaking to a particular audience. What you want to accomplish specifically with your audience rests with you. For example, assume you are asked to introduce yourself to the rest of the class. What do you want your classmates to think and feel about you? Do you want them to like, respect, and admire you? Then your specific purpose might be "to have the class develop a favorable opinion of me." Clearly this is a persuasive effort. You are creating attitudes about yourself where none existed before. Thus, even in early speech assignments, you should try to articulate a specific purpose for your speech.

The specific purpose of a speech is typically expressed in terms of an infinitive phrase that begins with "to." Specific purposes usually fall under one of the general purposes: to inform, to persuade, or to entertain. If you were giving an informative speech on computer viruses, for example, you might express your specific purpose as "to inform my audience about the methods of transmission of computer viruses." This purpose, however, is somewhat vague. More specifically, you might express it as "to enable my audience to explain in their own words the ways a computer virus can be transmitted." Because this specific purpose includes a way of measuring your results—the audience should be able to describe how the virus is transmitted—it will point you toward a specified goal. The level of audience understanding should be realistic: One speech cannot make them computer experts, but they should know how to protect themselves against viruses.

On the same topic, you might have as a persuasive specific purpose "to convince my audience to purchase a virus-detection program for their personal computer." Thus, a successful speech given this goal would lead to a number of audience members eventually purchasing such a program. Of course, there is a difference in content as well as purpose between a speech to inform the audience on computer virus transmission and one designed to persuade them to purchase a particular virus-detection software product. The persuasive speech would probably require the speaker to compare products, prices, and ease of use. The informative speech would not. Both speeches, however, would need to explain the nature of the threat to computer data from viruses. The persuasive presentation might do more to raise the level of concern among audience members so as to motivate them to purchase software to combat the threat.

Speeches to entertain have the advantage of instantaneous feedback. Speakers know by the audience's laughter or applause whether they have succeeded. So, a speaker might express a specific entertainment purpose as "to entertain my audience with the story of my worst computer nightmares." It is not necessary to state how you will measure whether this goal has been met because success or failure is immediately evident.

As you continue to give speeches in your class, work on developing specific purposes that are realistic, that are worthwhile for the audience, and that fulfill your goals as a speaker. Realistic specific purposes are those that can be accomplished in the brief time you have to present your speech considering the views of the audience you are addressing. For example, you might well motivate your audience to drink alcohol responsibly—something that is noncontroversial for most people. But to convince an audience that disagrees with your point of view to change its opinion on a topic like gun control or abortion is unrealistic. On such topics your specific purpose should be more modest—perhaps to have the audience become more open to your point of view.

Thus, examples of realistic specific purposes for persuasive speeches would include:

- To persuade audience members to avoid binge drinking.
- To persuade audience members to consider that a prison sentence is not always the best punishment for youthful offenders.
- To persuade the audience that privatization of social security is or isn't a good idea.

For informative speeches, examples of specific purposes would include:

- To teach my audience the basic principles involved in the Heimlich maneuver.
- To have my audience learn the basic steps of swing dancing.
- To have my audience learn about the earliest contributors to hip-hop culture.

Again, your specific purpose must be realistic. It is one thing to explain the basics of the Heimlich maneuver, and quite another to successfully instruct people in using the maneuver in a brief time without any hands-on practice. You can explain the basic steps of swing dancing in a few minutes, but teaching someone to really "swing" takes much longer.

In addition to ensuring that your specific purposes are realistic, make sure they are worthwhile. For example, the Heimlich maneuver can save a life. But unless your audience has some interest in swing or hip-hop, why would audience members be motivated to listen to your speech?

Finally, you need to assess your specific purpose carefully in terms of your own goals. What, exactly, do you want to achieve (other than a passing grade on your speech)? For example, what is your reason for teaching the steps of swing? Do you go swing dancing every Saturday night? Do you want to encourage others to join you? Or are you just a fan of the style, but not a participant? Understanding your own goals can help you write a clear and useful specific purpose.

As you develop your specific purpose, keep in mind these factors and the four guidelines listed below.

- Describe the results you seek.
- Be as specific as possible.
- Express your goal in measurable terms.
- Set a realistic goal.

Whatever speech topic you select, therefore, you need to clarify in your own mind and for your instructor what specific purpose you intend to achieve through the speech. Make sure the specific purpose is realistic, is worthwhile for your audience, and helps you achieve your own goals as a speaker.

Writing Your Thesis Statement

thesis statement A single declarative sentence that focuses the audience's attention on the central point of a speech.

Every speech should have a central idea or point that it makes. If you want people to save for their retirement at the earliest age possible, your point might be that doing so can make an early retirement possible. You should be able to express this point in a single declarative sentence. We call this a **thesis statement,** a sentence that focuses your audience's attention on the central point of your speech. A thesis statement should make your central point clear; express your point of view on that point; and, if accepted, fulfill your specific purpose.

Your thesis statement should help the audience understand what response you seek from them. As a case in point, you might be opposed to further restrictions on what you can do in dorm rooms. Assuming you are speaking to a group of student colleagues, you may wish to focus your speech on what they can do to fight the restrictions. Thus, your thesis statement might be, "We need to lobby the board of trustees of the university to stop this unjustified and harmful plan." Notice that the thesis statement here is directly related to the specific purpose of your speech. In this instance, your specific purpose is "to convince other students to lobby the board of trustees to stop the proposed restrictions." The thesis statement, if accepted and acted upon by the audience, will fulfill your specific purpose. While the specific purpose expresses your goal for the audience's response to the speech, the thesis statement expresses the essential message that is designed to fulfill that purpose.

Although the specific purpose is not normally stated explicitly to the audience, the thesis statement should be sufficiently related to that purpose to allow the audience to know what you want to accomplish. As an example, consider a speech on binge drinking. If your specific purpose was to persuade audience members to drink responsibly, your thesis statement might be, "Binge drinking can destroy lives." Or if you wanted to inform your audience of the basic principles of the Heimlich maneuver, your thesis statement might be, "The Heimlich maneuver involves applying pressure to the victim's diaphragm to expel air from the lungs and thus dislodge what is caught in the throat."

The thesis statement is usually stated in the introduction to the speech. There are some exceptions to this guideline, which will be discussed in later chapters. But as a general rule, letting your audience know your central point is important if you are to fulfill your goals as a speaker.

Even a speech to entertain should have a clear thesis. Obviously, there's no easier way to turn off an audience than to say, "Today I'm going to make you laugh." But it would be logical to say, "First dates are often a disaster, and mine was no different." Unlike a David Letterman monologue, which is often just a string of jokes, a speech to entertain should have a clear purpose, thesis, and structure.

PREPARING YOUR SPEECH

To classical speakers, **invention** was the creative process by which the substance of a speech is generated. It may seem odd, at first, to think of a speech as an invention. However, just as it was not enough for Thomas Edison simply to have the idea for the lightbulb, it is not enough for you just to have an idea for a speech. You need to invest time and effort in inventing the substance of what you plan to say. Where do you go for the substance of your speech? Here are some general suggestions, which we will develop in more detail in Chapter 7.

invention The creative process by which the substance of a speech is generated.

Personal Experience

Begin with your own experiences. Each of us has had experiences that make us unique. Many early speech assignments require you to look no further than to the things that have happened in your own life. For example, you may be asked to introduce yourself or tell a story about a personally significant experience. You may be able to rely on hobbies or past job experiences for an early informative speech. Even if you cannot rely solely on personal experience, it is the logical place to begin searching for information.

Speaking about matters with which you have firsthand experience connects you to your message. What's more, this personal connection may also tell you how to connect your message to the personal and professional needs of your audience. For example, a successful actress, who was enrolled in one of the author's classes at the University of Southern California, gave a speech on how to break into "show biz." Unfortunately, she failed to mention her own experience, which included a role in a Clint Eastwood movie and a recurring role on the sitcom *The Odd Couple*. Had she done so, her speech would have connected more effectively to the audience, in effect saying, "If I can do this, so can you!"

Even though your personal experience and knowledge are good sources with which to start, don't stop there. No matter how intense your experience or extensive your knowledge, there is always more to learn. In the effort to augment personal experience and knowledge, then, consult other sources as well.

Outside Sources

Look to general sources of information. Books, reference books, general-circulation periodicals (*Time, Newsweek, U.S. News & World Report*, etc.), and even public affairs programs such as *60 Minutes, Dateline*, or *20/20* are good places to look for information on topics of general interest. Keep in mind that books may have a long lead time before they are published. Thus, on topics that require up-to-date information, you need to rely on more recent sources, such as periodicals, rather than books. A speech on why the United States got involved in the Gulf War, for example, might well rely on books and encyclopedias, whereas a speech on the current situation in the Middle East would require the most recent sources available.

Sometimes you can interview an expert on the topic of your speech. You may not have to look any further than the other classes you are taking. An interview with an environmental-science instructor, for example, could provide a wealth of information for a unique speech about global warming. Further, experts often provide leads to other sources of information the speaker can obtain. Be sure to prepare thoroughly for your interview so that you know what questions to ask. Chapter 7 contains specific guidelines for conducting interviews, which you should consult before interviewing sources for any speech.

Conduct computerized searches, including the Internet. At one time the beginning public speaker relied primarily on print indexes, such as the *Readers' Guide to Periodical Literature*. In some libraries, these may still be the best means of access. However, more and more libraries are providing computerized databases, such as the Academic Search. In addition, many students now have access to the Internet either through their universities or through private Internet service providers (ISPs). Although you must be cautious about the reliability of many Web sites on the Internet, there is a wealth of information available to the average citizen. You can learn everything from the latest sports scores to up-to-the-minute political news. However, the Internet is also rife with misinformation and outright fraud. Imagine that you are doing research on cloning, and you go to the Web site at http://www.d-b.net/dti/. At first you might think human cloning is a reality. It's only when you read the fine print that you discover "DreamTech does not exist in this dimension; this site is a spoof site, intended to simulate one possible manifestation of reproductive cloning technology, and stimulate thought on the pros and cons of reproductive cloning."[2]

Your school may also have access to Lexis-Nexis Academic Universe, a service that allows for searches of newspapers, magazines, wire service reports, court transcripts, law digests, and even television program transcripts. If you have access to such resources, they will provide a systematic way to find articles on your topic. Further, they will save you time and improve the quality of your research.

Finally, consider specialized sources of information. Every discipline has specialized journals and books, as well as indexes to provide access to them. Chapter 7 discusses some of the more commonly used indexes. If you are dealing with a specialized topic early in the class, you probably should skip ahead to that chapter or meet with a reference librarian to help familiarize yourself with the resources available at your school. You might also consider other types of specialized sources, such as trade publications and government publications, if they are appropriate to your topic. For your early speeches, such specialization probably will not be necessary, but you should be aware that there is more to researching a speech than simply consulting the general books and periodicals found in most libraries.

TIPS AND TACTICS   *Resources for Your Speech*

1. Begin with your own experiences.
2. Look to outside sources of information:
   a. Search general sources of information, such as books and periodicals.
   b. Interview experts.
   c. Conduct computerized searches.
   d. Consider specialized sources of information.

As you gather information, whether from written sources or interviews, be sure to carefully record the facts and quotations you discover. Note not only what was said but also who said it, when, and where. As we discuss in Chapter 7, documenting your evidence for an audience will build your credibility, which will enhance the likelihood you will be effective in delivering your speech.

ORGANIZING YOUR SPEECH

Someone once said that every speech has three tell 'ems. First you tell 'em what you are going to tell 'em; then you tell 'em; and, finally, you tell 'em what you told 'em. That's a bit simplistic, but nevertheless, it captures the basic idea of the three parts of every speech: the introduction, the body, and the conclusion.

Though there are many ways to organize your speech, one of the most helpful patterns we have found for our own students is an adaptation of a system developed by Dr. Loretta Malandro for the business executives she coaches.[3] According to Dr. Malandro, the traditional introduction, body, and conclusion of a speech should include several important steps. Steps 1–4 are the introduction, step 5 is the body of the speech, and steps 6 and 7 are the conclusion. None of these steps should be skipped, and they should nearly always be presented in the order given here.

Seven Steps for Organizing Your Speech   **TIPS AND TACTICS**

1. *Open with impact.* In this step you capture your audience's attention.
2. *Focus on your thesis statement.* In this step you draw the audience's attention to the central point of your speech.
3. *Connect with your audience.* In this step you let the audience know "what's in it for them."
4. *Preview the body of your speech.* This is where you tell your audience what you are going to tell them in the body of the speech.
5. *Present your main points.* In this step you present the body of your speech. This step constitutes the bulk of your presentation.
6. *Summarize your main points.* In this step you tell the audience what you've told them.
7. *Close with impact.* In this step you leave your audience with a lasting impression.

 SPEECH COACH

To hear more about these Tips and Tactics, go to Audio Tips and Tactics on your CD.

Let's briefly examine each of these steps and how they relate to the traditional introduction–body–conclusion format of a speech. This relationship is illustrated in Figure 2.1.

 **SPEECH COACH**

To help you prepare your speech outline, see the Outline Tutor on your CD.

Introduction

To present an effective introduction, you should follow four steps.

Open With Impact   Introduce your presentation dramatically or humorously. There's no surer turnoff than beginning a speech, "Uh, um, well, I guess I'll talk about dorm food today." Begin the speech with something that captures your audience's attention, such as an appropriate joke, a startling statistic, an anecdote, or a reference to current affairs.

**FIGURE 2.1
Organizing Your
Speech.** The seven-step organizational pattern relates closely to the traditional introduction–body–conclusion pattern.

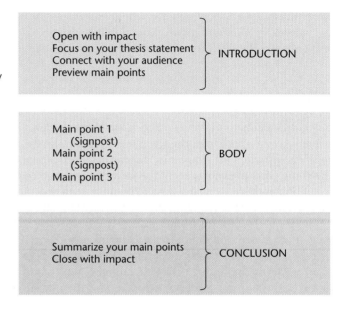

Open with impact
Focus on your thesis statement
Connect with your audience
Preview main points } INTRODUCTION

Main point 1
   (Signpost)
Main point 2
   (Signpost)
Main point 3 } BODY

Summarize your main points
Close with impact } CONCLUSION

TIPS AND TACTICS *Ways to Open Your Speech With Impact*

 SPEECH COACH

To learn more about these Tips and Tactics, see Audio Tips and Tactics on your CD.

1. Tell a brief story.
2. Use a quotation.
3. Make a startling statement.
4. Refer to the audience, the occasion, or a current event.
5. Use appropriate humor.
6. Relate a personal experience.
7. Ask a thought-provoking question.

Focus on Your Thesis Statement As we noted earlier, the thesis statement captures the central point of your speech. For example, if you are opposed to a planned tuition hike on your campus, you should state clearly, "The students of this campus should not be forced to pay more for less." On the other hand, you might want to inform your audience about the variety of financial assistance available to them: "With effort and persistence, you can obtain a student loan or scholarship to help meet your college expenses."

Connect With Your Audience Answer the questions "What's in this for my audience? Why is it in their personal and/or professional interest to listen to me?" For example, will the proposed tuition hike keep some in your audience from completing their degrees? Make the connection to your specific audience clear in the introduction to the speech. This is also a good place to build your credibility as a speaker. Let the audience know you understand their concerns and have their best interests at heart. If you have expertise on the topic, let your audience know this now so that they can appreciate what is to come.

Preview   Most people like a map of the territory they're entering. The **preview** provides your audience with a map to where you are taking them. It forecasts the **main points** of a speech. You should mention all your main points briefly before treating each one in detail. This is the "tell 'em what you're going to tell 'em" part of the speech. It may be as simple as saying, "I'm going to present three ways to save money on your groceries: clipping coupons, watching for store ads, and buying generic brands." On the other hand, a preview may specifically enumerate the three main points of the speech: "You can save money on your groceries, first, by clipping coupons; second, by watching for store ads; and third, by buying generic brands." The preview helps reduce the audience's uncertainty about what is to follow, and it helps them see the relationship among your various points.

preview A forecast of the main points of a speech.

main points The key ideas that support the thesis statement of a speech.

Body

The majority of your speech should develop the thesis you are trying to convey. Usually, the body of the speech is divided into three to five main points that in aggregate develop the thesis of your speech.

Organize Your Main Points   A speech that wanders off the topic or whose main points don't follow a logical pattern of development is likely to lose the audience. The same is true of an overly complex speech. Here are some basic patterns for organizing your main points:

- *Time pattern*. Most stories are arranged chronologically. One event follows another until the climax unfolds. Often speeches deal with topics in terms of past, present, and future.

- *Spatial pattern*. Some topics are best dealt with spatially. A speech on the solar system might begin with the sun and work out to the most distant planets.

- *Categorical pattern*. Many topics fall into obvious categories. A teacher explaining the federal government to a civics class, for example, is likely to talk about the legislative, judicial, and executive branches. This is sometimes called a topical pattern of organization. If a topic lends itself to natural divisions, this is an excellent way to arrange your speech.

- *Problem–solution pattern*. The problem–solution pattern is a natural way to organize persuasive speeches. What's wrong and why are followed by how to solve the problem and how the solution will benefit the audience. Many sales pitches are built around a problem–solution pattern. For example, a salesperson selling water softeners would begin with the problems caused by "hard water," such as water spots on dishes and excessive use of expensive detergent. Then she would propose a solution: buying her company's product.

These four ways to organize a speech are summarized in Figure 2.2. Other ways to organize a speech are discussed at length in Chapter 8. For now, this will give you a start. The key thing to remember in this regard is to pick a simple pattern and stick with it for the entire speech.

Provide Signposts   We also want to emphasize the importance of using **signposts,** transitional statements that bridge your main points. For example, you might say

signposts Transitional statements that bridge main points.

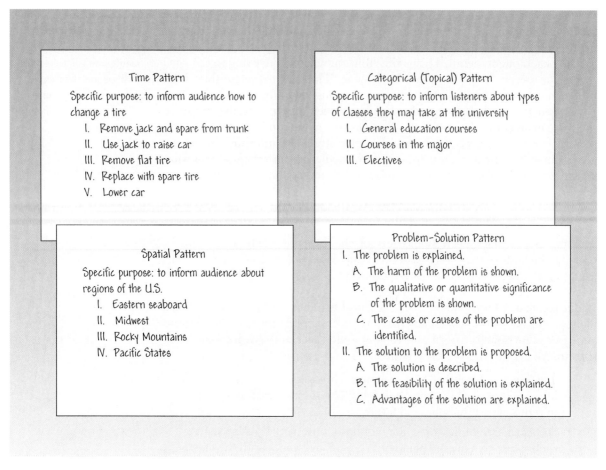

FIGURE 2.2 Common Patterns for Organizing the Main Points of a Speech

something as simple as, "My second point is . . ." or "Now that you understand the problem, let's examine some possible solutions." The goal in using signposts is to provide your audience with guides along the path of your speech so that they will know where you have been, where you are, and where you are going next.

Conclusion

All too often, speakers invest so much energy in developing the introduction and body of their speeches that they run out of gas at the end. The impact with which you conclude a speech is just as important as the impact with which you began.

Summarize Your Main Points   Tell 'em what you've told 'em. That is the first and most important function of a conclusion. Remind the listeners of what they've heard.

Close With Impact   Just as a salesperson doesn't like the customer to walk out the door without buying something, you don't want your audience to leave without at least thinking about doing what you've asked them to do. So, find a way to reinforce your specific purpose. It's also your last chance to leave a favorable impression. Just as listeners are turned off by an introduction that begins "Today I want to tell you about . . . ," you can undermine the effectiveness of an excellent speech with a poor conclusion, such as "Well, I guess that's about it." Finish with a flourish that is as powerful as your opening.

Ways to Close Your Speech Effectively

TIPS AND TACTICS

- Present a short, memorable *quotation*.
- Use an *anecdote* or a brief *story* that illustrates your point and leaves a lasting impression on your audience.
- Make a *direct appeal* or "call to action."
- *Return to your opening*. This is one of the best ways to end a speech because it brings the listeners full circle.

SPEECH COACH
To hear more about these Tips and Tactics, go to Audio Tips and Tactics on your CD.

So, conclude your speech by *summarizing* your main points and *closing with impact*.

The speech outline in the box "Go Sun Smart" by Shelly Lee follows the steps we have just discussed. Notice how the speaker begins the speech by asking a thought-provoking question most of us can relate to. The speaker connects with the audience by relating to an almost universal experience of getting a bad sunburn. The speech is built around three main points, and concludes with a summary and call to action. We have noted a number of these features in the margin.

SPEECH COACH
To view a video of this speech, see segment 2.2 on your CD.

PRESENTING YOUR SPEECH

There's a story told about the great speaker of ancient Greece, Demosthenes, who said that the first, second, and third most important things in rhetoric were—delivery, delivery, and delivery.[4] Although the story is probably apocryphal, it does illustrate the importance of effective delivery. No matter how well thought out your speech, or how many hours you put in at the library, or how elegant your outline, unless the speech is effectively presented, your message will not have its desired impact. In Chapter 10 we deal at length with the nature of delivery, including the important functions nonverbal communication serves for a speaker. In the meantime, however, the following guidelines will help you present your beginning speeches.

Keep in mind that you have three tools as a public speaker: your *voice*, your *face and eyes*, and your *body*. If you manage these effectively, you will be able to get your message across to your audience.

Use Your Voice Effectively

How you use your voice is critical to effective communication. Some basic guidelines will enable you to speak most effectively.

Breathe Properly   Breathe deeply, from your diaphragm. Give your voice enough support to be heard, but avoid straining your voice or shouting.

Speak Conversationally   Think of public speaking as heightened conversation. Don't attempt to emulate political orators: Most audiences are put off by their techniques. Speak as you do in conversation, but enlarge your voice sufficiently

Sample Speech Outline

GO SUN SMART
by Shelly Lee

General purpose: To inform

Specific purpose: To inform the audience how to protect themselves from deadly skin cancer.

Introduction

I. **Open with impact:** How many of you can remember a sunburn so bad you could barely put your clothes on? How many of you have simply been burned while spending the day at the beach, tubing on the river, water skiing at the lake, or even skiing or riding your board on a fresh powder day at your favorite mountain?

  A. Did you know that there are over 1 million new cases of skin cancer each year in the United States, including over 51,000 cases of melanoma (Kalb, 2001)?

  B. Did you know that many of these cases can be directly linked to the cumulative effects of the sun?

  C. Did you know that there is no such thing as a safe tan, despite what the indoor tanning industry would like you to believe (Young and Walker, 1998)?

II. **Connect with audience:** Every one of you who raised your hand needs to know that those sunburns you got put you at increased risk for skin cancer. Further, even if you've never burned or you are dark skinned, the information I'll share in a moment is important to you as well.

III. **Thesis:** Skin cancer is not only the fastest growing form of cancer in the United States, it also is one of the easiest forms of cancer to prevent (American Cancer Society, 1996).

IV. **Preview:** As a result, I'd like to look at three important things we all need to know to reduce our risk for skin cancer. First, there are three basic forms of skin cancer. Second, skin cancer is all too often a by-product of too much fun in the sun. And third, you can reduce your risk for developing skin cancer by following some easy steps.

Body

I. There are three types of skin cancer: basal cell, squamous, and melanoma (Kalb, 2001).

  A. Basal cell is the most common and easily treated and is rarely life threatening.

  B. Squamous cell cancer is the next most common, and it too is easily treated and seldom fatal unless completely unattended.

  C. Melanoma, which is the form of skin cancer Maureen Reagan died from, is increasing at an alarming rate in the United States. It is deadly if not treated early in its growth.

(**Signpost:** So what causes skin cancer?)

II. Much as we may like the sun, too much of this good thing is bad for us.

  A. The sun's rays contain ultraviolet radiation.

B. Science has linked ultraviolet radiation from the sun with basal cell and squamous cell skin cancer (Kalb, 2001).

   1. Scientists at the National Cancer Institute also believe that ultraviolet radiation is linked to melanoma, although the relationship is not as clear (Kalb, 2001).

   2. Melanoma can show up anywhere on the skin and can develop in even dark-skinned people.

   3. For example, did you know that Bob Marley died from melanoma skin cancer?

C. As few as three severe sunburns in childhood put you at increased risk for skin cancer.

(**Signpost:** Even though the incidence of skin cancer is increasing, you have considerable control over this risk.)

III. The American Cancer Society and the American Dermatological Association have developed some simple guidelines to follow: (American Cancer Society, 1996)

A. Avoid the sun between 10 A.M. and 4 P.M. when possible.

B. Always wear a sunscreen with sun protection factor of 15 or better, and wear sun-protective clothing such as a wide-brimmed hat, long-sleeved shirt, and long pants.

C. Know the early warning signs of skin cancer, which are A for *asymmetry*, B for irregular *borders*, and C for irregular *color* on moles and freckles especially.

D. Finally, give yourself a full body check every six months or have someone do it for you.

Conclusion begins with a summary of main points.

(**Signpost:** In conclusion)

Conclusion

I. **Summarize:** Remember these important facts:

A. Skin cancer comes in three types: basal, squamous, and melanoma.

B. Also, keep in mind that while we need the sun, a little sunning is actually a lot.

Speech closes with impact. Ask yourself if it matches the impact with which the speech opened.

C. Finally, be sun smart by practicing sun-safe behaviors such as those suggested by the ADA.

II. **Close with impact:** Skin cancer can kill. With a little common sense, however, it is easily prevented. Please be sun smart.

References

American Cancer Society (1996). *Cancer facts and figures*. Atlanta, GA: The American Cancer Society.

Kalb, C. (2001, August 20). Overexposed. *Newsweek*, 35–38.

Young, J. C. and Walker, R. (1998). Understanding students' indoor tanning beliefs and practices, *American Journal of Health Studies*, 14, 120–128.

Speaker lists references at end of speech with full bibliographic citation. We discuss American Psychological Association (APA) and Modern Language Association (MLA) methods of source citation in Chapter 7. Your instructor may prefer a different method of citing sources. Whatever method is used, accurate source citation is important.

to be heard by all in the room. It is certainly appropriate and even advisable to ask those in the back of the room if they can hear you, should there be any doubt.

Vary Your Voice   Nothing is more deadly to a speech than a monotone voice. Vary the rate at which you speak, the pitch (high or low) at which you speak, and the volume (loudness). The goal is to present your speech enthusiastically, sincerely, and energetically. Let the audience know you care about your topic.

Use Your Face and Eyes Effectively

The face is one of the most complex and expressive parts of our anatomy, capable of communicating thousands of messages. Use your facial expression to reinforce your verbal message. The eyes, in particular, convey a great deal. Consider a person who gazes at you without pause. This will tend to make you uncomfortable. On the other hand, in our North American culture, a person who refuses to look at us communicates a negative message. (In some other cultures, such as certain Asian societies, no such negative message is communicated by avoiding eye contact.) As a speaker communicating to an American audience, therefore, maintain eye contact with your audience. This does not mean staring at just one portion of the room or shifting your eyes randomly. Rather, look at one member of your audience, then shift your gaze to another member, and so on. Be alert for audience responses to what you are saying. Are they restless, interested, puzzled? Such feedback can help you adapt to the audience as you speak.

Use Your Body Effectively

Your body is the third tool you use to communicate your message. Your body communicates to your audience through *posture, movement, gestures,* and *dress.*

Posture   How do you want to stand during your speech? Some speakers are comfortable behind a lectern, whereas others prefer to move away from it or dispense with it entirely. Choosing not to use a lectern can be an effective way of lessening the physical and psychological distance between yourself and the audience. If your preference is to use a lectern, do not use it as a crutch or bass drum. Avoid leaning on or clutching the stand, as well as beating on it with your open palm. Instead, find a comfortable, erect posture and stand slightly behind the lectern. Keep in mind that to breathe effectively, you need to have good body posture.

Movement   Movement should be spontaneous and meaningful. Though good speakers avoid pacing and random movements, it is perfectly appropriate—in fact, desirable—to move to emphasize an important idea or a transition between points. There is no reason a speaker's feet have to be nailed to the floor. Use your body to communicate your message whenever possible and practical.

Gestures   It is common in everyday conversation to gesture with your hands. In fact, try this experiment: Give someone directions from your school to your home *without* moving your hands. You will find it virtually impossible. The key to effective use of gestures in a public speech is that they should be appropriate to the point you are making and clearly visible to your audience. The larger the room, the larger the gesture needs to be for your audience to see it. On the other hand, too many gestures, especially if they appear to be the result of nervous-

Using your face, eyes, and hands can add to the effectiveness of your presentation.

ness, such as fidgeting, can be distracting to an audience. Finally, your gestures should be natural extensions of what you do in everyday conversation.

Dress   Your dress as a speaker should be *appropriate* to the situation and the audience. A good rule of thumb is to dress as you might for a job interview. People make instant judgments about other people and, as one shampoo ad proclaims, "You never get a second chance to make a first impression." In no case should your dress detract from the message you want to convey.

Methods of Delivery

There are four common ways to deliver a speech:

- Write out a *manuscript* and read it to your audience.
- *Memorize* your speech and recite it from memory.
- Present a spontaneous, unrehearsed *impromptu* presentation.
- Combine preparation and spontaneity in an *extemporaneous* presentation.

We discuss each type of delivery in turn, along with its advantages and limitations. For a discussion of how an experienced speaker chose to deliver her most famous speech, see the box "The Dole Stroll."

Manuscript Delivery   When a speaker uses **manuscript delivery,** the speech is written out completely and read to the audience. Few speakers are very good at reading a speech. In fact, except for politicians and other officials who rely on ghostwriters to prepare their speeches, most of us will not have occasion to give a manuscript speech.

Though it might seem easy to write out your speech in advance and read it to the audience, this is easier said than done. One disadvantage of written speeches is that most people don't write as they speak. Speeches delivered from

manuscript delivery A mode of presentation that involves writing out a speech completely and reading it to the audience.

"The Dole Stroll": *Dr. Nichola D. Gutgold**

Former secretary of labor and transportation, former president of the American Red Cross, and wife of presidential nominee Bob Dole, Elizabeth Dole is one of the most polished and prepared public speakers in America. She made history and captivated the American public when, at the Republican National Convention, she abandoned the podium and walked among the delegates to speak. Mrs. Dole explains why she chose to break with tradition:

I was told by two experts that I could not walk around at the 1996 GOP convention successfully. . . . Walking down 12 steps in heels was something to think about twice before you do it! But I think when the audience saw me come down, they all got quiet. They hadn't seen this before. They all wondered "what is she doing?" And because of that, they were more attentive and cooperative as I walked around the audience. . . . That walking around really works well for me in other speeches as well. I like doing that, and I frequently use that style when I speak for the American Red Cross and I speak to victims and their families. I think that it is a very effective way for me to reach the audience. The audience seems to respond so much better when I move around and I am not behind the podium with bright lights glaring at me. I now feel that the podium is a barrier between the audience and me. What we found during the campaign was that a fascinating thing to do was to interview people—stop them and have them tell their story and then tell them what Bob Dole would do. . . . I found that the reason that I started moving from the podium is about three months before I left for my leave of absence from the Red Cross, when I was trying to get

people to give money to the Red Cross, or blood or their time, if I could get close to them—if I could talk to them like it was a conversation, it worked much better.

Source: Elizabeth Dole, interview in Hershey, Pennsylvania, 7 April 1998.

*Dr. Gutgold is an assistant professor of speech communication at Penn State Berks-Lehigh Valley College and is writing a book about the public speaking of Elizabeth Dole.

a manuscript have an artificial quality. Sentences are often too long and complex. The audience often loses track of the point being made. "Oral essays" are not an effective way to communicate with an audience.

If the manuscript pages get out of order or some are missing, you may be forced to improvise or stop your speech altogether. Most teachers have had the painful experience of watching a speaker fumble for words as he or she looks frantically for the next page of the speech. Overreliance on a manuscript can lead to such embarrassing moments.

Another disadvantage of manuscript delivery is that you lose eye contact with your audience. Not only does this inhibit feedback, it reduces your contact with the audience, which, as we will see later, is a major factor in establishing your credibility as a speaker.

The principal situation in which you will want to deliver a speech from a manuscript is if it is critical that you be quoted accurately. For example, public officials usually speak from a manuscript to ensure that they are accurately quoted in the media, to which copies are usually provided. For your first speeches, however, you should avoid the manuscript speech.

Overreliance on a speech manuscript can cause a speaker to lose contact with the audience.

Memorized Delivery An alternative to reading a speech is to memorize it. **Memorized delivery** is a mode of presentation in which the speech is written out and committed to memory before being presented to the audience without the use of notes. This method of delivery does eliminate the problems associated with maintaining eye contact. And, presumably, an able speaker can quickly drop a section of a memorized speech should time run short. But, on the whole, memorized speeches today are confined to the theater and speech tournaments. The reason is simple: Memorization requires an enormous investment of time for even a brief speech. Further, if you forget the speech, you are faced with either a very noticeable silence or "winging it." Finally, memorized speeches usually sound memorized. They are simply oral essays without the physical manuscript.

memorized delivery A mode of presentation in which a speech is written out and committed to memory before being presented to the audience without the use of notes.

Impromptu Delivery A spontaneous, unrehearsed mode of presenting a speech is termed **impromptu delivery.** We are frequently called on to give impromptu speeches, although we usually don't think of them as speeches. For example, when your instructor calls on you to explain the day's reading assignment—or when you explain to your bank why you really aren't overdrawn—you are making an impromptu speech. In fact, most of our everyday conversations are spontaneous.

impromptu delivery A spontaneous, unrehearsed mode of presenting a speech.

Nevertheless, for most speaking situations, the impromptu method of speaking is of limited usefulness. Even experienced public speakers usually have "canned" or set pieces on which they rely when they are called on to make impromptu presentations. For example, candidates for public office prepare for their debates and press conferences for days beforehand. Every conceivable question is asked in rehearsal, and possible answers are practiced. The unprepared candidate is often caught off guard, and his or her attempt to ad lib can backfire, as when Bob Dole spoke about the "Brooklyn Dodgers" during the 1996 presidential campaign. Of course, the Dodgers haven't played in Brooklyn since the early 1950s, and Dole's flub was taken by many as a sign that he was out of touch.

For beginning speakers, impromptu speeches should be approached as a learning tool to enhance the principles that apply to other speeches. To rely on impromptu speeches for all of your assignments is not wise.

Impromptu speaking is discussed in more detail in Chapter 15, but here are a few pointers to keep in mind if you are called on to give an impromptu presentation early in the semester.

TIPS AND TACTICS   *Making an Impromptu Presentation*

- Think about what basic point you want to make about the topic. Are you for or against it? If you don't know, you might list the pros and cons of the issue and let the audience reach its own conclusion. If you are not informed on the topic, try linking it to something on which you do have information.

- Think of one or more points that support your position.

- If you have time, think of an attention-getter as an introduction.

- State your topic in the introduction: It buys you time and then you are sure the audience knows what you are saying.

- As a conclusion, summarize what you've said.

If you do not have time to organize your thoughts, at least take a moment to think of your thesis and two or three main points. Believe it or not, in a few seconds you can organize a fairly decent impromptu speech. We engage in spontaneous conversations all the time. Thinking and speaking are not mutually exclusive.

Extemporaneous Delivery   The best mode of presentation for most beginning speakers is **extemporaneous delivery,** which combines careful preparation with spontaneous speaking. The speaker generally uses brief notes rather than a manuscript or an outline. Some instructors require students to first outline their speech in a formal way, in which case the outline should serve as a preparatory tool, not an abbreviated speech manuscript. Other instructors require only that students prepare note cards to help them recall their main and supporting points. (For an example of a speaker's note cards, see Figure 2.3.) Practicing the speech in advance allows you to fix the ideas in your head without memorizing the exact wording.

The extemporaneous method allows you to be prepared yet flexible. If you see from the audience feedback that people are disagreeing with you, you can re-explain a point or add another example. If the audience seems bored, you might skip ahead to your most interesting example. Most teachers employ an extemporaneous method when lecturing to their classes. Students are invited to interact with their instructor, ask questions, and perhaps challenge a point. An extemporaneous speech should be a true transaction between speaker and listener.

extemporaneous delivery
A mode of presentation that combines careful preparation with spontaneous speaking. The speaker generally uses brief notes rather than a full manuscript or an outline.

SUMMARY

The essential steps in developing an effective speech are to:

- Analyze the situation with which you are faced, including both the nature of your assignment and the audience.

 **SPEECH COACH**
To evaluate your understanding of this chapter, see the Quizzes on your CD.

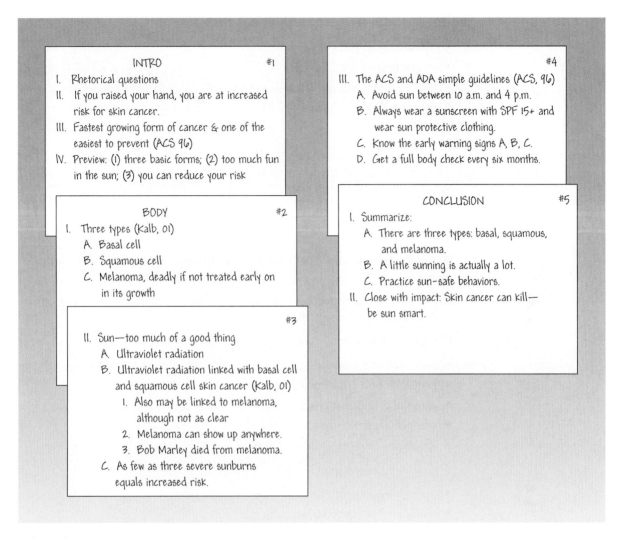

FIGURE 2.3 Speaker's Note Cards

- Choose a topic that is suitable to both the situation and the audience.
- Decide on a general and specific purpose.
- Write a clear thesis statement.
- Prepare the substance of your speech.
- Organize your speech.
- Present your speech effectively.

There are many ways to come up with an appropriate topic, including:

- making a personal inventory
- talking to friends
- reading widely
- checking the Internet
- brainstorming

An appropriate speech topic should be:

- interesting to you
- interesting to your audience
- appropriate to the situation
- appropriate to the time available
- manageable
- worthwhile

The primary function of a speech is expressed as a general purpose:

- to inform
- to persuade
- to entertain

A specific purpose describes your goal or objective in speaking to a particular audience.

The thesis statement focuses your audience's attention on the central point you wish to make in your speech.

Resources for preparing your speech include:

- your own experiences
- general sources of information
- interviews with experts
- computerized searches
- specialized sources of information

A clearly organized speech:

- opens with impact
- focuses on your thesis statement
- connects with your audience
- previews your main points
- organizes your ideas with three to five main points
- summarizes your main points
- closes with impact

Common organizational patterns include:

- chronological
- spatial
- categorical
- problem–solution

Transitional statements are called signposts.

In presenting your speech use your voice, face, and body.

Of the four methods of speech delivery, we recommend the extemporaneous method.

CHECK YOUR UNDERSTANDING: EXERCISES AND ACTIVITIES

1. Write a one- or two-page analysis of the audience for your first speech. What characteristics do your classmates seem to have in common? Are they similar to or dissimilar from you in age, social status, and background? What assumptions can you make about them based on their attendance at your university or college? How will what you know about your classmates affect your choice of speech topic and specific purpose?

2. Come up with three possible topics for your first speech. For each topic, consider whether it is (a) interesting to you, (b) interesting to your audience, (c) appropriate to the situation, (d) appropriate to the time available, (e) manageable, and (f) worthwhile. Based on this analysis, which topic do you believe is best for your first speech?

3. Once you have selected the best topic, determine what general purpose it would fulfill and phrase a specific purpose that you would hope to achieve in presenting the speech.

4. Make a list of appropriate sources for information about the topic you have chosen for your first speech.

5. Using the format discussed in this chapter, prepare an outline that organizes your speech so that it (a) opens with impact, (b) focuses on your thesis statement, (c) connects with your audience, (d) previews your main points, (e) organizes your ideas with three to five main points, (f) summarizes your main points, and (g) closes with impact.

6. View a speech on videotape and then read a transcript of the speech. Appendix A contains a transcript for a speech available on the CD that accompanies this book. After both reading and viewing the speech, write a short paper that answers the following questions: (a) What seemed to be the greatest strength of this speech? (b) What seemed to be the greatest weakness of this speech? (c) What differences did you note between reading an outline or transcript of the speech and actually seeing the speech delivered?

    Alternatively, review the transcript of a famous speech, such as Earl Spencer's eulogy of Princess Diana or Mary Fisher's speech on AIDS (in Appendix B). Then answer questions (a) and (b).

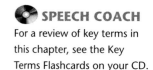 **SPEECH COACH**

For a review of key terms in this chapter, see the Key Terms Flashcards on your CD.

NOTES

1. Claudia Kalb, "Overexposed," *Newsweek*, 20 August 2001, 34–39.
2. "Clones R Us" [http://www.d-b.net/dti/, 26 August 2001].
3. The formula was originally developed by Dr. Loretta Malandro and is taught in her program "Speak With Impact," offered by Malandro Communication Inc., Scottsdale, Arizona. We have modified it to add a preview to the introduction.
4. George Kennedy, *The Art of Persuasion in Greece* (Princeton, N.J.: Princeton University Press, 1963), 283.

Practice helps
relieve anxiety
about speaking.

Managing Speech Anxiety

 OBJECTIVES

After reading this chapter and reviewing the learning resources on your CD-ROM and at the Online Learning Center, you should be able to:

- Explain the relationship between arousal and anxiety.
- Distinguish speech anxiety from communication apprehension.
- Define anxiety and distinguish it from speech anxiety.
- Identify common sources of speech anxiety.
- Understand and use skills that have proved effective in controlling arousal and speech anxiety.

 KEY CONCEPTS

communication apprehension	coping skills	self-talk
	negative self-talk	speech anxiety
constructive self-talk	physiological arousal	visual imagery

If your stomach disputes you—lie down and pacify it with cool thoughts.

—SATCHEL PAIGE

It often begins with butterflies in the pit of your stomach. Then your heart begins to palpitate. Your head starts to swim, making it difficult for you to concentrate, and a veil of perspiration begins to form on the palms of your hands. It may result from being asked to pinch-hit during a game of summer softball, from anticipating an important test you need to pass for your major, or from thinking about an interview for a needed internship. As pointed out in an episode of ABC Television's *20/20*, however, for more than 40 percent of the adult population, these feelings are the result of people's anxiety about public speaking.[1]

Emotional and physical discomfort with public speaking has been called everything from stage fright and speech anxiety to shyness and communication apprehension. For our purpose, we'll call it speech anxiety. We define **speech anxiety** as the unpleasant thoughts and feelings aroused by the anticipation of a real or imagined speech in public.[2] It is different from stage fright because it concerns public speaking rather than acting. It is different from shyness because it is not the result of general discomfort with social situations. Further, it is different from communication apprehension because it affects at least twice as many people, and because highly communication apprehensive people are fearful about communicating interpersonally and in groups, not just in public.[3]

There is another important distinction between speech anxiety and communication apprehension. **Communication apprehension,** which is the fear of real or anticipated communication with others regardless of the situation, is difficult to change with skills training. In contrast, research shows that speech anxiety can be managed with mental and behavioral skills you can learn both inside and outside of your class.[4]

Seventy-five years of solid research have taught us much about the nature, effects, and constructive management of speech anxiety. In this chapter, we pass some of the most relevant research along to you, as well as the aforementioned skills. Topics discussed include (1) the physiological and psychological origins of speech anxiety, (2) how speech anxiety most commonly expresses itself in the speech process, and (3) the specific skills you can begin using to make your emotions work for you rather than against you before, during, and after your speeches. To assess your own level of communication apprehension and speech anxiety, fill out the scales in the box "How Anxious Are You About Public Speaking?" and follow the scoring guide when you are finished.

PHYSIOLOGICAL AROUSAL AND SPEECH ANXIETY

The relationship between physiological arousal and speech anxiety is paradoxical. When we speak of **physiological arousal,** we mean the physical changes that occur when a person is aroused, such as an increased pulse rate, greater alertness, and more energy. On the one hand, moderate arousal is necessary for everything from spiking volleyballs and kicking field goals to writing a good essay and delivering a powerful speech. The adrenaline charge from moderate arousal makes you more motivated and alert, energized, and ready to perform the activity at hand. While a little arousal helps you to perform physical behav-

speech anxiety Feelings of discomfort that people experience before, during, and after speaking in public.

communication apprehension Fear about communicating interpersonally and in groups, not just in public.

physiological arousal The physical changes that occur when a person is aroused, such as increased pulse, greater alertness, and more energy.

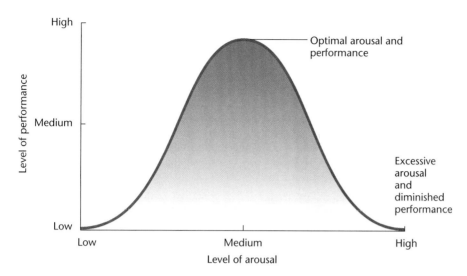

FIGURE 3.1 Arousal and Performance

iors especially, too much arousal can produce undesirable side effects (see Figure 3.1).[5] Too much arousal causes excessive adrenaline in the body, which can cause constricted muscles and vocal cords, rapid and shallow breathing, and light-headedness. For the speaker who feels constricted, short of breath, and on the verge of passing out, delivering a speech becomes an ordeal. The trick then is not to make feelings of arousal disappear, but to keep these feelings in check so that they do not unnecessarily interfere with the ability to speak effectively.

THE PSYCHOLOGY OF AROUSAL AND PERFORMANCE

The body does what the brain tells it to do. The body, moreover, does not distinguish what the brain communicates as real or imagined, exciting or terrifying. People sometimes cry out during a bad dream or jump in their seat during a scary movie because their imagination produces a physical response, even though they are not really in harm's way.

Physical reactions to stimuli help us when we are actually threatened. They can hinder us, however, when the threat is more psychological than real. For many people, the anticipation and act of speaking are perceived quite negatively. Even though their physical well-being isn't truly threatened by the task of speaking, their highly negative view of the task causes their bodies to react as if it were. As a result, they may tremble, blush, and perspire. Such a reaction would be justified if they were running away from a knife-wielding attacker. But that is not the case. They are standing in front of a group of people who actually want them to succeed.

The key to overcoming this undesirable and illogical reaction is to find a way for people to alter their interpretation of the situation and their physical response to it. While that may not be easy, it can be done. In fact, thousands of people each year are able to go out in a crowd or give a speech because they have learned **coping skills** that help them to control their fear of large groups or fear of speaking.

coping skills Mental and physical techniques used to control arousal and anxiety in the course of speaking in public.

How Anxious Are You About Public Speaking?

The following scale measures communication anxiety in general, as well as anxiety resulting from communication in four specific contexts: (1) dyads, (2) small groups, (3) meetings, and (4) public settings. You may find upon completion of the measure that although your overall score is indicative of mild levels of communication anxiety, you are moderately to highly anxious about communicating in one or more specific contexts. Some research, for example, indicates that communicating in groups, meetings, and public settings is most anxiety arousing for students much like you. In any case, the techniques introduced in this chapter will help you cope with your communication anxieties, regardless of their contextual source.

PERSONAL REPORT OF COMMUNICATION APPREHENSION (PRCA-24)

Directions: This instrument is composed of 24 statements concerning your feelings about communication with other people. Please indicate in the space provided the degree to which each statement applies to you by marking whether you (1) Strongly Agree, (2) Agree, (3) Are Undecided, (4) Disagree, or (5) Strongly Disagree with each statement. There are no right or wrong answers. Many of the statements are similar to other statements. Do not be concerned about this. Work quickly; just record your first impression.

_____ 1. I dislike participating in group discussions.
_____ 2. Generally, I am comfortable while participating in a group discussion.
_____ 3. I am tense and nervous while participating in group discussions.
_____ 4. I like to get involved in group discussions.
_____ 5. Engaging in a group discussion with new people makes me tense and nervous.
_____ 6. I am calm and relaxed while participating in group discussions.
_____ 7. Generally, I am nervous when I have to participate in a meeting.
_____ 8. Usually I am calm and relaxed while participating in meetings.
_____ 9. I am very calm and relaxed when I am called upon to express an opinion at a meeting.
_____ 10. I am afraid to express myself at meetings.
_____ 11. Communicating at meetings usually makes me uncomfortable.
_____ 12. I am very relaxed when answering questions at a meeting.
_____ 13. While participating in a conversation with a new acquaintance, I feel very nervous.
_____ 14. I have no fear of speaking up in conversations.
_____ 15. Ordinarily I am very tense and nervous in conversations.

Roots: Why Some People Are More Anxious Than Others

Not all people have the same reason for being anxious about speaking in public. The underlying sources of speech anxiety are varied. Still, research over the past three decades has given a good picture of the most common sources of anxieties about speaking in public. Further, recent studies reveal that the picture laypeople give for speech anxiety roughly corresponds to that uncovered in scholarly research.[6] College students much like you, for example, report that lack of preparation, the fear of making mistakes, appearance concerns, projections about audience interest, and lack of previous experience can feed speech anxiety. In a sense, these

_____ 16. Ordinarily I am very calm and relaxed in conversations.

_____ 17. While conversing with a new acquaintance, I feel very relaxed.

_____ 18. I'm afraid to speak up in conversations.

_____ 19. I have no fear of giving a speech.

_____ 20. Certain parts of my body feel very tense and rigid while giving a speech.

_____ 21. I feel relaxed while giving a speech.

_____ 22. My thoughts become confused and jumbled when I am giving a speech.

_____ 23. I face the prospect of giving a speech with confidence.

_____ 24. While giving a speech I get so nervous, I forget facts I really know.

SCORING

To determine your anxiety level, compute the following formulas. The higher your score, the more significant your level of anxiety. (The numbers in parentheses in the formulas refer to the numbered questions above.)

Group = 18 – (1) + (2) – (3) + (4) – (5) + (6)

Meeting = 18 – (7) + (8) + (9) – (10) – (11) + (12)

Dyadic = 18 – (13) + (14) – (15) + (16) + (17) – (18)

Public = 18 + (19) – (20) + (21) – (22) + (23) – (24)

Overall CA = Group + Meeting + Dyadic + Public

MAKING SENSE OF YOUR SCORE

Your combined score for all 24 items should fall somewhere between 24 and 120. If your score is lower than 24 or higher than 120, you need to recalculate it. A score above 83 indicates high communication apprehension; a score between 55 and 83 indicates moderate apprehension, which is the norm for most people. Low apprehension is anything less than 55. Your subscores indicate the degree to which you are anxious when speaking in public, talking in a group, or engaged in conversation with another person. These scores can range between 6 and 30. The higher your score is, the more anxiety you feel. A score above 18 on the public speaking subset suggests you feel a manageable level of speech anxiety. Regardless of your score on this subset, you can significantly benefit from the skills and techniques presented in this chapter. A score of 18 or above on the other two subsets also suggests you feel some anxiety about interpersonal and group communication.

Source: James C. McCroskey, _An Introduction to Rhetorical Communication,_ 7th ed. (Needham Heights, Mass.: Allyn & Bacon, 1997).

"reasons" reflect three stages in the process of becoming anxious. Stage one reflects concerns before speaking. Stage two reflects concerns that come up immediately before and during a speech. And stage three concerns what happens after speaking.

STAGE ONE: MANAGING ANXIETY BEFORE YOU SPEAK

Many factors can preoccupy your mind and influence your behavior before you speak. Major ones include a pessimistic attitude, inadequate preparation and practice, negative or insufficient experience, unrealistic goals, negative self-talk, and misdirected concerns about what a speaker should focus on in preparing to speak. First we will discuss each of these sources of anxiety in turn. Then we will discuss two useful skills, visual imagery and relaxation techniques, that can help you manage your level of arousal.

Pessimistic Attitude

Though actual physiological arousal is neither positive nor negative in itself, your perception of it can be either positive or negative. If you perceive and react to a situation positively, the arousal you feel will be perceived as a pleasant rather than an aversive sensation. What's more, it is not likely to exceed its optimal level. Conversely, if you perceive a situation negatively, you will perceive the arousal you feel as an unpleasant, even worrisome sensation. This increases the chances of arousal exceeding the optimal level for performance.

Research shows that the difference between being positively excited or negatively threatened by a situation such as public speaking is not a matter of arousal per se. It is a matter of how the arousal is initially interpreted. Consider riding a roller coaster. Some people love it; others hate it. If you were to measure arousal while people actually rode a roller coaster, however, you would find, in the beginning, very little difference in their level of physiological arousal. But as the ride progressed and their positive or negative interpretation of the experience began to kick in, differences in arousal would begin to appear. So it is with public speaking. If you perceive it as an opportunity to become a more skilled communicator, chances are you will be able to maintain an optimal level of arousal before, during, and following your speeches. Of course, the reverse is also true. If you perceive public speaking as a task you prefer to avoid, you may begin to experience mental and physical signs of anxiety well in advance of speaking.

Inadequate Preparation and Practice

One reason for developing a pessimistic attitude about speaking is inadequate preparation and practice. Whereas most students would never dream of entering an athletic competition or taking a test crucial to their success in their major without preparation and practice, many seem to think that public speaking is different in this regard. So they put off preparing and practicing their speech until the last moment. Then they wonder why the act of speaking itself makes them nervous, prone to making mistakes, and negative about the overall experience.

Minimizing the importance of preparation and practice to the speaking experience only increases the amount of uncertainty surrounding the upcoming speech. Further, this uncertainty is a chief cause of the excessive arousal and anxiety that students begin to feel in the course of preparing to speak. Frequently, then, the real source of their discomfort when they actually do speak is a result of their own shortsightedness.

Sometimes students recognize the importance of preparation and practice but simply cannot confront the public speaking assignment. Much like writer's block, this aversion to preparing and practicing a speech occurs because students are afraid of what they'll feel when getting started. Perhaps they fear failure, or they just don't know where to begin. Whatever the reason, procrastination only postpones genuine speech anxiety. Procrastination also gives you less time to

The difference between a "thrill ride" and a "chill ride" is a matter of perception.

prepare. To avoid this vicious circle, we make the following two suggestions. First, choose the right topic. You should already know something about it, and you should be excited about it. This will help motivate you and keep you in a positive frame of mind. Second, overprepare. Always give yourself plenty of time to work on your speech. Make a commitment to become an expert on your topic. Then carry out the commitment with research that informs you. Don't be satisfied with knowing only enough about your topic to "just get by."

Negative or Insufficient Experience

Your prior experiences with any task influence how you approach and complete your present task. If your past experiences with public speaking proved both successful and personally rewarding, chances are you look forward to your speaking assignments in this class. But if your prior experiences with public speaking were unpleasant, you may harbor some doubt about your ability to succeed in this class. Finally, if you have had little or no opportunity to speak in public, you may be mildly or even considerably anxious about speaking before your teacher and peers.

The fact that your past efforts as a speaker were unrewarding, or even unpleasant, need not mean that your efforts in this class will prove likewise.

Practicing your speech is essential to building confidence.

The past need not dictate your future, assuming you are serious about becoming an effective speaker. Be realistic about your previous experience. You didn't learn to read and write overnight. Chances are you received a few psychological bumps and bruises in the process. You cannot expect to be an overnight speaking sensation, either. It takes commitment and effort. Thus, the fact that your previous experience with speaking was unpleasant does not mean that you cannot become an effective speaker by the end of this class.

By the same token, the fact that you think you have had little experience with the skills necessary for effective public speaking shouldn't make you overly anxious. Just as running is an extension of walking, public speaking is an extension and refinement of the communication skills you put to use daily. Through your class and this book, you can learn to successfully extend your everyday communication skills to the task of speaking in public.

Practice delivering your speech well in advance of presenting it. Athletes practice much more than they formally compete. They realize there is a crucial connection between practice and performance on game day.

Unrealistic Goals

Another common source of anxiety for beginning speakers involves the goals they set for themselves. Though it is important to set high goals, they should also be realistic. Unrealistic goals can lead to irrational fears about the speaking situation. Research shows that people who set realistic goals for themselves are less anxious and more successful than their counterparts with unrealistic goals.[7] This finding has also been reported in studies of elite athletes, businesspeople, and students enrolled in public speaking courses.

Speech-anxious students often hurt themselves by establishing goals that are not only unrealistic but also well beyond their reach or commitment. They tell themselves that despite their inexperience and unwillingness to make their speech class a priority, they must be the best in their class or get As exclusively. Such illogical and unrealistic goals, the research shows, harm much more than help students in coping with their speech anxiety.

Negative Self-Talk

Closely aligned with the problem of unrealistic personal goals is the more widespread problem of self-defeating patterns of self-talk before the speech transaction. **Self-talk,** or communicating silently to yourself, is natural before you speak, while you speak, and even after you speak. However, it is neither natural nor helpful to beat up on yourself verbally in this process. **Negative self-talk,** a self-defeating pattern of intrapersonal communication, is common among people who report that they experience speech anxiety.[8] Negative self-talk can result from several causes, including the following:

- Worrying about factors beyond your control, including how other students are preparing for their speeches.

- Dwelling excessively on negative past experiences with public speaking.

- Spending too much time thinking about the alternative approaches you might take in preparing your speech.

- Becoming preoccupied with feelings of mental and physical anxiety, such as the inability to concentrate as you try to prepare for your speech.

- Thinking about the worst and usually most unlikely consequences of your speech—people laughing at you or ridiculing your speech.

- Having thoughts about or feelings of inadequacy as a public speaker.

Such negative thinking usually leads to three specific types of negative self-talk: self-criticizing, self-pressuring, and catastrophizing. Let's look at each.

Self-Criticizing   Though realistic self-evaluation is important in self-improvement, it is well documented that many of us verbally question our self-worth or communication skills without sufficient cause. Without much evidence at all, we say negative things about ourselves, including that we're stupid and hopeless when it comes to speaking.

Not only students but people in all walks of life tell themselves they are poor speakers. Many of them do so despite the fact that they have never received any training in public speaking and have had few if any opportunities to speak in public. Their lack of skill doesn't justify their self-criticism.

Self-Pressuring   We also bring undue and added pressure on ourselves through our self-talk, never once thinking about whether such added pressure will help us to perform better. We tell ourselves, for example, that we must be "the best speaker in the class" without first considering why. As it is, you invariably will

self-talk (sometimes referred to as intrapersonal communication) Communicating silently with oneself.

negative self-talk A self-defeating pattern of intrapersonal communication, including self-criticizing, self-pressuring, and catastrophizing statements.

experience moderate pressure and arousal when speaking publicly. Moderate pressure can help you reach the optimal level of arousal needed to deliver your speeches effectively. If you feel no pressure at all, you will lack the motivation to properly prepare and practice. However, telling yourself that you must be the best speaker in class, or that your speech has to be perfect, can add unnecessary and harmful pressure with which you will be unable to cope. Such added pressure, in fact, is like throwing fuel on a raging fire!

Catastrophizing   People often blow things out of proportion when talking to themselves. They project that the consequences of their actions are likely to be far more drastic than is realistic. Anxious public speakers can be guilty of the same thing. For example, they may tell themselves that an upcoming speech is the worst assignment they have ever had. Or they may convince themselves that the low grade they are bound to receive will keep them out of graduate school.

As is the case with unrealistic goals, this kind of self-talk increases arousal and speech anxiety. The more negative your self-talk about the ultimate outcome of your speech, the more probable it is that you will exceed your optimal level of arousal.

Misdirected Concerns

Finally, some research suggests that students who are highly anxious about speaking express very different concerns about an upcoming speech than do those who are only moderately anxious. For example, researchers found that highly anxious students were most concerned with how they would be evaluated, how long they should speak, what specific topic they should choose, whether they could use notes, and how much time they had to prepare.[9] In short, these students were concerned primarily with immediate factors that affect how they will be evaluated in the classroom situation. These concerns are classic signs of mental anxiety. Moreover, they suggest that truly anxious students may be so preoccupied with their misdirected concerns, they may neglect the preparation of their actual speech.

These researchers also found that students who reported little anxiety about speaking were most concerned with factors that would enable them to successfully attain their goals as speakers. In fact, these are the kinds of issues that even professional and highly paid speakers want to know about—for instance, the arrangement of the room, the availability of a microphone, and whether the audience would ask questions. To get a clearer idea of the concerns that make you most anxious, see the box "What Are the Sources of Your Speech Anxiety?"

TIPS AND TACTICS   *Before Speaking*

SPEECH COACH
To hear more about these Tips and Tactics, go to Audio Tips and Tactics on your CD.

If you are overly anxious before you speak, it's likely you will be even more so when you are actually called on to speak. Fortunately, there are some helpful tips you can follow to moderate your before-speaking anxiety.

- Be realistic about your goals and write them down. Becoming an effective speaker is a process. The goals for your first speech should be different from

What Are the Sources of Your Speech Anxiety?

Listed below are common sources of speech anxiety. As you read each item, consider how much it contributes to the anxiety you experience about public speaking. Rate each item on a scale of 1 to 10, from least important to most important.

Sources of Speech Anxiety	Least Important/Most Important
	1 2 3 4 5 6 7 8 9 10
Your attitude toward speaking	__ __ __ __ __ __ __ __ __ __
Lack of preparation and practice	__ __ __ __ __ __ __ __ __ __
Previous experiences with speaking —lack of or bad experiences	__ __ __ __ __ __ __ __ __ __
Unrealistic goals	__ __ __ __ __ __ __ __ __ __
Perception of your audience as hostile or unsympathetic	__ __ __ __ __ __ __ __ __ __
Negative self-talk	__ __ __ __ __ __ __ __ __ __
Misdirected concerns with how you will be evaluated	__ __ __ __ __ __ __ __ __ __

Rearrange the items in order of importance. Use this hierarchy to better understand the sources of your speech anxiety. What steps can you take to address and change your patterns of thought and behavior?

1. _____
2. _____
3. _____
4. _____
5. _____
6. _____
7. _____

those you write down before your second and third speeches. Regardless of which speech you are making, your goals must be grounded in your potential to improve as a speaker, as well as how much effort you are willing to make to realize your potential.

• Inventory your routine self-talk as you prepare to speak. Note what kinds of things you routinely say to yourself and ask yourself: Do these statements make me more or less anxious about my speech? Substitute negative statements you routinely make with **constructive self-talk** modeled after the examples in Table 3.1.

• Consult with your instructor about your concerns and the degree to which they are valid. Don't assume your instructor shares your beliefs about what is and isn't essential to your success. Finally, do not fall victim to the misguided idea that you will appear stupid if you seek your instructor's counsel.

constructive self-talk The use of positive coping statements instead of negative self-talk.

There are at least two other skills you can use in advance of speaking: (1) visual imagery and (2) relaxation techniques. These skills are excellent complements to the preceding tips and deserve additional comment.

TABLE 3.1 Constructive Self-Talk Before You Speak

Prior to Practice	Actual Practice	During Behavioral Rehearsal
Get off to a good start: Prepare early . . . don't put it off.	Time for some imagery.	Use my coping statements.
This will be good for me.	Let's run through this in my mind's eye.	Speak slowly and clearly.
I like this topic.	Visualize the opening and hear myself sharing the thesis statement.	First work on knowing content.
Rough outline first . . . there's time to polish later.	Visualize the connect and preview.	Okay, now I know it.
I have plenty of information.	Okay, hear and see myself make each point	Make eye contact with people.
I bet my information will be pretty new to my classmates.	Try to see myself from the audience's point of view.	Speak conversationally.
I've uncovered a lot of interesting facts.	Visualize the summary and close.	Have fun with it.
Lay it out logically.	Try it again, but this time use relaxation imagery too.	Be myself but under control.
Time to rewrite.		

Visual Imagery

visual imagery The process of mentally seeing (imagining) oneself confidently and successfully performing an action or a series of actions.

Visual imagery is another way to rehearse your speech. It is the process of mentally seeing (imagining) yourself performing an action or a series of actions. Instead of practicing your speech out loud, you visually imagine yourself confidently and successfully giving the speech. At the 1998 Winter Olympiad, TV viewers were treated to pictures of Tara Lipinski and Michele Kwan, the gold and silver medalists in figure skating, both rehearsing through visual imagery before their performances. You may have caught a glimpse of them as they moved their heads from side to side and up and down with eyes closed, while seated backstage. Ice skating is the tip of the iceberg in terms of sports in which elite athletes include visual imagery as a part of their everyday practice. Visual imagery is widely practiced in archery, baseball, basketball, football, golf, gymnastics, hockey, kayaking, skiing, and snow boarding. Athletes who use visual imagery include golfer Tiger Woods, quarterback Payton Mannington, and professional ice skater Kristi Yamaguchi (see the box "An Athlete's Approach to Anxiety").

More to the point of this book, however, is the case of Dr. Loretta Malandro. The founder of a successful communication-consulting firm, Dr. Malandro travels worldwide as a professional speaker. One of the things she tries to do before each speaking engagement is to visually imagine herself giving the speech. Even if it means getting up before dawn, for example, she tries to run five miles and visualize her upcoming presentation as she runs. Because Dr. Malandro does this routinely, she sees not only herself as she shares her message but also the positive feedback she is receiving from her audience.

Because it is yet another way to reduce your uncertainty about an upcoming speech, visual imagery can also assist you in controlling your level of anxiety and arousal. This technique works best when you are in a relaxed state and familiar

An Athlete's Approach to Anxiety: *Kristi Yamaguchi*

Champion figure skater Kristi Yamaguchi not only practices physically for a performance, she practices mentally in order to cope with anxiety. Here, she describes her techniques:

> I usually get by myself before I go out for a routine. I walk through the program, visualizing myself completing all the moves. Right before a performance, I start talking to myself: "Okay, get out there, skate like it's an everyday practice."

The techniques Kristi Yamaguchi uses illustrate the importance of practice and mental imaging in dealing with anxiety. Notice that she mentally rehearses her moves right before a performance. She also engages in constructive self-talk when she tells herself that a competition is like an everyday practice. How do you think Yamaguchi's techniques could be successfully used by a public speaker? What can we learn as public speakers from the ways that elite athletes deal with the enormous pressure under which they must perform?

Source: American Health © 1992 by Steve McKee.

with the content of your speech. It involves controlled visualization of your actual speaking situation, which will require practice on your part. The idea is to see yourself during all phases of your speech. For example, you might first visualize yourself seated at your desk, relaxed but appropriately aroused as you wait your turn to speak. Next, you might visualize yourself leaving your desk, moving to the front of the room, confidently facing your audience, and introducing your speech. From here on, you would visualize yourself speaking—moving, gesturing, and making eye contact with individual members of your audience right up to your conclusion. Finally, you would see your audience and teacher enthusiastically responding to your presentation. Once you become adept at visualizing, you can even add sound to the picture in your mind's eye. Hearing yourself take command of an audience as you turn a phrase or smoothly make a transition from one point to another will enhance the impact of visual imagining.

Visual imagery works best as a complement to actual practice. Study after study shows that visual imagery actually enhances behavioral rehearsal.[10] As a result, you will want to include it as part of your preparation and practice routine.

Making Effective Use of Relaxation Techniques

As discussed earlier, butterflies, a racing heart, trembling hands, and weak knees are the result of the excessive adrenaline that is pumped into your system when you are overly aroused. One of the best ways to prevent these symptoms is to condition your body to relax in situations that are, characteristically, overly arousing. You can accomplish this in one of several ways.

Exercise is a great way to manage the stress and anxiety you feel in anticipation of speaking.

Exercise   The first way to help your body relax is to engage in some form of intense exercise one to two hours before you speak. The effects of physical exercise on physical and mental well-being are well known. Intense exercise assists us in decreasing signs of stress and has been linked to improved thinking and performance, regardless of the task.

Relaxation Imagery   If exercise is either inconvenient or impractical, another way to induce relaxation before you speak is to use relaxation imagery. Imagery is not the same as merely thinking. Imagery involves pictures, whereas thinking is a verbal process. Relaxation imagery involves visualizing pleasant and calming situations. Lying in a hammock or on the beach during a warm summer day are two examples of such pleasant and calming situations. If you were to visually linger on such situations, you would find your body becoming increasingly relaxed. As a result, you would significantly lower the level of arousal customarily felt as a result of the day's activities.

This latter point is important. As a busy college student, you may find your upcoming speech to be the most significant but not the sole source of arousal you experience during the day. By practicing relaxation imagery before you speak, you can reduce the arousal that began to climb with the start of your day.

Muscular Relaxation   This technique involves systematically tensing and relaxing the various muscle groups, as is visually demonstrated on your CD. It usually begins with the muscles in your face and neck, then gradually moves to your middle and lower torso. The idea behind this technique is to teach your body the difference between tension and relaxation. By first tensing and then relaxing your muscles systematically, you can also condition your muscles to relax even under the most stressful circumstances.

There's a good reason for practicing muscular relaxation. When we tense up, the range of movement in our muscles is restricted. They don't work as they are intended. In a game of basketball, this is seen when a free-throw shooter hits the front of the rim, loses "touch," or puts up an air ball. With a speaker, this is evident either in the absence of movement or gesturing or in movement and gesturing that are awkward and unnecessary.

Combining Techniques

By combining relaxation with visual imagery, you can enhance the effectiveness of both techniques. You will come to associate the speaking situation with relaxing images rather than anxiety-producing ones.

These techniques also work best when they become a habitual routine that you practice as you prepare to speak. Elite athletes don't use them only before they are about to compete; speakers shouldn't put off using them until the night before they speak. The research is clear. These techniques will serve you well only if you commit to their systematic use.

STAGE TWO: MANAGING ANXIETY DURING YOUR SPEECH

Some of the same factors that give rise to pessimism before a speech also undermine the speech transaction itself. Negative self-talk frequently plagues speakers as they speak. But there are other factors we haven't discussed, for example, inaccurate perceptions of the audience and unjustified concerns about appearance.

The Audience

A recent study confirms that many beginning speakers view their audience as hostile toward them.[11] They convince themselves that the members of their audience are just waiting for them to trip over their feet, lose their train of thought, blow a quotation, or mumble through a sentence. Along the same lines, it is not uncommon for beginning speakers to read into the nonverbal feedback they receive from their audience such false conclusions as "they're bored to tears" or "they think I'm terrible." This is anything but the case, of course. Audiences, with rare exception, want speakers to succeed and are silently rooting for them to do so.

In recognition of this fact, consider the case of the late Mary Martin, a well-known and highly praised stage actress who first popularized the Broadway productions of *Peter Pan* and *Annie Get Your Gun*. She used to do something before a performance that you may wish to try. Just before going on stage, she would close her eyes, take a deep breath, and say 100 times to herself, "I love

SPEECH COACH

For an example of relaxation techniques, see segment 3.1 on your CD.

Appropriate dress can greatly enhance your feelings of confidence.

my audience." Next she would repeat the process, but this time tell herself, "My audience loves me."

Beginning speakers also may convince themselves that their audience expects more from them than they can deliver. Such expectations about an audience can easily become a self-fulfilling prophecy. The students you face are in the same boat with you and want you to succeed as much as you do. If you still need convincing, consider how you feel when you are a member of an audience gathered to watch a public performance. Do you silently root for the performer to fail miserably? Do you take perverse joy in seeing the performer make an obvious mistake? Do you expect more from the person than he or she could ever deliver? We didn't think so!

Appearance

This is an appearance-obsessed culture. We are not so naïve as to recommend that you try to convince yourself that appearance is unimportant. However, we do recommend that you try to be reasonable in this regard. Although you cannot transform your body type or radically alter your appearance for your speech class, you can dress appropriately for the occasion. All too often we see students

TABLE 3.2 Constructive Self-Talk During Your Speech

Get comfortable.

Speak slowly.

I know my speech.

I was nervous to start, but I've calmed down.

It's okay if I'm not perfect.

The audience is interested in what I have to say.

This is easier than I thought.

Make eye contact.

Just like I practiced.

So far so good.

Don't rush it.

Time to summarize.

Take your time.

Not bad . . . not bad at all.

in our own classes whose inappropriate dress detracts unnecessarily from what they hope to say. They become self-conscious in the process, increasing their chances of becoming overly anxious.

Appropriate dress enhances your credibility. It also can help you feel more confident. Both are positive outcomes, ones that should reduce rather than increase feelings of speech anxiety. Thus, the easiest way to overcome concerns about your physical appearance is to dress for the occasion.

Self-Talk

Just as you use self-talk before a speech, you may also talk to yourself as you actually deliver a speech. Again, you want to avoid negative self-talk in this regard. It's important to note that your audience will not be nearly as critical of you as you will be of yourself. Your audience is also less likely to pick up on mistakes than you are, because they don't know your speech like you know it. When you make mistakes, which even the most polished speakers do, avoid criticizing yourself. Refrain from saying such things as, "Way to go, stupid," or, "Why am I screwing up?"

Instead, as you speak, try to use statements such as those suggested in Table 3.2. These *process statements* will help to keep you in the moment and on track. They will also help to keep your mind from wandering or dwelling on minor mistakes your audience probably did not catch.

While You Speak

- Take time to get comfortable before you start to speak. Take a couple of deep breaths, make eye contact with a friendly face, and smile. Also take a shoulders-width stance and try to stand tall.

- Don't obsess on your audience. Important as the audience is to your success, you need to keep their importance in perspective. Remember that your

TIPS AND TACTICS

 SPEECH COACH

To hear more about these Tips and Tactics, go to Audio Tips and Tactics on your CD.

FOXTROT © 1995 Bill Amend. Reprinted with permission of Universal Press Syndicate. All rights reserved.

audience wants you to succeed and that the audience is uncomfortable when you are uncomfortable.

- Dress appropriately for the occasion. Not only will it help make you feel more confident, but it will also increase your credibility with your audience.

- If you engage in self-talk, follow the advice in Table 3.2. Talk to yourself about what's going well. Tell yourself that you are okay and that your audience is with you.

STAGE THREE: MANAGING ANXIETY AFTER YOUR SPEECH

Even experienced speakers can find themselves in a mental fog following their speech. They may find it hard to concentrate or stay focused on the comments directed toward them.

What takes place after a speech will affect the way you approach and deliver your next speech. Comments directed to you by peers and your instructor can help you prepare your next speech, including: (1) the goals you set, (2) preparation and practice, and (3) your level of confidence as you take on these tasks. Constructive comments cannot help you, however, if you fail to hear and process them in the first place.

Anxiety interferes with the ability to listen and accurately process what you hear. To get the most out of immediate feedback following a speech, we offer the following tips.

TIPS AND TACTICS   *After Speaking*

 **SPEECH COACH**
To hear more about these Tips and Tactics, go to Audio Tips and Tactics on your CD.

- Take several deep breaths when you go back to your seat. This will help to bring down your heart rate.

- Minimize self-talk. You can mentally review your presentation later.

- Look for your instructor's eye contact and tell yourself to relax as you listen to your instructor and classmates.

- Write down what is said. You can check with your instructor later to determine the accuracy of the feedback you recorded.

TABLE 3.3 Constructive Self-Talk After You Speak
That wasn't half-bad.
Find your seat.
Smile, take some deep breaths.
Don't forget to take notes from the feedback I get.
Talk with my instructor.
Don't forget the "did well" and "room to improve" list.
Go back over the speech tonight in my mind's eye.
Write down goals for next time.

- Within 24 hours review the entire process, and make a list with two columns: (1) things I did well and (2) areas where I realistically can improve. Refer to this list as you prepare for your next assignment.
- Practice self-talk patterned after the statements you see in Table 3.3.

SUMMARY

Speech anxiety is a result of our subjective interpretation of the arousal we experience when called on to speak publicly. Although some degree of arousal is necessary to prepare and deliver an effective speech, too much of it can lead to psychological side effects, such as excessive worry, and physical side effects, such as trembling hands. Too much arousal can lead to a debilitating level of speech anxiety. Managing speech anxiety involves:

- developing a positive attitude toward speaking
- committing to practice and preparation and avoiding procrastination
- replacing negative self-talk before, during, and following a speech with constructive self-talk
- establishing realistic goals given your commitment to your class
- recognizing and accepting the fact that your audience wants you to succeed
- focusing on what you and your instructor agree are important considerations in the development and delivery of your speech
- combining visual imagery with behavioral rehearsal
- combining imagery with relaxation techniques
- making the preceding skills and techniques part of your routine before, during, and after a speech

CHECK YOUR UNDERSTANDING: EXERCISES AND ACTIVITIES

1. In a short paper, describe the relationship between physiological arousal and speech anxiety and give examples of both physical and mental symptoms of anxiety. Be sure to define anxiety and distinguish it from speech anxiety.

SPEECH COACH

To evaluate your understanding of this chapter, see the Quizzes on your CD.

SPEECH COACH

For a review of key terms in this chapter, see the Key Terms Flashcards on your CD.

2. The chapter lists six common sources of speech anxiety and steps for controlling them. For your next speaking assignment, identify at least one such source of anxiety that concerns you and make an effort to remedy it. For example, if you have a tendency to procrastinate, make sure you start your speech sooner than usual. After the speech, assess how the remedy worked in alleviating at least one source of public speaking anxiety.

3. Before your next speech, make a list of the negative self-talk you have engaged in regarding speech assignments. Then come up with a series of constructive self-talk statements you will use in preparing for and while giving your next speech. Your instructor may ask you to turn in your list before you speak.

4. Two of the most convenient relaxation techniques you can use are relaxation imagery and muscular relaxation. Both initially require a quiet place and time where you will not be interrupted. This exercise allows you to practice relaxation on your own or with a friend. It is sometimes useful to have someone read the steps to you so that you can completely relax.

   a. Find a reclining chair or couch where you can make yourself comfortable.

   b. Lower or turn off bright lights.

   c. With your eyes closed, tense and then relax your muscles in this order: face, neck and shoulders, biceps and triceps, forearms, wrists and hands, chest, solar plexus, buttocks/hamstrings, quadriceps, calves, ankles and feet.

   d. Once you are completely relaxed, imagine a peaceful setting in which you feel calm. Learn to hold this image for as long as you can. After a minute or two, move on to the next step.

   e. Imagine your speech class. If you feel any sign of anxiety, return to the preceding image.

   f. Continue to imagine your speech class and add yourself to the picture. See yourself calmly seated, enjoying others as they speak.

   g. See yourself writing down the requirements of an assigned speech. See yourself involved with the various stages of preparation, including seeing yourself practice.

   h. See yourself waiting to be called on, aroused but not anxious.

   i. See yourself walking to the front of the room, turning to face your audience, smiling, and opening your presentation with impact.

   j. See yourself speaking energetically, gesturing, and using your eyes, face, and voice.

   k. See students and your instructor listening attentively.

   l. See yourself concluding and your audience responding with genuine applause.

Practice this series of steps at least twice a week for 15–25 minutes each time. Remember, any time you begin to feel anxious during this exercise, replace whatever image you're holding with a pleasant and relaxing one.

NOTES

1. *20/20.* ABC Television, 20 June 1990. Bruskin Associates, "What Are Americans Afraid Of?" The Bruskin Report 53 (July 1973).

2. J. A. Daly and J. C. McCroskey, eds., *Avoiding Communication: Shyness, Reticence and Communication Apprehension* (Beverly Hills, Calif.: Sage, 1984).

3. Karen K. Dwyer, "The Multidimensional Model: Teaching Students to Self-Manage High Communication Apprehension by Self-Selecting Treatments," *Communication Education,* 49 (2000): 72–81; Lynne Kelly and James A. Keaton, "Treating Communication Apprehension Anxiety: Implications of the Communibiological Paradigm," *Communication Education,* 49 (2000): 45–57. Research on this chapter's topic is ongoing; as a result, we have used multiple sources to support our claims. Some of these sources represent very early research, but others alert you to more contemporary research.

4. Michael J. Beatty and Kristen Marie Valencic, "Context-Based Apprehension Versus Planning Demands: A Communibiological Analysis of Anticipatory Public Speaking Anxiety," *Communication Education,* 49 (2000): 58–71. Ralph R. Behnke and Chris R. Sawyer, "Milestones of Anticipatory Public Speaking Anxiety," *Communication Education,* 48 (1999): 165–71.

5. R. M. Yerkes and J. D. Dodson, "The Relation of Strength Stimulus to Rapidity of Habit Formation," *Journal of Comparative Neurology and Psychology,* 18 (1908): 459–82.

6. Amy M. Bippus and John A. Daly, "What Do People Think Causes Stage Fright? Naïve Attributions About the Reasons for Public Speaking Anxiety," *Communication Education,* 48 (1999): 63–72.

7. William J. Fremouw and Michael D. Scott, "Cognitive Restructuring: An Alternative Method for the Treatment of Communication Apprehension," *Communication Education,* 28 (1979): 129–33; William J. Fremouw and M. G. Harmatz, "A Helper Model for Behavioral Treatment of Speech Anxiety," *Journal of Consulting and Clinical Psychology,* 43 (1975): 652–60.

8. Albert Ellis and Robert A. Harper, *A New Guide to Rational Living* (Hollywood, Calif.: Wilshire Book Company, 1975).

9. William J. Fremouw and Michael D. Scott, "Cognitive Restructuring"; William J. Fremouw and M. G. Harmatz, "A Helper Model for Behavioral Treatment of Speech Anxiety."

10. J. A. Daly, A. L. Vangelisti, H. L. Neel, and P. D. Cavanaugh, "Pre-Performance Concerns Associated With Public Speaking Anxiety," *Communication Quarterly,* 37 (1989): 39–53; J. A. Daly, A. L. Vangelisti, and D. J. Weber, "Speech Anxiety Affects How People Prepare Speeches: A Protocol Analysis of the Preparation Process of Speakers," *Communication Monographs,* 62 (1995): 383–97.

11. T. Freeman, C. R. Sawyer, and R. R. Behnke, "Behavioral Inhibition and Attribution of Public Speaking State Anxiety," *Communication Education,* 46 (1997): 175–87.

Listening is an
important part
of the speech
transaction.

Listening

  OBJECTIVES

After reading this chapter and reviewing the learning resources on your CD-ROM and at the Online Learning Center, you should be able to:

- Explain what listening involves.
- Describe the significant role that listening plays for both speakers and audience members.
- Recognize and demonstrate the difference between hearing and listening.
- Identify common misconceptions about listening.
- Exhibit behaviors consistent with those of an active listener.
- Demonstrate understanding, appreciative, and critical listening skills.
- Identify and overcome obstacles to listening.

  KEY CONCEPTS

active listening	critical listening	pinpoint concentration
active mindfulness	cross cue–checking	retention
appreciative listening	culture	selective attention
comprehension	denotative meanings	sensorial involvement
connotative meanings	listening	wide-band concentration
context	metacommunication	

> *To listen is an effort, and just to hear has no merit. A duck hears also.*
>
> —IGOR STRAVINSKY

Nationally syndicated humorist Dave Barry wrote about traveling in Japan. To illustrate how "the Japanese tend to communicate via nuance and euphemism," he described an encounter between Beth and a Japanese travel agent just prior to a trip to Japan:

> **Beth:** . . . and then we want to take a plane from Point A to Point B.
>
> **Travel Agent:** I see. You want to take a plane.
>
> **Beth:** Yes.
>
> **Travel Agent:** From Point A?
>
> **Beth:** Yes.
>
> **Travel Agent:** To Point B?
>
> **Beth:** Yes.
>
> **Travel Agent:** Ah.
>
> **Beth:** Can we do that?
>
> **Travel Agent:** Perhaps you would prefer to take a train.
>
> **Beth:** No, we would prefer to take a plane.
>
> **Travel Agent:** Ah-hah. You would prefer to take a plane?
>
> **Beth:** Yes. A plane.
>
> **Travel Agent:** I see. From Point A.

This exchange continued along these lines with Beth still seeking an answer to what she perceived to be a straightforward and simple question. Hearing no answer, she broke off the exchange, perplexed by what she perceived to be the agent's evasive and unresponsive behavior.[1]

Scenarios such as this one can be common between communicators from different societies that have different norms for appropriate communication behavior. In this case, it wasn't that the Japanese agent was purposely trying to evade Beth's question. To the contrary, coming from a society where it is impolite to tell others "no" explicitly, the agent was trying to assist Beth in coming to the realization that her request was impossible because there was no plane between Points A and B. To come to such a realization, though, Beth would have had to realize that to understand the Japanese it is not enough to *hear* the content of the message. In a collectivist culture like Japan, where the context often contains more information than the words, you must *listen* for the nuance of the message as well.

Of course, we don't need a cross-cultural example to know that simply hearing what people say isn't the same as listening to them. Most of us have had plenty of experiences where our understanding of what we heard didn't correspond to the message the speaker intended. This is because although we may have heard what was said, we weren't listening for the underlying message that was being sent. *Hearing* is a physical process that in no way guarantees understanding. *Listening,* which is paramount to understanding, is both physical and psychological.

Listening is one of those concepts to which we all pay lip service. Yet how many of us truly understand what it means to listen, what listening involves, and what a significant role it can play in making us more competent communicators, as both speakers and interested audience members? Research suggests that fewer of us understand than we might think.

There are tremendous benefits to learning to be a good listener. On a daily basis, we are given directions, instructions, and advice that can be very important to our personal well-being. Anyone who's ever been lost and had to follow directions from a stranger knows how important it is to fully understand what is said. Few bosses are tolerant of employees who say, "Sorry, I didn't hear you tell me to do that." Whether seeking financial, career, or even personal advice, it is important to understand fully what is being said. Listening is one of those skills people take for granted, yet their very lives can depend on it.

Listening to other people is essential not only to our daily lives but also to our development as speakers and responsible audience members. Further, the information we receive in our daily lives is often rich in cues about the nature of our potential audiences. Thus we are more likely to achieve our speaking goals if we have listened carefully to the people around us.

This chapter is designed to assist you in becoming a better public speaker and audience member by first becoming a better listener. We discuss (1) the nature of listening, including its importance to overall communication competence; (2) misconceptions about listening; (3) obstacles to effective listening; (4) types of listening especially relevant to the speech transaction; and (5) a series of interdependent techniques you can begin to use immediately in the effort to improve your listening behavior.

EVERYDAY IMPORTANCE OF LISTENING

The ability to listen effectively is important to succeeding (1) in school, (2) at work, (3) in relationships with friends and family, and (4) in situations where we need to share information with others. First, consider the fact that as a college student you are exposed to hundreds of hours of lectures, group discussions, and mediated communication. The ability to process and absorb information is the essence of learning. Not every professor is a brilliant speaker, holding your attention with ease. You need to listen especially well if you are to obtain the maximum benefit from your college career.

Second, effective listening is essential to success in the workforce. One of the key complaints of many employers is that employees do not listen effectively, costing millions of dollars each year in mistakes and inefficiencies. Among the skills employers value in listeners are "listening for content; listening to conversations; listening for long-term contexts; listening for emotional meaning; and listening to follow directions."[2]

Third, listening is essential to interpersonal communication, especially in families. How many times have you heard children or parents complain that no one listens to what they say? In interpersonal contexts, listening must go well beyond content, focusing on the emotional and relational components of the communication transaction.

Fourth, listening is essential to effectively communicate information to others. You need to adapt your own messages to the feedback you receive from others. Understanding what others need is essential to successfully influencing their beliefs, attitudes, and actions through the speeches you share.

Research tells us that because we are accustomed to receiving information in the form of a story, storytelling is an excellent way to communicate information. In our public speaking classes, we usually begin the semester with a speech of introduction and a storytelling speech, which allows students to relate a personal

FIGURE 4.1
Listening Relative to Other Types of Communication

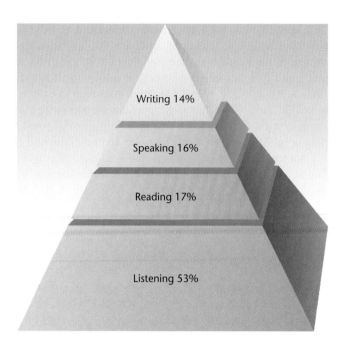

Writing 14%

Speaking 16%

Reading 17%

Listening 53%

experience to their classmates. Both of these speeches are excellent listening opportunities for the rest of the class to learn about their classmates' backgrounds and interests. The information gleaned from listening to such early speeches can be used later in analyzing the audience to which you will be speaking throughout the semester.

As you can see in Figure 4.1, which shows the types of communication activities in which people engage daily, listening is by far the most dominant. But it also may be the activity at which people are the least skilled. The average listener remembers only about half of what was said immediately after it was said. And, as if that weren't bad enough, after 48 hours the average listener remembers only about one quarter of what was said.[3]

THE NATURE OF LISTENING

listening The process of receiving, attending to, and assigning meaning to aural as well as visual and tactile stimuli.

active listening Listening that involves conscious and responsive participation in the communication transaction.

There is no universally accepted definition of listening. For our purposes, though, **listening** is the process of receiving, attending to, and assigning meaning to aural as well as visual and tactile stimuli.[4] Important to this comprehensive definition is the idea of **active listening,** which involves conscious and responsive participation in the communication transaction.[5] Such active and complete participation encompasses the following:

- active mindfulness
- selective attention
- sensorial involvement
- comprehension
- retention

Active Mindfulness

Active mindfulness involves the degree to which speakers and audiences are consciously aware of the transactions between them. For example, the fact that someone responds to your message with a look of puzzlement doesn't automatically mean the person is hard of hearing. Yet, many people automatically speak louder when their message is greeted with such a look, rather than considering the alternatives. Before raising their voice, such people should at least consider the possibility that they were unclear or that the other person speaks another language. This kind of consideration, though, demands complex instead of simplistic thinking.

Active mindfulness also requires open-mindedness to ideas contrary or unfamiliar to the way you customarily think. This doesn't mean that you have to accept such ideas uncritically. Instead, it means that you do not automatically reject these ideas.

active mindfulness The degree to which speakers and audiences are consciously aware of the transactions between them.

Selective Attention

As the discussion of mindfulness suggests, people are most likely to seek out and pay attention to speakers and messages that they perceive to be reinforcing. A person whose speech reflects your viewpoint, therefore, is more likely to get your undivided attention than one whose speech presents a diametrically opposed viewpoint. Similarly, professors whose lectures involve your major are more likely to "have your ear" than those who lecture on topics you perceive to be less important to your future.

Understanding **selective attention** is important to your development as an audience-focused speaker and as an attentive and responsive audience member. You cannot learn to effectively communicate to your audience, for example, unless you first selectively choose to pay attention to the thoughts and concerns of the people in it. You can't be a responsive audience member unless you make the conscious choice to pay attention to what a speaker shares.

selective attention Making a conscious choice to focus on some people and some messages, rather than others.

Listening to others speak, moreover, is one of the best ways to improve your own speaking ability. For instance, listening for such things as the developmental pattern a speaker follows, changes in pitch and rate, and the sources a speaker cites can assist you tremendously in preparing and delivering your own speeches. In a sense, listening facilitates the "modeling" of effective speakers and their speeches. However, you first must decide to consciously pay attention—selectively attend—to these models of effective public speaking.

Sensorial Involvement

Once you've chosen to pay close attention to the speech transaction, you then need to practice **sensorial involvement,** that is, to involve all of your senses in the transaction. As noted in Chapter 1, every message has two dimensions: a content and a relationship dimension. Reading the text of a speech is not the same as physically participating in the transaction. Simply reading text limits you to the *content* of the message and its compositional elements. While *what* a speaker says is important, *how* a speaker says it is equally important. Gestures, movements, facial expressions, and eye contact serve to visually punctuate the content of a speech and suggest nuances of meaning, including what a speaker

sensorial involvement A process that involves listening with all the senses, not simply the sense of hearing.

is saying "between the lines." The reaction of people to a speaker's message and the physical setting in which it's shared also affect the meaning of the message.

To truly appreciate the speech transaction, therefore, you need to involve as many of your senses as you can. Not only must you try to hear what is being said, but you also must try to see and feel what is being said. Only then will you be in a position to measure the totality of the message that has been communicated.

Comprehension

comprehension The act of understanding what has been communicated.

Comprehension is the act of understanding what has been communicated. Careful listeners make sure that they truly understand what a speaker means and do not hesitate to ask for clarification if the speaker's message is unclear. It is also important to make sure that understanding includes not just the explicit content of a message, but the relational component as well. And speakers need to make sure that their choice of words is appropriate for their audience. Speaking in technical language to a nontechnical audience, for example, is a sure way to guarantee noncomprehension of your message.

Retention

retention The act of storing what was communicated in either short- or long-term memory.

Retention is the act of storing what has been communicated in either short- or long-term memory. Often what is viewed as a failure to remember is actually a failure to comprehend or attend to the original message. But assuming a listener fully attends to and comprehends a speaker's message, there is still the important issue of retaining that message. The use of careful note-taking can help a listener to retain messages that would otherwise be forgotten. And a good speaker will repeat and reinforce the key concepts of a message to help the audience remember it.

MISCONCEPTIONS ABOUT LISTENING

There are a number of common misconceptions about effective listening. These include but are not limited to the idea that listening (1) is easy, (2) is correlated with intelligence, (3) does not need to be planned, and (4) is related to skill in reading.[6]

"It's Easy to Listen"

Some people think that listening is like breathing, that we are born competent listeners. Of course, that is just as fallacious as assuming that because we breathe, we all breathe well enough to become professional singers. Just because someone can carry a tune and sing in the shower doesn't mean the person is ready for the New York Metropolitan Opera. Similarly, just because we've heard others talk to us all of our lives does not mean we are effective listeners. Quite the contrary, our complacency about listening is one of the very things that makes us susceptible to poor listening habits. Have you ever had the experience of hearing a song on the radio and thinking the lyrics said one thing and, when you later read the lyrics, found out they were quite different? Most of us have either misheard lyrics or know someone who has. One of our kids thought Iron Butterfly's heavy-metal classic "In-A-Gadda-Da-Vida" was "In the Garden of Eden." A friend thought the Beatles' "Lucy in the Sky with Diamonds" was "Lucy in Disguise with Diamonds." Gavin Edwards actually wrote two books of such "misheard lyrics." The title of his first book, 'Scuse Me While I Kiss This Guy and Other Misheard Lyrics, comes from a mishearing of the Jimi Hendrix lyric, "Scuse me while I kiss the sky."[7] Edwards' second book title, He's Got the Whole World in His Pants and More Misheard Lyrics, is based on a mishearing of the old gospel song, "He's Got the Whole World in His Hands."[8]

"I'm Smart, So I'm a Good Listener"

Even highly intelligent people can fail to listen. For example, submarine crew members are among the most intelligent, tested, and trained members of the Navy. But failure to listen caused the submarine U.S.S. Stickleback to collide with a destroyer escort and sink off Hawaii in May 1958. Although no personnel were lost, tragedy was narrowly avoided. And it all happened because an electrician's mate thought he heard the order "Come on" when the actual order was "Come off." Instead of turning his rheostat down, as he was ordered, therefore, he turned it up, tripping the circuit breakers, cutting off power, and causing the sub to lose control, plunging it directly into the path of the destroyer escort.[9]

Intelligence far from guarantees effective listening. Although some highly intelligent people have been trained to use effective listening skills, equal numbers have not. As the U.S.S. Stickleback incident illustrates so well, some people may fail to listen carefully in spite of their intelligence.

"There's No Need to Plan Ahead"

A third common misconception is that listening just happens—that there's no need to plan for it. Of course, sometimes you will end up listening to an unexpected conversation. But if you know in advance that you will be in a listening

 **SPEECH COACH**

To evaluate speeches, see the
Speech Critique program on
your CD.

situation such as the one you face in your speech class, you should plan ahead. For example, in most introductory speech courses, students provide each other with both oral and written feedback. Who do you think will do a better job: the student who prepares in advance, including a review of criteria for the speech, checklists for speech evaluation, and a clear understanding of the speech assignment, or the one who shows up to class only to be surprised by the fact that he or she will be responsible for providing classmates with feedback about their speeches? Finally, when the tables are turned, whose speeches do you think most likely will benefit from critical evaluation by classmates?

"I Can Read, So I Can Listen"

Although reading and listening skills might seem to be correlated, that is not the case. In fact, the skills required are quite different. The reader controls the pace of communication, whereas a listener is at the mercy of the person speaking. A reader can reread a confusing passage, whereas a listener may have only one chance to get the point. Reading is typically a solitary activity; listening most often takes place in groups, where it might be hard to hear the speaker or there might be distractions. Listening skills, as you can begin to see, require development in their own right.

OBSTACLES TO LISTENING

Several factors can intervene to prevent effective listening. Six of the most important obstacles to listening are physical conditions, cultural differences, personal problems, bias, connotative meanings, and anxiety.[10] Most of these obstacles are directly influenced by our perceptions. Thus the discussion of perception and communication in Chapter 1 directly relates to problems in listening.

Physical Conditions

The physical environment clearly affects our ability to listen. Among the factors that can inhibit listening are noise, an unpleasant room temperature, poor lighting, physical obstacles, and uncomfortable chairs. A noisy, hot, poorly lit room, with uncomfortable chairs and a post blocking your view, is hardly an ideal listening environment. On the other hand, a quiet, well-lit room with a clear line of sight, comfortable (but not too comfortable) chairs, and a pleasant temperature allows you to concentrate on the speaker. Although there is usually not much the listener can do about the physical environment, being aware of its impact on listening helps you know how much you need to focus. In addition, you can often choose your location to listen. Students who sit in the back of the classroom, where their view is limited, often are tempted to let their attention drift. Those who move front and center clearly are interested in listening to what is said.

The best speakers try to minimize the effects of a troublesome physical environment on audience listening. If the acoustics are bad, they may raise or amplify their voice so that it is more audible. If their line of sight is blocked from some audience members, they may move toward audience members in the back of a room. If some loud activity is occurring within earshot of the audience,

Some situations make it very difficult to listen to others.

they may make light of the situation rather than show that the noise bothers them. No matter what a speaker does to overcome a problem environment, however, audience members also bear some responsibility in this regard.

Cultural Differences

Communication patterns vary from culture to culture. **Culture** is a learned system of beliefs, customs, and values with which specific people identify. The relative importance of the context in which listening takes place differs from one culture to another. Anthropologists Edward T. Hall and Mildred Reed Hall define **context** as the information that surrounds an event and contributes to the meaning of that event.[11] For example, suppose you receive a message on your answering machine from a relative you almost never hear from except in an emergency. The message simply says, "Call me right away." Needless to say, you would be alarmed, because you know this person never calls you unless there is a serious problem. On the other hand, if you received the same message from a friend with whom you often get together, you might assume he or she just wants to set up a meeting. The same message has a very different meaning because of the context in which it occurs.

As our opening story illustrated, some cultures rely more than others on unspoken information contained in the context to determine the meaning of a message. In high-context (HC) cultures, such as Japan, the Arab states, and the Mediterranean countries, the context of statements can be extremely important. Much of the meaning in such cultures is carried not only by the words that are spoken but also by the situation in which they are uttered. On the other hand, in low-context (LC) cultures, such as the United States, Germany, and most northern European countries, people rely less on the overall communication situation and more on the words spoken to convey meaning.

culture A learned system of beliefs, customs, and values with which people identify.

context Information that surrounds an event and contributes to the meaning of that event.

When high- and low-context cultures meet, listening often becomes more difficult.

When low- and high-context people communicate with each other, the results can be frustrating. Hall and Hall note that HC people are apt to become impatient and irritated when LC people insist on giving them information they don't need. Conversely, low-context people are at a loss when high-context people do not provide *enough* information. Too much information frequently leads people to feel they are being talked down to; too little information can mystify them or make them feel left out.[12]

Although we cannot give you any simple rule of thumb for dealing with cultural differences in listening, our best advice is to be aware of the culture of the person(s) to whom you are listening or with whom you are speaking. Then, take differences from your own culture into account and try to adjust your behavior accordingly. Finally, if you expect to be listening or speaking to someone from a different culture, which is increasingly likely on a college campus, learn as much as you can in advance about the person's culture.

Personal Problems

Most people have had the experience of being so preoccupied with a personal problem they couldn't pay attention to what someone was saying. Personal problems can easily detract from listening to what is being said. The best advice

Listening in High- and Low-Context Cultures

As discussed in this chapter, some cultures place greater emphasis on the context in which communication occurs than on what is actually said. In such high-context cultures, as they are called, people realize that what one hears while listening must be deciphered only after thoroughly considering the context in which it is heard. Yes may mean no and vice versa, for example, depending on where and under what circumstances they are uttered. The opposite is true in low-context cultures, where the greatest emphasis is given to the spoken word. People trust what they think they hear without giving undue attention to the context in which it is heard.

One of the major stumbling blocks to the Paris Peace Conference, which laid the foundation for ending the war in Vietnam, was the shape of the conference table. Why? Because the North Vietnamese were concerned about the "message it would send" to those observing the negotiations. Vietnam is a high-context culture.

What kinds of problems do you see occurring when people from high- and low-context cultures listen to each other's speeches? Which of the listening skills discussed in this chapter do you think would most help in overcoming these problems? Be specific!

Source: Edward T. Hall and Mildred R. Hall, *Hidden Differences: Doing Business With the Japanese* (Garden City, N.Y.: Anchor/Doubleday, 1987)

---

for overcoming this obstacle is to recognize the situation and to focus on what is being said, as difficult as that may be. For example, if you were plagued by a personal problem prior to an important job interview, chances are you would tell yourself to "get your act together." You need to do exactly the same thing before listening to (or giving) a speech.

Bias

As you might suspect, bias gets in the way of active mindfulness. All people are biased, though not to an equal degree. Bias reflects an opinion formed without evidence, usually about a person or group of people. Racial, religious, sexual, and other such biases, although forbidden by law, often exist in the reality of people's opinions. Recognizing bias is an important step to overcoming it.

Bias isn't always based exclusively on false generalizations about groups of people. Prior, but incomplete, knowledge can cause people to form hasty judgments. Such was the case with the man who shot and killed a Sikh gas station owner in Arizona shortly after the September 11, 2001, terrorist attacks on the World Trade Center and Pentagon.[13] Not only is it wrong to assume all Arabs and Muslims are terrorists or support terrorists' goals, Sikhs are neither Arab nor Muslim, but actually are a different religious group originating in India.

Regardless of its source, bias is a serious impediment to listening. To overcome bias, listeners need to first recognize its existence, mentally set it aside, and recognize its irrationality. Although this may seem easier said than done, the ability to put bias in its rightful place is one of the keys to critical thinking and decision making.

Connotative Meanings

Important to this discussion are the related concepts of denotation and connotation. **Denotation** involves the objective, conventional meanings you find in a dictionary for a word. **Connotation** involves meanings you won't always find in

denotation The generally agreed upon meaning of a word, usually found in the dictionary.

connotation The secondary meaning of a word, often with a strong emotional, personal, and subjective component.

What Is Your Level of Receiver Apprehension?

The following statements apply to how various people feel about receiving communication. Although this measure was developed specifically for persons without hearing disabilities, people who are hard of hearing may think about analogous situations in which they become anxious while receiving messages through nonaural means, such as sign language, closed captions, reading lips, or via a TDD. Indicate if these statements apply to how you feel by noting whether you (5) strongly agree, (4) agree, (3) are undecided, (2) disagree, or (1) strongly disagree.

_____ 1. I feel comfortable when listening to others on the phone.

_____ 2. It is often difficult for me to concentrate on what others are saying.

_____ 3. When listening to members of the opposite sex, I find it easy to concentrate on what is being said.

_____ 4. I have no fear of being a listener as a member of an audience.

_____ 5. I feel relaxed when listening to new ideas.

_____ 6. I would rather not have to listen to other people at all.

_____ 7. I am generally overexcited and rattled when others are speaking to me.

_____ 8. I often feel uncomfortable when listening to others.

_____ 9. My thoughts become confused and jumbled when reading important information.

_____ 10. I often have difficulty concentrating on what others are saying.

_____ 11. Receiving new information makes me feel restless.

_____ 12. Watching television makes me nervous.

_____ 13. When on a date, I find myself tense and self-conscious when listening to my date.

_____ 14. I enjoy being a good listener.

_____ 15. I generally find it easy to concentrate on what is being said.

_____ 16. I seek out the opportunity to listen to new ideas.

_____ 17. I have difficulty concentrating on instructions others give to me.

_____ 18. It is hard to listen or concentrate on what other people are saying unless I know them well.

_____ 19. I feel tense when listening as a member of a social gathering.

_____ 20. Television programs that attempt to change my mind about something make me nervous.

To determine your score, first total the scores you gave yourself for statements 2, 6–13, and 17–20, and *add* 42 to that total (maximum 107, minimum 55). From this result, *subtract* the total of the scores you gave yourself for statements 1, 3–5, and 14–16. Your score should be in the range of 20 to 100. The higher your score, the more apprehensive you are about listening. Scores above 80 indicate a relatively high level of receiver apprehension. A midrange score would be about 60. Scores below 40 indicate a relatively low level of receiver apprehension.

Based on your score, what sorts of listening behaviors do you think you could improve? For example, do your answers suggest a need to work harder at concentration? Should you seek greater opportunities to practice listening skills and learn new information? Could the same type of relaxation exercises suggested in Chapter 3 be useful in listening situations, as well as when you are a public speaker?

Source: Copyright by the Speech Communication Association, 1975, from Lawrence R. Wheeless, "An Investigation of Receiver Apprehension and Social Context Dimensions of Communication Apprehension," *The Speech Teacher* 24 (1975): 261–268, by permission.

a dictionary for a word, or the ideas, images, and emotions people associate with a word. Although denotative meanings can be learned by reading a dictionary, connotations, which are largely determined by cultural usage, are learned over time from seeing and listening to examples. As an illustration of connotation, consider some of the various words used to describe a person who weighs more than average. The word *chubby* is appropriate when describing a baby or toddler, but would prove hurtful when used to describe a teenager. The word *stocky* doesn't mean the same when used to describe a man as when it is used to describe a woman. And, although it would be okay for a physician to write on a chart that a patient was overweight, it wouldn't be appropriate to write "tubby."

Anxiety

As discussed in Chapter 3, anxiety significantly detracts from our ability to process the information to which we are exposed. Anxious speakers often are unable to focus on audience feedback as they speak or actively listen to an instructor's feedback when they finish speaking. Likewise, anxious audience members have difficulty listening actively. To evaluate yourself in this area, see the box "What Is Your Level of Receiver Apprehension?"

GOALS OF LISTENING

The purpose or goal of a listener shapes the context in which listening occurs. It is one thing to listen to a stand-up comic and another to sit through a lecture on the theory of relativity. Just as speakers can have different general purposes, such as speaking to entertain, inform, or persuade, listeners can approach the public speaking transaction with different goals. The three listening goals most relevant to our purposes are (1) listening to understand, (2) listening to appreciate, and (3) critical listening (Table 4.1).

Listening to Understand

Understanding, in the truest sense of the word, is a multistep process. Further, there are different levels of understanding, depending on the goal of the listener. The first step in the process of understanding is to discriminate between

TABLE 4.1 Goals of Listening		
Type	*Goal*	*Example*
Listening to understand	To recognize meaning based on auditory and visual cues and to comprehend meaning	Listening to a lecture on Einstein's theory of relativity
Appreciative listening	To experience stimulation and enjoyment	Listening to a speech to entertain
Critical listening	To arrive at an informed judgment	Listening to candidates to determine how to vote

differing auditory and/or visual stimuli.[14] As infants we first recognize parental voices, then sounds, words, and eventually the complex structures of language. Visual stimuli, such as facial expression, gesture, and movement, become part of meaning for us, as does touch. The careful listener is sensitive to both the verbal and the nonverbal nuances of messages. This is especially true for public speaking. Listeners in the audience need to look beyond just the words of a speaker's message. By the same token, speakers need to listen to the entire message received from the audience. This means they should listen not only for aural feedback but for feedback from other sources as well. These sources include the expressions on audience members' faces, their body orientation, and head movements such as nodding in agreement.

Once you have discriminated among various sounds and sights, the next step to understanding is making sense of the aural and visual stimuli received.[15] Successful listening to understand demands that the meaning you assign to a message closely approximates that of the source of the message. How well you understand depends on several factors. Chief among them are vocabulary, concentration, and memory.[16]

Vocabulary   Obviously, you cannot comprehend something for which you don't have meaning. Thus a limited vocabulary has the undesirable effect of limiting your ability to understand messages. In fact, failure to master the necessary vocabulary can lead to disaster. For example, both authors of this text were high school debaters. One of us recalls a particularly embarrassing incident that resulted from not knowing the meaning of the word *superfluous*. Unaware that the other team's plan to remove all "superfluous United States tariffs" meant that they would remove only the unnecessary ones, the author's team produced several examples of tariffs that were essential to American industries. During cross-examination, an opposing team member asked the author, "Do you know what *superfluous* means?" Of course, the author did not know. When the opposition pointed out that every tariff the author's team had cited was, by definition, *not* superfluous, and that only superfluous tariffs would be removed, the debate was, for all practical purposes, lost. Needless to say, a dictionary became standard material for all future debates.

Concentration   A second important factor in listening to understand is concentration. As we know all too well, our minds are easily distracted from the task at hand. If you doubt that, think back to the last time you immediately forgot the name of someone to whom you had just been introduced.

There are two types of concentration: wide-band and pinpoint (Figure 4.2). Whereas pinpoint concentration is most relevant to critical listening, wide-band concentration is most central to listening to understand. **Pinpoint concentration** focuses on specific details. **Wide-band concentration** focuses on patterns rather than details. As a result, wide-band concentration assists you in listening for the tone of the speech, or its larger meaning in a particular context.

Both types of concentration, however, demand that you try to block out stimuli that compete with the message on which you are trying to focus. These competing stimuli range from the obvious, such as a heavy-metal band playing in the free-speech area outside your classroom, to the subtle, such as the gastrointestinal growls your stomach makes when you are hungry.

pinpoint concentration
Listening that focuses on specific details rather than patterns in a message.

wide-band concentration
Listening that focuses on patterns rather than details.

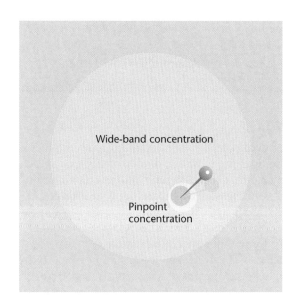

FIGURE 4.2 Wide-Band Versus Pinpoint Concentration. If you were listening to a symphony orchestra, you would use wide-band concentration to focus on the total sound of the orchestra. Pinpoint concentration would involve focusing on a single section of the orchestra.

Memory   Closely related to concentration is the third factor that influences listening to understand: memory. Often failure to remember reflects the fact that you also failed to concentrate. Consider the example of forgetting the name of someone to whom you have just been introduced. Although this very common experience simply may be the result of "mental laziness," most often it is the product of the anxiety accompanying the situation. Both anxiety and preoccupation with feelings of anxiety have a devastating effect on our powers of concentration and memory. As you are being introduced to someone, you may be too busy thinking about how you are being perceived to concentrate on the person's name. It isn't that you forgot the name—it's that you didn't listen for and process the name in the first place.

Much of your day is spent in situations that require comprehensive listening. And nowhere is this more likely to be true than in your speech class. Here are some skills that will help you improve your listening to understand.[17]

Improving Listening to Understand   **TIPS AND TACTICS**

- *Utilize the time difference between speech and thought effectively.* Most people speak at a rate of about 125 to 150 words per minute, but the human brain can process 400 to 500 spoken words per minute, although that is possible only with a special process known as "compressed speech." By using the time differential to think about what you are hearing, you can better interpret and understand the significance of what is said.

- *Listen for main ideas.* Don't get bogged down in insignificant detail. Rather, focus on understanding the main ideas and principles a speaker is discussing.

- *Listen for significant details.* Though not as important as main ideas, some details are fairly significant. Try to determine which details are illustrative of the main ideas and have significance for understanding what is being said.

- *Learn to draw valid inferences.* What does it all mean? Try to determine what conclusions you can draw from the speech.

Listening to Appreciate

Appreciative listening involves obtaining sensory stimulation or enjoyment from others.[18] This could include listening to music, drama, poetry, or a speech to entertain. Though it might appear that such listening "just comes naturally," the fact is that you can enhance your pleasure by expanding your listening experiences, improving your understanding of what you are listening to, and developing your powers of concentration. Music appreciation classes, for example, help students learn what to listen for in different kinds of music.

This is also true of your speech class. Learning about the various types, styles, and structures of speeches should help you appreciate what a rarity a good speech is. Learning how important it is to construct and share a good speech, moreover, should reinforce your appreciation and give you a more finely tuned ear. Here are some skills that will help you improve your appreciative listening.[19]

TIPS AND TACTICS   *Improving Appreciative Listening*

- *Use opportunities to gain experience with appreciative listening.* Listening appreciatively, as with all forms of listening, requires experience with different situations.

- *Be willing to listen appreciatively to a variety of writers, speakers, composers, and so on.* Even if you've developed preconceptions about a particular composer or type of music, for example, be willing to listen with an open mind. You may not appreciate Beethoven, and someone else may not appreciate The Deftones. Chances are that with a proper frame of mind you can learn what it is that makes them both appealing to large numbers of people.

- *Develop the ability to concentrate while listening appreciatively.* Many forms of appreciative listening depend on not letting your mind wander. Of course, the greater your experience with a variety of situations that involve listening, the more ability you will have to concentrate on the important aspects of the experience.

Critical Listening

Critical listening, which is an extension and refinement of the two types of listening just discussed, often requires skills similar to those required by listening to understand as well as to appreciate. There is a crucial difference, however: **Critical listening** is listening for the purpose of making reasoned judgments about speakers and the credibility of their messages. As we will discuss in Chapter 13, when listeners are motivated to think critically and elaborately about what a speaker says, they are likely to reach conclusions with more staying power. They are more confident in what they believe and are less susceptible to having their views changed by subsequent speakers.

Advertisers (such as the tobacco and alcoholic beverage industries) would go broke if people listened critically to their messages.

Much of the daily information we receive is targeted at influencing us, as well as making us compliant to the wishes of others. If information directed at influencing us or making us comply was always in our own self-interest, this wouldn't be a problem. Of course, this is anything but the case. Cigarette advertising, for example, is notorious for encouraging people to pursue a habit that can cost them their health or even their life. Beer companies, moreover, glamorize drinking to excess, even though alcohol is the single most abused substance in the United States.

Thus learning to listen critically is a form of self-protection. It guards us against being taken advantage of by unscrupulous salespeople, politicians, and plain-old con artists. But learning to listen critically also enhances our ability to communicate while delivering a speech.

At a minimum, critical listening involves focusing on both the speaker and the message in the attempt to verify the validity of what is being said. Is the speaker competent and trustworthy? If you think so, what evidence have you been given that makes this the case? Is the message directed at getting you to change, stay the same, or buy something? Is it merely informative, or is it argumentative? In either case, how do you know the information is representative of the facts? Is it logical? Is it supported with evidence, and are the sources clearly cited?

Here are some skills that will help you improve your critical listening.[20]

Improving Critical Listening   **TIPS AND TACTICS**

- *Consider the credibility of the source.* How much confidence do you have in the goodwill, trustworthiness, and competence of the person to whom you are listening?

- *Recognize that the credibility of the source can influence you.* Although credibility is important and can be influential in and of itself, do not let another person's judgment automatically replace your own thinking. Even the most credible sources can be wrong.
- *Evaluate the validity of arguments.* Are the arguments presented reasonable? Don't be afraid to question the logic of a speaker if it seems fallacious.
- *Evaluate the evidence presented in support of arguments.* Is the evidence presented believable, from reliable sources, and documented for you?
- *Recognize fallacies of reasoning.* In Chapter 14 we discuss a number of ways arguments that appear to be valid can be deceptive or fallacious.
- *Identify emotional appeals.* Determine the type of emotions the speaker appeals to. Are these appeals ones with which you are proud to identify? Whereas appealing to legitimate human emotions is a necessary aspect of persuasion (as we see in Chapter 13), misguided appeals can be destructive. Use of appeals to hate, irrational fears, and prejudice should be rejected.

The critical perspective you bring to bear when listening to speakers and their messages is just as relevant to you and the message you ultimately share with others. Thus, learning to listen critically to others will help you become more objectively critical of yourself. This will assist you in both the preparation and the delivery of your own speeches because it will force you to apply a similar set of critical questions to yourself.

TECHNIQUES TO IMPROVE YOUR LISTENING SKILLS

Actually, listening begins within our own minds. We all carry on an internal dialogue. Sometimes this is limited to our own thoughts, whereas at other times, it is in response to what someone else has said. For example, imagine you are about to ask a friend for money. You might hear yourself saying silently, "Oh no, he'll never loan me the money. All I will do is tick him off." On the other hand, you might think, "I've helped her out before. She knows I'm good for it. What have I got to lose?"

Sometimes we listen to our thoughts in response to another's words, although we don't verbalize them. For example, suppose you listen to someone speaking about a controversial topic. If you agree with the speaker, you may find yourself thinking, "Yeah . . . yes!" On the other hand, if you disagree with the speaker, you may mentally hear yourself saying things like, "You've got to be kidding." Listening to your own thoughts affects how you listen to others and can interfere with your processing of the message you are receiving. For example, if you think you already know what a speaker is going to say, you might say to yourself, "Heard that before" and tune out, missing an important message you did not anticipate. Or thinking about what you are going to say to another person can cause you to miss what he or she is saying to you.

To begin with, no one can make you listen. The decision to actively attend to speakers and their messages is yours and yours alone. The same is true for speakers listening to their audiences. All the techniques in the world, therefore, won't help you become a better listener unless you consciously choose to attend to a specific speaking transaction.

The techniques that follow are best viewed as a collection or system of techniques that are interdependent. Your skill in using one of these techniques, consequently, will have a direct bearing on your skill in using them all. The techniques we discuss are setting goals, blocking out distracting stimuli, suspending judgment, focusing on main points, recognizing highlights and signposts, taking effective notes, being sensitive to metacommunication, paraphrasing, and questioning.

Setting Goals

The first technique is straightforward: Establish a goal you hope to achieve as a consequence of listening. This goes back to the goals of listening described earlier. The goal of appreciative listening is not the same as the goal of critical listening.

Your goal guides your behavior as you listen. When listening critically, for example, much of your attention will be focused on distinguishing what part of a speaker's message is fact from what part of it is opinion. In contrast, when you are listening appreciatively, your attention will be more general, focused on the gist of the message's meaning, not on each and every fact offered by a speaker. The listening goal established tends to dictate the listening behaviors in which people engage. Thus, when people fail to establish a goal at the outset of the listening process, they run the risk of focusing on what is peripheral rather than central to their needs.

Blocking Out Distracting Stimuli

The second technique is even more straightforward: To listen actively, you must clear your mind of distracting stimuli. Trying to force yourself to rid your mind of distracting thoughts, however, is not the answer. Relaxation may be.

Research suggests that a relaxed mind is a receptive mind. Moreover, we know that there is a mind-body relationship in this regard. When the body feels relaxed, so does the mind. As a result, anything you do to promote self-relaxation prior to listening should help you diminish the potential impact of distracting stimuli. In Chapter 3 we provided a number of ways to help you relax before speaking. The same techniques can also help you relax so that you can become a more receptive listener.

Suspending Judgment

People can be excessively judgmental, even when they have been provided with little concrete evidence on which to base their judgments. People cannot listen when they prematurely judge others and their messages. They may hear what they want to hear, but they cannot listen. Critical listening especially demands an open mind.

In the attempt to suspend judgment when you are listening to a speaker, you can do three things. First, recognize and accept the fact that you—and everyone else—bring subjective experience and bias to the speech transaction. This subjective experience colors and filters your perceptions of the speaker and the message. Second, try not to judge a book by its cover. Stereotypes on the basis of physical appearance are notoriously unreliable. Finally, try to process the message rather than immediately reacting to the speaker and the message.

Focusing on Main Points

You may also find it helpful to prioritize what you listen for in a communication transaction. The content of all messages varies in importance. Some ideas expressed are central, whereas others are more peripheral. As mentioned earlier, listening to the main ideas in a message is most important.

Some students make the mistake of trying to write down verbatim everything a professor says in class. They risk missing the main points of the lecture. For example, one of the authors had a classmate in college who tape-recorded and then transcribed every class lecture. Despite an extraordinary effort on her part, she rarely earned better than a C. Why? Because she focused so much on trying to record and memorize every word her professors said, she never learned to separate the important points from the insignificant ones.

Recognizing Highlights and Signposts

Two things you can look for in the attempt to make sure you are listening for main ideas are highlights and signposts. Highlights and signposts also are something you'll want to include in your own speeches to assist the listeners in your audience. The best speakers go out of their way to highlight what is most important in their message. They might say:

> "Of the three ideas I've shared, this one is far and away the most important."

> "In my mind, the most precious freedom we enjoy is the freedom of speech."

> "How can anyone ignore the magnitude of environmental problems caused by automobiles?"

Signposts are transitional statements that tell people when one main idea is ending and another is beginning. Examples of such signposts might be:

> "Having established the importance of a speaker's credibility, let's now look at . . ."

> "This key to understanding the poetry of Edgar Allan Poe leads me to my second point about the interpretation of *The Raven*."

> "Equally important to this idea is the notion that an open society demands a free press."

Taking Effective Notes

Much as professors might like to think otherwise, not every word they utter in their lectures deserves to be recorded. Yet they routinely have to ask students to quit writing, sit back in their seats, and listen to an idea before writing it down. Effective note-taking is a science. Like any other science, it demands an appropriate methodology. Ralph G. Nichols and Thomas R. Lewis, two of the earliest researchers on the process of listening, describe four basic note-taking methods for listening to speeches and lectures.[21] They point out that no one method will work with every situation. The four methods are outlining, annotating a book or manuscript, précis writing, and recording fact versus principle.

Outlining   We will discuss outlining from the point of view of the speaker at greater length in Chapter 8, so we won't go over the details of the process here. The listener using outlining basically tries to capture the main points of the speech as they are presented, as well as the subordinate or supporting ideas under each point. A well-done outline is a good guide to what has been said. But outlining requires considerable effort on the part of the listener and can distract attention from what is being said. It also depends on the speaker using clear signposts and a consistent organizational pattern. Trying to outline a disorganized speech is the height of frustration.

Annotation   This technique works well only when a speaker or lecturer is going over material you have already read. For example, if a literature professor is discussing a short story you have been assigned to read, you would write marginal comments called annotations at each place in the book the professor discusses. Although the technique does not require great effort on the part of the listener, it can be messy and there is no way to organize your notes for later review.

Précis Writing   With this technique, you listen for a few minutes, get the gist of what the speaker is saying, and then write a brief paragraph to yourself summarizing what has been said. This technique involves alternating between intense listening for three- or four-minute intervals and brief periods of note-taking. While listening to the speaker, you should be focusing on what is being said and how to summarize it for your notes. Though the notes produced are brief, clear, and easy to review, the downside is that you must divert your attention from the speaker to write your précis.

Recording Fact Versus Principle   First, you divide your page vertically down the middle. On the left write "facts"; on the right, "principles." As you listen to the speaker, list each important fact presented on the left, numbering them 1, 2, 3, and so on. On the right, list only broad general principles, using roman numerals (I, II, III, etc.) to distinguish them from facts. Under each principle, list the numbers of the facts that correspond to the principles. This method of note-taking is illustrated in Figure 4.3. The system avoids excessive writing and requires the listener to think about what the speaker has said. In addition, you can leave space at the bottom for ideas and questions that occur to you as you listen. Although this is a very useful technique, it works better for the social sciences and humanities than for the natural sciences.

   Whatever note-taking system you employ, the important thing is to focus attention on the speaker's ideas and try to think about what is being said, not simply try to produce a transcript. Writing down too much can cause you to miss the most important ideas and get bogged down in minute details.

Being Sensitive to Metacommunication

Another important technique involves listening for metacommunication. **Metacommunication** is the message about the message. It is generally conveyed nonverbally. You can listen for metacommunication in a speaker's eyes, voice, gestures, movements, posture, and use of time. You can also listen for metacommunication in other people's reaction to your message.

metacommunication The message about the message; generally conveyed nonverbally.

FIGURE 4.3 Recording Fact Versus Principle While Listening

	FACTS	PRINCIPLES
	1. 1455, Gutenberg invented moveable-type printing	I. Technological developments in communication have accelerated at an ever more rapid pace.
	2. 1920s, first radio broadcasts	
	3. 1952, 9% of households had TV	(1, 2, 3, 4, 5, 6)
	4. 1960, 85% of households had TV	
	5. 1980s, 1.1% of households had VCRs	II. TV & radio are becoming more important to average Americans than print.
	6. 1995, 67% had VCRs	
	7. Average American watches TV 7 hours a day	(7, 8, 9)
	8. 96% of population listens to radio	
	9. Newspaper subscriptions per household are about half of what they were in 1960	IDEAS & QUESTIONS
		Has the increase in VCRs cut into broadcast TV?

cross cue–checking Gauging what a person says verbally against the nonverbal behaviors that make up metacommunication.

Chief among the reasons for listening carefully to metacommunication is cross cue–checking. **Cross cue–checking** involves gauging what a person says verbally against the nonverbal behaviors that make up metacommunication. Cross cue–checking enables people to ferret out the subtleties in a speaker's message—for example, irony, sarcasm, and sometimes deception. Metacommunication is a potentially rich source of meaning. Because shared meaning is the bottom-line goal of listening, it would make no sense to ignore this source.

A word of caution is in order. At the outset of this discussion, we stated that techniques for listening are interdependent. This is especially true of metacommunication. Never infer the meaning of a speaker's or an audience member's message on the basis of metacommunication alone. It is not a substitute for the spoken word. It also can be tremendously misleading when isolated from its spoken counterpart.

Listening should involve both sight and sound. What do you "hear" in this speaker's metacommunication?

Paraphrasing

One of the techniques you may use when researching your speeches is the interview. Successful interviewing depends on active listening. A key element of active listening is seeking confirmation from people that you have understood their message. The techniques of paraphrasing and questioning (discussed next) are valuable tools for ensuring accurate communication. Moreover, paraphrasing encourages the interviewee to talk because it reinforces the fact that you are actively engaged with what the interviewee is saying.

To paraphrase a message, you briefly repeat in your own words the essence of what has been said. Paraphrasing should be nonevaluative. Your goal is not to convey your opinion of what was said, but merely to confirm that you understand it. Often you will paraphrase not only the denotative content of the message but the emotional aspects as well. For example: "What I'm hearing you say is . . . ," "Let me make sure I understand what you are saying . . . ," or "You seem to be feeling . . . ."

Questioning

Similar to paraphrasing, questioning is another way of determining if you correctly understand the message. But rather than simply repeating back what you think you have heard, you ask the other person for information as well as confirmation. Avoid hostile and loaded questions. A *hostile question* signals your strong disagreement with the other person: for example, "How can you possibly say such a stupid thing?" *Loaded questions* assume something that is not necessarily the case. The classic loaded question is "Have you stopped beating your wife (or husband)?" Your goal is not to embarrass or trap people, but to give them an opportunity to clarify and elaborate on what they have said.

When listening to a speech, you should not interrupt to ask a question unless the speaker has clearly indicated a willingness to take questions during the presentation. Even then, the common courtesy of raising a hand to indicate you wish to ask a question is recommended. Some public speakers ask people to hold their questions until the end of a speech. When interviewing people, of course, the flow of questions is much freer. But you should still wait until the opportunity arises to ask your question without interrupting the other person mid-sentence. Often, paying close attention to nonverbal behaviors will help you know when it is appropriate to interrupt with a question. A pause, a glance, or a facial expression that indicates finality are all ways of signaling that a person is waiting for a response.

SUMMARY

 **SPEECH COACH**
To evaluate your understanding of this chapter, see the Quizzes on your CD.

Listening is necessary to becoming a competent speaker and audience member. Keep the following principles in mind:

- Hearing and listening are not the same.
- Listening is the process of receiving, attending to, and assigning meaning to aural as well as visual and tactile stimuli.
- Active listening involves conscious and responsive participation.
- Active mindfulness involves conscious awareness of the transactions between speakers and listeners.
- Selective attention involves a conscious choice to focus on certain people and some messages.
- Sensorial involvement means listening with *all* the senses.
- Comprehension is understanding what was said.
- Retention is storing what was said in memory.

You should avoid common misconceptions about listening, such as:

- Listening is easy; it is not.
- Intelligence guarantees effective listening; it does not.
- There is no need to plan ahead; planning is essential.
- Reading skills correlate with listening skills. Such is not the case.

Obstacles to effective listening include:

- physical conditions
- cultural differences
- personal problems
- bias
- connotative meanings
- anxiety

Listening can have one of three goals:

- understanding
- appreciation
- critical listening

Techniques you can use to increase your overall listening skill include:

- setting goals
- blocking out distracting stimuli
- suspending judgment
- focusing on main points
- recognizing highlights and signposts
- taking effective notes
- being sensitive to metacommunication
- paraphrasing
- questioning

CHECK YOUR UNDERSTANDING: EXERCISES AND ACTIVITIES

1. In a short paper or speech, describe an incident in which your message was misunderstood or you misunderstood another person's intended message. Were there any tip-offs that the speech transaction was not effective? How could the misunderstanding have been avoided?

2. Planning for upcoming listening situations is important. Consider one of your classes in which the instructor regularly lectures. In what ways can you prepare for listening to the next lecture? Are there any specific listening obstacles you need to overcome? After attending the lecture, see if your understanding was enhanced by your preparation for the class.

3. In a short paper, describe a situation you have experienced in which bias affected the listening process. Choose a situation in which you feel your meaning was distorted due to bias or a situation in which you feel your own biases handicapped you in the listening process.

4. Make a list of 10 words that have varying connotations to different people or in different situations. Be prepared to share your list with classmates in small groups or before the full class, depending on your instructor's directions.

5. Describe three times in a given day during which you engaged in critical listening. Be prepared to share your list with classmates in small groups or before the full class.

 **SPEECH COACH**

For a review of key terms in this chapter, see the Key Terms Flashcards on your CD.

NOTES

1. Dave Barry, *Dave Barry Does Japan* (New York: Random House, 1992), 35–36.
2. Anthony P. Carnevale, Leila J. Gainer, and Ann S. Meltzer, *Workplace Basics: The Skills Employers Want* (Washington, D.C.: American Society for Training and Development and U.S. Department of Labor, 1988), 12.
3. Lyman K. Steil, Larry Barker, and Kittie W. Watson, *Effective Listening* (New York: Random House, 1993), 12–13.
4. Andrew D. Wolvin and Carolyn Gwynn Coakley, *Listening*, 3rd ed. (Dubuque, Iowa: W. C. Brown, 1988), 93.
5. Wolvin and Coakley, *Listening*, 115.

6. Melvin L. DeFleur, Patricia Kearney, and Timothy G. Plax, *Fundamentals of Human Communication* (Mountain View, Calif.: Mayfield, 1993), 112–113.

7. Gavin Edwards, *'Scuse Me While I Kiss This Guy and Other Misheard Lyrics* (New York: Simon & Schuster, 1995).

8. Gavin Edwards, *He's Got the Whole World in His Pants and More Misheard Lyrics* (New York: Simon & Schuster, 1996).

9. Robert Haakenson, *The Art of Listening* (Philadelphia: Smith Kline & French Laboratories, n.d.), 3.

10. DeFleur, Kearney, and Plax, *Fundamentals of Human Communication*, 113–117.

11. Edward T. Hall and Mildred Reed Hall, *Hidden Differences: Doing Business With the Japanese* (Garden City, N.Y.: Anchor Press/Doubleday, 1987), 7.

12. Hall and Hall, *Hidden Differences*, 10–11.

13. Tamar Lewin, "Sikh Owner of Gas Station Is Fatally Shot in Rampage" [from Lexis-Nexis, 24 September 2001] (*New York Times*, 17 September 2001, B16).

14. Wolvin and Coakley, *Listening*, 140.

15. Wolvin and Coakley, *Listening*, 188.

16. Wolvin and Coakley, *Listening*, 189–206.

17. Wolvin and Coakley, *Listening*, 207–225.

18. Wolvin and Coakley, *Listening*, 320.

19. Wolvin and Coakley, *Listening*, 330–333.

20. Wolvin and Coakley, *Listening*, 287–313.

21. Ralph G. Nichols and Thomas R. Lewis, *Listening and Speaking: A Guide to Effective Oral Communication* (Dubuque, Iowa: W. C. Brown, 1954), 41–53.

Adapting to
the Audience

PART TWO

Effective public
speakers adapt
their message to
their audience.

Adapting to
Your Audience

 OBJECTIVES

After reading this chapter and reviewing the learning resources on your CD-ROM and at the Online Learning Center, you should be able to:

- Analyze your audience in terms of cultural variables, common demographic characteristics, and individual attributes.
- Adapt to audience diversity in terms of individual, demographic, and cultural variables.
- Identify the basic elements of the public speaking situation, including your goals, audience, and constraints on achieving your goals.

 KEY CONCEPTS

attitude	culture	primitive beliefs
audience diversity	demographic diversity	rhetorical situation
belief	demographics	short-term goals
central beliefs	individual diversity	socioeconomic status
constraints	long-term goals	values
cultural diversity	peripheral beliefs	

I was not planning on speaking here tonight, but this is where my journey has taken me. . . .

—CAROLYN McCARTHY, wife and mother of victims of the Long Island Railroad massacre, speaking to the 1996 Democratic National Convention.

Mary Fisher, who contracted the HIV virus from her husband, riveted the 1992 Republican Convention with her speech about AIDS.

If necessity is the mother of invention, then circumstance may be the father of public speaking. Consider two cases: Mary Fisher and Carolyn McCarthy. Their lives were dramatically altered by circumstances beyond their control. And both of them became powerful public voices in the process.

Mary Fisher appeared to have a life most people can only dream about. She was a rising star in the campaign machinery of the Republican Party, counted famous people among her friends, was married to a much admired artist, and was the mother of two adoring children. Even though her marriage ultimately failed, her success as a political adviser and as a mother continued to flourish. Then something terrible happened, threatening her very being. Her ex-husband was diagnosed with AIDS. Shortly thereafter, Mary tested positive for HIV, something she had never feared, given her sexual orientation, monogamous relationship with her husband, and drug-free lifestyle.

Carolyn McCarthy's life was less glamorous than Mary Fisher's, but was still admirable. A registered nurse, wife, and mother, she was widowed by a deranged gunman who shot her husband and critically wounded her son on December 7, 1993. It was Carolyn's 50th birthday. What should have been a day of joy for Carolyn and the two people she loved most, turned into one of inexplicable loss.

What happened next in the lives of these two remarkable people is what makes their stories worth telling. Instead of giving in to HIV and AIDS, Mary

Mary Fisher Speaks Out on AIDS

The AIDS virus is not a political creature. It does not care whether you are Democratic or Republican; it does not ask whether you are black or white, male or female, gay or straight, young or old. Tonight, I represent an AIDS community whose members have been reluctantly drafted from every segment of American society.

Though I am white and a mother, I am one with a black infant struggling with tubes in a Philadelphia hospital.

Though I am female and contracted this disease in marriage and enjoy the warm support of my family, I am one with the lonely gay man sheltering a flickering candle from the cold wind of his family's rejection.

Source: Official Report of the Proceedings of the Thirty-Fifth Republican National Convention, August 19, 1992.

Fisher became a prominent AIDS activist as a result of the moving speech she was motivated to give at the 1992 Republican National Convention. You can read excerpts of her speech in the box "Mary Fisher Speaks Out on AIDS." Read her full speech in Appendix B. To this day, she is one of the most sought after speakers in the world on the topic of AIDS.

Carolyn McCarthy, whose pleas to her congressman for tighter gun controls fell on deaf ears following her personal tragedy, also became an activist. In her case, however, she switched political parties, ran against the congressman who rebuffed her, and was elected in a huge upset. Like Mary Fisher, Carolyn also took advantage of an opportunity to address the national convention of her party, which established Carolyn as a national voice on the topic of gun control. You can read her speech in Appendix B.

Neither Mary Fisher nor Carolyn McCarthy planned on becoming a highly visible public speaker. Circumstances demanded that they take action. Although we hope you never have to face circumstances even remotely similar to Mary Fisher's or Carolyn McCarthy's, the chances are good that you will one day find yourself speaking to an audience on a topic that you cannot possibly imagine today. The circumstance may be as ordinary as speaking out in favor or against a development project in your community or as compelling as speaking out on behalf of yourself and co-workers about the necessity of change in the management style at the company where you work. It's not a question of if, but when, the right circumstance will present itself.

This chapter is meant to help you prepare not only for these unforeseen circumstances in the future, but also for the one in which you find yourself right now: your speech class. In the pages that follow we focus on a variety of topics, all of which are related to the task of analyzing and adapting to your audience. These topics include:

- The importance of thinking about the purpose and goals of your speech relative to your audience.
- How your purpose and goals are mediated by audience diversity.
- How best to adapt your speech to diverse audiences.
- The importance of identifying and adapting to your potential audience and situational constraints you may encounter.

Carolyn McCarthy, a homemaker and nurse, never expected that one day her personal tragedy would lead her to address the 1996 Democratic National Convention about gun violence.

GOALS AND SPECIFIC PURPOSE

All too often, beginning speakers get ahead of themselves in the planning process: For example, they start with the challenges an audience poses without first considering their own purpose in speaking and the goal they hope to achieve. If you have no clear goal to start with, no amount of audience analysis is going to help. We want you to be able to reasonably predict how your audience is likely to respond to your speech. This begins with deciding on your goal and then selecting a specific purpose that will make sense in light of the audience you know awaits you and the goal you hope to achieve.

You can have both **short-term goals** and **long-term goals.** For example, Mary Fisher sought in her speech to have her audience realize that AIDS is not a virus that only attacks gays, intravenous drug users, or the sexually promiscuous. She was a married professional, faithful to her spouse, and she contracted the virus from her husband. If audience members recognized that AIDS could infect anyone, not just a few groups, then she would fulfill her short-term goal. In the long term, of course, she desired more—an end to the epidemic and the stigma associated with it. But with one speech she had to choose an attainable goal. As with Carolyn McCarthy's campaign against gun violence, her long-term goals have yet to be realized, but progress has been made.

short-term goals Those ends that we can reasonably expect to achieve in the near term.

long-term goals Those ends that we can hope to achieve only over an extended period of time.

Your specific purpose, as discussed in Chapter 2, is the objective you hope to achieve in speaking to a particular audience on a particular occasion. While your instructor will probably assign you a general purpose for each speech, such as to persuade, to inform, or to entertain, the specific purpose is up to you. The specific purpose should be chosen to fulfill a specific goal.

THE AUDIENCE

Given the specific purpose and goals you have tentatively established for your speech, you now want to be able to predict whether they make sense in light of your audience. Analyzing your audience is an extension of the process we all go through when meeting and getting to know new people. It begins on a general level and then becomes increasingly specific. When we meet new people we try to gauge the degree to which they are similar to us; for example, do they share our language and dialect? We then use this information as a basis for predictions about how to introduce ourselves and what topics of conversation and questions would be appropriate. As we get to know people better, we learn more about what makes them unique. We then use this new, more sophisticated knowledge to guide us in broaching more sensitive topics with them.

You do much the same thing with an audience. Instead of focusing on a single person, however, you have the more difficult task of focusing on many. What you discover about them helps you decide what to say and how to say it. You can never know all there is to know about even a small audience. Still, if you are systematic in your analysis, you can learn a tremendous amount about the increasingly diverse people you encounter. You can profitably use what you learn about such people to adapt your purpose, goal, and eventual message so that they welcome rather than reject your speech.

Audience Diversity

Audience analysis begins with recognition and acceptance of the fact that today's audience is more diverse than ever. **Audience diversity** represents the cultural, demographic, and individual characteristics that vary among audience members. According to an analysis of the most recent U.S. census by *USA Today*, "The nation's diversity increased dramatically over the past decade.... There is nearly a 1 in 2 chance that two people selected at random are racially or ethnically different."[1] We see this increasing diversity daily in the classes we teach, and it is in these classes that our students present their speeches.

Recently, for example, one of us taught a public speaking class whose members resembled a small United Nations assembly. There were 15 men and 9 women, although statistically most classes at our university have more women than men. While the median age was about 20, one class member was almost 50, and another was in his 30s. Five students were from Japan. One was from Indonesia, and two others were from Malaysia. Another student was from the former Soviet Republic of Kyrgyzstan. One native-born American student was of Chinese origin, and another traced her ancestry to the Philippines. A number of students were hard-core science majors, while others were pursuing music, public relations, and graphic design. Hobbies ranged from scuba diving and fishing to origami and batik. Although this class's diversity was more dramatic than most, we think it is a preview of a not too distant future.

SPEECH COACH

For an overview of audience analysis, view video segment 5.1 on your CD.

audience diversity The cultural, demographic, and individual characteristics that vary among audience members.

Today's college students are more diverse culturally, demographically, and individually than ever before.

Once you have recognized and accepted the fact that the people in your audience are not clones of each other, you need to learn about and adapt to their diversity. There are three levels of audience diversity, which we have depicted for you in Figure 5.1. We will begin at the most general level, looking at the cultures to which members of your audience belong. Then we will look at some observable differences in what are termed **demographics**—differences such as age, sex and gender. Finally, we will look at your audience members as individuals. The more you can learn about your audience at each level, the better you can predict their response to your speech.

demographics Basic and vital data regarding any population.

Discovering Cultural Diversity

Culture is a learned system of beliefs, customs, and values with which people identify. Culture also is more a product of language than geography. French-speaking Canadians, for example, think of themselves as more French than English, even though Canada has mainly English traditions. Barcelonians think of themselves as Castilians rather than Spaniards, because they speak a dialect that is distinct from the rest of their country. **Cultural diversity** refers mainly to differences among people in terms of beliefs, customs, and values—in a sense, their world view.

cultural diversity Differences among people in terms of beliefs, customs, and values—in a sense, their world view.

Because culture is learned, what is appropriate in one culture may not be appropriate in another. The list of specific things that make one culture unique from another is inexhaustible. However, recognizing and responding to cultural diversity does not demand that you try to learn everything about a specific culture. To the contrary, discovering what is common but variable among cultures is the key to culturally responsive speaking.

Dutch communication scholar Geert Hofstede says that all cultures vary in terms of at least four dimensions: "power distance (from small to large), collectivism versus individualism, femininity versus masculinity, and uncertainty avoidance (from weak to strong)."[2] In addition, Hofstede notes that a fifth

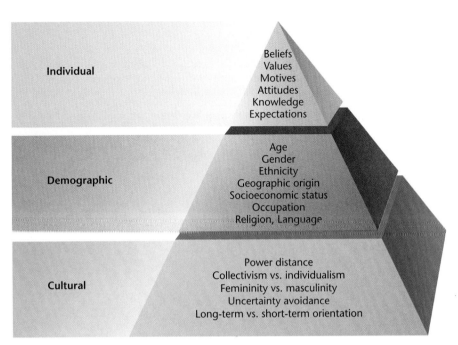

FIGURE 5.1 Levels of Diversity

Individual
Beliefs
Values
Motives
Attitudes
Knowledge
Expectations

Demographic
Age
Gender
Ethnicity
Geographic origin
Socioeconomic status
Occupation
Religion, Language

Cultural
Power distance
Collectivism vs. individualism
Femininity vs. masculinity
Uncertainty avoidance
Long-term vs. short-term orientation

dimension has recently been discovered: long-term orientation versus short-term orientation to life.[3] We think Hofstede's dimensions are a useful guide for analyzing an audience's cultural diversity.

Power Distance   Power distance is "the extent to which the less powerful members of institutions and organizations within a country expect and accept that power is distributed unequally."[4] All societies are unequal, some more than others. However, different societies handle inequality in different ways. For example, there are large power distances in countries in Latin America, Asia, and Africa and in some European countries such as Spain. On the other hand, countries such as the United States and Great Britain and some parts of Europe have smaller power distances. Sweden is an egalitarian country with a small power distance, whereas France has a large power distance.

Power-distance differences have important implications for you as a public speaker. Suppose you are a manager in an international organization announcing company downsizing. You could not assume that an audience from a small-power-distance culture, such as Sweden, would react in the same way to your speech as would one from a large-power-distance culture, such as Japan. Similarly, teachers are treated with deference in large-power-distance cultures, whereas they are treated as near equals in small-power-distance cultures. For example, a professor from a Japanese university teaching in the United States might be surprised to be called by his or her first name, though such a practice is not uncommon at American universities. Conversely, a Japanese student studying in the United States might find it odd that professors expect students to treat them less formally than professors are treated in Japan. Interestingly, this respect is reciprocal. One of us was informed by a Japanese student that not only do students call their professors by last name as a sign of respect, but professors in Japan address students by their last names as well.

Between Two Cultures: Tomoko Mukawa

Tomoko Mukawa was born in Japan and lived there until she was 15, when she first came to the United States as a high school exchange student. When she returned to the United States as a college student, Tomoko was struck by the differences in the way students and professors communicate in the two different cultures. Tomoko gives an example of differences between the two cultures:

> I wanted to keep my fluency in Japanese, so I took a class from a Japanese professor. Although the American students were allowed to call the professor by his American nickname, I was required to follow the Japanese tradition of always using his title and surname. He stressed that, as a Japanese student, I needed to preserve my cultural heritage.

Tomoko also noticed that the language in which she spoke made a difference in how she was treated. As an English tutor for Japanese students coming to America, Tomoko discovered that when she spoke English she was perceived as more assertive than when she spoke Japanese. "You are like a different person when you speak Japanese," she was told by one of her students.

These experiences illustrate the differences between a large-power-distance culture like Japan and a small-power-distance culture like the United States. In Japan, students would never be familiar with professors, and women are generally not assertive. Simply speaking in her native language changed the way Tomoko was perceived. Language and culture are closely intertwined, as her experience has shown.

For an example of how one Japanese student reacts to the culture of an American university, see the box "Between Two Cultures: Tomoko Mukawa."

Collectivism Versus Individualism   The second dimension common to all cultures is collectivism versus individualism. "Collectivism stands for a society in which people from birth onwards are integrated into strong, cohesive ingroups, which throughout people's lifetime continue to protect them in exchange for unquestioning loyalty."[5] In an individualistic society, on the other hand, "everyone is expected to look after himself or herself and his or her immediate family only."[6] Some cultures, notably Asian and Native American, believe the good of the many far outweighs the good of the few. In these collectivist cultures, people shun the individual spotlight. Singling out a member of a collectivist culture while you're giving a speech is likely to embarrass the person.

In cultures where so-called rugged individualism is admired and encouraged, the opposite is true. In the United States, for example, the dominant culture is very individualistic. We champion lone-wolf entrepreneurs who strike it rich, quarterbacks who stand alone in the pocket, and politicians who march to the beat of a different drummer. There is evidence to believe, in fact, that the United States is the most individualistic nation on Earth.[7]

In speaking to an audience whose members are largely individualistic, you would be wise to point out how your recommendations will benefit them individually. For example, when faced with an energy crisis and the threat of rolling blackouts in California in the summer of 2001, the state instituted what it called the 20/20 program. Those who used 20 percent less electricity than they had the previous year earned a 20 percent reduction in their electric bill. A speaker encouraging energy conservation would be wise to stress the potential savings individuals could have on their electric bill by conserving energy.

In speaking to a predominantly collectivistic audience, however, appealing solely to individual benefits may be counterproductive. Audience members may feel that the speaker is appealing to selfish motives. Thus, appealing to the greater good for the state might well be the most effective strategy to promote energy conservation for collectivistic audiences. Of course, if a speaker can combine both individualistic and collectivistic appeals, then the speech is more likely to succeed whatever the cultural background of the audience.

The highly individualistic orientation of Americans may be slightly changing given immigration patterns and birth rates. Census data show that more people from collectivist cultures such as Asia reside in the United States today than at any other time in history. American college students today find that people from collectivist cultures are an increasing part of their audience. To find out where you stand as an individual on this dimension, see the box "How Collectivistic or Individualistic Are You?"

Femininity Versus Masculinity   The third dimension of culture in Hofstede's scheme is femininity versus masculinity. Hofstede explains: "Femininity stands for a society in which social gender roles overlap: both men and women are supposed to be modest, tender, and concerned with the quality of life."[8] Masculinity, on the other hand, "stands for a society in which social gender roles are clearly distinct: men are supposed to be assertive, tough, and focused on material success."[9] The United States ranks relatively high on measures of masculinity, ranking 15th out of 53 countries. Despite being traditionally a highly masculine country, this is changing slowly, as evidenced by the recent selection of female CEOs by Hewlett-Packard and Xerox. Nevertheless, the majority of CEOs in the United States continue to be male. The most feminine cultures are found in Scandinavia and tend not to assign one set of roles to men and another set of roles to women. In these cultures, the professional role a person assumes is a product of ability rather than biological sex. Thus, when imagining a physician or chief executive officer of a company, people don't automatically see a man. In imagining a nurse or secretary, they don't automatically see a woman.

The opposite is true for many other cultures. Some go to extremes in the degree to which one's sex decides one's role. Countries such as Austria, Venezuela, and Japan (which ranks highest on masculinity) have few women in positions of corporate or public authority. Women are assigned roles out of view and out of power. Thus, an audience of Japanese men would be polite but predictably unreceptive to a woman speaking on a topic such as reengineering the Japanese corporation. By the same token, a Scandinavian audience would be wary of a male speaker suggesting women belong in the home.

This dimension can be a factor in a number of settings. For example, in masculine cultures, children in school tend to speak out and compete openly. Failure is viewed as a disaster and can even lead to suicide. Boys and girls tend to

How Collectivistic or Individualistic Are You?

The purpose of this questionnaire is to help you assess your individualistic and collectivistic tendencies. Respond by indicating the degree to which the values reflected in each phrase are important to you: Opposed to My Values (answer 1), Not Important to Me (answer 2), Somewhat Important to Me (answer 3), Important to Me (answer 4), or Very Important to Me (answer 5).

_____ 1. Obtaining pleasure or sensuous gratification
_____ 2. Preserving the welfare of others
_____ 3. Being successful by demonstrating my individual competency
_____ 4. Restraining my behavior if it is going to harm others
_____ 5. Being independent in thought and action
_____ 6. Having safety and stability of people with whom I identify
_____ 7. Obtaining status and prestige
_____ 8. Having harmony in my relations with others
_____ 9. Having an exciting and challenging life
_____ 10. Accepting cultural and religious traditions
_____ 11. Being recognized for my individual work
_____ 12. Avoiding the violation of social norms
_____ 13. Leading a comfortable life
_____ 14. Living in a stable society
_____ 15. Being logical in my approach to work
_____ 16. Being polite to others
_____ 17. Being ambitious
_____ 18. Being self-controlled
_____ 19. Being able to choose what I do
_____ 20. Enhancing the welfare of others

To find your individualism score, add your responses to the *odd-numbered* items. To find your collectivism score, add your responses to the *even-numbered* items. Both scores will range from 10 to 50. The higher your scores, the more individualistic and/or collectivistic you are.

Source: William Gudykunst, *Bridging Differences,* 2nd ed. Copyright © 1994 by Sage Publications. Reprinted by permission of Sage Publications, Inc.

study different subjects. On the other hand, in feminine cultures, students tend to behave less competitively, failure is not viewed as a catastrophe, and boys and girls tend to study the same subjects. The more you know about which type of culture you are dealing with, the more effective speaker you will be. Even with an American audience, there are likely to be differences in masculinity and femininity based on cultural heritage, age, and progress in gender equity.

Uncertainty Avoidance The fourth dimension Hofstede discusses is uncertainty avoidance, which is "the extent to which the members of a culture feel threatened by uncertain or unknown situations."[10] As a student you know all about uncertainty and the feelings of discomfort that can accompany it. Instructors who are vague about assignments, tests, due dates, and evaluation not only create uncertainty but also are the ones you probably try to avoid. Just as people vary in terms of the amount of uncertainty they can tolerate, so it is with whole cultures. People who live in "low-uncertainty-avoidance cultures" have considerable tolerance for the kind of ambiguity that can drive some people nuts.

Among societies that *avoid* uncertainty are Greece, Portugal, Guatemala, and Japan. Societies that tend to tolerate uncertainty include Singapore, Jamaica, Denmark, Sweden, Great Britain, India, Philippines, and the United States. If you think about it, if it were not for the tolerance of a certain amount of uncertainty, it is unlikely that new businesses would ever secure the funding of venture capitalists. The United States is by and large a nation of immigrants and their descendants, people who by coming to the "new world" were prepared to accept a very high level of uncertainty.

How is this important to you as a speaker? If you have an audience that can tolerate at least a moderate amount of uncertainty, you do not need to promise certainty. Highly probable outcomes may be sufficient to gain their support. Imagine during the dot-com boom of the late 1990s how entrepreneurs could have obtained funding if they had been forced to guarantee results. On the other hand, total uncertainty is likely to result in rejection of your ideas, particularly in those societies that do not tolerate such ambiguity. You should tailor your appeals to the likely level of uncertainty that your audience is willing to accept.

Long-Term Versus Short-Term Orientation   The final dimension Hofstede discusses is long-term versus short-term orientation to life. "Long-term orientation stands for the fostering of virtues oriented toward future rewards, in particular perseverance and thrift."[11] "Short-term orientation stands for the fostering of virtues related to the past and the present, in particular respect for tradition, preservation of 'face,' and fulfilling social obligations."[12]

Asian countries, such as China, Hong Kong, Taiwan, and Japan, tend to rank very high on the long-term dimension. In fact, this dimension is sometimes called Confucian because many of the values, on both sides of the dimension, are the same as the teachings of Confucius. The United States is in the lower third of countries, and Pakistan is at the bottom of the list, meaning both have a short-term orientation.

Those cultures with a long-term orientation to life tend to adapt long-standing traditions to modern situations, are willing to save and persevere to achieve long-term goals, are willing to subordinate themselves for a purpose, and are thrifty in their use of resources. Short-term-oriented societies respect traditions, are willing to overspend to maintain their lifestyle, and expect quick results. It is revealing that when President Bush and Congress wanted to stimulate the economy in the summer of 2001, they fashioned a $300 to $600 tax rebate, hoping that people would spend the money, rather than save it for the future. In fact, many stores featured ads promising to stretch the rebate if people spent it at their business. Had Americans a longer-term orientation, the immediate tax rebates may have proved less appealing to the politicians promoting them.

Knowing whether your audience members share a short- or a long-term culture can significantly affect the content of your speech. Appeals to thrift and patience are likely to be effective in those societies with a long-term orientation, whereas appeals to instant gratification are more effective in societies that have a short-term view of the world. The current debate in the United States over the need to change the Social Security system to protect future generations reflects the results of years of a short-term orientation on the part of American society. That this issue is now being seriously debated suggests that both short- and long-term orientations are competing within the American culture.

Adapting to Cultural Diversity

All five of Hofstede's dimensions are important to analyzing cultural diversity. You shouldn't automatically give one greater credence than another. Rather, you should tailor your speech to fit with those dimensions that are most relevant to your topic. For example, a speech encouraging students to avoid accumulating credit card debt while in college is going to be better received by those with a long-term orientation than a short-term one.

Further, in a world where cultural diversity is the norm rather than the exception, you can count on audience membership that is not only culturally diverse but also variable with regard to such dimensions as femininity versus masculinity. Thus, developing and delivering a speech that appeals to a majority of the cultures represented in your audience is tougher than ever. The wider the range of reasons you present for your position, therefore, the better your chances of success.

Demographic Diversity

After cultural diversity, the second major factor you will want to examine to better understand your audience is how people vary in terms of demographics, which are the basic and vital data regarding any population. Demographic factors include age, gender, ethnicity, geographic origin, socioeconomic status, occupational role, religion, and language usage. **Demographic diversity** refers to the differences among people in terms of such factors. Many of these, such as age and ethnicity, are usually readily observable. Others, such as religion, occupation, and socioeconomic status, may be less obvious. We'll start with some of the easier ones to observe and move to the less obvious.

demographic diversity
Variations among people in terms of such attributes as socioeconomic background and level of education.

Age   You should know not only the median age of your audience, but also their range of ages and how those ages compare to your own. The age demography of the United States is changing at an accelerated rate; so is the demography of the classroom. At one time, college classrooms consisted of a relatively homogeneous group of 18- to 22-year-olds. Today's classroom comprises a much more diverse mix of students. For example, college classes in a state university in the 21st century are likely to be of mixed gender and age. It's common for students to be as young as 17 or as old as 75. As a speaker, you need to take into account this demographic diversity in both the preparation and delivery of your speech. You have to consider not only how 18- to 22-year-olds are likely to respond to your presentation, but also how continuing and reentry students are likely to respond. Likewise, you will also have to think through the response of students who may or may not be similar to you or other members of your audience. This makes it especially important that you compare your audience with yourself.

Some of the most effective speakers are similar but not too similar to their audience. Reentry students in their 40s can be somewhat intimidated by speaking to classes of 18- to 22-year-old classmates. Similarly, a 20-year-old asked to speak to a group of middle-aged people may feel uneasy. In situations where there is a big difference in age between speaker and audience, points of similarity can be stressed. For example, older students speaking to a younger audience can discuss their children, who might be the same age as the rest of the class. Similarly, younger persons facing an older audience can make reference to parents or grandparents in an effort to find a common thread linking them with the audience.

Gender   Whether or not you agree that "men are from Mars and women are from Venus,"[13] you cannot deny that men and women often have difficulty communicating with each other. Gender's influence on how people perceive themselves and others is a subject receiving considerable attention. As scholars such as Julia Wood point out, gender is much more than your biological sex.[14] Gender is the blend of social and cultural characteristics associated with maleness or femaleness in a particular culture. Individuals learn gender roles—the expectations their cultures have of them as males or females—in the course of growing up.

As you look out at an audience, you can usually tell who is male and who is female by such outward signs as dress and hairstyle. But unless you have more specific information, you cannot tell who is gay and who is straight, or who is in a committed relationship and who is single. Much gender-related information is probably beyond your knowledge in most public speaking situations.

Some audiences will be predominately one gender or the other, and they may be the opposite of your own. Thus a male speaker facing a largely male audience is in a different situation than one facing a largely female or evenly mixed audience.

One of the first issues you will face is topic selection. For example, one of our students gave a speech about the dangers of breast enhancement surgery. She and the female members of the audience obviously had an interest in the topic. Why should the males care? She made a specific effort to include the men in her audience. She talked in terms of their girlfriends or wives, and made a strong plea to men to accept their mates as they are. While this topic obviously had a greater direct relevance to the women in her audience, she was careful not to ignore her male audience members.

Ethnicity   Although closely related to culture, ethnicity is not the same thing. For example, in one of our classes recently, we had both a Japanese exchange student and a fifth-generation Japanese American. While both might appear outwardly to share the same ethnic background, they identified with very different cultures. With the exception of Native Americans, in fact, all of us can trace our ethnic roots to other places on the globe. The ethnic origins of many of your classmates may be significant to their self-concept. These same classmates may be actively involved in maintaining and passing on the traditions that define their ethnicity. Thus, if you are ignorant of the ethnic diversity present on your campus, you may inadvertently violate or be insensitive to one or more of these traditions. For example, although born in the United States, one of our students was very proud of her Filipino heritage. Knowing that was important to predicting how she would respond to certain topics, for example, the crisis that was occurring at the time in the Philippines, where hostages had been taken by a rebel group.

It is also important to recognize that many Americans have multiple ethnic backgrounds. Tiger Woods, who is Asian, African American, Native American, and Caucasian, is one of the most prominent examples of this trend. According to the most recent U.S. census, Woods is not alone. "About 2.4% of Americans, some 6.8 million people, reported themselves as belonging to more than one racial group."[15]

Geographic Origin   The varied makeup of today's audience is also reflected in the geographic origins of the audience members. One of our international students, when asked where she was born, said she was born in the USSR, but lived in Kyrgyzstan without ever moving. Of course when the Soviet Union fell she became a citizen of a new country. Given that none of her classmates had ever heard of Kyrgyzstan, this student devoted her informative speech to telling us about her homeland.

Look around your campus. The chances are good that the population reflects national and regional demographic diversity. International student attendance at U.S. colleges and universities is at an all-time high. Faculties are becoming more international as well. To deny or ignore how this national diversity influences people's perceptions of each other, including how you are perceived as a public speaker, is foolish. The same can be said for the regional diversity reflected in your student body. Some campuses are near-mirror images of the region in which they exist. Others look more like international cities than like their regional environment.

A speaker can unknowingly offend audience members by using a reference that may be taken as a slight regarding their geographic home. For example, we recall a Texan who was offended by the phrase "going south," made in reference to a falling economy. Although the speaker was referring to the downward slope of the stock market index, the Texan assumed it was a reference to poverty in the American South. Knowing as much as you can about the geographic origin of your audience can help you not only to avoid mistakes, but also to incorporate relevant and positive references into your speeches.

Socioeconomic Status   The social grouping and economic class to which people belong is termed their **socioeconomic status.** Socioeconomic status is not always directly observable. Most universities want diversity of social and economic backgrounds of their students. Thus, in your speech class there may be students who come from impoverished backgrounds as well as students from affluent families. Although you can sometimes make inferences regarding the social status of your audience, these are not always reliable. For example, one of us once suggested to his class that a proposed tuition increase might lead to fewer minority students attending California universities. An African American student objected, pointing out that one cannot assume that all African Americans are necessarily too poor to afford higher tuition.

Knowing the socioeconomic background of an audience is important particularly in speeches that are designed to persuade them to buy some product. For example, both of the authors earned degrees from the University of Southern California, which at the time had students drawn heavily from higher economic backgrounds. One of the authors recalls a speech encouraging classmates to spend their spring break on a cruise ship. Although the audience in this class was very responsive to this student's topic, imagine the irrelevance of the same

socioeconomic status Social grouping and economic class to which people belong.

speech at a community college in a poorer section of Los Angeles, where most of the students worked full time in addition to taking classes.

Occupation   Demographic diversity is also reflected by the kind of work people do. On a residential campus, occupational roles are generally expressed in terms of major. At many schools, however, students are already involved in an occupation and pursuing a degree for purposes of advancement or career change. This is especially true of urban and metropolitan schools in or near major cities. One cannot always assume from outward appearances what a person's occupation or former occupation might be. For example, we recall one female student, barely five feet tall, who revealed in one of her speeches that she had been a truck driver for several years. Obviously, her perspective on many issues was affected by that experience. To assume she was uninformed about basic auto mechanics, for example, would have been a clear mistake.

Occupations and co-workers influence how people see the world. Self-employed people, for example, probably see things differently than do people working in the public sector, at a large corporation, or in the home. Just as it is important for speakers to analyze age and social diversity, so it is important to respect the full range of occupations represented in audiences. As you get to know your classmates, you may be able to incorporate references to their majors or jobs when it fits your speech. For example, one student in our classes was a DJ. Other students often mentioned this when it fit with their speech topic, such as how to organize a special event. Audience members appreciate positive references to their occupations, while they can be potentially offended by negative ones. For example, had a student made a derogatory remark about DJs, it could have alienated the audience member who earned his livelihood that way.

Religion   You need to consider religious diversity as a sensitive feature of your audience. At public colleges and universities, you can assume that almost every type of religious belief is represented. Even at universities like Notre Dame, which is affiliated with the Catholic Church, you will find diversity in the religious beliefs of groups of students. In some cases, a person's religion can be identified on the basis of apparel and appearance. Such cases include the Amish, Hasidic Jews, some Muslims, and Hindu Sikhs. Usually, religious affiliations will not be easily visible. You cannot tell a devout Catholic from an atheist by outward appearances. In one of our classes, several students were Muslims. One of the students spoke on common misconceptions about Islam. Moreover, he related his frustrations with American restaurants that did not disclose that some of their dishes contained pork, which he was forbidden to eat by his religious beliefs.

We want to point out, however, that religious beliefs do not always predict actual attitudes. For example, despite official opposition by many churches to using human embryos for stem cell research, a Harris poll of over 1,000 Americans revealed that "slightly more than 60% of Catholics and half of born-again Christians surveyed agreed that scientists should be allowed to use stem cells in their medical research."[16]

Perhaps the most important advice we can give about religious beliefs is to be tolerant and respectful of those who do not share your own views. A speech class is a captive audience. A speech that attacks one set of religious beliefs or seeks to proselytize class members is not appropriate for most colleges and universities. Say, for example, that a student gave a speech accusing those who have abortions of committing murder. Imagine the effect on a student in a class who has herself had an abortion. You most likely won't know this sort of fact about your classmates; thus you should always assume that there may be audience members who will be deeply offended by religious topics. Although our Muslim student dealt with a religious topic, he did so in a nonjudgmental way. He did not attempt to challenge the religious beliefs of Christians and Jews in the class, but rather sought to show that his beliefs were not what many Americans thought they were.

Language   Finally, audience members may differ in terms of how they use language in the reference group with which they most identify. Even people with a common native tongue often create a variation of their language that identifies them as a member of a specific reference group. Every generation of young people, for example, creates a shared vocabulary and syntax that distinguishes it from preceding generations. In the early 1950s college students referred to an object they liked as "real George." Generations that came later replaced *George* with *hip, cool, bitchin'*, and even *hella' bitchin'* in Northern California.

People of Mexican descent in the United States may refer to themselves as Mexican American, Chicano/Chicana, or Latino/Latina, depending on when they were born and where they were raised. And people of African descent may refer to themselves as Blacks or African Americans for similar reasons.

Language groups are not necessarily based on age or ethnicity, however. Special usage and vocabularies also can develop around an activity or interest. Surfers and sailboarders, snowboarders and skiers all have a vocabulary peculiar to their sport, as well as a way of using this vocabulary that is distinctive. The same can be said about computer hackers, photographers, serious backpackers, and white-water enthusiasts. What's more, these groups use their vocabulary not only to identify their own kind but also to differentiate themselves from others.

As the world becomes smaller and linguistic diversity grows even within the borders of the United States, it is important that speakers learn to adapt to their audience's linguistic background. According to the 2000 U.S. census, while 20 years ago only one in ten Americans primarily spoke a language other than English, today that number has reached 17.6 percent, nearly one in five.[17] You may want to learn a few phrases in another language if you are speaking to an audience that doesn't share your primary language. One of the advantages George W. Bush had in his campaign for president was his proficiency in the Spanish language. Taking the time and making the commitment to learn another language signals to members of the language community that you are truly interested in them.

Individual Diversity

For most public speakers, the most difficult aspect of audience diversity is predicting how individual members of the audience will respond to them and their message. What are some of the specific things you should look for in analyzing the individuals who make up your audience? **Individual diversity** is deeply embedded in people's knowledge, beliefs, attitudes, values, motives, and expectations. What makes people truly unique is their individual diversity, which cannot be determined on the basis of their culture or demography alone. When you know people as individuals rather than simply as members of a culture or group, you can make far more sensitive predictions about how they will respond

individual diversity How individuals in an audience differ in terms of knowledge, beliefs, attitudes, values, motives, and expectations.

to your speeches and to you. You can also use this knowledge to plan your speeches and decide whether your purpose and goal are realistic.

One of the great advantages of most public speaking classes is that you will learn to know your audience members as individuals. In a class of 25, you will spend about 96 percent of your class speaking time listening to your classmates give their speeches. If you actively listen to them, you will learn a great deal about what they know and think about the world around them. You can use this information as you prepare your own speeches.

Although many of your public speaking situations after college may not allow you to hear all of your audience members speak, you can endeavor to learn as much about them as individuals as possible before you speak. Even in situations where you face an audience "cold," you may be able to make certain assumptions about their interests and belief systems beforehand. For example, if you are asked to speak to the Lion's Club, it is useful to know in advance that they are concerned about raising funds to combat blindness and that they sponsor a public speaking contest for high school students. Any clues you can obtain about the individuals to whom you will be speaking can be valuable in crafting an effective speech.

Knowledge   One of the first things you'll want to know about your audience is what they know—about you and your topic. This is particularly important in selecting a topic for an informative speech. You have probably had the experience of listening to a speaker who simply tells you what you already know. Chances are you were impatient and bored. You have also probably had the experience of listening to a speaker who was almost incomprehensible because he or she used vocabulary you had never heard before, or assumed you had prior knowledge you didn't have about the topic.

Learn as much as you can about your audience's knowledge. Chances are there may be a range of knowledge on the topic you have chosen. If the difference in audience knowledge levels is too varied, preparing your speech may be very difficult. You will find yourself boring some members while losing others. For example, a speech on the federal reserve board may be old hat to economics majors, while leaving humanities majors mystified. If possible, speak on topics about which audience members are likely to have similar levels of knowledge. If you must rehash certain facts, at least try to put a new spin on them to keep the interest of well-informed audience members. In any event, you want to be sure you are the best-informed person in the room. It's embarrassing, to say the least, to be corrected on the facts by a member of your audience.

Beliefs   We all hold certain beliefs about a wide variety of topics. A **belief** is "an assertion about the properties or characteristics of an object."[18] Some beliefs are relatively obvious and undeniable. For example, we all (presumably) share a belief that the earth is round and revolves around the sun. On the other hand, some beliefs are controversial—for instance, those concerning life after death, abortion, and evolution. When you are dealing with matters on which people hold beliefs different from yours, you face a serious obstacle. You must either change their relevant beliefs or convince them that such beliefs are not relevant and not necessarily in opposition to your own point of view.

Convincing her congressman, who had strong beliefs on the subject, to change his stand on gun control proved impossible for Carolyn McCarthy.

belief An assertion about the properties or characteristics of an object.

FIGURE 5.2 A Belief System

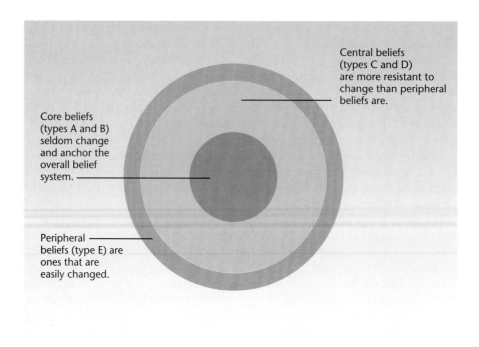

Central beliefs (types C and D) are more resistant to change than peripheral beliefs are.

Core beliefs (types A and B) seldom change and anchor the overall belief system.

Peripheral beliefs (type E) are ones that are easily changed.

So, rather than trying to move his position through speech, she used her newfound public voice to move him out of office. Simply put, all speakers must carefully choose their battles. That requires that you learn as soon as possible whether you have even the slightest chance to engage your audience positively on your topic.

Social psychologist Milton Rokeach pointed out that some beliefs are more resistant to change than others.[19] **Primitive beliefs,** also known as type A beliefs, are learned by direct contact with the object of belief and reinforced by unanimous social consensus. A primitive belief would be that "death is inevitable." Type B, or zero consensus, beliefs are based on direct experience, but do not require social support. These beliefs are also very resistant to change. For example, "I like myself" is a type B belief; it is not reinforceable by social consensus. Together, type A and B beliefs are core beliefs, which are very resistant to change.

The next two types of beliefs are known as **central beliefs** and are still difficult to change. Type C beliefs are authority beliefs. For example, beliefs in the truth of the Bible or Torah or Quran would be a type C belief. Type Ds are derived beliefs, based on authorities' beliefs. For example, Muslims who believe they should abstain from drinking alcohol and eating pork are said to hold derived beliefs. Changing a type D belief requires an understanding of the type C belief from which it is derived. Thus, a speaker might point to scripture to try to change a believer's views on a religious matter, but such an argument would have no impact on an atheist or a practitioner of a different religion.

The least central type of beliefs, type E, are called **peripheral beliefs.** For example, someone might like rap music, whereas another detests it. These are the most inconsequential of beliefs. Figure 5.2 illustrates the relationship among these levels of belief. Clearly, your chances of changing an audience member's core beliefs are far less than changing central or peripheral beliefs.

primitive beliefs (also known as type A beliefs) Those beliefs learned by direct contact with the object of belief and reinforced by unanimous social consensus.

central beliefs Beliefs based directly or indirectly on authority.

peripheral beliefs The least central type of beliefs, the easiest to change.

How can you learn what people believe? One way is simply to ask. In a speech about cell phone safety, for example, one student asked for a show of hands on how many of her classmates owned cell phones and how many used them while driving. Politicians and pollsters are always asking the American public what it believes about a variety of issues. Every year the Cooperative Institutional Research Program at UCLA sponsors a national study of thousands of incoming first-year college students. You may learn from such sources, in a general way at least, what audience members are likely to believe. For example, among entering freshmen in 2000, the national survey showed that 34.2 percent believe that marijuana should be legalized, 31.2 percent oppose the death penalty, and 56 percent believe in legal marital status for same-sex couples.[20] You might use this information in one of your own speeches, knowing that the survey represents students at colleges throughout the United States

Attitudes   An **attitude** is "a learned predisposition to respond in a consistently favorable or unfavorable manner with respect to a given object."[21] Attitudes are not simply beliefs, but rather ways of responding, based in part on beliefs. Over the course of our lives, we develop innumerable attitudes on everything from our favorite brand of soft drink to globalization of world business. These attitudes affect how we respond to the messages we hear. Thus, knowing your audience's attitudes toward your topic is crucial to your success as a speaker, as one speaker learned when she tried to challenge her classmates' aversion to eating a certain type of food—insects. Eating insects is rare in American culture, and most of her classmates groaned when they heard her topic. She attempted to convince her classmates that eating "bugs" actually could be healthy. Not everyone was convinced, but several of her classmates (and even the professor) ended up sampling her "mealybug chocolate chip cookies." While not dramatically changing her audience's attitudes, the speaker did induce at least some class members to soften their strong attitude against this type of food.

How do you learn your audience's attitudes? Sometimes they are fairly predictable. Most Americans don't eat bugs. On the other hand, without asking, it's not easy to know what your classmates think about the Kyoto Protocol on global warming, or how many of them are vegetarians. Never assume that all members of a particular group of people share the same attitudes: Not all Republicans think alike, any more than Democrats do. Nor do all members of a religion—whether Catholics, Protestants, Jews, Baptists, or Muslims—subscribe to exactly the same religious convictions.

It is entirely possible, in fact probable, that in a diverse audience, individuals will have conflicting and even contradictory attitudes. The more you know about the predominant or prevailing attitudes of the group, the better are your chances of a majority of the audience responding positively to what you say in your speech. When an audience is fairly evenly divided, you need to attempt to find some middle ground. Finding areas of common agreement while recognizing and respecting differences of opinion is essential to dealing with an audience of mixed attitudes.

Values   One scholar describes **values** as "more general than attitudes, . . . enduring beliefs that hold that some ways of behaving and some goals are preferable to others."[22] Underlying someone's opposition to animal testing in research, for example, is both a belief about how animals are treated in doing research and a value system that believes all life is important, not just human life.

attitude A learned predisposition to respond in a consistently favorable or unfavorable manner with respect to a given object.

values Our most enduring beliefs about right and wrong.

Although both call them-selves Republicans, Colin Powell and Trent Lott do not always see eye to eye.

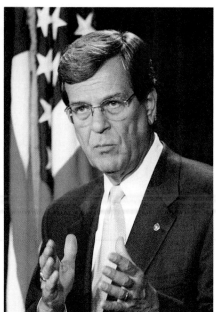

Rokeach classifies values as either terminal (ends in themselves) or instrumental (those that help achieve the ends we seek as humans). [23] Examples of terminal values include a comfortable life, an exciting life, a sense of accomplishment, a world at peace, a world of beauty, equality, family security, freedom, and happiness. Instrumental values are guides to behavior, the means to achieve the ends specified in the terminal values. Examples of instrumental values include ambitiousness, broad-mindedness, capableness, cheerfulness, cleanliness, courage, forgiveness, helpfulness, and honesty.

Although one might not always agree with Rokeach's classification—for example, honesty can certainly be viewed as an end in itself—the basic notion is useful. Some values are desirable in and of themselves, whereas others are instruments for achieving higher, terminal values. For example, forgiveness and courage may be seen as means to achieving a world at peace.

Values, particularly terminal values, are difficult to change because they are learned at an early age and widely shared among people. Such values as fairness, justice, life, patriotism, and so on, not only are fundamental but also are taught to us in our most formative years. In fact, our basic value system probably is pretty well determined at a very young age, as Robert Fulghum points out in his best-selling book, *All I Really Need to Know I Learned in Kindergarten*.[24]

Speakers are best advised to appeal to known values shared by their audience rather than try to convince their audience to adopt new values. Some speeches don't just appeal to existing values, they seek to reinforce those values. A Fourth of July speech, a eulogy honoring a great hero, or an inspirational speech can be thought of as fulfilling a value-strengthening function. For the most part, speakers need to treat values as a given and build on them. For example, Martin Luther King, Jr.'s "I Have a Dream" speech was not so much a call for new values as for Americans to live up to the values stated in the Declaration of Independence and the Bill of Rights.

On Independence Day, many Americans celebrate the values embodied in the Declaration of Independence.

Motives   Humans are motivated by a wide variety of desires, for example, popularity, financial security, love, peace, and so on. You should learn as much as you can about the likely motives of your audience relative to your topic. For example, a speaker at a graduation ceremony can assume that the audience is there to be inspired and to receive their diplomas. A lengthy speech on the Magna Carta would be inappropriate for this audience. On the other hand, a graduation speech focusing on the successes of graduates from the same school might be just what the audience wants.

One specific type of motive concerns why your audience members are attending your speech. In most classroom situations, the answer is simple: because they have to. In those situations, you have to work harder at holding the audience's interest and connecting to their needs than if they had come especially to hear you speak. In Chapter 8 we offer some suggestions that will help you connect with an audience and gain their attention. Even an audience member who has come to hear you needs to be held. It is easy to lose an audience and very difficult to recapture their attention, as any experienced speaker can testify.

Expectations   Closely tied to their motives for attending the speech are your audience's specific expectations. If audience members expect to be entertained, and you deliver a serious speech on the dangers of ozone depletion, you are unlikely to receive a favorable reception. Similarly, if most audience members expect a serious lesson on a topic not to be taken lightly, you owe it to them to meet this expectation. It is usually wise to match your speech as much to the audience members' expectations as is possible, while still achieving your goals.

Generally, speeches contrary to a majority of audience members' expectations may backfire or, at the very least, be apathetically received. For example, we once attended a graduation ceremony where the speaker used the opportunity to preach his view on "political correctness." Families and friends were there to honor and celebrate the graduates' accomplishments, but they were instead treated to a political statement. Whereas such an address might have been appropriate at a meeting of the faculty senate, it missed the mark for the assembled graduates and their guests. The fact that the audience prematurely applauded and shouted loudly at what they thought was the conclusion of the speech reinforced how inappropriate the speech was.

THE SITUATION

rhetorical situation A natural context of persons, events, objects, relations, and an exigence (goal) which strongly invites utterance.

Once you have determined your goals and analyzed the audience, you must next consider the broader public speaking situation or context in which you'll speak. Another term for this is what professor Lloyd Bitzer calls the "**rhetorical situation.**" He defines it as "a natural context of persons, events, objects, relations, and an exigence [goal] which strongly invites utterance."[25] Bitzer sees the major elements of a rhetorical situation as an exigence (what we have called goal), an audience, and a set of constraints that limit the speaker's response. We have already examined your goals and the audience in detail. What needs to be determined is how you can adapt those goals to your audience and how you can deal with the inevitable constraints you will face as a speaker.

How Your Audience Can Help You Achieve Your Goals

Any hope you have of achieving your speaking goals depends on whether your audience is "capable of being influenced by discourse and of being mediators of change."[26] We have already discussed the importance of knowing your audience, not only as individuals, but also as members of different demographic groups and representatives of various cultures. To achieve your goals, however, you also need to know what power they have to help you achieve them. You also need to know whether they favor, oppose, or are indifferent to those goals.

Suppose you are concerned that the Greek system on your campus is about to be eliminated as a result of concerns about binge drinking. Who are the decision-makers? Speaking to members of your fraternity or sorority may not be enough if the decision rests in the hands of a faculty committee. You might enlist members' support, but ultimately you would have to convince the faculty committee in charge. In seeking audiences to support your campaign, obviously alumni of the Greek organizations and representatives from the national chapters are likely to support your goals. On the other hand, faculty in general may see fraternities and sororities as competing with academics for student attention, which would mean they would be less than sympathetic to your goals. Thus, finding a way to protect the Greek system that would meet teachers' concerns about controlling binge drinking and preserving academics would be essential to achieving your goals.

Confronting Constraints

We all face certain constraints on action. A **constraint** is a limitation on your choices. Among the common constraints you may face in giving your speech are the facts pertaining to the situation, legal constraints, ethical constraints, nature of the occasion, traditions, time, and resources. Let's examine each of these.

constraint A limitation on choices in a speech situation.

Facts Pertaining to the Situation   President John Adams observed that "facts are stubborn things."[27] Although some people seem oblivious to the facts governing their situation, sooner or later they must face reality. A speaker who hasn't done research is likely to be embarrassed by the lack of knowledge. As we noted earlier, part of preparing for a speech is to find out what it is that your audience knows, and make sure you know more. Furthermore, it is important to cite the sources from which you have learned your facts. Your audience will perceive you as a more knowledgeable speaker if they know you have solid sources for your facts.

Legal Constraints   We all must abide by certain legal constraints in our speaking. Libel and slander laws, for example, forbid certain types of speech. Other laws cover when and where groups may peaceably assemble. Some anti-abortion activists have been successfully prosecuted, for example, for blocking the entrances to abortion clinics. Although the First Amendment guarantees freedom of speech and assembly, these rights are not license to do what you please.

Some speakers, however, have effectively challenged and even broken laws for a purpose. Nelson Mandela was willing to spend much of his life in jail to bring about the end of apartheid in South Africa. Ultimately, this self-sacrifice helped to sway world opinion against the White minority government of South Africa and led to Mandela's election as South Africa's president.

In your case, it is highly unlikely that you will choose to purposefully break the law to further the cause advanced in one of your speeches. Yet, unless you check on the legal constraints relevant to your situation, you may accidentally break a law of which you are unaware. In our own experience, we've had students show up to class with everything from exotic beers to poisonous pets, both of which are illegal on our campus. We've learned, consequently, that it is necessary for us to check on the topics and plans of our students well before their time to actually speak. So, check with your instructor before you unintentionally pit yourself against the law.

Legal constraints may also affect the range of topics and positions you take on topics. For example, we recently heard a speech on why sharing of music files on the Internet through services such as Napster should be totally free of charge. Of course, at the time there had been a great deal of litigation on the issue, and the courts had ruled that such unfettered distribution of music on the Internet, without paying royalties to the artists, violated U.S. copyright laws. Thus, the speech was about a topic on which the audience had no power to effect change.

Ethical Constraints   We discuss ethical considerations for public speaking in detail in Chapter 6. At this point, we simply want to alert you to the fact that as a speaker and as a listener, you will face ethical constraints. Although something may be technically legal, that doesn't make it ethical.

Nature of the Occasion   What is the nature of the occasion prompting you to speak? You probably remember the day the world learned that Princess Diana had been killed in an automobile accident in France. When her brother, Earl Spencer, delivered her eulogy on September 6, 1997, he sought both to honor her and to make the point that the paparazzi bore a share of the responsibility for her death. Was Diana's state funeral an appropriate forum for making this point? While some Britons applauded his efforts, others were shocked at his breach of etiquette.

You will most likely give speeches to classes during normal class times. Your audience is a captive one. Given that unavoidable fact, you must always decide whether your topic and presentation are appropriate to this context and occasion. One of our students made his classmates extremely uncomfortable by discussing his own first sexual experience. Such personal disclosure is inappropriate in a classroom setting. Similarly, vulgarity, profanity, and the like are obviously not suitable for the class. Even excessively casual slang is probably not appropriate for an academic environment. When you have a doubt as to the appropriateness of your speech for your class, it is always wise to check with your instructor.

Traditions   Many speeches are governed by tradition. Whereas this is not a major factor in most classroom speeches, it could be when you are called on to speak in situations outside the classroom. For example, many service clubs, such as Rotary or Lions, have a whole set of traditions that may seem puzzling to the outsider. For instance, there is a good deal of good-natured poking fun at certain members, "fines" are levied for infractions such as getting your name in the paper, and so forth. Major corporations, such as IBM and Apple, each have their own set of traditions. IBM is formal; Apple is much less so. In speaking to either group, therefore, you would want to reflect the degree of formality each expected in terms of dress, demeanor, and style of presentation.

Time   How much time do you have to give your speech? If you have been asked to speak for 5 minutes and you ramble on for an hour, the response will be predictably negative. On the other hand, imagine paying to hear an hour lecture by a major public figure and having the speech end in 10 minutes. You need to know and respect time limits, as well as match how much information you cover in your speech to your allotted time. For instance, it is generally better to cover a narrow topic thoroughly than to try to cover a wide range of points superficially.

Time is also a factor to consider in your preparation. If you have a week to prepare a speech, you probably don't have time to send for information from outside sources. If you have a month, you probably do. You also will need time for practice. Public speaking deserves the same degree of practice as shooting free throws, swinging a golf club, or learning a new exercise in gymnastics. Simply put, it cannot possibly be mastered without some degree of repetition. And this means committing time to practice as far in advance of the speech as possible. Relaxation techniques and other approaches to managing anxiety also require time to master.

Resources   Two questions are involved here. First, what resources do you have available to you? Resources include money, information sources, other people who might assist you, and the like. Second, what resources do you need to accomplish your speaking goal? If your resources match or exceed what you need, you are fine. If you lack the necessary resources, however, you must either redefine your goal or obtain more resources.

Suppose you are assigned to give a speech with at least three visual aids. How do you go about getting these? If you have enough money, you may be able to pay to have pictures enlarged to poster size or to have overhead transparencies prepared. If your classroom is equipped with a computer and projector, you may be able to use special software to present part of your speech. If not, what alternative resources do you have? If you have a friend who is an art major, perhaps he or she can help you make posters. Whatever your situation, you need to give careful consideration to the resources you have or will need to obtain to achieve your goal.

SUMMARY

In this chapter, we have provided the tools to analyze your audience and adapt your speech goals, both long and short term, to the audience and the situation. Here, we recap the four major areas to consider.

Analyze your audience in terms of cultural variables:

- power distance
- collectivism versus individualism
- femininity versus masculinity
- uncertainty avoidance
- long-term orientation versus short-term orientation

Analyze your audience in terms of demographic characteristics:

- age
- gender
- ethnicity
- geographic origin
- socioeconomic status
- occupation
- religion
- language usage

Analyze your audience in terms of individual diversity, including their:

- knowledge
- beliefs
- attitudes
- values
- motives
- expectations

SPEECH COACH

To evaluate your understanding of this chapter, see the Quizzes on your CD.

Adapt your goals to the audience and the total rhetorical situation. Consider the following constraints:

- facts
- legal constraints
- ethical constraints
- nature of the occasion
- traditions
- time
- resources

CHECK YOUR UNDERSTANDING: EXERCISES AND ACTIVITIES

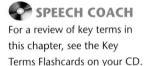 **SPEECH COACH**

For a review of key terms in this chapter, see the Key Terms Flashcards on your CD.

1. Given the topic of alcohol abuse, how might you develop your speech presentation differently if your audience were made up of (a) high school students, (b) students your own age, (c) bar and tavern owners in your community, or (d) recovering alcoholics? In a short paper, explain how your approach and purpose would differ in each case.

2. Create a model of your belief system, including your core beliefs, authority beliefs, and representative derived beliefs, on one of the following topics: gun control, the importance of voting, abortion, civil rights. What does your belief system say about how susceptible you are to being influenced on the topic selected?

3. Interview a student from another country who is studying at your university. What most surprised him or her about American culture? What would Americans be most surprised to know about his or her culture? Write a short paper or give a short talk about what you have discovered.

4. Learn as much as you can about the cultural, demographic, and individual diversity of your classmates. Construct a short questionnaire that will guide you in preparing for an upcoming speech. After obtaining your instructor's approval, write a survey about your chosen topic. You might ask questions about what your audience already knows about the topic, their attitudes for or against your position, and their level of interest in the topic. Distribute the questionnaire to your classmates and collect their responses (anonymously, of course). Tabulate the results. For example, if your topic is banning the sale of handguns known as Saturday night specials, you might report that 60 percent of your classmates were familiar with the term, while 40 percent were not; that 50 percent agreed with a ban, 20 percent opposed one, and the remainder had no opinion; and that 30 percent felt gun violence was a major issue, while 70 percent did not. Based on these results, write a short paper on how you used this information to shape your speech. Also indicate how your plans for your speech may have changed based on the information from your survey.

NOTES

1. Haya El Nasser and Paul Overberg, "Index Charts Growth in Diversity Despite 23% Jump, Segregation Is Still Going on, Researchers Say" [Lexis-Nexis, 5 August 2001] (*USA Today*, 15 March 2001, 3A).

2. Geert Hofstede, *Cultures and Organizations: Software of the Mind* (London: McGraw-Hill, 1991), 14.

3. Hofstede, *Cultures and Organizations*, 14.

4. Hofstede, *Cultures and Organizations*, 262.

5. Hofstede, *Cultures and Organizations*, 260.

6. Hofstede, *Cultures and Organizations*, 261.

7. Hofstede, *Cultures and Organizations*, 53.

8. Hofstede, *Cultures and Organizations*, 261.

9. Hofstede, *Cultures and Organizations*, 262.

10. Hofstede, *Cultures and Organizations*, 263.

11. Hofstede, *Cultures and Organizations*, 261.

12. Hofstede, *Cultures and Organizations*, 262–263.

13. John Gray, *Men Are from Mars, Women Are from Venus: A Practical Guide for Improving Communication and Getting What You Want in Your Relationships* (New York: HarperCollins, 1992).

14. Julia T. Wood, *Gendered Lives* (Belmont, Calif.: Wadsworth, 1994).

15. Robert A. Rosenblatt, "Census Illustrates Diversity From Sea to Shining Sea; Population: Massive Surge of Immigration in '90s Makes Nearly One in Every Three U.S. Residents a Minority, Report Says. Trend Is Nationwide" [Lexis-Nexis, 5 August 2001] (*Los Angeles Times*, 13 March 2001, Part A; Part 1; Page 16).

16. Reuters News Service, "Six in Ten Americans Favor Stem Cell Research" [Yahoo News, http://dailynews.yahoo.com/h/nm/20010726/hl/stemcell_3.html, 26 July 2001].

17. David Westphal, "More Speak Spanish in U.S.," *Sacramento Bee*, 6 August 2001, A12.

18. Sarah Trenholm, *Persuasion and Social Influence* (Englewood Cliffs, N.J.: Prentice Hall, 1989), 6.

19. Milton Rokeach, *Beliefs, Attitudes and Values* (San Francisco: Jossey-Bass, 1968), 6–21.

20. Cooperative Institutional Research Program, *The American Freshman: 2000 Executive Summary*. [http://www.gseis.ucla.edu/heri/00_exec_summary.htm, 24 July 2001] Los Angeles: Higher Education Research Institute, University of California at Los Angeles.

21. Martin Fishbein and Icek Ajzen, *Belief, Attitude, Intention, and Behavior: An Introduction to Theory and Research* (Reading, Mass.: Addison-Wesley, 1975), 6.

22. Trenholm, *Persuasion and Social Influence*, 11, based on Rokeach, *Beliefs, Attitudes and Values*.

23. Milton Rokeach, "Change and Stability in American Value Systems, 1968–1971," in *Understanding Human Values: Individual and Societal*, ed. Milton Rokeach (New York: Free Press, 1979), 129–153.

24. Robert Fulghum, *All I Really Need to Know I Learned in Kindergarten* (New York: Ivy Books, 1988).

25. Lloyd Bitzer, "The Rhetorical Situation," *Philosophy and Rhetoric* 1 (1968): 5. Bitzer further defines an exigence as "an imperfection marked by urgency; it is a defect, an obstacle, something waiting to be done, a thing which is other than it should be." In this text we prefer to focus on the speaker's goal, which, strictly speaking, is to overcome the exigence present in the rhetorical situation.

26. Bitzer, "The Rhetorical Situation," 8.

27. John Adams used this phrase in a summation to a jury. You can read a more complete text at http://www.law.umkc.edu/faculty/projects/ftrials/trialheroes/HEROSEARCH5.htm.

Police, firefighters, and rescue workers risked their own lives to save others in a display of the highest ethical principles.

Ethical Speaking

CHAPTER 6

 OBJECTIVES

After reading this chapter and reviewing the learning resources on your CD-ROM and at the Online Learning Center, you should be able to:

- Demonstrate an understanding of the differences among ethical relativism, universalism, utilitarianism, and situational ethics.
- Apply ethical principles to a variety of different public speaking situations.
- Explain plagiarism and the role of attribution in avoiding plagiarism.
- Explain and apply the basic ethical obligations of both speakers and listeners.

 KEY CONCEPTS

categorical imperative	goodwill	trustworthiness
cultural relativism	good reasons	universalism
ethical relativism	plagiarism	utilitarianism
ethics	situational ethics	

The time is always right to do what is right.

—MARTIN LUTHER KING, JR.[1]

Tom Burnett and other passengers on Flight 93 sacrificed their own lives to save countless others from terrorists, who intended to use the plane as a weapon.

Thomas Burnett, Jr., was on his way home from the East Coast to San Ramon, California, where he was chief operating officer of Thoratec Corp., a medical research and development company. He'd been scheduled to depart from Newark Airport on a later flight but was able to change his booking to get home to his wife, Deena, and three daughters sooner by taking United Airlines Flight 93. Of course, as the world now knows, on September 11, 2001, Flight 93 never made it to California. It was hijacked by terrorists bent on destroying an American landmark, as had their cohorts, who destroyed the World Trade Center twin towers and damaged the Pentagon. But Flight 93 never reached its intended target. Rather, it crashed in rural Pennsylvania. As Burnett told his wife in the last of four cell phone calls made from the plane, he and other passengers had decided to retake the plane from the hijackers, knowing that they would undoubtedly lose their own lives, but would prevent an attack on another

American landmark, killing many more innocent citizens. Although his wife told him to "sit down and not draw attention to himself," he said, "no."[2]

How Burnett and other passengers resisted the hijackers, resulting in the plane plummeting to its destruction and killing all aboard, will forever remain a mystery. But what we do know is that they sacrificed their own lives for the greater good—to save the lives of countless others. In acting decisively, they embodied the highest of ethical principles, sacrificing their own good for the greater good.

Their sacrifices were the first of many spawned by the tragedies of September 11, 2001. Hundreds of police, firefighters, and rescue workers in New York City risked and even lost their lives trying to rescue victims in the World Trade Center. They entered the buildings at great risk to their own lives, and many were lost when the buildings collapsed around them from the intense heat.

These courageous acts represented not only heroism, but also the manifestation of ethics in action. **Ethics** is a system of principles of right and wrong that govern human conduct. Ethical standards and practices should not be viewed as all-or-nothing propositions. In fact, there are degrees of ethical behavior, from highly ethical to totally unethical.[3]

ethics A system of principles of right and wrong that govern human conduct.

In this chapter we treat ethics as an important concern of all participants in the public speaking transaction, speakers and audience members alike. The same standards that govern our everyday conduct apply to the public speaking transaction. In addition, because speakers can potentially influence a great many people, they have to face some special concerns. Thus, we begin this chapter with a review of some basic ethical questions. Next, we suggest a set of norms, or guidelines, for public speaking. We then focus on ethical issues faced by public speakers, including plagiarism. Finally, we discuss specific ethical obligations of both speakers and listeners.

BASIC ETHICAL QUESTIONS

As a speaker you will often be grappling with topics that involve ethical considerations: Why should you care about ethics? How will you adapt to differences in groups and cultures that have different standards of ethical conduct? Are there some universal principles that simply cannot be compromised? What constitutes the greatest good for the greatest number, and to what extent should some people be asked to sacrifice for the greater happiness? What are the situational constraints that impinge on your ethical decision making? What means are ethically acceptable in seeking to achieve ethical ends? These are some of the questions we address in this section.

Why Care About Ethics?

Perhaps the most basic ethical question of all is "Why care about ethics?" After all, why shouldn't everyone just look out for number one? There is, of course, no way that reading a book or enrolling in a class will make a person who doesn't care about ethics into Mother Teresa. However, we believe that most people are fundamentally ethical and seek to do the right thing. Ask yourself about your own motives. Have you ever sacrificed something you really wanted in order to help out someone less fortunate than yourself? Have you ever helped a friend through a difficult situation or talked someone out of harming him- or herself or others? If you have done any of these or countless other ethical things,

American women played an important role in Operation Desert Storm, which conflicted with the norms for women in Saudi culture.

you know the feeling that comes from doing what is right. The next question is "How do ethical principles apply to the public speaking situation?" Our goal in this chapter is to help you answer that question. It doesn't mean we can give you pat answers for every situation. But we do hope to provide you with guidelines for "doing the right thing."

Is Everything Relative?

ethical relativism A philosophy based on the belief that there are no universal ethical principles.

Ethical relativism is a philosophy based on the belief that there are no universal ethical principles. This theory goes back at least as far as the Sophists, who believed that truth was relative and depended on circumstances.[4]

The most radical version of relativism asserts that any one person's ethical standards are as good as the next person's. Although this philosophy has the advantage of simplicity, it makes a civilized society impossible. Life would be, essentially, a free-for-all. When a group of people holds such a radical view, the consequences for society are potentially disastrous. After all, the Nazis believed they were entitled to enslave and kill Jews and other "undesirables." No doubt the street gangs in many cities believe it is expedient but moral to shoot members of rival gangs. Whatever the rationale, an individual- or group-based ethics is untenable.

Culture and Credit

It is sometimes surprising to speakers who come from a traditional Euro-American background that practices they take for granted as being acceptable are held to be morally wrong in other cultures. For example, taking out a loan for college expenses, a car, or a new wardrobe is routine for most Americans. However, those who practice the religion of Islam may find such practices morally unacceptable. As reporter Fahizah Alim explains in an article about a Sacramento, California, restaurant owner, Khaled Umbashi, many Muslims view the interest charged today by banks as *riba* (usury), which is forbidden by the Quran. Umbashi refuses to borrow money to improve or advertise his restaurant because "his Islamic religion forbids him from borrowing the funds and paying interest on that loan. . . . 'Our Islamic religion prohibits paying or charging compounded interest,' says Umbashi, a native of Libya."

Not all Muslims agree with this interpretation of the Quran. For example, Asghar Aboobaker, a Muslim who has written on the topic, holds that "this is a very complicated issue, and there are many, many camps." On the other hand, Irfan Ul Haq, a Muslim businessman, economist, and author, believes, "Much of the world's financial crisis has to do with the interest based system."

Thus, although most of those raised in a Western culture find nothing wrong with borrowing money, some Muslims consider such a practice not just unwise, but morally objectionable.

We make mention of this story because we have heard countless speeches on topics that involve credit or paying interest on a loan. We actually heard a student boast in a speech how he capitalized on the "bull market" by using money from student loans to purchase stock. This student emphasized that with a rate of return of 22 percent on one stock pick, he was making 14 percent on the $5,000 student loan on which he was being charged 8 percent interest.

Clever as our stock-wise student was, his ethics might be questioned by students in general. Certainly the Muslim students in his audience were given pause by his speech.

Knowing and respecting culturally diverse moral principles is often essential to your success in a culturally diverse society.

Source: Fahizah Alim, "No Credit: For Muslims, Asking for a Loan Is a Question of Religion," *Sacramento Bee*, 29 August 1998, Scene, 1, 3.

On the other hand, many people endorse **cultural relativism,** the notion that the criteria for ethical behavior in one culture should not necessarily be applied to other cultures. This was the position of the Sophist Protagoras, who argued that moral laws are based on the conventions of a given society. Examples of such differences among cultures are easy to find. (See the box "Culture and Credit" for one.) In many cultures women are treated as second-class citizens or worse, at least in light of the standards to which Americans aspire. Cultural relativists, with whom the authors disagree, argue that the standards of our culture cannot and should not be applied when making judgments about those in which women's rights are ignored. Differences between two cultures were starkly apparent during the U.S. involvement in the Persian Gulf War in 1991. Female American officers often commanded male soldiers, something unthinkable in Saudi Arabia. Saudi women are not even allowed to drive cars, much less serve in the army or issue commands to men.

Similarly, there are cultural differences in ethical standards governing communication. One such difference involves the extent to which people should be explicit or "brutally honest" in certain situations. In collectivist cultures, "saving face" is important to the good of all society, so people are often indirect and may stretch the bounds of truthfulness in certain situations. To do either in an individualistic culture such as that of the United States could be regarded as unethical communication. Can either culture claim superiority over the routine communication practices of the other? Not really.

cultural relativism The notion that the criteria for ethical behavior in one culture should not necessarily be applied to other cultures.

At the same time, there are limits to what most people will accept as culturally relative ethics. Even within a society, customs change over time as people reexamine their ethical values. Human sacrifice was once a routine part of some religions, yet no one today would consider such behavior ethical. Less than a century and a half ago, a significant number of Americans believed that slavery was ethical and gave their lives to defend the institution. A mere 50 years ago, during World War II, American citizens of Japanese ancestry were interned in "relocation" camps. And today, female infants are routinely killed or allowed to die in a number of countries around the world. What makes one culture or one time period ethically superior or inferior to other cultures or other times? Or is it all relative?

We need to be careful not to exaggerate cultural differences, however. Philosophy professor James Rachels, for example, points out that different cultures often agree on underlying principles but disagree on how they are to be applied. For example, he notes that even apparently inhumane practices, such as that of the Eskimos, who once left the elderly to die in the snow, are grounded in the need of the family to survive in a harsh environment. Rachels argues that "the Eskimos' values are not all that different from our values. It is only that life forces upon them choices that we do not have to make."[5]

Are There Rules for Every Situation?

universalism The philosophy that there are ethical standards that apply to all situations regardless of the individual, group, or culture.

categorical imperative Immanuel Kant's ethical principle that we should act only in a way that we would will to be a universal law.

An alternative to ethical relativism is **universalism,** the philosophy that there are ethical standards that apply to all situations regardless of the individual, group, or culture. Immanuel Kant, an 18th-century philosopher, developed such a philosophy. He proposed the **categorical imperative:** *"Act only on that maxim through which you can at the same time will that it should become a universal law."*[6] To will the maxim be universally applicable means that you would want everyone to obey the same rule as you are proposing.

Suppose, for example, that you think it's acceptable for anybody to lie at any time, so you propose, as a universal rule, that lying is permissible for any reason. What would the result be? Lies would deceive no one, because lying had become the rule. Thus, a universal law that lying is permissible would in fact make lies ineffective. Consider voting as another example. You might think you don't need to vote, because your own vote doesn't make a difference. But imagine that as a universal rule: "Since individual votes don't matter, voting is unnecessary." If not voting were a universal rule, democracy would collapse. So Kant gives us a test for specific ethical rules. To be an ethical principle, a rule or maxim must be capable of being applied universally.

One of the most important ethical rules that Kant proposed relates directly to the public speaker. Kant proposed the maxim *"Act in such a way that you always treat humanity whether in your own person or in the person of any other, never simply as a means, but always at the same time as an end."*[7] One practical implication of this maxim is that speakers should treat audience members with respect, not simply as a means of achieving their goals. Conversely, audience members should respect and treat speakers as fellow human beings, not as objects of derision. Obviously, then, tactics that deceive or demean either an audience or a speaker would be unacceptable.

Kant's categorical imperative is not without drawbacks. Consider truth telling. If lying is unacceptable in any circumstance, innocent people may suffer as a con-

When Is It Acceptable to Lie?

Read the following scenarios carefully. Put a check mark next to the scenarios in which you think it would be acceptable to lie. Be prepared to present your responses in class and to discuss any differences between your responses and those of your classmates.

_____ 1. You know your best friend is cheating on a lover. The lover is suspicious and asks you, "Is Jane/Joe cheating on me?"

_____ 2. The person seated next to you during an exam appears to be copying your answers. As you turn your exam in, the instructor asks, "Was X copying from your exam?"

_____ 3. A casual friend misses several lectures in a class you both attend. He asks to borrow your notes to copy them. You don't want to hand over your hard work, but you also don't want to appear unsympathetic.

_____ 4. A person repeatedly asks you out on a date. You've run out of excuses, but to be honest about it, you find the person completely unattractive.

_____ 5. Your parents have always trusted you. Over a break from school they ask you whether you've experimented with marijuana. Even though you have used marijuana, you are of the opinion that what your parents don't know won't hurt them.

sequence. Miep Gies, for example, lied to authorities throughout World War II to protect the Jews she was hiding from the Nazis, including a young girl named Anne Frank. And this isn't an isolated example. History is replete with cases demonstrating that it's sometimes better to bend the truth to fit the situation.

Of course, one can reformulate Kant's rule and say people shouldn't lie except under certain circumstances, such as when necessary to save lives. But that creates another problem: How do we know which actions fall under these conditions? Rachels points out a key problem with Kant's universalism: "For any action a person might contemplate, it is possible to specify more than one rule that he or she would be following; some of these rules will be 'universalizable' and some will not. . . . For we can always get around any such rule by describing our action in such a way that it does not fall under that rule but instead comes under a different one."[8] To examine your own principles, see the box "When Is It Acceptable to Lie?"

Does the Good of the Many Outweigh the Good of the Few?

Another ethical standard, utilitarianism, was proposed by English philosophers Jeremy Bentham, John Stuart Mill, and Henry Sidgwick. **Utilitarianism** is based on the principle that the aim of any action should be to provide the greatest amount of happiness for the greatest number of people. These philosophers sought the greatest good for the greatest number. And they specifically defined the good as that which creates happiness—"not the agent's own greatest happiness, but the greatest amount of happiness altogether."[9]

This certainly is a useful standard for the public speaker. Most topics on which you will speak are about choices and trade-offs. If we trim social spending to fund a tax cut, some people will suffer while others will benefit. If we

utilitarianism The philosophy based on the principle that the aim of any action should be to provide the greatest amount of happiness for the greatest number of people.

crack down on crime and build more prisons, there will be less money for schools and colleges. What constitutes the greatest good for the greatest number? As a speaker, you have an obligation to your audience to thoroughly research your subject to determine what position will ensure the greatest good and to put that greatest good ahead of mere personal gain. If you fail to fully inform your audience of the facts, if you lie to or deceive them, how can *they* rationally decide what will promote the general good?

Utilitarianism, of course, has its critics. Many would say it promotes ethical relativism. After all, if the greatest good for the greatest number means that some minority of people are oppressed, would not utilitarianism justify that oppression? Could not a Hitler rationalize his extermination of the Jews in the name of the greater good for all of Germany? Certainly that is not what the utilitarians contemplated. But critics of utilitarianism have a point. Seeking the greatest happiness for all does not guarantee that particular individuals will not suffer unjustly.

If you think these issues are mere philosophical musings, think again. Consider the case of a newborn baby who suffers from a genetic abnormality that will cause its death in a short time. The parents want to donate the baby's organs to help other ill children. However, in the process of dying, the baby's organs will so deteriorate that they will not be usable for transplantation. The parents seek to have the baby's life support disconnected, but they are overruled by a judge. Here a utilitarian would have no difficulty justifying "pulling the plug." The baby is brain-dead and can enjoy no happiness. Several other babies can benefit from the transplantation of the organs. But those with other philosophical views might argue that all human life is sacred. They can claim that this is the first step on the road to disconnecting life support from viable infants to save the lives of others. These sorts of dilemmas have led to the emergence of a new field, known as biomedical ethics. Many hospitals now have review boards that deal with ethical dilemmas in medicine.

How Do Specific Situations Affect Ethical Principles?

situational ethics The philosophy that there are overriding ethical maxims, but that sometimes it is necessary to set them aside in particular situations to fulfill a higher law or principle.

Another approach to ethics is known as **situational ethics.** According to this philosophy, there are overriding ethical maxims, but sometimes it is necessary to set them aside in particular situations to fulfill a higher law or principle, such as love. As one writer put it, "What acts are right may depend on circumstances . . . but there is an absolute obligation to will whatever may on each occasion be right."[10]

Situational ethics is particularly useful in explaining how what appears to be the same kind of act can be ethical in one case and unethical in another. For example, most people agree that giving a classroom speech written by someone else is unethical. The principle that a student should do his or her own work is embedded in American education. At the same time, no one expects Jay Leno to write all of his own jokes or the president of the United States to write all of his own speeches. In those situations, everybody knows that Leno has comedy writers and the president has ghostwriters.

Critics of situational ethics argue that this is just relativism in another guise and thus provides no criteria for ethical judgment.[11] However, situationists do not mean we should abandon all ethical principles. As ethicist Joseph Fletcher writes: "The situationist enters into every decision-making situation fully armed with the ethical maxims of his community and its heritage, and he treats them with respect as illuminators of his problems. Just the same he is prepared in any situation to compromise them or set them aside *in the situation* if love seems better served by doing so."[12]

One problem with situational ethics, however, is that it would allow the use of unethical means to achieve ethical goals.[13] That brings us to our final question.

Do the Ends Justify the Means?

You may have heard the old saying "The ends don't justify the means." This means that it is not acceptable to do something wrong just because it will produce a good result. Of course, some people will use a good result as the justification for behavior normally considered immoral. But to do so raises serious ethical concerns. As a speaker you need to concern yourself with ends (goals) as well as the means you use to achieve them.

In terms of ends, many of your topics are likely to be about issues of right and wrong, morality and immorality, the weighing of the good of the many against the good of the few. Understanding how people make ethical decisions is important to your choice of topic and the goals you seek. Obviously, the first and foremost ethical obligation of any speaker is to seek ethical ends, that is, to make sure you are striving to achieve a goal that is ethical and just. So, as you choose your topics, adapt to your audience, and seek to fulfill your goals as a speaker, you should always focus on accomplishing ethical ends.

Not only should your goals be ethically sound, but how you seek to reach those goals should also be ethical. Consider the example of a speaker who wants to raise money for a worthy cause, such as finding a cure for AIDS. Certainly the end is admirable. But suppose the speaker knows the audience is strongly homophobic and so tells them that the money will be used for cancer research. Does the end—raising money to fight AIDS—justify the means—lying about how the money will be spent? Would it not be a greater good to educate the audience about AIDS, letting them know that it is not just a disease that gay men get, rather than giving in to their phobia? Further, once you accept the premise that it's acceptable to lie to raise money for AIDS research, why not for the homeless, for the poor, or for communication majors at the local college? No matter what the goal, the ethical speaker uses ethical means to achieve his or her ends.

ETHICAL NORMS FOR PUBLIC SPEAKERS

Developing standards for ethical public speaking is not an easy task. Probably the closest thing to a code of conduct for public speakers is the National Communication Association's Credo for Free and Responsible Communication in a Democratic Society, reprinted in the box "Codes of Conduct for Public Speaking." More than by any specific code of conduct, however, ethical public speakers are guided by the traditional standards of rhetoric that date back over 2,000 years. Sophists were known for their philosophical relativism. Some Sophists carried this philosophy to its logical extreme, arguing that virtually any rhetorical deception was justified if it furthered their cause.[14]

Codes of Conduct for Public Speaking

Although it is not a full-fledged ethical code, such as those found in law and medicine, the National Communication Association's Credo for Free and Responsible Communication in a Democratic Society forms an important touchstone for the ethical public speaker. Other guidelines that may be of help to the public speaker are found in the American Advertising Association's Code of Ethics, the Code of Ethics of the International Association of Business Communicators, and the Public Relations Society of America's Code of Professional Standards for the Practice of Public Relations.[1]

CREDO FOR FREE AND RESPONSIBLE COMMUNICATION IN A DEMOCRATIC SOCIETY[2]

Recognizing the essential place of free and responsible communication in a democratic society, and recognizing the distinction between the freedoms our legal system should respect and the responsibilities our education system should cultivate, we the members of the National Communication Association endorse the following statement of principles:

We believe that freedom of speech and assembly must hold a central position among American constitutional principles, and we express our determined support for the right of peaceful expression by any communicative means available.

We support the proposition that a free society can absorb with equanimity speech which exceeds the boundaries of generally accepted beliefs and mores; that much good and little harm can ensue if we err on the side of freedom, whereas much harm and little good may follow if we err on the side of suppression.

We criticize as misguided those who believe that the justice of their cause confers license to interfere physically and coercively with the speech of others, and we condemn intimidation, whether by powerful majorities or strident minorities, which attempts to restrict free expression.

We accept the responsibility of cultivating by precept and example, in our classrooms and in our communities, enlightened uses of communication; of developing in our students a respect for precision and accuracy in communication, and for reasoning based upon evidence and a judicious discrimination among values.

We encourage our students to accept the role of well-informed and articulate citizens, to defend the communication rights of those with whom they may disagree, and to expose abuses of the communication process.

We dedicate ourselves fully to these principles, confident in the belief that reason will ultimately prevail in a free marketplace of ideas.

[1]Richard L. Johannesen, *Ethics in Human Communication*, 4th ed. (Prospect Heights, Ill.: Waveland Press, 1996), chap. 10.

[2]Used by permission of the National Communication Association.

Such philosophical relativism ran counter to the philosophy of Socrates, who taught that absolute truth was knowable through a question-and-answer technique known as dialectic. Socrates' student Plato wrote two dialogues, the *Gorgias* and the *Phaedrus*, that expounded this Socratic view of rhetoric. To Plato, rhetoric, as practiced by the Sophists, was a sham, with no truth to it, designed to deceive listeners. In the *Phaedrus*, Plato proposes an ideal rhetoric, one based on philosophical truths. The basic function of this rhetoric is to take the truth discovered through dialectic and energize it for the masses.

The best-known response to Plato came from his student Aristotle, whose *Rhetoric* is probably the most influential book on communication to this day. To Aristotle, rhetoric was not the opposite of dialectic but rather its counterpart. Aristotle did not view rhetoric as either moral or immoral. Rather, it was an art that could be put to both good and bad uses. The moral purpose of the speaker was the determining factor. Aristotle believed that "things that are true and things that are just have a natural tendency to prevail over their opposites."[15] Therefore, he stressed the importance of training in rhetoric. Even arguing both sides of a question was not immoral; rather, it was a way of learning how to refute someone who misstates the facts on the other side of an issue. For Aristotle, in sum, rhetoric was an art, not a sham.

In the 1st century A.D., the Roman orator and rhetorician Quintilian provided an ethical standard that many emulate to this day. To Quintilian, the ideal citizen-orator is a good person, speaking well. As he put it, "Oratory is the science of speaking well."[16] Further, because no one "can speak well who is not good,"[17] the moral quality of the speaker is not irrelevant. Rather, it is central to the ideal orator.

Today, the issue of ethical standards for public speaking has once again become a central concern for communication educators. What constitutes ethical communication? Most of us would agree that speakers should not lie or distort the truth. Beyond that, however, what are the moral obligations of speaker to audience and audience to speaker? Based on the work of the philosophers discussed, as well as several communication scholars, we suggest the following norms or guidelines for the public speaker: (1) Be truthful. (2) Show respect for the power of words. (3) Invoke participatory democracy. (4) Demonstrate tolerance for cultural diversity. (5) Treat people as ends, not means. (6) Provide good reasons. Let's look at each of these more closely.

Be Truthful

James Jaksa and Michael Pritchard of Western Michigan University have developed a set of ethical norms for speakers. Three of these seem particularly relevant to us. The first is the norm of truthfulness, which is fundamental to all communication.[18] The speaker caught in a lie loses his or her credibility and the goodwill of the audience, which are essential to belief. As former presidential spokesman Larry Speakes learned, the loss of credibility can be disastrous. After acknowledging in his 1988 book, *Speaking Out*, that he made up quotations and attributed them to President Reagan, he lost his prestigious position at Merrill Lynch. In retrospect he admitted, "It was wrong—wrong then and wrong now."[19]

Of course one does not have to tell an outright lie to deceive listeners. As we discuss in more detail in Chapter 14, distortions and omissions can sometimes be as harmful to the truth as outright lies. If you doubt that, we invite you to check out the "facts" in many political ads. Although most are based on a kernel of truth, often what's left out changes the whole meaning of the ad. We recall one political challenger who showed a video clip of the incumbent saying, "I'll do anything to get reelected." What the ad failed to mention was that the incumbent was playing the part of the challenger! The video clip was edited to reflect the exact opposite of the meaning intended by the incumbent. Of course the ad didn't lie outright—the words were actually said—but because the context was omitted, the result was the same as a lie.

A speaker who is unsure of the facts must learn the truth before speaking. Even a speaker who is simply misinformed, not consciously lying, can cause considerable harm. One of the authors heard a student speech based on the theory that AIDS is not caused by a virus but is a result of the homosexual lifestyle. That thesis flies in the face of every reputable medical study done on the disease. Documented cases of AIDS transmitted from mother to baby at birth or through blood transfusions clearly disprove the theory. Yet students in the class seemed to believe every word of the speech. Although a guest in the class, the author finally intervened and questioned some of the student's claims.

Talk shows such as the "Jerry Springer Show" feed on the power of inflammatory language.

Such misinformation, if believed, can have serious, even fatal consequences for audience members who come to believe they are immune to a lethal disease because they are heterosexual.

Show Respect for the Power of Words

Another norm cited by Jaksa and Pritchard is respect for the word.[20] The power of words is undeniable. Consider the reaction of people to certain emotionally laden words. Even words and usages that were once acceptable, such as referring to a woman as a "girl," or an African American man as "boy," have come to be viewed as sexist and racist. Emotionally charged words can cause severe damage.

Although freedom of speech is central to our democracy, the courts have recognized that there are limits. As Chief Justice of the Supreme Court Oliver Wendell Holmes, Jr., once said, freedom of speech does not give you the right to shout "fire!" in a crowded theater. Although Justice Holmes was speaking metaphorically, the principle he was expressing is as relevant to the current debate about speech codes as it was nearly a century ago. The fact that you can say almost anything that comes to mind in this country doesn't make the content of what you say either ethical or wise. The old saying "Sticks and stones can break my bones, but words can never hurt me" is incorrect. In fact, words are very powerful and can cause great harm as well as great good. The ethical speaker recognizes that words have consequences.

Invoke Participatory Democracy

Jaksa and Pritchard discuss the importance of participatory democracy, which rests on a foundation of choice and respect for people.[21] Citizens must have accurate and ample information in order to make informed choices. Further, the golden rule of treating others as we would have them treat us applies to public speaking as well as to interpersonal communication. Speakers should put themselves in the shoes of listeners and ask if they are treating them as they would like to be treated. The ethical speaker recognizes the audience as an equal participant in the communication transaction. Similarly, listeners need to show respect and tolerance for speakers, even if their views are different from their own. Shouting down a speaker, for example, infringes on the speaker's freedom of speech and the public's right to hear a full spectrum of viewpoints.

In other words, ethics in communication is a joint responsibility. For example, there have been many complaints in recent years about negative and deceptive political advertising. Yet political consultants say they are only giving the public what it wants. Although that is no ethical defense for their behavior, we must also realize that deceptive advertising succeeds only because voters fail to protest against it and continue to vote for candidates who engage in such practices.

Demonstrate Tolerance for Cultural Diversity

Clearly, what people regard as ethical or unethical depends a great deal on their culture and the set of beliefs that inhere in it. It is difficult for people to avoid using their own culture's ethical standards when judging the behavior of people in another culture. In North America, for example, we generally like people to be "up front" with us, that is, to communicate honestly and directly, even if we don't like the message. We generally don't want people to beat around the bush on matters we personally perceive as significant.

But what we call beating around the bush is the norm in many cultures around the world. Physicians, businesspeople, and even family members may be less than direct or forthright in their transactions with each other. In Japan, physicians and family members commonly hide the truth from a terminally ill patient. They believe that telling the truth in this case will undermine the power of the person's mind to intervene and perhaps divert the disease's course.

Some cultures, groups, and individuals are more tolerant of diversity than others. Ethical speakers recognize that the customary criteria they use in making ethical judgments may be inappropriate in judging the behavior of people from other cultures. This tolerance guides ethical speakers in both interpreting and responding to the communication behaviors of those who are culturally dissimilar to them. Tolerance is not synonymous with unconditional approval, however. Ethical speakers may tolerate ethical norms with which they disagree, but they may also engage in constructive dialogue with the individuals who follow those norms.

Treat People as Ends, Not Means

To these principles we wish to add one taken from Kant, namely, that people should never be treated as mere means to an end. Their best interests should be the ends sought by the speaker. Using people as objects, manipulating them even to achieve desirable ends, is never justified. Consider the case of the *Jenny Jones Show*, a TV talk show. In 1994, Jones invited people to go on the air and meet their secret admirers. What the producers didn't tell these people, however, was that these secret admirers could be heterosexual, gay, or lesbian. You may recall the tragic results of this attempt to "entertain" the viewing audience. One guest discovered that his secret admirer was gay and later stalked and murdered the admirer.

Of course the guest's tragic overreaction was also unethical and far out of proportion to the deception perpetrated by Jones. Nevertheless, the television show was widely criticized as having gone too far. Embarrassing people on national TV as a means of simply building program ratings is clearly unethical.

Provide Good Reasons

Another principle of ethical speaking has been articulated by Karl Wallace, scholar and former president of the Speech Communication Association (now known as the National Communication Association). Wallace believes that the public speaker must offer his or her audience "good reasons" for believing, valuing, and acting.[22] **Good reasons** are statements, based on moral principles, offered in support of propositions concerning what people should believe or how people should act. Wallace believes that ethical and moral values, as well as relevant information, are the basic materials of rhetoric. Speakers who rely on "good reasons" value all people and the ethical principles to which they adhere. Not only does the use of good reasons help ensure that the speaker uses ethical means, it is also far more likely to be successful in accomplishing the ethical ends sought by the speaker.

good reasons Statements, based on moral principles, offered in support of propositions concerning what we should believe or how we should act.

SPECIAL ISSUES FOR SPEAKERS

As a public speaker, you face some special issues that might not be as relevant in other communication situations. A speech is a uniquely personal event. Unlike a written essay, for example, in which the author may be unknown to the reader, a speaker stands as one with his or her words. In fact, Aristotle said that character "may almost be called the most effective means of persuasion" possessed by a speaker.[23] Four important issues need to be addressed, therefore, because of their special significance for public speakers: (1) plagiarism and source attribution, (2) building goodwill and trustworthiness, (3) revealing or concealing true intentions, and (4) discussing both sides of a controversial issue.

Plagiarism and Source Attribution

plagiarism Stealing the ideas of others and presenting them as your own.

Plagiarism—stealing the ideas of others and presenting them as your own—is highly unethical. What makes it a particular sin for speakers is that they are jeopardizing their most important asset—their character. Few students begin their speech assignment intending to plagiarize. But other pressing assignments, poor time management, sloppy note-taking, or just plain laziness often intervene. Students are tempted to use someone else's words or ideas without credit, assuming that no one will be the wiser. The consequences of such behavior can be severe. An example from the authors' own experience illustrates what can happen.

One of our teaching associates (we'll call him Jack) was ill and asked another TA (Jane) to cover his class. It happened that one of the students in Jack's class was the roommate of a student in Jane's. When Jane heard the same speech in Jack's class that she had heard earlier in the week in her own section, bells went off. Of course, it turned out that one roommate had appropriated the other student's speech. The plagiarizer was caught red-handed, but it didn't end there. The original speech writer was guilty of aiding and abetting the roommate.

Both students had to face disciplinary action from the university as well as failure in the class.

Although it's true, of course, that this act might have gone undetected had Jack not become ill, this is not the only way plagiarism is discovered. At our university, and we suspect this is true at others as well, professors often talk about speeches they have heard in class. In fact, every speech at our university is recorded on videotape. Over the years, we have discovered several instances of plagiarism. Each time the students have been shocked and repentant. They have come to realize that they have put their college careers at risk for a few extra points on a speech. The negative consequences of plagiarism are not confined to students. Plagiarism can also destroy a reputation or even a career.

How can you avoid plagiarism? First, you need to recognize that there are varying degrees of the offense. Because plagiarism is a form of theft, we call these variations "the total rip-off," "the partial rip-off," and "the accidental rip-off."

The Total Rip-Off   The case of the roommates who used the same speech is an example of a total rip-off. Here a student simply gives someone else's speech. Usually it is not a speech from a published source, because such speeches don't often fulfill the assignment. Further, if the speech is well known, it is likely to be spotted instantly as a phony. More common is the use of a speech from a classmate who took the class in a previous term or who is in another section. This is clearly academic dishonesty equivalent to cheating on an exam or turning in someone else's term paper. Most universities and colleges suspend or even expel students caught in this sort of dishonesty. If the speech was knowingly given to the plagiarist, the original author can face the same penalties.

Avoiding this type of plagiarism is easy: Don't offer a speech or accept the speech of another person to present as your own. Most students who use other students' speeches do so out of desperation. Our advice is not to put off writing your speech until the last minute. Give yourself as much time to research and prepare as you would to write a paper for an English class. Realize also that giving a speech you don't really know is likely to be a disaster. You will stumble over words and be unable to answer questions. Even if you escape detection, you'll do yourself little good. If you simply cannot get a speech ready to deliver on time, talk to your instructor. Policies will vary, but your own speech, given late, even with a penalty, is far superior to a ripped-off speech given on time.

The Partial Rip-Off   More common than the total rip-off is the partial rip-off. Here a student creates a speech by patching together material from different sources. Rather than quoting the sources, the speaker presents the ideas as if they were original. The irony is that the speaker has done a lot of work. The problem was not that time ran out. Rather, the speaker wanted to be credited with the ideas.

The way to avoid this type of plagiarism is to give credit to your sources orally and to make sure that you use material from these sources only to enhance your own speech. Rather than simply using the words of another, tell the audience who made the statement or where the idea originated. Interestingly, research has shown that under many circumstances, citing sources in your speech enhances your persuasiveness.[24] Audiences are impressed that you have done your homework. It is important to cite sources as you speak, not just in the bibliography of your written outline. Only by citing sources orally can you inform your audience of where the words, phrases, and ideas came from, which is what you need to do to build your credibility as a speaker.

Citing sources is important for direct quotations as well as for specific facts, statistics, and ideas derived from the work of others. Thus, you might not quote Martin Luther King, Jr., directly, but you would still refer to him as the author of the idea that people should be judged by their character, not their skin color.

The Accidental Rip-Off   Perhaps the most frustrating thing for an instructor who discovers a student's plagiarism is when the student simply doesn't understand what he or she has done wrong. For example, a student may take significant ideas or even quotes from sources listed in a bibliography accompanying the speech, without saying so in the speech. The student sees no problem, responding, "I did cite my sources—they are right there in the bibliography." For the listener, however, there is no way to know which ideas came from outside sources and which are the speaker's own, as mentioned in the previous section. A common variant of this is that the speaker attributes ideas to a source but actually uses a word-for-word quotation without making that clear to the audience. The written version of the speech outline should include quotation marks to distinguish between paraphrased ideas and direct quotations. Further, you should use "oral" quotation marks. Either state that you are quoting someone, or make it clear from your tone of voice that you are in fact quoting someone else's words. Use such phrases as "To quote Martin Luther King, Jr., . . ." or "As Martin Luther King, Jr., said . . . ."

Finally, be careful of letting ideas become disassociated from their source. We've all had the experience of remembering an idea or a quote but forgetting where we heard it. Unfortunately, the tendency in a speech is just to use the words. By taking careful notes as you research your speech, you are less likely to accidentally borrow an idea from another source without attribution.

Whether a full-scale rip-off, an incremental theft, or an accidental violation, plagiarism is a serious ethical offense for the public speaker. Our best advice is to resist the temptation, cite the sources of your ideas for your audience, and take pride in those ideas that are your own. In Chapter 7 we discuss how to record and cite sources in a speech. But the general principle is to let your audience know exactly where your ideas are coming from.

Building Goodwill and Trustworthiness

goodwill The perception by the audience that a speaker cares about their needs and concerns.

A speaker's credibility has several components. Two of the most important are goodwill and trustworthiness. **Goodwill** is the perception by the audience that a speaker cares about their needs and concerns. A speaker who truly cares about his or her audience's needs, and who can communicate that to the audience, not only is more likely to be effective but also is much more likely to behave ethically. There is a huge difference, for example, between the speaker who is trying to put one over on the audience and the speaker who really cares about the well-being of the audience. If speakers apply the principle developed by Kant of treating people as ends and not means to ends, then that is a mark of goodwill.

trustworthiness The perception by the audience that they can rely on a speaker's word.

Trustworthiness is the perception by the audience that they can rely on a speaker's word. A promise made is as good as done. The effect on a speaker's trustworthiness of a broken promise or a revealed lie is devastating. In recent years, there has perhaps been no clearer example of the importance of telling the truth than President Clinton's problems following his categorical denial in January 1998 of having had "sexual relations with that woman, Monica Lewinsky." His subsequent televised admission of an improper relationship following his Grand Jury testimony fell short of an admission that he had lied, and was followed by numerous attempts at public contrition. Clinton ultimately became only the second president ever impeached in the history of the United States, based on allegations of perjury and obstruction of justice. One reason politicians in general are held in such low regard by the public is that so many of them have broken their promises and become untrustworthy in people's eyes.

As a speaker, you need to realize that you rarely can accomplish your purpose in one speech or even a short series of speeches. Often your goals will require a long-term commitment. And your relationship to your audience needs to be one of trustworthiness. If you violate their trust, not only have you behaved unethically, you have jeopardized your chances of achieving your goals as well. The solution to this problem is twofold. First, don't make promises you cannot or do not intend to keep. And second, if circumstances might require you to deviate from prior promises, make it clear what limits there are on your promise.

Revealing or Concealing Intentions

One of the thorniest issues you face as a speaker is whether or not to reveal your intentions to your audience. Sometimes, to begin your speech by announcing a position that you know your audience drastically opposes is to deny yourself the opportunity to be heard. On the other hand, to conceal your true intentions can be unethical, particularly if those intentions violate what the audience perceives as its best interests. In some ways, this decision requires the application of "situational ethics." Consider a couple of examples.

You are speaking to a potentially hostile audience about a controversial issue. Let's say you want to convince a group like the Moral Majority that we should not have state-sanctioned prayer in school. Should you begin by announcing your position? What is the likelihood that your argument would be heard? On the other hand, suppose you begin by describing a scenario in which the state requires everybody in school to study the Quran and pray to Allah. "How would you react?" you ask them. "Well, now reverse the situation," you continue. "What if Muslim students are required to study the Bible and say the Lord's Prayer?" The idea would be to work from a common ground—that Christians should not be forced to pray to a Muslim God—to the logical application of that principle to the issue of state-sanctioned school prayer.

Certainly this approach is no guarantee of persuading the audience of your viewpoint. But it is hard to argue that it is ethically wrong to begin with points of agreement before moving to areas of disagreement. The intentions of your speech are revealed to the audience. When and how those intentions are revealed is a strategic rather than an ethical issue.

On the other hand, consider the case of the person who knocks on your door and asks you if you would be willing to participate in a survey. Sure, you reply, always happy to help out. After going through a series of questions, you realize that the "pollster" is actually a salesperson for an encyclopedia company. Your time has been wasted, and now you have to figure out how to get the person to leave. The clear misrepresentation of intent—pollster as opposed to salesperson—is ethically wrong. And you have been harmed, if for no other reason than the salesperson stole your time. And, as many sellers know, once they get their foot in the door, the likelihood of closing the sale increases.

What makes these two cases different? Both people begin by concealing their intentions, and both eventually do reveal their goals. But in the first case, the speaker does not misrepresent his or her intentions; rather, they are deferred until after some common ground is established. In the second case, a direct misrepresentation is made—there is no poll. While the two cases seem on the surface to be similar, we would argue that the situations are far different and that that difference is ethically relevant.

These types of cases are not always easy or clear-cut. A universal rule—always state your purpose up front—cannot be applied. Speakers must sincerely ask themselves in what ways their interests and those of their audience intersect. They must then decide the best approach to take in any given case, at the same time striving to maintain goodwill and trustworthiness.

Discussing Both Sides of a Controversial Issue

One question with both ethical and practical implications is whether you should provide an audience with only your side of an issue or mention arguments on the other side of the issue as well. For a number of years, speech experts answered this question pragmatically: It depends on the makeup of your audience. If the general level of education in your audience is high school or less, stick to your side only. If the level of education in your audience is beyond high school, introduce the other side as well. Of course this raises some real ethical concerns. It smacks of using the audience as a means rather than treating them as ends. Basically, it says if you can fool enough of the people, no need to worry about fooling all of them.

The authors have never thought much of the recommendation to present only one side of an issue. What's more, we now have research on our side. This research, which combined the findings of more than 25 studies done over the past four decades, suggests that speakers should use a two-sided persuasive message regardless of the audience's level of education. Specifically, the most effective persuasive strategy is to present both sides of a controversial issue along with a refutation of the opposing point of view.[25] If you think about it, this makes good sense. In general, your audience will have heard or will eventually hear the other side of the story. What does it do to the audience's perception of your credibility if they believe they've not been told the whole truth? Two-sided presentations are not only more ethical, they are also more effective. We discuss the issue of "message sidedness" in more detail in Chapter 13.

TIPS AND TACTICS   *Ethical Guidelines for Speakers*[26]

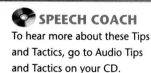
SPEECH COACH
To hear more about these Tips and Tactics, go to Audio Tips and Tactics on your CD.

- Provide truthful, relevant, and sufficient information to allow audience members to make informed choices.
- Present "good reasons," not just those that may work. Appeal to the best, not the worst, in people.
- Reinforce and be consistent with democratic processes. Recognize the importance of free speech in a democratic society and the right of others to disagree.

- Demonstrate goodwill and trustworthiness toward the audience.
- Put yourself in the position of the listeners and treat them with the same respect you would expect were the roles reversed.
- Recognize that both the means and the ends of a speech should be ethical. Be concerned with the possible consequences of accepting the message as well as with its truthfulness and accuracy.
- Take responsibility for your own work. Plagiarism is the ultimate in intellectual dishonesty.

ETHICAL NORMS FOR LISTENERS

People who find themselves in the primary role of listeners also need to think about their ethical obligations. Remember, audience members are very much a party to the public speaking transaction. When you are a listener, you too bear some responsibility for the consequences of the speech. Thus, we suggest these norms for ethical listening: (1) Take responsibility for the choices you make. (2) Stay informed on the issues of the day. (3) Speak out when you are convinced that a speaker is misinforming or misleading people. (4) Be aware of your own biases.

Take Responsibility for Choices

The first guideline for listeners is to recognize that unless coerced, they are responsible for the choices they make during and following a communication transaction. This means listeners cannot blame a speaker for the decision to riot following a speech or for violating human rights because they were persuaded to do so by a charismatic communicator. Just as the judges at the Nuremberg trials following World War II concluded that "following orders" was not an excuse for war crimes, audience members cannot excuse their unethical behavior on the grounds that they were complying with a speaker's request.

Stay Informed

A second guideline, which logically follows from the first, is that listeners are responsible for keeping themselves informed on issues of the day. People who are uninformed about important topics and vital issues are easy prey for propagandists. History is replete with examples of people who have tried to attribute unethical behavior to ignorance, real or imagined. They range from the people who said they didn't know the Nazis were sending millions of Jews to their death during World War II to the tobacco company executives who claimed tobacco was not addictive. Simply put, ignorance is no excuse for unethical behavior.

Speak Out

The third guideline for listeners is related to the first two. It involves the audience members' ethical obligation to speak up when convinced that a speaker is misinforming or misleading people. Most of us have been in situations where we knew someone was bending the truth, leaving out pertinent details, or passing off another's ideas as original. Under some unique set of circumstances, keeping this knowledge to ourselves may be justified. In most circumstances,

Ethics and economic profit are not always compatible, as the congressional testimony of tobacco industry executives clearly demonstrated.

however, listeners owe it to themselves and others to speak up. Speaking up can take the form of a question for the speaker following a presentation, asking the appropriate agency for equal time to speak, writing a letter to the editor of a newspaper or magazine, or confronting the speaker one on one. Whatever the appropriate medium, constructive objections are generally preferable to silence.

Be Aware of Biases

The final guideline for listeners concerns their subjective view and the manner in which it biases how they receive and process a speaker's message. Perception is colored by our experiences, both real and vicarious. Rather than denying the fact, it's much healthier and realistic for us to admit this to ourselves. Only then can we determine how much of our reaction to a speech is based on its content and relational dynamic and how much is attributable to our individual biases.

Is it ethical to stand up in silent protest or to shout another speaker down?

Ethical Guidelines for Listeners[27]

TIPS AND TACTICS

SPEECH COACH

To hear more about these Tips and Tactics, see Audio Tips and Tactics on your CD.

- Be aware that all communication is potentially influential and that there are consequences to accepting any message. Ask what influence the speaker is seeking to exert.
- Stay informed on important topics so that you can judge the accuracy of the communication provided by others. Be willing to independently confirm information that appears questionable.
- Be aware of your personal biases to reduce your susceptibility to appeals to prejudices. Be willing to listen to opposing views with an open mind.

- Be aware of deceptive communication ploys and work to expose those guilty of fallacious reasoning, propaganda ploys, and outright deception. Be willing to speak out in response to deceptive speech.
- Put yourself in the position of the speaker and treat him or her with the same respect you would expect were the roles reversed.
- Provide constructive feedback to the speaker if the opportunity is given.

SUMMARY

 SPEECH COACH
To evaluate your understanding of this chapter, see the Quizzes on your CD.

Several basic ethical questions are of concern to speakers:

- Why care about ethics? Most people fundamentally want to do what is right.
- Is everything relative? Ethical relativists believe there are no universal ethical principles.
- Are there rules for every situation? Universalists believe there are ethical standards that apply to all situations regardless of the individual, group, or culture.
- Does the good of the many outweigh the good of the few? Utilitarianism is based on this principle.
- How do specific situations affect ethics? Situational ethicists believe it is sometimes necessary to set aside one ethical principle to fulfill a higher law or principle.
- Do the ends justify the means? Speakers should seek ethical ends utilizing ethical means, such as those found in the National Communication Association's Credo for Free and Responsible Communication in a Democratic Society.

Ethical norms for public speaking are:

- Be truthful.
- Show respect for the power of words.
- Invoke participatory democracy.
- Demonstrate tolerance for cultural diversity where consistent with ethical principles.
- Treat people as ends, not means.
- Provide good reasons.

Public speakers face special issues:

- Plagiarism—the stealing of words or ideas of another—is considered a serious ethical violation.
- Building goodwill and trustworthiness is essential to successful and ethical public speech.
- Whether to reveal or conceal one's intentions can present an ethical as well as practical dilemma for speakers.
- Giving a two-sided presentation is both ethically sound and pragmatically more effective.

Listeners should adhere to the following ethical norms:

- Take responsibility for the choices they make.
- Stay informed on the issues of the day.
- Speak out when they are convinced that a speaker is misinforming or misleading people.
- Be aware of their own biases.

CHECK YOUR UNDERSTANDING: EXERCISES AND ACTIVITIES

1. In a brief speech or short paper, explain the reason you believe the best ethical standard for the public speaker is (a) relativism, (b) universalism, (c) utilitarianism, or (d) situational ethics. Define the version of ethics you endorse, and explain why you feel it is the best alternative for public speakers.

2. Read the following cases and answer the questions about each one. Depending on your instructor's directions, either write a short paper responding to one or more of the scenarios or discuss one or more of them in a small group.

    Case A: A student in your public speaking class presents a speech that contains glaring factual errors. As an audience member who is familiar with the topic, you realize that the speaker has not done research and has "made up" certain "facts." What should you do? What do you think the instructor should do?

    Case B: You are preparing a speech arguing against a tuition increase at your college. In your research, you discover strong arguments against your position. Nevertheless, you still believe the tuition increase is a bad idea. Should you share the arguments against your position with your audience, or present only your side of the story?

    Case C: You are required by your instructor to attend a speech outside of class time. You discover on arriving at the lecture hall that the speaker holds views precisely the opposite of your own. What should you do?

    Case D: You are assigned by your teacher to speak for a position you fundamentally oppose on a question about which you hold strong moral beliefs, such as abortion. What should you do?

3. In a short paper, discuss the differences and similarities between the ethical obligations of speakers and listeners. As a speaker, how would you deal with listeners who are unwilling to meet their basic ethical obligations? As a listener, how would you respond to a speaker you felt was unethical?

4. In a short paper, discuss whether you agree with Quintilian that "no one can speak well who is not good." Cite some contemporary or historical examples to support your position.

5. In a short paper, consider the question of whether there can be any situation in which it is ethical to "shock people into action" through the use of especially horrifying or unpleasant images. Give examples to support your position.

6. In your view, what modern politician is most successful at eliciting feelings of goodwill and trustworthiness? Why do you think this person is successful in doing so? Be prepared to discuss your example in class.

7. Administrators, faculty, and students on campuses across the United States are trying to come up with speech codes that strike a balance between First

SPEECH COACH
For a review of key terms in this chapter, see the Key Terms Flashcards on your CD.

Amendment rights and the right of people in the college community to be protected from hateful and demoralizing language. Working either on your own or in an instructor-assigned group, find out if your school has a speech code that prohibits the use of certain types of words and language. If it does, how would you amend it to fit your or your group's thinking? If it doesn't, what would you include in such a code? Write a short paper on your findings or thoughts, or be prepared to discuss them in class.

NOTES

1. "Quotations About Integrity, Ethics, Behavior, Character" [http://www.geocities.com/quotegarden/integrty.html, 2 October 2001].
2. Michelle Locke (AP), "Passengers Had a Plan," *Chico Enterprise-Record,* 13 September 2001, 1A, 9A.
3. J. Vernon Jensen, "Ethical Tension Points in Whistleblowing," in *Ethics in Human Communication,* 3rd ed., ed. Richard L. Johannesen (Prospect Heights, Ill.: Waveland Press, 1990), 281.
4. Samuel Enoch Stumpf, *Socrates to Sartre: A History of Philosophy* (New York: McGraw-Hill, 1966), 35.
5. James Rachels, *The Elements of Moral Philosophy* (New York: Random House, 1986), 21.
6. Immanuel Kant, *Groundwork of the Metaphysics of Morals,* trans. H. J. Paton (New York: Harper & Row, 1964), 88.
7. Kant, *Groundwork of the Metaphysics of Morals,* 96.
8. Rachels, *Elements of Moral Philosophy,* 108–109.
9. John Stuart Mill, *Utilitarianism,* in *Essential Works of John Stuart Mill,* ed. Max Lerner (New York: Bantam Books, 1961), 198–199.
10. William Temple, *Nature, Man and God* (New York: Macmillan, 1934), 405, as cited in Joseph Fletcher, *Situation Ethics: The New Morality* (Philadelphia: Westminster Press, 1966), 27.
11. James A. Jaksa and Michael S. Pritchard, *Communication Ethics: Methods of Analysis,* 2nd ed. (Belmont, Calif.: Wadsworth, 1994), 21.
12. Fletcher, *Situation Ethics,* 26.
13. Fletcher, *Situation Ethics,* 121.
14. Stumpf, *Socrates to Sartre,* 36.
15. Aristotle, *Rhetoric,* trans. W. Rhys Roberts (New York: Modern Library, 1954), 22.
16. Quintilian, *Institutio Oratoria,* trans. H. E. Butler (Cambridge, Mass.: Harvard University Press, 1920), 317.
17. Quintilian, *Institutio Oratoria,* 315.
18. Jaksa and Pritchard, *Communication Ethics,* 65.
19. Larry Speakes, *Speaking Out: The Reagan Presidency From Inside the White House* (New York: Avon Books, 1988), 400.
20. Jaksa and Pritchard, *Communication Ethics,* 64.
21. Jaksa and Pritchard, *Communication Ethics,* 74.
22. Karl R. Wallace, "The Substance of Rhetoric: Good Reasons," *Quarterly Journal of Speech* 49 (1963): 239–249.
23. Aristotle, *Rhetoric,* 25.
24. James C. McCroskey, "A Summary of Experimental Research on the Effects of Evidence in Persuasive Communication," *Quarterly Journal of Speech* 55 (1969): 169–176.
25. Mike Allen, "Meta-Analysis Comparing the Persuasiveness of One-Sided and Two-Sided Messages," *Western Journal of Communication* 55 (1991): 390–404.
26. Several of these speaker responsibilities are derived from Sarah Trenholm, *Persuasion and Social Influence* (Englewood Cliffs, N.J.: Prentice Hall, 1989), 18–20.
27. Several of these listener responsibilities are also derived from Sarah Trenholm, *Persuasion and Social Influence.*

Putting Theory
Into Practice

PART THREE

The key to a
successful speech
is research.

Researching and Supporting Your Message

 OBJECTIVES

After reading this chapter and reviewing the learning resources on your CD-ROM and at the Online Learning Center, you should be able to:

- Explain the benefits of focusing on the audience when you choose an appropriate topic, formulate a specific purpose, and research a speech.
- Recognize the types of supporting materials you can use for a speech.
- Conduct systematic library research to find support for a speech.
- Conduct a search of the Internet to find support for a speech.
- Conduct a meaningful interview with an expert on the topic of a speech.
- Prepare a bibliography for your speech using one of two academic styles (APA or MLA).
- Record information in a usable form for your speech.

 KEY CONCEPTS

abstract	narrative	research
Boolean operators	narrative fidelity	search term
expert opinion	narrative probability	secondary sources
fact	online catalog	statistics
index	primary sources	

Genius is one percent inspiration and ninety-nine percent perspiration.

—THOMAS EDISON

This chapter is about the hard work that is essential to transforming thought into public speech. It looks at the process set into motion when your instructor first explains the nature of the speaking assignment you must complete. The specific topics we'll examine include focusing on the audience, topic, and specific purpose; supporting your speech with examples, facts, statistics, expert opinion, explanations, descriptions, and narratives; finding support, including library resources, the Internet, and interviews; and finally, preparing a bibliography and recording information.

FOCUSING ON YOUR AUDIENCE, TOPIC, AND SPECIFIC PURPOSE

As we discussed in Chapter 5, the situation you face as a speaker includes your goals, the audience, and constraints. To successfully prepare a speech that fulfills your goals, you need to understand whether your audience favors, opposes, or is undecided about your goals. You need to understand the diversity of your audience, including cultural, demographic, and individual differences. Understanding your audience does not mean simply telling them what they want to hear; it means knowing whether your basic message is likely to fall on receptive ears or to be tuned out.

In addition to an audience's attitude toward your topic, you need to consider their level of knowledge about and interest in the topic. If they already know most of what you are going to say, they are likely to think your speech is a waste of time. On the other hand, if the audience members know nothing about your topic, they may not be able to understand your speech. So you need to meet your audience's level of knowledge—presenting them with something new and worthwhile, yet not going beyond what they can absorb in a short time. As you select your topic, do your research, and construct your speech, always keep your audience in mind. Focusing on the audience is the hallmark of the successful speaker.

As we discussed in Chapter 2, a good speech topic should be interesting to you, interesting to your audience, appropriate to the situation, appropriate to the time available, manageable, and worthwhile. A thorough analysis of the situation should help you meet these standards. Understanding the needs you share with your audience, the situation, the time available, and your resources should help you in determining a topic your audience is likely to find involving.

The question for many students, though, is "Where do I find the ideas for a speech topic?" As we discussed in Chapter 2, you may begin with your own knowledge or turn to the popular media, the Internet, or a number of other sources available to you.

In an introductory speech class, the general purpose of your speech—to inform, persuade, or entertain—probably will be assigned. What you will not be assigned is a specific purpose, which, as discussed in Chapter 2, is your goal or objective in speaking to a particular audience. If, for example, your general purpose is to inform, your specific purpose might be "to inform the audience on how to scuba dive."

SUPPORTING YOUR SPEECH

You may have decided on a topic and a specific purpose, but a speech involves more than your own opinion. You need to find ways to support the points you make in your speech. Possible types of support include examples, facts, statistics, expert opinion, explanations, descriptions, and narratives. The important thing to recognize is that not all forms of support are equal. Not all examples, for instance, carry equal impact.

Examples

An example is a specific instance that represents some larger class. Thus, you might cite a recycling program in your hometown as an example of how curbside recycling can work. The test of an example is whether it is actually representative of the larger category. To test whether an example is representative, ask the following questions:

- *What is the relevance of the example to the larger category?* If you are talking about products made from recycled material, then a cardboard box made from new materials, although it could be recycled by the consumer, is not relevant to your point.

- *Are there enough instances to support the generalization?* A few years ago, a disposable-diaper manufacturer ran an ad campaign claiming that its diapers could be turned into compost. However, according to a *Consumer Reports* article, only about a dozen cities had the capability to compost disposable diapers.[1] Thus, if you were listing products that can be set out for curbside recycling, disposable diapers wouldn't be a good example.

- *Is the example typical of the larger category?* Be careful of isolated and atypical examples. Just because some types of plastic can be recycled doesn't mean that *all* plastic is recyclable.

- *Are there counterexamples that disprove the generalization?* A counterexample is an example that contradicts the generalization. Whereas several examples can only suggest the truth of a generalization, even one example to the contrary can disprove it. If a speaker claims all American cars are unreliable, then pointing to just one car line—for example, the Saturn—as having been shown to be reliable disproves that generalization. If counterexamples exist, either the generalization is false or it needs to be reformulated to be less inclusive. Thus, a speaker might say, "Many American cars are unreliable," a generalization that one counterexample would not disprove.

Facts

fact Something that is verifiable as true.

A **fact** is something that is verifiable as true. It is a fact that there are 50 states in the United States. As former baseball great Yogi Berra might say, "You can look it up." On the other hand, the statement that Texas is the best state in which to live is not a fact, though it may be widely believed by Texans.

A fact, of course, is only as good as the source of that fact. To evaluate a fact, ask the following questions:

- *Does the fact come from a reliable source?* Encyclopedias, almanacs, authoritative books, and scholarly articles are usually reliable. On the other hand, if the "fact" comes from someone who has a clear bias about the topic, you should be suspicious. For example, many Internet sites claim to contain facts, such as the existence of extraterrestrials or that there are "black helicopters" waiting to take over control of the United States. Just because you find something on the Internet, do not assume that it is true. Later in this chapter we will suggest some specific tests for Internet-based information.

- *Is the fact verifiable?* You should be suspicious of facts that are difficult to verify. For example, there are widely varying estimates of certain types of crime, such as rape. Part of the discrepancy is that many rapes go unreported. Thus, the number of reported rapes is multiplied by some factor assumed to represent the number of unreported rapes for every reported rape. However, these numbers are impossible to verify for the very reason that the unreported rapes are, by definition, unverifiable. Although these estimates may be useful, they are not facts in the sense of being verifiable.

- *Is the fact the most recent available?* Until recently, statistics about the federal budget projected a large annual surplus. Yet as this book is being written, these projected surpluses are likely to evaporate. A speech built around the existence of budget surpluses would clearly be out of date in the current economic climate.

- *Is the fact consistent with other known facts?* Facts do not stand alone. You should be suspicious of alleged "facts" that seem to be inconsistent with other known facts. For example, many tobacco manufacturers claim that nicotine is not addictive. However, not only the surgeon general but anyone who has tried to give up smoking can tell you that such a "fact" is suspect. Double-check your sources for possible error. Be particularly careful with **secondary sources,** which rely on another source rather than gathering the information firsthand. It is always better to look at **primary sources,** which are the original sources of information, because there may be honest mistakes in transferring information from one source to another. Finally, keep in mind what facts your audience

secondary sources Information sources that rely on other (primary) sources rather than gathering information firsthand.

primary sources Original sources of information.

already knows. If your facts are inconsistent with what the audience believes to be true, you first have to convince them that yours are more reliable if you are to have any success.

Statistics

Numerical summaries of data, such as percentages, ratios, and averages, that are classified in a meaningful way are known as **statistics.** These can be a rich source of information; yet they can also be confusing and misleading. For example, an American automobile manufacturer announced a survey showing that its cars were preferred overwhelmingly to foreign cars. However, it turns out that the company included only 200 people in its survey, none of whom even owned a foreign car.[2]

We are constantly bombarded by statistics that seem authoritative but are of dubious value. Some questions to ask about statistics are the following:

- *Is the source of the statistics reliable and unbiased?* The tip-off to the problem with the survey on foreign versus American cars is that it was sponsored by an American car company. Statistics found through general searches of commercial, individual, or organizational Internet sites are often particularly suspect. On the other hand, statistics found in official sources, such as www.fedstats.gov, are less likely to be biased, since this site collects official government statistics.[3]

- *Were unbiased questions asked?* A poll asking whether disposable diapers should be banned was preceded by a statement that disposable diapers account for only 2 percent of trash in landfills. Not surprisingly, 84 percent of those polled felt disposable diapers should not be banned.[4]

- *Was the sample representative?* A representative sample is absolutely necessary for a statistic to be reliable and valid. A representative sample is one made up of people who possess the same attributes as the people in the population from which the sample is drawn. Your speech class, for example, could be representative of the student body at your college. But unless your class was drawn randomly from the entire student body, you do not know for certain.

    There are many ways to obtain a representative sample, but the most common way is to randomly select people from the population in which you are interested: for example, college students between the ages of 18 and 25; all single mothers in the state; or members of your state bar association. Generally speaking, the larger the sample randomly drawn from a population, the more representative the sample.

    The complexities of statistical sampling are beyond the scope of this book, much less a single section of a single chapter. Still, we want you to know that the value of any statistic depends on sampling. Thus, at a minimum, you should never accept a statistic at face value; demand from the source of the statistic information about the sample on which the statistic is based.

- *Is the statistic based on a poll?* Polls are statistically driven. A meaningful poll calls participants, not the other way around. Based on sophisticated sampling techniques and random selection, a national poll can predict a presidential election with about a four-percentage-point margin of error.

statistics Numerical summaries of data, such as percentages, ratios, and averages, that are classified in a meaningful way. Age, height, and weight are not statistics, although they are commonly mistaken as such.

But when your local television station or newspaper conducts an "unscientific poll," in which people call in to record their views, the results are meaningless. Only people who are interested in the topic will call, and there is nothing to prevent someone from calling a hundred times. In short, such polls are worse than worthless, because they undermine confidence in legitimate polls.

- *Are the differences in the poll greater than the margin of error?* Good polling results state the margin of error. Keep in mind that the margin of error increases as the sample gets smaller. Whereas the margin of error for a sample of 1,067 people is about 3 percent, for 150 people the margin of error is about 8 percent.[5] Suppose a poll has a margin of error of 4 percent. Thus, if a poll shows a political candidate ahead of her opponent by 51 to 49 percent, she could be ahead by as much as 55 to 45 percent, or behind by 47 to 53 percent—or any number in between. Subgroups within a sample may have even greater margins of error than the larger group. For example, large-scale national polls on the Clarence Thomas and Anita Hill controversy showed that most people believed Thomas. An ABC–*Washington Post* poll showed 38 percent of women believed Thomas, whereas 28 percent believed Hill, a 10-point difference. However, the margin of error of this particular subgroup was reported as 12 percent![6]

- *What are the percentages based on?* "There's been a 10 percent increase in the rate of inflation!" Sounds pretty alarming, doesn't it? However, unless you know what the underlying rate of inflation is, this is a meaningless figure. Inflation rates are themselves a percentage. Say that inflation is running at 4 percent. That means what cost $100 last year now costs $104. A 10 percent increase in the rate of inflation means that it would cost $104.40—not too bad. On the other hand, a 10 percent rate of inflation means that what cost $100 a year ago now costs $110. Sound confusing? It is. The point is that you need to be sure of what percentages are based on before relying on them to prove a point.

- *What is meant by average?* One of the most frequently reported statistics is the average, or mean. Although easily computed, the average, or mean, is often misleading because it is commonly distorted by numerical extremes.

  Consider a newspaper report that states the average salary for new college graduates is $40,000 a year. That doesn't mean a majority of college graduates are paid $40,000 a year. It simply means that when you add the salaries paid to all college graduates surveyed and divide that sum by the number of graduates in the sample, that's the mean (the arithmetic average) you get. The number likely has been distorted by graduates in engineering, computer science, and information systems management, who though few in number, start at salaries two to three times as much as their more numerous counterparts in the liberal arts and social sciences. The most telling statistic is always the *median*, which is the midpoint in a distribution of numbers. Knowing the median tells you that half of the numbers in the distribution are larger, and half are smaller. In Chapter 14, we discuss the mean and median in more detail.

Using a visual aid helps your audience visualize statistics.

This list of questions is not meant to discourage you from using statistics. They can be a powerful form of support. The key is to know what your statistics mean and how they were collected, and to avoid biased sources and questionable sampling techniques. Most important, you need to explain enough about the statistics to your audience so that they will have confidence in the claims you are using the statistics to support. In Chapter 11, we discuss the use of visual media, which are particularly helpful in explaining statistics to an audience.

Expert Opinion

One very useful source of support is **expert opinion**—a quotation from someone with special credentials in the subject matter. Quotations from experts, whether gathered from a personal interview or from written sources, can be a persuasive way of supporting your points. However, you need to ask three basic questions about expert opinion:

expert opinion A quotation from someone with special credentials in the subject matter.

- *What is the source's expertise?* How do you know this person is an expert? Look at biographical sources (such as *Who's Who*) if you do not know who the person is. Look for marks of expertise, such as academic credentials, official positions, or references from other authorities. Finally, make sure your source is an expert in the subject matter of your speech. It is important to explain to your audience why the person you are quoting is an expert they should believe. Sting is an environmental activist devoting time, money, and his fame to campaigns to save the world's rain forests. No doubt he has learned much about environmental science as a result of his activism. He is not, however, an expert, in the sense that we use the term here.

- *Does the expert have a reputation for reliability?* How accurate have the expert's previous statements been? If someone has a record of either false or mistaken statements in the past, it is misguided to rely on that person's statements today. For example, many of the spokespeople who defended Representative Gary Condit as not having had an affair with Chandra Levy were badly embarrassed when the truth became known.

- *Is the source unbiased?* If a source has a vested interest in one side of a topic, his or her opinions are automatically suspect. Your audience needs to be assured that you are not relying on sources who have an ax to grind.

Explanations

An explanation is an account, an interpretation, or a meaning given to something. Detailed explanations may prove useful in a speech. But to be effective, explanations must meet two tests:

- *Is the explanation clear?* A complex or unclear explanation may only confuse your audience. One way to clarify an explanation is to use comparisons and contrasts. Thus, someone might explain a nuclear power plant by comparing it to a tea kettle whose source of heat is a nuclear reaction.
- *Is the explanation accurate?* An explanation that is clear is not necessarily complete or correct. You must also make sure that your explanations are as complete and accurate as possible, given the limitations of a speech situation.

Descriptions

A description is a word picture of something. For example, you might describe a place you have visited or researched. Consider the following statement from a speech by one of our students, Chalsey Phariss: "Imagine a place where the rivers are flowing, the sun is shining, and the fun is unlimited, where there is never a dull moment, and the freedom of the outdoors will captivate your mind." This description leads into a speech about the "Lake of the Sky," Lake Tahoe.[7]

Descriptions should meet the following tests:

- *Is the description accurate?* Descriptions can be tested for accuracy by comparing them with the thing being described. Thus, for the Tahoe example, looking at pictures of the lake or actually visiting it would help to verify the description.
- *Is the description vivid?* To hold an audience's attention, you need to paint a word picture. Calling Lake Tahoe by its Indian name, "Lake of the Sky," is much more vivid than simply describing the blueness of the water. Photographs and other visual materials, which are discussed in Chapter 11, can sometimes supplement descriptions in a speech.

narrative An extended story that is fully developed, with characters, scene, action, and plot.

Narratives

A **narrative** is an extended story that is fully developed, with characters, scene, action, and plot. Narratives sometimes provide an effective way of driving home a point to an audience. An effective narrative builds gradually from the begin-

Can you find words to accurately describe the beauty of Lake Tahoe?

ning, through conflict, to a climax. The conflict is then resolved, and the ending of the story often ties back into the beginning. For example, consider the highly successful *Scream* series. The story begins with Neve Campbell "home alone." Conflict develops when she begins to receive threatening phone calls from an anonymous caller. Tension begins to build as her safety is jeopardized by the intruder. The climax occurs when the intruder is killed and his identity revealed; or so we're led to believe. Often the ending of a narrative ties into the beginning. In the case of *Scream*, the phone calls come again as the movie ends, and the tension begins to build for the next film.

Narratives can be more than a useful supporting tool for a speech; in some cultures, narrative is an organizing principle of speaking. The storyteller in North and Central American culture, for example, is revered. We were in the audience when actor-activist Edward James Olmos spoke at our university. His speech was largely a series of stories—about his career, his family, how people of different cultures can come to understand one another. Award-winning rhetorical scholar Walter Fisher has argued, in fact, that human beings are fundamentally storytellers. Fisher believes that reasoning is done in the form of narrative. Even if you don't accept Fisher's narrative paradigm, it is undoubtedly the case that a well-told story, real or fictional, can captivate an audience. Fisher claims that two basic tests apply to narrative reasoning:[8]

The movie *Saving Private Ryan* had both narrative probability and narrative fidelity for those who had actually experienced combat during World War II.

narrative probability The internal coherence or believability of a narrative.

- *Does the narrative have probability?* **Narrative probability** is the internal coherence or believability of a narrative. Does a story make sense in and of itself? A hallmark of the success of Academy Award–winning director Stephen Spielberg's movie *Saving Private Ryan* is his attention to detail, in an effort to make the movie historically accurate.

narrative fidelity The degree to which a narrative rings true to real-life experience.

- *Does the narrative have fidelity?* **Narrative fidelity** is the degree to which a narrative rings true to real-life experience. Even if a story makes sense internally, it may not make sense in terms of the real world. Many World War II veterans emerged from the theater after watching *Saving Private Ryan* with tears in their eyes. Clearly, this film "rang true" to those who had experienced combat during the Second World War.

When you tell a story to an audience, you should let them know if it is true or hypothetical. But either type of story needs to ring true to the audience's own experience if it is to have impact. Although people may enjoy hypothetical stories for their entertainment value, they don't find these narratives real. For a speech to have impact, the narratives need to have probability and fidelity.

FINDING SUPPORT

research The process of gathering supporting materials for a speech.

Examples, facts, statistics, expert opinions, explanations, descriptions, and narratives constitute the supporting materials from which you will construct your speech. The process of gathering these supporting materials is called **research.** There are two basic steps to research. First there is the search, whereby you find the sources likely to contain information on your topic. Then there is the research, in which you examine these sources for materials you can use. Many people mistakenly rely on the first source they find on their topic, jotting down a few notes and then writing their speech. In other words, they skip to the research phase of the process before they have done a thorough search of information available on their topic. To avoid this mistake, which can lead to an incomplete and even deceptive speech, look for as many sources as you can before deciding about the materials on which you'll most rely.

There are innumerable sources from which to gather materials on a topic, including personal experience and knowledge, nonprint media, library resources, interviews, and the Internet. In this section we will focus on three of these sources: the library, the Internet, and interviews with experts. This does not mean that you shouldn't use personal experience or other sources of information. However, to build a well-supported speech, authoritative sources, such as those discussed in the following section, are essential.

The Library

Most research for your public speaking class will involve a trip to your campus or community library. The library is the intellectual center of most universities and colleges—the repository of the history of ideas and thought. Although campus libraries vary in their extensiveness and degree of sophistication, the basic principles of a library search are the same.

The first step in using your library is familiarization. Most campus libraries feature guided tours, handouts, and special seminars for groups interested in a particular area of research. Your instructor may have your class take a library tour or send you on a library scavenger hunt to familiarize you with the library. Whatever you do, though, don't wait until you are facing a deadline before familiarizing yourself with your library. If you didn't do it during your first few weeks on campus, make it a priority now.

We recommend the following four steps when you do library research.

Four Steps of Library Research   **TIPS AND TACTICS**

1. Select search terms.
2. Search the library catalog.
3. Search relevant indexes, abstracts, and other databases.
4. Consult reference sources.

Although you may not need to use each step every time you do library research, it's useful to know about each step and how they are connected. Let's look at each step in detail.

Select Search Terms   A **search term** is a word or phrase used in a database such as a library catalog or indexes to identify a subject. Search terms are like the combination to a safe: If you have the right combination, you can easily open the door; without it, your chances of opening the door are slim. Thus, the most effective library search begins with a search term or terms on the topic of interest.

search term A word or phrase used in library catalogs and indexes to identify a subject.

Search the Library Catalog   Although some libraries still use a physical card catalog to list their book holdings, an increasing number use computerized online catalogs, which ease your task and allow you to construct more complex searches. An **online catalog** is a computerized listing of library holdings. Some

online catalog A computerized listing of library holdings.

FIGURE 7.1 Boolean Operators

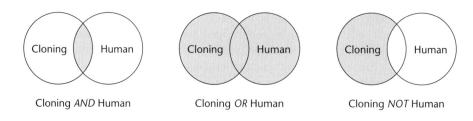

Cloning *AND* Human   Cloning *OR* Human   Cloning *NOT* Human

Boolean operators Terms, such as *and, or,* and *not,* used to narrow or broaden a computerized search of two or more related terms.

libraries may require you to be in the building to search their online catalogs, whereas other catalogs may be accessible from a remote computer terminal or even through the Internet. Whether they use physical cards or a computerized system, library catalogs are built on the same principles. Catalogs are arranged by subject, author, and title. Some online catalogs may also permit searching by call number or allow you to search for a term that appears anywhere in the record. Because you are just beginning a search on your topic, it is unlikely that you will know specific authors, titles, or call numbers. Thus, the subject heading or the "anywhere in the record" search is the most likely basis for your search.

If you are using an online catalog or similar database, one additional advantage is that you may use what are called **Boolean operators.** These are terms, such as *and, or,* and *not,* used to narrow or broaden a computerized search of two or more related terms. You should know, however, that some databases and library catalogs will *assume* the Boolean operator *and,* unless you supply another, while others will require you to type in *and* or +. For example, if you enter search terms *human cloning* and your database assumes the *and,* it will locate all sources that use both the word *human* and the word *cloning,* even if they are not used together. On the other hand, if the *and* is not assumed, your database may only locate sources where the phrase *human cloning* appears. Depending on your search needs, you'll need to determine which method is used in your library catalog. Check with a librarian at your school to learn whether you need to use Boolean operators, or experiment with different search combinations until you discover which way your library catalog operates. How Boolean operators can be used to broaden or narrow a search is shown in Figure 7.1.

An additional tip for using library catalogs is that when you locate a book or other source that is interesting to you, check and see what subject headings are used by the library to index the book in addition to the one you used to find it. These subject headings can then provide new search terms to expand your search and locate additional sources on your topic.

As you can see, the online catalog provides increased capabilities to expand, limit, and speed up your search. Some online terminals are connected to printers so that you can print out the results of your search and use that to locate the books you need. If you cannot get a printed copy of your search, note the author, title, date, and call number of each source that seems promising. Simply going into the stacks with a series of call numbers can be confusing; you will soon forget which call number goes with which book.

When you visit the stacks, it is a good idea to do a little browsing as you find the specific books you have noted. Because books are shelved by subject, it is not unusual to find a book closely related to your topic that you overlooked in your search. This serendipitous search for information often turns up better sources than those you originally found.

TABLE 7.1 Representative List of Databases

Academic Search	The Grove Dictionary of Art
Academic Universe (Lexis-Nexis)	GROVEmusic
America: History and Life	Health Reference Center
Anthropological Index Online	Historical Abstracts
Applied Science & Technology Index	Library of Congress
Art Abstracts	MEDLINE [NLM Gateway] or PubMed
Bioethicsline	The New Grove Dictionary of Music & Musicians
Biological Abstracts	BIOSIS	
Biological & Agricultural Index	[Proquest] Newsstand
Britannica Online	P.A.I.S. [Public Affairs Information Service]
Congressional Universe	Philosopher's Index
Contemporary Authors	PsycINFO
Contemporary Women's Issues	Religion Index	ATLA Religion DB
Country Watch	ScienceDirect
Dow Jones Interactive	Stat-USA
Encyclopedia Britannica	Wiley InterScience
Ethnic NewsWatch	

One great advantage of going to books for information first is that the authors have done much of your work for you. Most books have a bibliography or footnotes that lead to other sources. Obviously, the more recent the books you read first, the more up-to-date their bibliographies. In many ways, a researcher is like a detective looking for clues. A good general book on a topic is like a room full of clues. The author will have left fingerprints all over the place. Follow the leads suggested by general books.

Search Relevant Indexes, Abstracts, and Databases An **index** is a listing of sources of information, usually in newspapers, journals, and magazines, alphabetically by topic. An **abstract** is a summary of an article or a report. Numerous paper, or *hard copy*, indexes and abstracts are commonly found in libraries. For example, the *Readers' Guide to Periodical Literature* is an old standby for those seeking articles in general-interest magazines. In addition, every topic you can imagine is classified in one or more specialized indexes. A good library has hundreds or even thousands of indexes related to specialized fields. Some indexes list and abstract articles in journals. Today, more and more indexes are available in the form of computerized databases. For example, a partial list of databases available at our university library is provided in Table 7.1.

You can probably guess from the titles what the subject matter is of most of these indexes. Whether your topic is art, science, religion, philosophy, or health and medicine, there are computerized databases that can assist you in finding reliable information. Your library will undoubtedly differ from ours in the available indexes. However, the basic search principles will be the same regardless of the index used.

We will illustrate how to do a search using two popular databases. The first, Academic Search, is an excellent source for searching scholarly and professional

index A listing of sources of information, usually in newspapers, journals, and magazines, alphabetically by topic.

abstract A summary of an article or a report.

journals in the social sciences, humanities, and physical sciences. This database contains information on everything from astronomy to religion, law, psychology, and current events. Not only are citations and abstracts of articles available, but Academic Search also allows you to access the full texts of many articles. To search, you simply follow easy on-screen directions to enter appropriate search terms. The same Boolean operators you would use in an online catalog search can be used with most computerized databases. When you enter your search, a list of citations will be produced, and you will be able to mark the ones that interest you for viewing. Depending on your library's facilities, you may be able to print, copy to a disk, or even e-mail the results of your search to yourself or a classmate.

To illustrate the power of Academic Search, in late 2001 we did a search for articles on human cloning. First we typed in the words *cloning and human*, which would retrieve any article in which both words appeared, even if they were not together. We got 1,408 hits, far too many to be useful. By limiting the search to the exact phrase *human cloning*, our search netted 579 citations, still more than we could use. Academic Search allows you to further refine your search, which we did by limiting it to only those articles that were peer reviewed or refereed. That means experts in the field had authenticated the article for publication. That narrowed our search to 182 sources, still more than we needed. Finally, we decided to limit our search to articles from the last six months, which reduced our results to a manageable 22 citations. Of these, 8 were available in full text, meaning we could actually print out a copy or e-mail them to ourselves without leaving our computer. Thus, while databases such as Academic Search may initially seem to produce far too many results to be usable, a careful narrowing of the parameters of your search can lead to productive and easily accessible results. Although your library may not have this exact database, chances are it has a similar database that can access reliable published information on a wide variety of topics.

Of course, not every library has a physical or electronic copy of every journal listed in any given index or database. Thus, you must compare the most promising articles from your search with your library's holding of journals. Some libraries provide listings of the journals they have. The card or online catalog may also list journals. You would look under the title, for example, to see if your library had a particular journal. Even if your library does not have it, you may be able to use interlibrary loan services to obtain a copy, if time permits. Also, some libraries subscribe to special services, such as Carl UnCover, which allow them to have copies of journals not held in their collections faxed to the library for a nominal charge.

Another powerful database is Lexis-Nexis, which is widely used in business, publishing, and law. The educational version of Lexis-Nexis is known as Academic Universe. You'll need to inquire at your library as to whether this database is available on your campus. If it is not, you may have access to a similar database, called ProQuest Newsstand. If your library has no database for searching newspapers and similar periodicals, you can go directly to the Web sites of most major newspapers, such as the *New York Times*. However, for articles more than a few days old, these databases normally charge a fee to download the articles you have found. The advantage to Lexis-Nexis is that it includes virtually all major newspapers, magazines, scripts of televised public affairs programs, newswire reports (such as Reuters), medical, and legal sources.

A database such as the one for the *New York Times* indexes only one paper. Lexis-Nexis is a full-text service. If you choose, it not only looks in titles for the words you search for, but anywhere in the text. Thus, if you are looking for a report of a speech in which someone made a particularly memorable statement, you can use Lexis-Nexis to search for that specific phrase in any of the newspapers, magazines, or TV news reports that covered the speech. Unlike subject searches, when you do a search for a word in a text, you are going to get dozens to thousands of "hits" unless you carefully narrow your search.

We tried our search on human cloning on Lexis-Nexis, using the major newspaper database. Typing in the words *human and cloning*, we got the following message: "This search has been interrupted because it will return more than 1,000 documents." Even the exact phrase, *human cloning*, got the same response. So we narrowed our search by asking for only the last six months. That search yielded 368 citations, again far too many. Then we shifted to the medical database. Looking for the words *human and cloning*, even if they didn't appear together, yielded six sources, while the phrase *human cloning* gave us two, one in the *American Journal of Law & Medicine* and another in the *Journal of Contemporary Health Law & Policy*. These are just examples of how powerful databases can help you find high-quality information that is readily accessible in your library or even in full-text form that can be downloaded on your computer.

Consult Reference Sources   Frequently you need to find a very specific fact—for example, how much plastic was produced in the United States in a certain year. You could search a dozen articles and never find that number. But a good reference book, such as the *Statistical Abstract of the United States*, puts that kind of information at your fingertips. For an online source of reliable government statistics, try the Web site http://www.fedstats.gov/, which bills itself as "the gateway to statistics from over 100 U.S. Federal agencies."[9] This site includes topics from A to Z, map statistics, links to various federal agencies, and even the ability to access the online version of the *Statistical Abstract of the United States*.

Perhaps you need a good quotation to begin or end your speech. Numerous books of quotations are available. In fact, because there are so many, a reference book called *Quotation Location* was written to help you find any of 900 published compilations of quotations.[10] Or you might go to a Web site, such as Bartleby.com's Great Books Online at http://www.bartleby.com/, which allows you to conduct computerized searches of sources such as *Bartlett's Quotations*.

There are countless reference books to which you can turn in the effort to track down information. For example, almanacs and yearbooks, such as *The World Almanac and Book of Facts* and *Information Please Almanac*, are useful sources of statistics and facts. Digests of information, such as *Facts on File* and *Editorial Research Reports*, are useful sources for information on current issues. Biographies, such as the *Who's Who* series, help you find out about the qualifications of various sources. You should not overlook encyclopedias, which are often available online or on CD-ROM. Although the information in them is likely to be general and dated for hard-copy versions, encyclopedias can provide a useful source for your early search. Atlases are valuable in learning about the world. By consulting an atlas, you can learn not only where a country is geographically but also important facts about it. Shortly after the attacks on the

World Trade Center and Pentagon, many Americans found themselves reaching for an atlas to find out exactly where Afghanistan was located.

The Internet

Most of you have probably used the Internet, if not for research, for fun. You can check the latest scores of your favorite team, find your favorite music, or see a trailer from the latest motion picture release. The virtually limitless access to information provided by the Internet is both its strength and its weakness. And, of course, the Internet is popular for e-mail and instant messaging.

Although e-mail is a time-saving and convenient way to keep in touch with friends and family, it is an unreliable source of information for your speeches. It is often the source of hoaxes, chain letters, and unwanted e-mail called *spam*. The terrorist attacks on the World Trade Center and Pentagon spawned a lot of e-mail, some of it distorted. Keep in mind that when an e-mail is forwarded, its content can be altered in a way that is undetectable to the next recipient. On September 13, 2001, an e-mail sent to about 20 people by Tamim Ansary, an Afghani writer from San Francisco, criticized callers to a San Francisco radio talk show host, Ronn Owens. The e-mail morphed from a discussion of how a religious war in Afghanistan would play into bin Laden's hands, into an attack on Owens himself, for calling for bombing Afghanistan into the Stone Age, which is something Owens never said. As the e-mail was forwarded, it was changed. Ansary, who is male and a writer, became an Afghani woman and a professor at Stanford. As Owens said on his own Web site a week after the e-mail first circulated, "It's been an eye-opening experience for me to see how a forwarded e-mail can be altered as it makes its way through cyberspace."[11]

The most useful aspect of the Internet to speakers is the World Wide Web. Within each Web page there are connections to other sites, which can link to even more sites. Sites cover everything from sports to literature to current events. You can find the latest scores of your favorite sports or the entire text of some books on the Web. Even items such as atlases, encyclopedias, and government publications may be available through your computer. In a sense, the Internet can be thought of as a "virtual library." Always exercise caution, however, in using materials from the Web. Unlike the materials in your library, no one has checked the authenticity or the reliability of the billions of pieces of information available on the Web.

We will not explain in this book how to access the World Wide Web or how to use your Web browser. Our experience has shown that the majority of college students use the Web on a regular basis. If you have not done so, consult your school's computer center and obtain the necessary instruction. With the most recent versions of Microsoft Internet Explorer and Netscape Navigator, the technical skill needed to find things on the Web is minimal. However, the ability to find reliable and authenticated information is not as common as basic computer skills. Thus, we will focus our attention not so much on how to use your computer to access the Web as on how to find the best information for your speeches.

Most people who search for Web sites use a search engine, such as Yahoo (www.yahoo.com) or Google (www.google.com). Figure 7.2 shows an example of Yahoo's home page. In fact, during the month of July 2001, Yahoo had 64.3 million users, compared to the second-place search engine, Terra Lycos, with

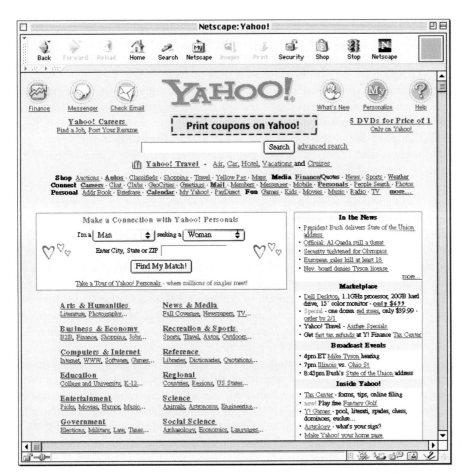

FIGURE 7.2 Yahoo Home Page Yahoo is one of the most used search engines. (Text and artwork copyright © 2002 by Yahoo! Inc. All rights reserved. Yahoo! and the Yahoo! logo are trademarks of Yahoo! Inc.)

37.6 million. Excite (28.6 million), Google (15.1 million), and Alta Vista (7.2 million) rounded out the top five most popular search sites.[12]

While they are powerful resources, it is important to realize that such search engines list Web sites based not on their quality, but on other criteria. For example, Google uses a system that ranks pages by a system called page rank, which interprets cross-links of Web sites as a "vote" for their importance. As we were writing this chapter, in late 2001, we typed the phrase (with no spaces between words) *martinlutherking* into the Google search box. Notice that there is no need to capitalize words in most search engines. The first Web site on the list at first appears to be a tribute to the late Dr. King, but closer examination reveals that it actually is a site sponsored by a hate group, Storm Front, whose motto is "white pride world wide." The site even promotes a book by former Nazi and Ku Klux Klan grand wizard, David Duke. The likely reason this page shows up first on Google's list is that librarians and others teaching about evaluating Web sites put this link on their own Web pages as an example of a misleading site. By listing the site on their own Web sites, these teachers inadvertently cause the site to rank very high in Google's system.

In fairness we should point out that Google normally returns highly useful results. For example, if you type *martin luther king* as separate words rather than running them together, in the Google search engine, you do not end up at the racist site, but rather at the Martin Luther King, Jr., papers project at Stanford University, a highly credible site (http://www.stanford.edu/group/King/).

Although we generally find search sites such as Google very useful (and in fact use it regularly), we caution that you must be critical of what you find, and not assume that a high ranking in the list of hits means that a site is more reliable than others. Also, you need to know that many search engines put Web sites that pay a fee at the top of their search results lists. One of the advantages of Google is that it doesn't do so, but rather clearly distinguishes which Web sites have advertised with them.

Every Web site has an address, called the URL (Uniform Resource Locator). Most addresses begin with http:// (which tells you it uses a hypertext transfer protocol). Sometimes you can pretty well guess the rest of the address, called the *domain*. For example, if you wanted to read the *New York Times* online, you would go to http://www.nytimes.com/, which is the URL for the newspaper's home page. The ".com" tells you it is a commercial site. To get past the home page, you'll need to subscribe to the online newspaper, which, as of this writing, is a free subscription. Other common endings for Web sites are ".edu" for educational, ".gov" for government, ".net" for network, and ".org" for organization. As we shall see later, knowing what type of a site you are visiting may be helpful in evaluating the validity of the information you obtain.

Keep in mind that computers are stupid beasts. They only look for the exact string of characters that you enter. If you misspell a word or use a different form of the word (*pollute* rather than *pollution*), you will often be disappointed in your search results. Always double-check your typing and the spelling of the words.

Suppose you conduct your search and have found a number of useful Web sites. Obviously you don't want to copy down the information on note cards for use in your speech. How can you save what you have found? First, if you are using your own computer, be sure to make a bookmark (or "favorite" in Internet Explorer) to save the site on your browser. Second, you can often highlight and cut and paste information into your word processing program. Third, you can print what you find, but that may leave you with reams of paper and undermine the very reason you want to search by computer—ease of manipulating the information. Fourth, some programs will allow you to e-mail either yourself or someone else the actual Web page as an attachment. Finally, you can often save a Web page to your computer or a floppy disk (using the Save command under the File menu). Our recommendation is to save the results of your search electronically and print only the things you know you need in hard copy. Once you have saved the material, particularly in your word processing program's format, it is easy to incorporate material from your search into your speech outline later. Of course, you will need to keep a full citation of where you found the information, so that it may be properly cited in the speech, a topic we will address later in this chapter. Keep in mind that the Web is also an excellent source for finding information about diverse cultures, as the box "Cultures on the Web" illustrates.

Evaluating Internet Information   Unlike published books and articles, which are usually subject to editing, fact checking, and peer review, the Internet is unregulated. Anyone can say anything and, short of outright pornography, there is no government regulation. You must be cautious with information gathered

Cultures on the Web

One of the great advantages of the Internet is that it is a global phenomenon. You can literally read newspapers from anywhere in the world. You can send e-mail to and receive it from people on the other side of the globe. In fact, Dr. Madeline Keaveney, a professor at our university, established an e-mail pen-pal program with students in Japan for her intercultural communication class. The possibilities of learning about other cultures and sharing information with people from these cultures is endless.

Although there are Web sites that deal with Native American, Latino, Asian, and African American cultures, any list of these sites would be incomplete and highly selective. Rather, we suggest that you do your own Internet surfing to learn about other cultures and then incorporate that information into your next speech. For starters, we suggest you try Yahoo!, which has numerous links dealing with society and culture (http://www.yahoo.com/Society_and_Culture/). For example, you can learn how different cultures deal with topics such as death and dying, disabilities, families, fashion, food and drink, gender, holidays, mythology and folklore, religion, sexuality, and weddings, just to name a few. So go ahead, reach out globally—from your own computer!

from the Internet because you have no assurance as to its reliability and verifiability. There have been instances of material being altered on the Net. As a speaker you have an ethical responsibility to ensure that such information is accurate, even if this requires tracking down the original source of the information. So, all the tests of supporting materials that apply to published materials apply doubly to computer information. Nevertheless, there is the advantage that because Internet-based information is unedited and uncensored, you can directly read the ideas of others, even controversial or unpopular ones that would never make it into print. In many ways the Internet is the ultimate marketplace of ideas. The following standards and criteria for electronic information are suggested by Courtright and Perse.[13]

- *Who is the source of the information?* Often the source of a Web site is not clear. For example, during a recent presidential election, we found a site that appeared to belong to the Republican Party. However, one of our students pointed out that an official Republican Party site would end with .org (organization), whereas the site in question ended with .com (commercial). In other words, someone was masquerading as the Republican Party site. During the election some sites were designed to parody or spoof real sites. So make sure you know who is the real source of the information. That source can then be subject to all the normal tests of evidence—bias, reliability, and the like.

- *Is the source primary or secondary?* If you go to the White House site, you can obtain primary reports of presidential speeches, proclamations, and important documents. A CNN report of a presidential speech, on the other hand, would be a secondary source. Whenever possible, primary sources are preferable. One of the great advantages of the Internet is that the average person can visit the sites of almost any organization imaginable, and thus obtain primary information that was previously available only by writing or calling the source—and hoping they would provide the needed material in time for your speech.

- *How old is the information?* Web sites usually have a line at the bottom of the page stating when they were last updated. If a site has not changed

FIGURE 7.3 "Get Page Info" Screen From a Web Page

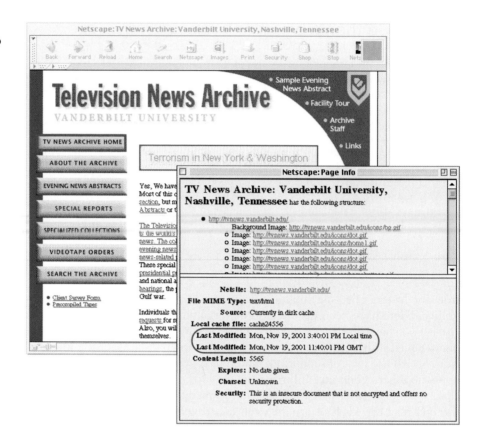

in several months, chances are the information is out of date. Also, you can use your browser to find out page information, which often includes the date the page was last updated. For example, in Netscape, go to the View menu and select Page Info. You will get a screen that looks something like Figure 7.3.

INTERVIEWS

We put off discussing interviews until now for a reason. Far too often students go into an interview before researching their topic. In a sense, they expect the expert they interview to write their speech for them. Although interviews with experts can offer useful information and may lead you to other sources of information, they cannot substitute for doing your own research. Thus, an interview should be conducted only after you have been to the library and searched the Internet so that you will have done the research necessary to ask the interviewee intelligent questions.

Finding potential interviewees on most topics is not as difficult as you may think. On the topic of recycling, you may be able to arrange an interview with the director of a local recycling center. Community leaders, including members of the city council, also may have information on topics such as recycling, traffic congestion, parking, and growth. At a university, most departments have experts on various topics. Often a call to the department asking if there is anyone familiar with your specific topic will elicit a name. In other cases, you may simply want to consult a department's course offerings. Someone who teaches a class on ecology, for example, most likely is an expert in that subject.

Another strategy is to contact organizations related to your topic and ask if someone there would be available to interview. For example, if you are researching the effects of secondhand smoke, the American Lung Association is a likely source of potential interviewees.

Sometimes you may already know a person who can help you. We recall the case of one student who was speaking about a "miracle" weight-loss product. After calling the company's home office and getting the runaround, she contacted her local pharmacist. He informed her that the ingredients in the product were in no way capable of helping a person lose weight—in fact, they were potentially harmful. A brief interview with the pharmacist gave her information she would have had great difficulty finding on her own.

Once you have decided on a person you would like to interview, the following basic guidelines for before, during, and after the interview should help you proceed. For additional advice, read the box "The Importance of Interviewing: Professor Rick Rigsby."

Before the Interview

- Contact the potential interviewee well in advance. Explain why you want to meet and how much time you think you will need. If the person agrees to be interviewed, ask for a convenient time and place for a meeting (usually at the interviewee's place of business). If possible, confirm your appointment in writing. Verify where and when you will meet and how much time you have to spend, which will guide you both in formulating questions and in ascertaining the number of questions you can reasonably pursue.

- Do some general reading on your topic. Read at least a book or two and some recent articles, or visit relevant Web sites. This will give you a basis for framing your questions and allow you to concentrate on those things you cannot easily find out for yourself.

- Prepare specific questions in advance. You should attempt to ask openended questions, which will allow the interviewee an opportunity to talk at some length. Of course, be prepared to deviate from your questions as answers suggest other avenues to follow. But at least you know you won't be wasting time trying to come up with questions on the spot.

During the Interview

- Show up on time, dressed professionally, and ready to begin. Introduce yourself and explain how you will use the interview in your speech. If you are planning to tape-record the interview, be sure to ask for permission. If an interview is by phone, you have a legal obligation to inform and gain consent from the other party if you are planning to tape the conversation.

- Using what you have learned about your topic as a guide, begin with general questions, and then move to specific ones. Be sure to let the interviewee talk. Don't monopolize the conversation; doing so defeats the purpose of the interview.

The Importance of Interviewing: *Professor Rick Rigsby*

Dr. Enrique D. "Rick" Rigsby teaches speech communication at Texas A&M University in College Station, Texas. He also serves as a mentor for A&M athletes and is in great demand as a motivational speaker. Before becoming a teacher, he was a television news reporter for seven years. Not only did Rick use the interview as a principal technique in television reporting, he continues to conduct interviews as part of his research, as he explains below. We asked Rick to explain the importance of interviewing to students of public speaking.

To appreciate the role interviewing performs, one must understand that we humans tend to be storytelling animals. Everyone has a history filled with commendations, successes, and struggles. These stories are marked by significant dates and may include a supporting cast of characters. The stories develop in basements and ballparks, departments and dormitories. We experience life, record dramas, and share the stories when called upon. Thus, our stories contribute to newscasts, government reports, research projects, even speeches in communication classes!

For the college student preparing a speech, interviewing someone with expertise on the subject might produce insights other sources cannot generate. Make sure to avoid this one pitfall: Refrain from interviewing the person most available. Rather, carefully select the individual who will enhance your work. A simple question to ask yourself is "Will the interview I conduct enlighten the audience about the subject and increase my credibility as a speaker?"

I have used the medium of interviewing in both my collegiate and professional careers. When I was a speech communication major in college, interviewing individuals for speeches allowed me to use real-life adventure to help inform, persuade, or entertain my audience. As a television news reporter, I interviewed thousands of people in a variety of situations. Imagine talking to a person who has just won the lottery or thrown the winning touchdown pass! Getting the right interview can make the difference between a presentation that few hear or a speech that few will ever forget. I continue to use interviewing today. A large part of my job as a

college professor is to conduct research. My research focuses on volunteers who participated in the civil rights demonstrations of the sixties. An essential part of my research task is to interview those former protesters and document their stories.

If your future includes the preparation of a presentation, you would be well advised to consider the medium of interviewing as a way of obtaining information. Remember, we're a storytelling culture. But what good is a story if it's never told? You know, interviewing a subject as a part of your speech preparation could make the difference between a mediocre speech and a memorable oration. But don't take my word for it . . . go interview your speech prof!

- Ask the interviewee if he or she can suggest other sources of information—books, pamphlets, periodicals, or other experts. Often an expert will lead you to sources you never would have thought of yourself. If you are lucky, your interviewee may even loan you some relevant journals or other publications.

- Use the active listening skills discussed in Chapter 4, especially setting goals, blocking out distracting stimuli, suspending judgment, being sensitive to metacommunication, and using paraphrasing and questioning.

- Either tape-record (with permission) or take complete notes during the interview. If you do not get something down, ask a follow-up question to make sure you get the essential points on paper. If you want to use quotes from the interview in your speech, make sure they are accurate.

- When your time is about up, ask the interviewee if there is anything he or she can add to what has been said. Perhaps there is some area you have completely overlooked.

- Thank the interviewee for his or her time and exit graciously.

After the Interview

- A follow-up thank-you letter is common courtesy and may help you get subsequent interviews.

- Transcribe your tape or your notes while the interview is fresh in your mind. Notes that may have been clear at the moment will quickly fade from memory unless you flesh them out soon after the interview.

- Follow up on leads or other interviews suggested by your interviewee.

Interviews can not only provide a rich source of information but also add credibility to your speaking. The fact that you have taken the time to speak directly to an expert shows your concern for your audience. Further, your own expertise is enhanced by virtue of the interview. And if you use the interview in presenting your speech, be sure to let your audience know why your interviewee is a credible source on your topic.

USING YOUR RESEARCH

Preparing a Bibliography

Before beginning in-depth reading on a topic, you should prepare a preliminary bibliography of the sources you have found. You might, for example, find 20 sources on cloning that look like they will be relevant. Using either your computer word processor or small note cards (4 by 6 inches is a good size), list the following information about each source:

> For all sources: author(s), preferably by full name, if an author is listed

> For books: exact title and the following facts of publication: location, publisher, and date

> For periodicals: article title, periodical title, volume number, date, and pages

> For government documents: the agency issuing the document, as well as the document's full title, date, and publication information

> For electronic resources: author, title, publication information, the e-mail address, Web site, or path by which the material was located and the date you found it

Leave space to add information to each citation as you read the source.

Because you will need all of this information for your formal speech outline, it is better to list it as you compile it, rather than having to go back to find it later. At the end of this chapter we provide samples of how to correctly cite sources according to the systems developed by the American Psychological Association (APA) and the Modern Language Association (MLA). If you use a computer word processor to prepare your bibliography, you will be able to edit and sort it as necessary for your final speech outline. If you use note cards, it is important to put only one source on each card, because you will need to shuffle their order to obtain an alphabetical listing for the final outline. If you need more space than one card provides for recording the information that you read, give each source a code number or a short title to use on additional cards for the same source.

Recording Information

As you gather materials, carefully record the facts and quotations you discover. It is important to note not only the substance of what was said but also who said it and where. Documenting such information will build your credibility with your audience and enhance your overall effectiveness as a speaker.

If you are doing a computerized search, such as on the Internet, you may be able to download information directly onto a computer. For example, transcripts of CNN programs can be found by going to the network's Web site; then follow the instructions of your Web browser for downloading files.[14] Although this technique makes for ease in writing your speech, it does not relieve you from the task of reading and absorbing the material; you will be able to cite or quote only a small portion of the material in a given speech. With this approach, though, you may be able to cut and paste quotations from your sources into your own computer files. These can later be edited and incorporated into your speech with proper citation. But if you are using print books or articles, interviews, and the like, you will first need to write the important facts, examples, quotations, and statistics on note cards for easy sorting. Cards need to be large enough to accommodate the information, yet small enough so that you won't be tempted to put more than one fact on each card. The advantage of this technique is that you can organize cards in any way that seems logical when you begin writing your speech.

Another strategy is to photocopy pages from articles or books that seem particularly useful. Then use a highlighter or marker to identify those things you may wish to use in the speech. At this point, cut out the quotations you plan to use and paste or tape them to cards. Again, be sure to note the source and page number on each card. The advantages of this technique over copying information onto note cards are twofold. First, it saves time. Second, it ensures that you will accurately quote the source; handwritten notes can be hard to read or even inaccurate.

Finally, if you have access to a scanner, you may be able to scan articles into computer files and then process them as if you had accessed them from a computerized source directly.

SUMMARY

 SPEECH COACH
To evaluate your understanding of this chapter, see the Quizzes on your CD.

The process of researching to support your speech is like the process of inventing a new product: You need both a source of inspiration and the willingness to engage in hard work.

- Begin by analyzing the situation and focusing on your audience.
- Choose an appropriate topic.
- Formulate a specific purpose you wish to accomplish.

Many types of support are effective in speeches:

- Examples should be relevant, of sufficient quantity, and typical, and without counterexamples.
- Facts should be from a reliable source, verifiable, recent, and consistent with other known facts.
- Statistics should be from a reliable and unbiased source, based on fair questions, from a representative sample. Polls should report the sample size and margin of error. Know what percentages are based on and if the average or mean is being cited exclusively.
- Expert opinion should come from a subject matter expert, who is reliable and unbiased.
- Explanations should be clear and accurate.
- Descriptions should be accurate and vivid.
- Narratives should have probability (coherence) and fidelity for the audience.

Possible sources of information for your speech include:

- library resources, such as books, periodicals, and databases
- the Internet, but with particular attention to distinguishing authentic and reliable Web sites from questionable ones
- interviews

Develop a recording system for both sources and data:

- Download computerized sources.
- Copy information onto note cards.
- Use selective photocopying to record information.
- Scan information directly into your computer.

CHECK YOUR UNDERSTANDING: EXERCISES AND ACTIVITIES

1. Check your understanding of the American Psychological Association and Modern Language Association guidelines for source citations on pages 179–183. Provide a correct source citation for each of the following hypothetical sources, using both APA and MLA guidelines:

   A book with one author named Jack Smith, titled College Life, published in New York by University Press in 1995. How would your citation change if Smith were the editor of the book? How would you list a second author, John Q. Doe? How would you list a third author, Mary A. Smith?

   An article titled Dorm Life in American Universities, by Peter Chu, published in the scholarly journal Universities and Colleges, volume 31, December 1995, pages 24–56.

   A chapter by Jose Sanchez titled The Nine Lives Myth, appearing on pages 99–109 in the book Cat Stories, edited by Morris T. Katt, published by Feline Press in San Francisco, California, in 1995.

   An article in Canine Magazine titled Snoopy and Me, by Charlie Brown, pages 56–57, on December 14, 1995, in volume 42. How would you list the article if no author were named?

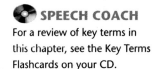

SPEECH COACH

For a review of key terms in this chapter, see the Key Terms Flashcards on your CD.

2. A speaker arguing that we should buy American products presents the following example: "I purchased a Japanese car last year. Since I purchased it, I have had nothing but trouble. I think this proves that you should buy American!" Compare this example with the tests of examples discussed in this chapter. Which of the tests does it fail to meet?

3. *Worksheet for speech topic choice.* One way to select an appropriate speech topic is to begin with an inventory of your own interests and those of your listeners as revealed by their self-introductions in class. Under each of the following headings, list at least three things that are important to you and to your audience.

	My interests	Audience interests
Hobbies	_____	_____
	_____	_____
	_____	_____
School	_____	_____
	_____	_____
Work	_____	_____
	_____	_____
Goals	_____	_____
	_____	_____

Situational factors _____

Nature of assignment _____

Time available _____

List of three possible topics _____

_____

_____

4. How would you go about verifying the "fact" that the leading causes of death in the United States are heart disease, cancer, and infectious diseases? What sources would you consult? Are these in fact the three leading causes of death?

5. Obtain a recent poll (one that appears in an article in, for example, *USA Today* or *Newsweek*). Does the poll meet the tests of statistical evidence outlined in this chapter? How large was the sample, and what was the margin of error? Did differences in the poll exceed the margin of error? What, if anything, does the article on the poll not tell you that you need to know to properly interpret the statistics in the poll?

6. How would you go about determining on what subject Arthur L. Schawlow and Charles H. Townes are experts? (Hint: They won Nobel Prizes for their discovery.)

7. Although the Internet is an invaluable source of information on almost any topic, it is also a notorious source of misinformation. As an exercise, try to locate the Web site of the Central Intelligence Agency (CIA). How many different Web sites did you find before locating the official page? How did you know when you were at the official site?

GUIDE TO SOURCE CITATIONS

American Psychological Association (APA) Style

The following information is based on the *Publication Manual of the American Psychological Association*, Fifth Edition, 2001, and on their Web site, www.apastyle.org. Please note that there are several changes in APA style from the fourth edition. Hanging indents (not tabs) are to be used in the references list, titles should be *italicized* rather than underlined, and the citation of online sources has changed. It is important that you fully document the sources of information you use in preparing a speech outline. Cite the source in parentheses in the actual body of the outline by name and date. Include page numbers for quotations or specific facts, for example, (Jones, 2001, p. 1).

Include a list of "References" at the end of your outline. Always include the author, date, title, and facts of publication. Personal communications, such as letters, phone calls, e-mail, and interviews, are cited only in the text, not the reference list; for example, J. Q. Jones (personal communication, April 1, 2001). The format varies depending on the type of work referenced.

Here are some of the most common types of works you may use in a speech. Notice that APA style does not place quotation marks around the titles of articles or book chapters. Also, titles of books and articles are not capitalized, except for the first word, the first word following a colon, and proper names. Periodical titles are capitalized. Authors are listed by last name first, followed by first and sometimes middle initials.

For more information on citing sources in APA or MLA style, go to the Online Learning Center.

Books

Single Author

Freeley, A. J. (1990). *Argumentation and debate: Critical thinking for reasoned decision making* (7th ed.). Belmont, CA: Wadsworth.

Multiple Authors

Germond, J. W., & Witcover, J. (1989). *Whose broad stripes and bright stars?* New York: Warner Books.

Corporate Author

American Psychological Association. (2001). *Publication manual of the American Psychological Association* (5th ed.). Washington, DC: Author.

Government Document

Department of Health and Human Services. (1989). *Smoking tobacco and health: A fact book.* (DHHS Publication No. CDC 87-8397). Washington, DC: U.S. Government Printing Office.

Chapter in a Book

Steeper, F. T. (1978). Public response to Gerald Ford's statements on Eastern Europe in the second debate. In

G. F. Bishop, R. G. Meadow, & M. Jackson-Beeck (Eds.), *The presidential debates: Media, electoral, and policy perspectives* (pp. 81–101). New York: Praeger.

Periodicals

Weekly Magazine

Alter, J. (1988, September 26). The expectations game. *Newsweek, 112,* 16–18.

If the author is unknown, you would list the article as follows:

The expectations game. (1988, September 26). *Newsweek, 112,* 16–18.

Scholarly Journal Divided by Volume Numbers

Vancil, D. L., & Pendell, S. D. (1984). Winning presidential debates: An analysis of criteria influencing audience response. *Western Journal of Speech Communication, 48,* 63–74.

[This means the article was published in 1984, in volume 48, on pages 63–74.]

Newspaper

Rosentiel, T. H. (1988, October 14). Minus a Dukakis home run, Bush is called winner. *Los Angeles Times,* p. A25.

If the author is unknown, you would list the article as follows:

Minus a Dukakis home run, Bush is called winner. (1988, October 14). *Los Angeles Times,* p. A25.

Pamphlet (published by author)

American Diabetes Association. (1987). *Diabetes and you.* Alexandria, VA: Author.

Internet

As computer sources multiply, the citation format has been evolving. APA guidelines ask that you include the type of medium, the necessary electronic information to permit retrieval, and then the date you accessed the information. You should consult the APA Web site at www.apastyle.org for the most recent information on how to cite Internet resources. Here are examples based on the fifth edition of the APA *Publication Manual.* If the date of the Web site is known, it goes in parentheses after the author; if unknown, use the abbreviation n.d. for no date.

Lichtblau, E., & Meyer, J. (2001, October 12). FBI warns of impending terrorist attacks. *Los Angeles Times.*

> Retrieved October 12, 2001 from http://www.latimes.com/
> news/nationworld/world/la-101201warning.story

For a Web site with no known author, list by title first:

> *An Overview of the 2000 Freshman* (2001, July 20). Retrieved
> October 11, 2001 from University of California Los
> Angeles Web Site: http://www.gseis.ucla.edu/heri/
> 00_exec_summary.htm

All references are listed in alphabetical order by authors' last names, regardless of type, at the end of the speech outline. Works listed by title, where the author is not known, are placed alphabetically by title. For an example of a reference list using APA style, see the outline in Chapter 8 on pages 208–209.

Modern Language Association (MLA) Style

This section is based on Joseph Gibaldi, *The MLA Handbook for Writers of Research Papers*, Fifth Edition, 1999. Also consult their Web site at www.mla.org. Although there are numerous similarities between APA and MLA style, there are also many differences. You may cite sources in parentheses in the actual body of the outline, as you do with APA, but you use only the author's name and the page number, not the date, for example, (Jones 1). Notice that in MLA style you do not separate the name and the page number by a comma, nor do you use the letter "p." MLA also allows you to incorporate the name of the author in your text and cite only the pages in parentheses. For example, John Jones tells us that "secondhand smoke is deadly" (1). Notice that the ending punctuation comes after the page number in this example.

Include a list of "Works Cited" at the end of your outline. Always include the author, title, facts of publication, and date. Personal communications are included in the Works Cited list, unlike in APA style. For example, an interview would be cited as follows: Jones, John Q. Personal interview. 1 Apr. 1992.

Here are some of the most common types of works you may use in a speech. Notice that MLA style does place quotation marks around the titles of articles or book chapters. Titles of books and periodicals are <u>underlined</u>, not *italicized*. Also, titles of books, articles, and periodicals are capitalized. Authors are listed by last name first, followed by full first names and sometimes middle initials. Finally, the date comes at or near the end of the citation, not right after the author's name, as in APA style.

Books

Single Author

> Freeley, Austin J. <u>Argumentation and Debate: Critical
> Thinking for Reasoned Decision Making</u>, 7th ed.
> Belmont, CA: Wadsworth, 1990.

Multiple Authors

> Germond, Jack W., and Jules Witcover. <u>Whose Broad Stripes
> and Bright Stars?</u> New York: Warner Books, 1989.

Corporate Author

American Psychological Association. <u>Publication Manual of the American Psychological Association</u>. 5th ed. Washington, DC: American Psychological Association, 2001.

Government Document

United States. Dept. of Health and Human Services. <u>Smoking Tobacco and Health: A Fact Book</u>. Washington: GPO, 1989.

Chapter in a Book

Steeper, Frederick T. "Public Response to Gerald Ford's Statements on Eastern Europe in the Second Debate." <u>The Presidential Debates: Media, Electoral, and Policy Perspectives</u>. Ed. George F. Bishop, Robert G. Meadow, and Marilyn Jackson-Beeck. New York: Praeger, 1978. 81-101.

Periodicals

Weekly Magazine

Alter, Jonathan. "The Expectations Game." <u>Newsweek</u> 26 Sep. 1988: 16-18.

If the author is unknown, you would list the article as follows:

"The Expectations Game." <u>Newsweek</u> 26 Sept. 1988: 16-18.

Scholarly Journal Divided by Volume Numbers

Vancil, David L., and Susan D. Pendell. "Winning Presidential Debates: An Analysis of Criteria Influencing Audience Response." <u>Western Journal of Speech Communication</u> 48 (1984): 63-74.

[This means the article was published in 1984, in volume 48, on pages 63–74.]

Newspaper

Rosentiel, Tom H. "Minus a Dukakis Home Run, Bush Is Called Winner." <u>Los Angeles Times</u> 14 Oct. 1988: A25.

If the author is unknown, you would list the article as follows:

"Minus a Dukakis Home Run, Bush Is Called Winner." <u>Los Angeles Times</u> 14 Oct. 1988: A25.

Pamphlet (published by author)

American Diabetes Association. <u>Diabetes and You</u>. Alexandria, VA: ADA, 1987.

Internet

MLA style for online citations is similar to that of APA, in that the online address and date accessed are included, but the rest of the citation is similar to MLA citations of other sources.

```
Lichtblau, Eric, and Josh Meyer. "FBI Warns of Impending
     Terrorist Attacks" Los Angeles Times.com 12 October
     2001. 12 October 2001 <http://www.latimes.com/news/
     nationworld/world/la-101201warning.story>
```

If there is no author, cite by the title of the Web page.

```
An Overview of the 2000 Freshman 20 July 2001. University
     of California Los Angeles Web Site 11 October 2001
     <http://www.gseis.ucla.edu/heri/00_exec_summary.htm>
```

The first date is the date of the Web page (which was obtained by viewing the page information on the browser), and the second date is the date it was accessed from the Web. The URL is placed in angle brackets < >.

As with APA, a complete list of sources—called "Works Cited"—in alphabetical order by author (if none, use title) should follow the text. If more than one work by the same author is included, replace the author's name with three hyphens (---) in all listings after the first.

NOTES

1. "Selling Green," *Consumer Reports*, October 1991, 687–692.
2. Cynthia Crossen, "Lies, Damned Lies—and 'Scientific' Studies," *Sacramento Bee*, Forum, 24 November 1991, 1–2. (Reprinted from the *Wall Street Journal*.)
3. Alice Jacobs, "Handling Religious Requests Can Be Tricky," *Sacramento Bee*, 4 September 2001, D2.
4. Crossen, "Lies, Damned Lies—and 'Scientific' Studies."
5. Robert S. Erikson and Kent L. Tedin, *American Public Opinion*, 5th ed. (Boston: Allyn & Bacon, 1994), 28.
6. Crossen, "Lies, Damned Lies—and 'Scientific' Studies."
7. Chalsey Phariss, "Lake Tahoe," speech delivered at California State University, Chico, April 18, 1998.
8. Walter R. Fisher, *Human Communication as Narration* (Columbia: University of South Carolina Press, 1987).
9. Fed Stats [http://www.fedstats.gov/, 30 September 2001].
10. Patricia McColl Bee and Walter Schneider, *Quotation Location* (Ottawa: Canadian Library Association, 1990).
11. Ronn Owens, "Ronn's New Site" [http://www.ronn.com/ronn.shtml, 20 September 2001]; and Tamim Ansary, "An Afghan-American Speaks" [http://www.ronn.com/email.html, 20 September 2001].
12. Jefferson Graham, "Straight-Shooting Google Gains Fans as Search Engine," *Sacramento Bee* (reprinted from *USA Today*), 18 September 2001, D3.
13. John A. Courtright and Elizabeth M. Perse, *The Mayfield Quick Guide to the Internet for Communication Students* (Mountain View, Calif.: Mayfield Publishing, 1998), 44–47.
14. See http://www.cnn.com/

Organization is one of the most important ingredients in successful public speaking.

Organizing Your Message

 OBJECTIVES

After reading this chapter and reviewing the learning resources on your CD-ROM and at the Online Learning Center, you should be able to:

- Develop an organizational strategy geared to your audience.
- Refine the specific purpose of your speech.
- Develop a clear thesis statement for your speech.
- Organize the body of your speech.
- Appreciate organizational patterns from diverse cultures.
- Utilize appropriate signposts to indicate transitions from one point to the next in your speech.
- Construct an effective introduction and conclusion for your speech.
- Prepare a formal outline for a speech to your class.
- Prepare and utilize speaker's notes for a speech to your class.

 KEY CONCEPTS

call and response pattern	problem–solution pattern	spiral pattern
categorical pattern	refutational pattern	star pattern
causal pattern	rhetorical question	stock issues pattern
extended narrative	spatial pattern	subpoint
formal outline	signposts	supporting point
main points	speaker's notes	time pattern
Monroe's motivated sequence		wave pattern

> *Every discourse, like a living creature, should be so put together that it has its own body and lacks neither head nor feet, middle nor extremities, all composed in such a way that they suit both each other and the whole.*
>
> —PLATO

It is easier for an audience to follow a speech when they know how it is organized.

In everyday conversation, we often speak in a random and seemingly disorganized fashion. Particularly in interpersonal conversation, one idea will trigger another, which will trigger another, and so on. We all have had the experience of wondering how we ended up talking about the latest music video when the conversation began with a question about weekend plans.

When engaged in casual conversation, we have no reason to worry about structuring our message. In fact, part of the fun of such conversations is that they are spontaneous and unpredictable. If we don't understand what someone has said, we can simply ask the person to explain what was meant. Feedback is immediate, verbal as well as nonverbal.

Unfortunately, as we move from engaging in conversation to speaking in public, such random and unpredictable speaking becomes a hindrance to effective communication. Rather than being fun, listening to the random thoughts of a disorganized speaker is frustrating. As listeners we desire structure. We want to know where speakers are going and when they get there. A stream-of-consciousness public speaker is usually an ineffective one.

In this chapter we assume that you already have a general notion of what you want to communicate in your speech. But, as Plato implied in the quotation at the beginning of this chapter, simply knowing what you want to communicate is not enough. You need to know how to structure that information for maximum effect. There are some specific things you can do organizationally to help you achieve your goals. They include developing an organizational strategy geared to your audience, refining your specific purpose, focusing on your thesis statement, organizing the body of your speech, introducing your speech, concluding your speech, communicating organization through previews and signposts, and preparing the formal outline and/or speaker's notes.

FOCUSING ON YOUR AUDIENCE

Just as with the process of researching and supporting your speech discussed in the preceding chapter, the organization of your speech should be grounded in your analysis of your speech situation in general, and your audience specifically. For example, should you put your best foot forward, so to speak, or save your best for last? A lot depends on the audience and your speech purpose. Suppose you have an audience that is either disinterested or hostile. If you save your most compelling material until the end, you are likely to lose the audience long before you have a chance to enlighten them or influence their opinion. On the other hand, if your audience already is greatly interested in your topic, you may want to build to a climax so that your best material will be fresh in their minds at the conclusion of the speech. A careful analysis of your audience is also crucial to refining your specific purpose and formulating your thesis statement.

Refining Your Specific Purpose

In Chapter 2 we defined specific purpose as a speaker's goal or objective in speaking to a particular audience. Although you will have a specific purpose in mind before you begin to construct your speech, you will need to refine your specific purpose in light of your research and your analysis of the audience. The specific purpose of a speech represents a compromise between the speaker's ideal goal and the constraints of the particular rhetorical situation. Let's suppose you know your audience is skeptical of your point of view. You may want to refine your specific purpose to a more achievable goal than your ideal. For example, if you want your audience to stop using cell phones while driving, but suspect that most audience members believe they can drive and talk at the same time, you might amend your purpose to convincing them to listen to you speak about traffic accidents in which cell phone use was a factor.

Focusing on Your Thesis Statement

Recall from Chapter 2 that a thesis statement focuses your audience's attention on the central point of your speech. Just as a photographer must clearly focus on the primary subject of a photo, you as a speaker must bring the principal thrust of your speech into clear focus for your audience. Your analysis of the audience may determine when and how you present your thesis statement.

Normally, the thesis statement comes early in the speech, right after the opening. It is frustrating to an audience not to know the central point of a speech early. However, there may be times when presenting the thesis statement early is not the best strategy. For example, in a persuasive speech, a hostile audience may tune you out as soon as they hear your position on a controversial issue. In that case, you may want to hold off stating your position until the end of the speech and instead begin with common ground. Again, audience-focused organization is a key to successful speech making.

Sometimes the thesis statement may be less specific than the specific purpose. For example, if you are dealing with a hostile audience, rather than saying, "I am speaking this afternoon to convince you that sex education needs to be part of the community's middle school curriculum," you might say, "Today's teens are becoming sexually active sooner than the generations ahead of them." You must be sensitive to your audience's attitudes, beliefs, and values in formulating a thesis statement that will both express the essence of your speech and allow the audience to give your views a fair hearing.

Once you know your specific purpose and have formulated your thesis statement, it is time to organize the body of your speech. Although you might think that the introduction should be written first, this is rarely the case. Until you have constructed the body of the speech, it is difficult to find an appropriate introduction. Also, in sifting through your ideas and the research you have done for the body of the speech, you might find something that strikes you as ideally suited to a strong introduction.

ORGANIZING THE BODY OF THE SPEECH

As Plato suggested, every speech needs parts that are "composed in such a way that they suit both each other and the whole." Thus, your speech needs not only a strong introduction and conclusion but also a well-organized body to support your thesis statement and achieve your purpose. Carefully thought-out main points, subpoints, and supporting points will provide that organization.

Main Points

main points The key ideas that support the thesis statement of a speech.

The key ideas that support the thesis statement of a speech are the **main points.** They should fully develop the thesis statement. As a result of understanding these points, your audience should be informed, persuaded, or entertained in accordance with your specific purpose. In developing your main points, keep five guidelines in mind. They are listed here and then described in more detail.

TIPS AND TACTICS   *Guidelines for Developing Your Main Points*

- Limit the number of main points.
- Focus each main point on one main idea.
- Construct main points so that they are parallel in structure.
- State main points as simply as the subject will allow.
- Give all main points equal treatment.

Number   Every speech needs to be anchored around two or more main points. (If there is only one main point, then that is, in effect, the same as your thesis statement, and what you think are subpoints are in fact the main points.) In our experience, more than five main points is too much for an audience to absorb. Three main points seems to be ideal. The audience (not to mention the speaker) usually can easily grasp three key ideas, especially if they are organized in a memorable way. As the number of points increases, each main idea tends to be devalued, and the chances of you or your audience forgetting one or more ideas tend to increase. Obviously, there can be no rule in this regard, because some topics do not fit into three neat pigeonholes. But if you find yourself with six, seven, or eight main points, your speech is likely to suffer. Either you are trying to cover too much in your speech, or what you really have are six to eight subpoints, which could be organized into fewer main points, each with two or three subpoints.

Focus   The main points should clearly relate to the thesis statement. They should fully develop the thesis statement, while not going beyond the focus of the speech. For example, if you are speaking about trends in contemporary music, your thesis statement might be "Pop music is more diverse than ever." This statement alerting your audience to your topic then could be divided into three main points:

I. Pop music is international.

II. Pop music is multicultural.

III. Pop music is multitongued.

Imagine, however, that your speech on diversity in pop music excluded a musical genre that people immediately think of as illustrative of your point, for example, hip-hop. Clearly, your thesis statement would have to account for the fact. If it didn't, you would most likely leave your audience wondering why you left out such a significant part of the pop music scene. On the other hand, suppose you decided to add another main point to the body of your speech, for example:

IV. Pop music is more profitable than ever.

Although this point is related to musical diversity, it is out of the focus suggested by the thesis statement. Thus, you need to reformulate your thesis statement, rethink your specific purpose, or drop the out-of-focus point.

Think of the thesis statement as limiting the territory covered by your speech. As you construct the body of the speech, include only those items that directly support your thesis statement. At the same time, do not allow your thesis statement to be incompletely supported. By the end of your speech, you should have fulfilled the promise of your thesis statement—no more, no less.

Each main point should focus on one main idea. For example, consider the potential confusion of this main point:

I. Today's pop music is international; the heart of the recording industry is in Los Angeles.

The first part of the statement clearly supports the thesis statement that pop music is more diverse than ever. The second concerns the fact that the recording industry is largely found in Los Angeles, California.

I. Today's pop music is international.

II. Even so, the heart of the recording industry remains in Los Angeles.

Using two separate points does not mean they are unrelated. The first and second points are related by virtue of the fact that both include Latino artists. But the two ideas expressed in the statements are clearly different.

Parallel Structure   Your main points form the essence of your speech, so they should be clear, concise, and memorable. One technique to help achieve this is to construct main points in parallel fashion. For example, which of the following versions of main points would work best for our pop music speech? Here is one version:

I. Today's pop music comes from all over the world.

II. Many cultures are represented in today's pop music.

III. The language of pop music is no longer simply English.

Or consider this version:

I. Pop music transcends the boundaries of a single nation.

II. Pop music transcends the limits of a single culture.

III. Pop music transcends the limits of a single language.

Obviously, the second example is easier to remember. The repetition of the phrase "pop music transcends the limits" in all three main points stresses the focus of this speech.

Simplicity Versus Complexity   Whereas a reader can reread anything that is complex or confusing, your audience has only a limited opportunity to process information. If you phrase your main points as complex sentences, you may lose your audience. Concise and simple language will help make the structure of your speech clear. Compare the following two examples, both of which attempt to communicate the same idea. The first example:

I. AIDS is transmitted through unprotected sexual relations, including homosexual and heterosexual encounters.

II. AIDS is transmitted when drug users, often desperate for their next fix, share dirty needles.

III. AIDS is transmitted by the exchange of blood, such as in a transfusion or between a mother and her unborn child.

The second example:

I. AIDS is transmitted through unprotected sex.

II. AIDS is transmitted through sharing of needles.

III. AIDS is transmitted by blood.

Which of the two sets of main points do you think the audience will remember? Although you will develop these main points in much more detail as you give the speech, statement of the main points should be as simple as the subject will allow.

Balance   You also should aim for balance among the main points of your speech. For example, if one main point composes two-thirds of the speech, audience members may become confused and wonder what they missed. Perhaps they will wonder why you think that one point is so much more important than the other. Or they may suspect that there is another main point you forgot to mention.

Subpoints

Subpoints are to main points what main points are to the thesis statement. A **subpoint** is an idea that supports a main point. Each main point should have at least two and no more than five subpoints. Consider, for example, our speech on diversity in pop music.

> **subpoint** An idea that supports a main point.

   I. Pop music transcends the boundaries of a single nation.   *[main point]*

     A. The pop music charts feature artists from not only the U.S. but Brazil, Canada, and France, to name a few.   *[subpoint]*

     B. The most popular recording artist in the world is from Spain.   *[subpoint]*

  II. Pop music transcends the limits of a single culture.

     A. African American and Caribbean cultures are well represented in today's pop music.

     B. Many Anglo musicians have adapted the music of their ancestral culture to the contemporary pop scene.

 III. Pop music transcends the limits of a single tongue.

     A. Ricky Martin sings in Spanish about La Vida Loca.

     B. Lil' Kim, Pink, and Christina Aguilera sing in French about Lady Marmalade.

It makes no sense to have only one subpoint under a main point. For example:

   I. Pop music transcends the boundaries of a single nation.

     A. The pop music charts feature artists from not only the U.S. but Brazil, Canada and France, to name a few.

If you wished to talk only about the United States, Brazil, Canada, and France, your main point would need to be adjusted to reflect the fact. But if a main point is not subject to division into at least two subpoints, it probably is not of sufficient merit to be a main point. Rather, it is likely to be a potential subpoint under another main point. Like main points, subpoints should be parallel in structure, simply stated, and given equal treatment.

Supporting Points

Sometimes the subpoints within your speech require further support and subdivision. Thus, you might choose supporting points for each subpoint. A **supporting point** is an idea that supports a subpoint. Returning to our example of pop music, the body of a speech might be organized as follows:

> **supporting point** An idea that supports a subpoint.

  II. Pop music transcends the limits of a single culture.   *[main point]*

     A. African American and Caribbean cultures are well represented in today's pop music.   *[subpoint]*

        1. Hip-hop music has obvious ties to African American culture.   *[supporting point]*

        2. Reggae and SKA have obvious ties to Caribbean culture.   *[supporting point]*

     B. Many Anglo musicians have adapted the music of their ancestral culture to the contemporary pop scene.

    1. Groups such as U2 and the Coors have been influenced by their Celtic roots.

    2. The lyrics of Sting are suggestive of traditional English ballads.

Each supporting point could be further subdivided, but such a detailed substructure probably would lose the audience. What's more, for a normal classroom speech, it is unlikely that you will have time to develop most points beyond this level. If a speech seems to lend itself to further substructure, ask yourself if some of your supporting points are really subpoints, as well as whether some of the subpoints might be better phrased as main points or whether you should narrow your topic further.

If you must further subdivide a supporting point, use lowercase letters in your outline as follows:

[main point]   II. Pop music transcends the limits of a single culture.

[subpoint]   A. African American and Caribbean cultures are well represented in today's pop music.

[supporting point]   1. Hip-hop music has obvious ties to African American culture.

[further support]   a. the rhythms are African American.

[further support]   b. the music fuses elements of rhythm and blues, soul, and rap.

                     2. Reggae and SKA have obvious ties to Caribbean culture.

                       a. Bob Marley continues to be popular.

                       b. as does his son Ziggy.

Patterns of Organization

There are a number of different patterns you can use to organize the body of your speech. In Chapter 2, we introduced four of those patterns. We now will add five traditional patterns of organization, for a total of nine: time, extended narrative, spatial, categorical, problem–solution, stock issues, refutational, causal, and Monroe's motivated sequence. In addition, we will introduce four nontraditional patterns common in the diverse cultures of our contemporary society: wave, spiral, star, and call and response.

time pattern A pattern of organization based on chronology or a sequence of events.

Time Many topics, especially for informative speeches, lend themselves naturally to a temporal sequence. A **time pattern** is a pattern of organization based on chronology or a sequence of events. Topics of a historical nature are likely to follow a time sequence. Suppose you were speaking about the history of the U.S. space program, as did Tom Wolfe in his book *The Right Stuff*. You might divide the speech into the following main points:

    I. The race begins in the 1950s with the launch of *Sputnik*.

   II. The U.S.S.R. puts the first men into space in the 1960s.

  III. The United States sets the goal to land on the moon by the end of the 1960s.

  IV. Neil Armstrong is the first human to land on the moon in July 1969.

Topics that deal with a process, such as how-to speeches, can frequently be ordered by a time pattern as well. You might sequence a speech on learning to ski in these terms:

I. Select the right equipment.

II. Invest in lessons.

III. Practice!

Extended Narrative   An **extended narrative** is a pattern of organization in which the entire body of the speech is the telling of a story. In Chapter 7, we introduced narrative as a form of support for a speech. As support, one main point of a speech might be a narrative, but the other main points might be in the form of statistics, expert opinions, facts, and the like. However, an extended narrative means the whole speech is one story. In this case you tell a story in sequence, with a climactic point near the end of the speech. This organizational pattern is often very useful, for example, in speeches to entertain. Thus, if you were to tell the story of your first blind date, you might pattern your speech after the following:

extended narrative A pattern of organization in which the entire body of the speech is the telling of a story.

I. I am asked to go out on a blind date.

II. I meet the date.

III. Disaster follows.

Sometimes a persuasive speech can also be built around an extended narrative of some incident that dramatizes the problem you are addressing in your speech. An example of an extended narrative in a persuasive speech might be the following:

I. Jim had too much to drink at a fraternity party.

II. His frat brothers dared him to hop a moving freight train.

III. Jim attempted to jump onto the moving train.

IV. He lost his balance and fell under the train; both of his legs were severed.

V. Jim lived and has dedicated his life to fighting alcohol abuse.

Notice that a story needs not only a plot line but also characters, including a central character with whom the audience can identify. In this particular story, the speaker would seek to create a sympathetic portrayal of Jim, who becomes the protagonist. Of course, each point would be developed in detail, and the audience should be held in suspense as the story unfolds. The moral of the story should not have to be stated explicitly but should be apparent to the audience. This is one of those speeches in which stating the thesis at the beginning would actually undermine the effectiveness of the speech. By the end of the speech, however, no one would doubt the speaker's central idea.

Spatial   A **spatial pattern** is a pattern of organization based on physical space or geography. Some topics, usually informative, lend themselves to a spatial or geographic order. Suppose you want to discuss weather patterns in the United States. You might divide your topic geographically into east, south, north, and west. If you were trying to explain how a ship is constructed, you might do so in terms of fore, midship, and aft. Or if you were giving a tour of your hometown, your points might look something like this:

spatial pattern A pattern of organization based on physical space or geography.

I. The east side is mostly residential.

II. The central part of town is the business district.

III. The west side is largely industrial.

TV meteorologists often use a spatial pattern to explain the weather.

categorical pattern A pattern of organization based on natural divisions in the subject matter.

Categorical   A **categorical pattern** is a pattern of organization based on natural divisions in the subject matter. Many topics, both informative and persuasive, naturally fall into categories. The federal government, for example, can be naturally divided into the legislative, executive, and judicial branches. The essential principle is that you divide your topic along its natural boundaries. Thus, a speech advocating solar energy might be organized as follows:

I. Fossil fuels pollute the atmosphere.

II. Nuclear energy creates radioactive wastes.

III. Solar energy is nonpolluting.

When using this pattern, however, be careful that you don't create false categories. Although it may be categorically convenient to cast people into some specific groups, for example, it also can be highly misleading or even offensive. Much social and ethnic prejudice is rooted in the stereotyping of people into arbitrary categories. All Muslims are not terrorists, for example, and all Christians are not peaceful, as the dispute in Northern Ireland sadly demonstrates.

problem–solution pattern A pattern of organization that analyzes a problem in terms of (1) harm, (2) significance, and (3) cause, and proposes a solution that is (1) described, (2) feasible, and (3) advantageous.

Problem–Solution   Sometimes we speak to propose a solution to an ongoing problem. This is frequently the case when we speak persuasively. One way to approach this type of speech is to use the **problem–solution pattern,** a pattern of organization that analyzes a problem in terms of (1) harm, (2) significance, and (3) cause, and proposes a solution that is (1) described, (2) feasible, and (3) advantageous. A specific example of this pattern might be a speech about the need for better health care. In this case, you might organize the speech in the following way:

I. Millions of Americans are denied access to adequate health care.   *[problem]*

   A. People suffer and die without this care.   *[harm]*

   B. More than 40 million Americans lack basic health insurance.   *[significance]*

   C. There is a gap between government-sponsored health care (Medicaid and Medicare) and private insurance.   *[cause]*

II. We need a program of national health insurance to fill the gap.   *[solution]*

   A. All businesses will be taxed to provide national health insurance.   *[description]*

   B. Similar programs exist in almost every other industrialized country in the world.   *[feasibility]*

   C. No longer will people be denied access to medical care simply because they cannot pay.   *[advantages]*

The relationship between harm and significance is important. Harm has to do with the bad consequences of the problem—in this case, potential suffering and death. Significance has to do with the extent of the problem. If 100 people in a nation of 250 million were at risk of suffering or death because of an inadequate health-care system, this would be unfortunate, but it would not be a significant problem relative to the population of the nation. If millions were at risk, then the problem would be significant.

You also need to recognize that there can be numerous different solutions to the same problem. Thus, it is important to stress both the feasibility and the advantages of the solution you propose, if you hope to have it adopted by your audience.

Stock Issues   Closely related to the problem–solution pattern is what is often called the **stock issues pattern,** which is well suited to persuasive speeches. This pattern is based on the model of deliberative debate, and addresses four key questions that must be answered affirmatively to support a policy proposal. For example, suppose you want to solve a parking problem on your campus. You would first want to know how serious the problem is, second, who is to blame, third, how it would be solved, and finally, whether the solution is worth the cost. These four stock issues are referred to as (1) ill, (2) blame, (3) cure, and (4) cost. In our example, your speech would have the following four main points:

> **stock issues pattern** A four-point pattern of organization that is based on (1) ill, (2) blame, (3) cure, and (4) cost.

I. The lack of parking is causing a serious problem on our campus.   *[ill]*

II. The problem exists because parking rules are not enforced, which allows many nonstudents to take up our parking spots.   *[blame]*

III. The problem can be cured by raising fines and increasing patrols.   *[cure]*

IV. The costs of the increased patrols will be paid for by higher fines.   *[cost]*

As with the problem–solution pattern, you'll need specific subpoints to show that the facts support the serious nature of the problem and that you have correctly identified the cause. The solution needs to be well thought out and explained. And you must be sure that the costs of your solution do not outweigh the benefits of solving the problem.

Refutational   Sometimes you are in a position to answer the arguments of another speaker. Perhaps you are involved in a debate. Alternatively, you may read or hear something with which you disagree. These types of persuasive speeches often call for the **refutational pattern** of organization, which involves the following steps:

> **refutational pattern** A pattern of organization that involves (1) stating the argument to be refuted, (2) stating the objection to the argument, (3) proving the objection to the argument, and (4) presenting the impact of the refutation.

I. State the argument you seek to refute.

II. State your objection to the argument.

III. Prove your objection to the argument.

IV. Present the impact of your refutation.

For example, if you wanted to refute the proposed national health insurance in the illustration of the problem–solution method, you might proceed with the following points:

[States the argument you seek to refute.]

I. The proponents of national health care say the government should control health care.

[States your objection to the argument.]

II. Government bureaucrats, not physicians or patients, will control medical choices.

[Presents proof for your objection.]

III. People from Canada, which has national health insurance, often have to come to the United States for medical care they are denied by their government-run program.

[Presents the impact of your objection.]

IV. The quality of American health care will decline in a program run by government bureaucrats.

causal pattern A pattern of organization that moves from cause to effect or from effect to cause.

Causal   The **causal pattern** is a pattern of organization that moves from cause to effect or from effect to cause. It is often useful in persuasive presentations. In cause-to-effect speeches, you are dealing with some known activity and showing your audience that it will produce certain effects. If these are desirable effects, you would be endorsing the activity. If they are undesirable, you would be suggesting that your audience avoid the activity. To illustrate this organizational pattern, suppose you wanted to convince your audience to quit smoking:

[Cause]

I. Cigarette smoke contains a number of harmful chemicals.

    A. Carbon monoxide reduces the body's ability to absorb oxygen.

    B. Nicotine is an addictive substance.

    C. Tar is made up of thousands of chemicals.

[Effect]

II. Cigarette smoking leads to significant health problems.

    A. Carbon monoxide has been linked to low-birth-weight babies.

    B. Nicotine makes quitting smoking difficult.

    C. Tar is the principal source of cancer-causing chemicals in tobacco.

On the other hand, if you wanted to convince your audience of the need to reduce the power of special interests in Washington, you might argue from various effects back to finding the cause:

[Effect]

I. The country is in economic trouble.

    A. Real wages are declining.

    B. Many industries are moving overseas.

    C. Our trade deficit is growing.

[Cause]

II. We have a system of government that is too tied to special interests.

    A. Lobbyists influence Congress to make bad economic decisions.

    B. Politicians are more interested in getting reelected than in solving problems.

C. Only by breaking the power of special interests can we get our economy back on track.

Whether you move from cause to effect or from effect to cause, you need to provide proof of the causal links asserted in your speech. Simply because two things occur one after the other does not prove one caused the other. For example, just because a car breaks down doesn't mean the last person to drive it is responsible for the breakdown.

Monroe's Motivated Sequence   A five-step organizational scheme developed by speech professor Alan Monroe, and thus termed **Monroe's motivated sequence,** is another pattern by which a speech can be structured.[1] These five steps overlap somewhat with the introduction and conclusion of a speech, as well as the body. They are as follows:

> **Monroe's motivated sequence** A five-step organizational scheme, developed by speech professor Alan Monroe, including (1) attention, (2) need, (3) satisfaction, (4) visualization, and (5) action.

I. *Attention:* Gain your audience's attention.   *[Introduction]*

II. *Need:* Show the audience that a need exists that affects them.   *[Body]*

III. *Satisfaction:* Present the solution to the need.   *[Body]*

IV. *Visualization:* Help the audience imagine how their need will be met in the future.   *[Body]*

V. *Action:* State what actions must be taken to fulfill the need.   *[Conclusion]*

To see how this motivated sequence might work, consider the earlier example concerning national health insurance:

I. *Attention:* A child dies when her parents can't afford to take her to the doctor.

II. *Need:* You could become one of millions of uninsured Americans who face financial ruin if they become seriously ill.

III. *Satisfaction:* National health insurance would guarantee all Americans the right to health care, regardless of their income.

IV. *Visualization:* The United States would join nations like Canada, where no one fears seeing a doctor because of the cost.

V. *Action:* Write your senator and representative today, urging the passage of national health insurance.

Obviously, the motivated-sequence pattern is most directly suited to persuasive presentations. However, an informative presentation could use at least some of these steps, because informative speaking typically is the first step in a persuasive campaign. In an informative presentation, it is important to show your audience why they need to learn the information you have presented and, of course, to satisfy that need. Helping an audience visualize how they will use the information is also valuable. And often you will then want them to put what they have learned into action.

These nine patterns of organization are primarily linear in nature and are well suited to audiences rooted in a Western European tradition. However, as the box "Organization and Culture" shows, there are other organizational patterns that are well suited to other cultures. We briefly discuss four of these patterns: wave, spiral, star, and call and response.

In constructing the body of your speech, choose one of the basic patterns of organization. As a reminder, we list them here.

Organization and Culture

Not all cultures and groups within a larger culture prefer the kind of linear organization patterns commonly discussed in public speaking classes. Cheryl Jorgensen-Earp has suggested that women and some ethnic speakers use less linear, more organic patterns. For example, one pattern found in the speeches of many women and African Americans is the **wave.** Much like a wave cresting, receding, and then cresting again, a speech following this pattern continually returns to the basic theme, repeating a phrase again and again throughout the speech. Perhaps the most familiar example is Dr. Martin Luther King, Jr.'s "I Have a Dream" speech, which gets its title from the constant repetition of the phrase. In addition, King uses the theme "Let freedom ring" repeatedly as he brings the speech to its dramatic conclusion.

Other patterns suggested by Jorgensen-Earp include a **spiral** pattern, which repeats points as does the wave, but with each point growing in intensity as the speech builds to its pinnacle at the conclusion. A third pattern she suggests is the **star,** in which all of the points of the star are of equal importance. Thus a speaker can present the points in any order in support of the common theme that encircles the star and holds the speech together.

A fourth pattern is the **call and response.** In this pattern, commonly found in African American churches, a call by the speaker is followed by a response from the audience. For example, the preacher might say, "Sinners repent, the day is at hand," and the congregation would respond, "Amen." Or the speaker might ask a real question, to which an audience response is expected. For example, a labor leader might ask, "What do we want?" to which the audience responds, "Jobs." "When do we want them?" "Now." Not only may a speech be organized around the call and response pattern, even speeches organized in another fashion can use this technique as a stylistic device to heighten audience involvement.

As a speaker, you should carefully consider both your audience's cultural background as it affects their organizational preferences and your own cultural affinity for certain patterns of organization. Although cultural diversity provides the opportunity to expand the ways in which speeches may be organized, it should not be used as an excuse for a lack of any coherent organizational pattern.

Source: The first three of these patterns are cited in Clella Jaffe, *Public Speaking: A Cultural Perspective* (Belmont, Calif.: Wadsworth, 1995), pp. 187–192. They are based on a telephone interview by Jaffe with Jorgensen-Earp, as well as the latter's unpublished works.

TIPS AND TACTICS *Patterns of Speech Organization*

call and response pattern A pattern of organization in which a call by the speaker is followed by a response from the audience.

spiral pattern A pattern of organization that employs repetition of points, with the points growing in intensity as the speech builds to its conclusion.

Time	Causal
Extended narrative	Monroe's motivated sequence
Spatial	Wave
Categorical	Spiral
Problem–solution	Star
Stock issues	Call and response
Refutational	

When constructing your speech, try to avoid mixing types of patterns. It is confusing to an audience to begin listening to a time sequence and then find themselves in the middle of a problem–solution speech.

Signposts

signposts Transitional statements that bridge main points.

In addition to constructing the actual body of the speech, it is important for you to help your audience follow your pattern of organization. A useful way to do so is through the use of signposts. As Chapter 2 explained, **signposts** are transitional statements that bridge your main points. They tell your audience where you have been and where you are going in your speech. By telling listeners where you are in the speech, signposts help those who have become lost or inattentive to pick up the thread of your speech.

Signposts tell your audience you are about to make or already have made a shift in direction. Signposts also serve to verbally link your thoughts as you speak. It's always a good idea to let your audience know that there is a sequence to your message—"Let's consider three important issues"—and then to remind your audience where you are in that sequence—"Having covered the first issue, let's now look at the second."

For example, if you want to add a point, use words or phrases such as *furthermore*, *in addition to*, and *besides*. To emphasize something, phrases such as *above all*, *indeed*, and *most important* are useful. To emphasize time, try words such as *then*, *afterwards*, *eventually*, *next*, *immediately*, *meanwhile*, *previously*, *often*, *usually*, and *later*. Cause and effect can be suggested by the words *consequently*, *therefore*, and *thus*. To stress that you are using an example, simply say, "for example" or "for instance." The progress from one point to another in your speech can be highlighted by terms such as *first*, *second*, *third*, or *furthermore*. Contrast can be indicated by use of words like *but*, *however*, *instead*, *nevertheless* and phrases such as *to the contrary*, *on the other hand*, and *in contrast*. The conclusion of a speech can be indicated by phrases such as *to sum up*, *for these reasons*, *in retrospect*, and *in conclusion*.[2]

star pattern A pattern of organization in which all of the points are of equal importance and can be presented in any order to support the common theme.

wave pattern A pattern of organization in which the basic theme, often represented by a phrase, is repeated again and again, much like a wave cresting, receding, and then cresting again.

Techniques for Signposting   **TIPS AND TACTICS**

- *Refer to preceding and upcoming ideas*. "Now that you know what computer viruses are, I'll discuss how to prevent their spread to your computer."

- *Enumerate key points*. If you number your points in the preview, stick with that numbering plan in the signposts. For example: "First, never assume that a program from a friend or computer bulletin board is virus free."

- *Give nonverbal reinforcement*. Changes in vocal inflection signal a change is coming. Movement can signal a signpost: Some speakers physically move from one place to another while speaking in order to emphasize that they are moving from one point to the next. Others hold up fingers to indicate number of points.

- *Use visual aids to reinforce signposts*. Moving to your next PowerPoint slide or putting up a new transparency clearly signals to your audience that you are moving on. It's also a way to help you remember the sequence of your speech.

- *Use words that cue your audience that you are changing points*. Words and phrases like the following suggest a signpost: *next*, *another*, *number*, *moving on*, *finally*, *therefore*, and *in summary*.

It's also a good idea to let your audience know that your speech is close to the end by using transitional words and phrases such as *finally*, *in sum*, *in conclusion*, and *to close*. Far too many times we've watched audiences guess whether they're hearing the end of the speech; the sign of their uncertainty is premature clapping.

After organizing the body of the speech, you can begin to construct your introduction and conclusion.

INTRODUCING YOUR SPEECH

You may recall from Chapter 2 that an introduction should do four things: open with impact, focus on the thesis statement, connect with the audience, and preview the rest of your speech. Let's look at each of these functions in turn.

Open With Impact

A speech should immediately grab the audience's attention. Within a few seconds, we begin forming impressions of others who come into our view. When you are speaking, your audience will form an immediate impression of you. One way to control this impression is to open your speech with impact. Of the numerous ways to do this, some of the most common are a story; a quotation; a startling statement; a reference to the audience, the occasion, or a current event; appropriate humor; a personal experience; or a thought-provoking question.

Story   A brief story, real or hypothetical, is often a good way to begin your speech. For example, a student in one of our classes began her speech by describing the strange behavior of a person who was staggering and incoherent, and who finally collapsed. The quick conclusion most of her audience drew as she was describing the person was that he was drunk. Not only was this conclusion wrong, the truth startled the class. The person had diabetes and was suffering from insulin shock. Needless to say, the class became far more interested in hearing the speech about diabetes than if the speaker had simply begun, "Today I'm going to tell you about diabetes."

Quotation   As we pointed out in Chapter 7, there are numerous anthologies of quotations, usually organized by topic. If you are having trouble deciding how to begin your speech, consider looking for a quotation that will captivate your audience and reinforce your main ideas.

Startling Statement   Humans are attracted naturally to surprising, startling, and unusual events. If you can tie the introduction of your speech to a surprising or startling statement, you will be assured of your audience's undivided attention. For example, we had a student in class who began her speech by announcing that her sister had died of toxic shock syndrome, which was the subject of the speech. Needless to say, her audience was startled and paid rapt attention to the speech that followed.

Reference to the Audience, Occasion, or Current Events   Professional speakers often tailor their speeches to a specific audience and situation, saying such things as "I'm so happy to be here at [fill in the blank] college" or "I join with you in praising your football team's come-from-behind victory last night."

Another possibility is to refer to a previous speaker. Consider an instance in one class when two students chose to speak on gun control, each taking the opposite side of the topic. The second speaker wisely incorporated a reference to the prior speech into her introduction. To ignore a speech on the same topic, particularly one at odds with your own speech, is likely to turn off an audience. Without attempting to refute the other speaker, she acknowledged those opposing views but also stated that she would present the other side of the issue.

Finally, current events often spark interest and controversy. If you are speaking on a topic of current interest, it is often a good idea to lead off with the most recent happenings. If you are speaking on alcohol abuse and a student at your school had recently died of alcohol poisoning, that would be an appropriate place to begin your speech.

Appropriate Humor   A classic *Far Side* cartoon shows Abraham Lincoln delivering the Gettysburg Address. His speech, however, begins with a joke, "And so the bartender says, 'Hey! That's not a duck!'" After a pause for laughter, Lincoln continues, "Fourscore and seven years ago . . . ."

Obviously, one would not begin a serious speech such as the Gettysburg Address with a joke. Humor, if not used properly, can backfire. It is best used on occasions when the audience will find it appropriate. An after-dinner speech, for example, is frequently an opportunity to employ humor.

However you use it, though, humor should be tied to the substance of your speech. Telling an irrelevant joke can detract from the main idea of your speech, rather than enhance it. It can also make you look foolish.

Finally, you need to be sensitive with regard to humor. Ethnic, sexist, and off-color jokes, for example, can get a speaker into justifiable trouble. The reputation of golfer Fuzzy Zoeller was deservedly damaged when he made a racially insensitive remark about the food preferences of golfer Tiger Woods after he won the Master's Tournament in 1997. Speakers need to err on the side of caution when they treat sensitive subjects with humor.

Writing humor is not as easy as it seems. Thus, we asked for the advice of an Emmy- and Golden Globe–winning professional comedy writer for shows such as *Murphy Brown, Cybill,* and *Becker.* You'll find his advice in the box "On Writing Comedy: Russ Woody."

Personal Experience   Often there is no other more compelling testimony on a topic than your own personal experience. Not only can a personal experience draw in your audience and get their attention, it also can serve to build your own credibility. For example, the speaker on diabetes referred to earlier had a brother who was diabetic. However, she did not mention this fact until she had finished her speech. Had she begun with her own experiences with a diabetic brother, she would have enhanced her credibility for the remainder of the speech.

Thought-Provoking Question   Sometimes you can use a question to open your speech. A **rhetorical question** is one that the audience isn't expected to answer out loud. For example, one student began a speech on secondhand smoke this way: "How many of you have ever returned home smelling as though you were a stand-in for the Marlboro Man?"[3] The attention-getting language worked well. However, beginning with a question can be ineffective if the question is not thought provoking. For example, beginning a speech with "How many of you would like to learn to snow ski?" isn't likely to have much impact

rhetorical question A question that the audience isn't expected to answer out loud.

On Writing Comedy: *Russ Woody*

As a college student, Russ Woody excelled in an event called "Speech to Entertain." Not only was humor Russ's hobby, it became his profession. Russ began his writing career at MTM productions, where he wrote episodes for shows such as *Newhart, St. Elsewhere,* and *Hill Street Blues.* For two years he was a producer and writer for *Murphy Brown,* for which he received an Emmy in 1990. He received a Golden Globe as co-executive producer of *Cybill.* He has also served as a consulting producer for *Foxworthy,* and is co-executive producer of *Becker,* currently airing on CBS. He is also working on a pilot called *Berkeley* for TriStar and writing a novel. We asked Russ to do the impossible: explain writing humor in 250 words or less. Here is the result.

WRITING HUMOR?
by Russ Woody

Two-hundred fifty words on how to write humor? Gee, can't I just whack myself in the forehead with a ball peen hammer? Trying to explain humor is a little like trying to wrest a ripe banana from an immense and bitter gorilla. If not handled correctly, you can end up looking rather foolish.

With that in mind, "Hello, Mr. Gorilla . . ."

The fact of the matter is, humor is more difficult to write than drama. Because, while both humor and drama rely heavily on emotional content, humor is much more difficult to break down mechanically. Therefore it's more difficult to construct initially. It's relatively easy to figure out what makes a person sad or angry or uneasy or embarrassed or happy. Yet it is, for the most part, difficult to say why a person laughs.

So I guess the first thing you've got to do is figure out what type of humor appeals most to you. Monty Python, Andrew "Dice" Clay, The Naked Gun, Murphy Brown, Full House, Spy Magazine, Mad Magazine, Saturday Night Live. Whichever it is, find it. Then—study it. Watch it, read it, take it apart, figure out how it's constructed, how it's set up, how it pays off—figure out the dynamics of humor. (Which will make it terribly unfunny when you do, but that's the perpetual hell comedy writers live in.)

For instance—one of my favorite jokes of all time is in one of the Pink Panther movies where Peter Sellers goes into a hotel and approaches a man at the desk who has a dog sitting beside him. Sellers says, "Does your dog bite?" The guy says no. So Sellers reaches over to pat the little pooch, and it tries to rip his arm off. Sellers then looks to the guy and says, "I thought you said your dog didn't bite?" The guy says, "It's not my dog."

I love that joke because every element of it is real, and nobody involved thinks it's funny. The man was quite correct in his literal interpretation of Sellers's question. Sellers is more than a little annoyed at the man for misunderstanding what seemed to be a logical and straightforward question. And the dog is just pissed off. In a more general sense, one person becomes a victim because the other is a stickler for precise wording. It is extreme focus on one character's part and vulnerability on the other character's part. In a way, it's like the movie The In-Laws, with Peter Falk and Alan Arkin. Falk is intensely focused on his job with the government, which, in turn makes Arkin's life a living hell. (If you've seen the movie, you know what I'm talking about—if you haven't, go see it, because I'm coming up on two-fifty pretty fast here, so I can't get into it.)

When you've taken enough jokes and stories apart, you may start to get an idea of how to construct your own. That's when it gets really tough. Just be sure you always remember the one, underlying key to writing humor—oops, outta time.

on your audience. Also, with rhetorical questions, audiences are sometimes unsure whether the question is meant to be answered out loud. On the other hand, we have seen speakers who effectively begin their speeches by asking audience members to respond to a series of questions with a show of hands. Questions, rhetorical or real, should be used only if they add impact to the opening of the speech.

Focus on the Thesis Statement

The central idea you want to convey to an audience should be captured by your thesis statement. Although you should have developed a thesis statement before writing the body of the speech, now is a good time to reflect on its phrasing. Have you really focused on the essential theme of your speech? Be sure your thesis statement is broad enough to incorporate all of your main points. At the same time, do not make your thesis statement so broad that your speech seems to leave something out.

As noted earlier, there may be situations, such as with a hostile audience, when you will not be ready to explicitly state your thesis early in the speech. In the introduction in these situations, indicate the general topic area of the speech, focusing on an area of common agreement, rather than the thesis, if it might provoke a defensive or hostile reaction from the audience. The thesis would then emerge toward the end of the speech, after you had made your case.

Connect With Your Audience

No speech should be constructed without asking yourself, "What's in it for the audience? What needs or desires will be fulfilled by listening to my speech?" The introduction is an opportunity to make the link between your speech topic and audience members. If you make this link in your introduction, you are much more likely to gain your audience's collective ear.

The introduction is another opportunity to build your credibility. Link your topic not only to your audience but to yourself as well, stressing your similarity to the audience. The student who spoke on toxic shock syndrome used her family's tragedy to stress that the same thing could happen to any woman. She not only made a connection with her classmates, she established her personal credibility by virtue of her experience and her subsequent research on the topic.

Although connecting with the audience is an important part of the introduction to your speech, the connection should not be made only once. In fact, throughout your speech you should draw a connection between your message and your audience whenever possible.

Preview Your Speech

Although no one knows who first said, "Tell 'em what you're going to tell 'em; tell 'em; and then tell 'em what you told 'em," it is a saying with more than a grain of truth. As we noted in Chapter 2, a *preview* is a forecast of the main points of a speech. It simply tells your audience members what they are going to hear. In many ways, it is a summary before the fact. By telling audience members what will follow, a preview helps them put your statements into a coherent frame of reference.

The way to preview a speech is rather simple: Cue the audience to the fact that you are previewing the main points of your speech, and then state the points in the same sequence they will be presented. A brief preview might be "In today's speech, I would like to share the definition, transmission, and prevention of computer viruses." Or you may want to enumerate your main points, saying, "Today, I want to first define computer viruses; second, explain how they are transmitted; and third, offer a way to prevent them from infecting your own computer."

THE WIZARD OF ID   **Brant parker and Johnny hart**

By permission of Johnny Hart and Creator's Syndicate, Inc.

It is not always necessary, however, to be so explicit. There are often subtler ways of previewing your speech. For example, "All computer owners need to know what computer viruses are, how they are transmitted, and how to detect and prevent them."

CONCLUDING YOUR SPEECH

The conclusion of a speech should be brief and memorable. The last thing an audience wants to hear after "In conclusion . . ." is a 10-minute dissertation on some new aspect of the topic. When you say those magic words "in conclusion" or "to wrap up," be prepared to conclude. Avoid introducing points that were not covered in the body of the speech. If you have another main point to cover, then it belongs in the body of the speech, not the conclusion. There are, consequently, only two basic things to do in concluding your speech: summarize and close with impact.

Summarize

Tell the audience, very briefly, what you have told them in the speech. This is where clear, concisely developed main points pay off. Going back to an earlier example, you might conclude your speech, "We have seen, therefore, that pop music is international, multicultural, and multitongued." Sometimes you may wish to explicitly number the main points in your summary. For example, "Remember there are three types of bikes you'll see on campus. First, there are cruisers; second, there are mountain bikes; and third, there are touring bikes."

Close With Impact

The final words of your speech should be memorable. The close is your last chance to make an impression on your audience. As with the opening, it should be relevant to the main thesis of your speech. A few of the common techniques for closing are a short, memorable quotation, an anecdote or a brief story, a direct appeal to action, and a return to your opening theme. If you have delayed presenting your thesis statement for strategic reasons, it should be incorporated

George Clooney utilizes a direct appeal to action when seeking donations for the September 11th Fund.

just prior to this point (right after the summary). If you stated the thesis earlier, it should be reiterated here.

Quotation   The same principles apply to a closing quotation as to an opening one. You want to capture the essence of your talk in a few words. If someone has said it better than you, then it is perfectly appropriate to quote that person. In the conclusion, it probably is best to state who you are quoting and then state the quotation. For example, it is less effective to say, "'I have a dream,' said Martin Luther King, Jr.," than to say, "As Martin Luther King, Jr., once stated, 'I have a dream.'"

Anecdote   The key in the closing is to be brief and to the point. A long, drawn-out story will undermine the effectiveness of the rest of your speech. A concluding anecdote should highlight your main focus, not detract from it. As with opening stories, such anecdotes can be real or hypothetical but should be clearly identified as such to your audience.

Direct Appeal to Action   Concluding with an appeal to action is typical of a persuasive speech and is an explicit part of the motivated sequence. It involves telling your audience members specifically what they can do to fulfill their needs or solve a problem—for example, sign a petition, write to Congress, or change their own behavior. A direct appeal to your audience is often the most appropriate way to conclude a persuasive presentation.

Return to Opening   One of the most effective ways to close a speech is to return to where you began. Not only does this remind the audience of your introduction, it also gives your speech a sense of closure. It takes both you and your audience full circle. For example, the speech that began by describing a person suffering from insulin shock ended by telling the audience that they would now know how to recognize when someone was in insulin shock and would be able to get that person the help he or she needed. If you can find a way to tie your opening and closing together, you can intensify the impact of both.

PREPARING THE FORMAL OUTLINE

Once you have a rough structure of your speech, including the body, introduction, and conclusion, your instructor may recommend that you prepare a formal outline of the speech. A **formal outline** is a detailed outline used in speech preparation but not, in most cases, in the actual presentation. Usually, such an outline should be typed or prepared on a computer, depending on your instructor's requirements. Such outlines help you put your ideas down in a clear and organized fashion. If submitted in advance of a speech, it also allows instructors to give you feedback and make suggestions.

There are two basic types of outlines. *Phrase* or *key word outlines* are meaningful to the speaker but probably would not make a lot of sense to anyone else. For example, a speaker might prepare the following outline for her own use:

Intro: Tell story
    I. Rock music
    II. Volume
    III. Deafness
Conclusion: Same story 10 years later

Because this outline probably would make sense only to the speaker, beginning speakers are frequently expected to prepare a *full-sentence outline*. In this type of outline, you include a full statement indicating what each main point and subpoint cover. All the parts of the speech are included, even signposts. Generally, a formal outline should include the following:

- Your specific purpose, phrased as an infinitive phrase (to . . .), describing exactly what you want your speech to accomplish.
- Three sections—labeled introduction, body, and conclusion—each separately outlined and beginning with the Roman numeral "I."

  The introduction, including your opening, focus on thesis statement, connection with the audience, and preview.

  The body, including main points, subpoints, supporting points, and further support, and, if your instructor requires them, signposts (in parentheses) between the main points.

  The conclusion, including a summary and a close.

- A bibliography of "References" or "Works Cited" (depending on whether you use APA or MLA style). Specific quotations or facts drawn from a source, as discussed in Chapter 7, should also be cited in the main outline. Of course, you should check with your instructor about the specific outlining requirements, if any, for your class. Some instructors prefer a different source citation system, for example, than the ones discussed in Chapter 7.

Outlines typically use a standard outline notation, which indicates the levels of subordination of points:

I. Main point
  A. Subpoint
    1. Supporting point
      a. Further support

Any subdivision should include at least two matching points. Thus, if you have an "A" subpoint under a main point, there should also be at least a "B." Supporting point "1" should be matched by at least a "2," and further support "a" should be followed by at least a "b."

Many instructors prefer that outlines be written in complete sentences, at least through the level of subpoints. This provides a clearer idea to both you and your instructor of what you are going to say. Divide separate ideas into different sentences. If you outline using paragraph form, what you really have is an essay with outline notation scattered throughout. Thus, the following is not really in outline form:

I. The first men on the moon were Americans. Neil Armstrong stepped out first. He was followed by Buzz Aldrin. At the same time, Michael Collins orbited the moon.

This paragraph could be turned into the following outline:

I. The first men on the moon were Americans.
  A. Neil Armstrong stepped out first.
  B. He was followed by Buzz Aldrin.
  C. At the same time, Michael Collins orbited the moon.

Notice how each sentence is placed in a separate point. The more general statement is the main point, and the specific instances are subpoints.

Some aspects of an outline do not need to be in complete-sentence form. For example, a speaker who wants to list the components of a larger whole, such as ingredients or tools, could use an outline like this:

  1. Cigarette smoke has three components:
    a. carbon monoxide
    b. nicotine
    c. tar

You need to use judgment, therefore, when you are asked to write a complete-sentence outline. Use complete sentences for your main points and subpoints and anywhere the meaning would not be clear if not expressed in complete-sentence form. The box "Sample Speech Outline: Accident or Suicide: Driving Without a Seatbelt by Karen Shirk" follows the suggested format. Remember, however, to check with your instructor for specific requirements in your class.

PREPARING SPEAKER'S NOTES

Of course, the outline is a preparation tool. When you are presenting a speech, we recommend that you use **speaker's notes,** which are brief notes with key words, usually written on cards. Your final notes should be meaningful to you as

SPEECH COACH

To see this speech, go to segment 8.1 on your CD.

speaker's notes Brief notes with key words, usually written on cards, used by a speaker when presenting a speech.

Sample Speech Outline

Title of speech.

ACCIDENT OR SUICIDE: DRIVING WITHOUT A SEATBELT
by Karen Shirk

Specific purpose is to motivate audience to do what they know is right.

Specific Purpose: To persuade my audience to wear their seatbelts.

Introduction

Speaker begins with startling statements and visual aids of actual objects that survived a crash.

I. **Open With Impact:** This may be recognized as a piece of a brake light, but to me, it is a piece of brake light from my mother's car. This may be recognized as a CD-player face, but to me, it's the only thing left from an accident that happened earlier this year.

    A. Many times I have seen people getting in cars and driving away without a seatbelt on.

    B. This concerns me because I know how quickly a little drive can turn into a big accident.

    C. It doesn't matter if you are an expert driver, your safety is put into other people's hands, whether you're the passenger or the driver.

Thesis statement and connect with audience are clearly labeled.

II. **Focus on Thesis Statement:** It's important to take what little control you have on the road and utilize it.

III. **Connect With the Audience:** That's why it's so important to wear your seatbelt.

Preview of speech is provided.

IV. **Preview:** Today I will discuss the importance of seatbelts, the benefits of wearing a seatbelt, why some people still aren't wearing seatbelts, and some ways to remind you to strap on your seatbelt.

Body

Body of speech is labeled.

Main points begin with Roman numeral I.

I. **Main Point:** Putting on your seatbelt may be the most important part of driving.

    A. After all, a seatbelt is defined as "an arrangement of straps designated to hold a person steady in a seat" (*Merriam-Webster's*, 1993, p. 1054).

Direct quotations are indicated by quotation marks and source is cited in parentheses. Your instructor may prefer a different method of citing sources.

    B. And, as Dr. Haddon says, "I would challenge those of you who do not use them to consider that . . . as persons sending something through the mail you would not ship things loose in an empty barrel to flop around with the barrel moving at high speed" (Haddon, 1968, p. 13).

    C. As an example, consider Barbie, who doesn't bother putting on her seatbelt (show overheads).

Speaker includes note to self to turn on overhead projector.

    D. Some important points to remember about seatbelts as listed online are:

        1. First, an adult can only hold back the weight of his body by the arms and legs at speeds of up to 7 kilometers per hour (*The seatbelt—a link with life*, 1998).

        2. Second, in a collision at 50 kilometers per hour, the force is the same as falling 10 meters.

Signposts are transitional statements between main points.

(**Signpost:** Now that you've been reminded of the importance of seatbelts, let's discuss how a seatbelt can benefit you.)

II. **Main Point:** A seatbelt can save you from serious or even fatal injury.

    A. First, if the vehicle you're in is rear-ended, a seatbelt will hold you from flying through the windshield.

    B. Second, if your vehicle rolls or flips, the seatbelt will keep you from banging into the sides and roof of the car.

C. And third, it can keep you from getting a hefty fine from the highway patrol.

(**Signpost:** Now that we've discussed the benefits, let's try to analyze why some people still aren't wearing seatbelts.)

III. **Main Point:** There could be several reasons why some people still aren't wearing seatbelts, although none of them serves as a valid excuse.
   A. One reason could be laziness.
   B. Another reason could be forgetfulness.
   C. One reason might be confidence.
   D. Some people are afraid that a seatbelt will trap them in the event of an accident.
   E. Finally, I've overheard someone say that wearing a seatbelt would wrinkle their clothes.

(**Signpost:** Basically, there's no excuse. But, instead of verbally abusing unsafe drivers, it's better to suggest a few solutions to remind yourself to strap on your seatbelt.)

IV. **Main Point:** These solutions are simple and don't require too much effort, considering the benefits involved.
   A. Make putting on your seatbelt the first thing you do upon entering a vehicle.
   B. Get into the habit of having it on.
   C. Wear it no matter how far you're driving—no exceptions.

Conclusion

I. **Summarize:** Today I've discussed seatbelts and the safety they offer.

Conclusion begins with a summary of main points.

   A. I've reinforced the importance of wearing a seatbelt.
   B. I've listed some of the immediate benefits of wearing a seatbelt.
   C. I've tried to explain some reasons why others may not wear a seatbelt.
   D. And I've tried to offer some useful suggestions on how to increase your control on the road by wearing a seatbelt.

II. **Close With Impact:** It shouldn't be necessary to have to persuade you to wear a seatbelt.

Speech closes with impact. Ask yourself if it matches the impact with which the speech opened.

   A. But, as seen in the numerous fatalities each year in cases where someone wasn't wearing theirs, sometimes the message doesn't get through.
   B. I hope I've reinforced that message enough so that you might think twice before driving unbuckled.
   C. That way, if you're ever in an accident, your chances are much higher that you'll walk away unharmed.

References

Haddon, W. (1968). The national highway safety program—18 months later. In J. O'Day (Ed.), *Driver behavior: Cause and effect*. Washington, DC: Insurance Institute for Highway Safety.

The seatbelt—a link with life. (1998). [Online]. Available: http://www.lycos.com/wguide/wire/wire_969214_2_0.html [1998, April 3].

Merriam-Webster's collegiate dictionary (10th ed.). (1993). Springfield, MA: Merriam-Webster.

Speaker lists references at end of speech with full bibliographic citation. We discuss American Psychological Association (APA) and Modern Language Association (MLA) methods of source citation in Chapter 7. Your instructor may prefer a different method of citing sources. Whatever method is used, accurate source citation is important.

Notice how this speaker has used highlighting to emphasize key points on these note cards.

a speaker, but not necessarily to anyone else. However, you should rehearse until you don't need to look at the note cards frequently. It is especially important to know your introduction and conclusion very well. The best open or close to a speech can be undone by a speaker who reads it from cards, rather than making direct eye contact with the audience.

Cards about 4 by 6 inches in size seem to work best. Larger cards are too obtrusive; smaller cards require you to strain to see your notes and to constantly be shuffling cards. The following are some helpful hints for preparing note cards.

TIPS AND TACTICS   *Tips for Preparing Note Cards*

- *Use bright colors and large, bold lettering.* This will make your notes easier to see.
- *Use no more than five or six lines per note card.* If you cram too much on one card, you'll end up confusing yourself.
- *Put each part of a speech on a separate card.* For example, your introduction might go on one card, the body on another, and the conclusion on a third.
- *Number your cards.* It is easy to lose track of your place while speaking. One way to help prevent this from happening is to number each card.
- *Write on only one side of a card.* If you write on both sides, you compound the chances of losing your place.
- *Highlight main ideas.* Just as you highlight key passages in books, highlight the points you wish to emphasize.
- *Use note cards to make comments to yourself.* It is perfectly appropriate, for example, to write prompts to yourself on your notes. For example, you might

write "O.H." to remind yourself to show an overhead at that point in your speech.

- *Don't try to write out your speech word for word.* This will only encourage you to read your speech, rather than present it in a conversational manner. The only exception to this rule would be exact quotations, facts, or statistics, which obviously you need to write out.

Speaker's notes contain all the same ideas as the complete outline, but the words are designed to cue you to what comes next. Only with practice can you speak from these notes and still be assured of covering all the ideas in the original outline. And this is the final point we wish to make: Successful speakers practice prior to an actual presentation. No matter how good your organization seems, it is only as good as your ability to deliver it. That takes practice. And practice doesn't mean running through your speech the night before or, even worse, the morning of your presentation. It means devoting significant amounts of time to practicing your speech until you have internalized its basic organization.

OVERHEAD TRANSPARENCIES OR POWERPOINT SLIDES

Finally, you also can use overhead transparencies or PowerPoint slides to guide you through your speech. Instead of note cards, you record the main points of your speech on transparencies, or list them on your slides, and use them as prompts. You may also want to record subpoints that support the main points. As was the case with note cards, you do not want to outline your entire speech on overheads or slides. Only the skeletal features of your speech should be included. Although we'll have more to say about using overheads and Power-Point slides in Chapter 11, here are some tips for making them and using them as prompts.

Preparing Overhead Transparencies and PowerPoint Slides as Prompts   **TIPS AND TACTICS**

- Dedicate one transparency or slide to previewing your main points.
- Use one transparency or slide for each main point and, possibly, supporting subpoints if their number is few.
- Follow the guidelines beginning on page 290 in Chapter 11 for preparing and using overhead transparencies effectively.

SUMMARY

To effectively organize your speech you should first:

- Focus on your audience when organizing your speech.
- Refine the specific purpose.
- Create a clear thesis statement.

 **SPEECH COACH**

To evaluate your understanding of this chapter, see the Quizzes on your CD.

Organize the body of the speech before tackling the introduction or conclusion. Remember that:

- Two to five focused main points should fully develop the thesis statement.
- Use parallel structure, simplicity, and balance.
- Develop main points by using subpoints, supporting points, and further support.

Organize the speech body in one of several patterns:

- time
- extended narrative
- spatial
- categorical
- problem–solution
- stock issues
- refutational
- causal
- motivated sequence
- wave
- spiral
- star
- call and response

Use signposts as transitional statements to help your audience follow the organization of your speech.

The introduction to a speech should:

- open with impact
- focus on the thesis statement
- connect with the audience
- preview the body of your speech

Effective openings may include:

- a brief story
- a quotation
- a startling statement
- reference to the audience
- the occasion, or a current event
- appropriate humor
- a personal experience
- a thought-provoking question

The conclusion to a speech should:

- summarize the main points of the speech
- close with impact

Ways to close include:

- quotation
- brief anecdote
- direct appeal to action
- return to the opening theme

A formal outline is sometimes required of beginning speakers. Many instructors prefer students to use standard outline notation and write a complete-sentence outline.

Speaker's notes, usually placed on small cards, can be used when presenting the speech, as can overhead transparencies or PowerPoint slides.

CHECK YOUR UNDERSTANDING: EXERCISES AND ACTIVITIES

1. Consider the following speech introductions. Rewrite them to fit the "open, focus, and connect" model suggested in this chapter.

   Today, I'm going to talk to you about pit bulls. I got attacked last week by a pit bull, and I think they are really dangerous. Something's got to be done!

   Have any of you ever thought about going snowboarding? I really like to snow-board, and that's what my speech is going to be about.

   I think capital punishment is wrong. What if somebody who was innocent got killed? I'm going to persuade all of you that life without parole is a better way to go.

2. View a speech on your CD. Using the format described in this chapter, construct a complete-sentence outline of the speech. How closely did the speech seem to follow the steps indicated in the chapter? Was the speech easy to outline? If not, how could the speaker have made the organization clearer?

3. Analyze a print ad in a magazine or newspaper, to see whether it uses a problem–solution, causal, or motivated sequence. If so, explain how each step is fulfilled. If not, discuss how the ad might be modified to fit one of these organizational patterns.

4. On the following pages is an outline of a speech, followed by a list of points in scrambled order. Your task is to match the appropriate sentence from the scrambled list with the points in the outline. This may be done as an individual or a group exercise, depending on your instructor's preference.

 **SPEECH COACH**

For a review of key terms in this chapter, see the Key Terms Flashcards on your CD.

Specific purpose: _____

Introduction

I. Open with impact: _____

II. Focus on the thesis statement: _____

III. Connect with your audience: _____

IV. Preview: _____

Body

I. Main point: _____

   A. _____

   B. _____

   C. _____

(*Signpost:* _____)

II. Main point: _____

   A. _____

   B. _____

   C. _____

(*Signpost:* _____)

III. Main point: _____

   A. _____

   B. _____

   C. _____

Conclusion

I. Summarize: _____

   A. _____

   B. _____

   C. _____

II. Close with impact: _____

Scrambled list:

1. Use fresh bread, preferably whole grain.
2. Use a quality jelly or jam, made without artificial additives.
3. Use either plain or chunky peanut butter.
4. You must have the necessary ingredients.
5. Fold the wax paper neatly around the sandwich.
6. Place the sandwich in a paper bag.
7. Use a biodegradable wrapper, such as wax paper, rather than plastic wrap.
8. You need to package the sandwich to take to school.
9. Put the two slices together.
10. Spread the first slice with peanut butter.
11. Spread the other slice with jelly or jam.
12. You need to assemble the sandwich.
13. To inform the class how to make a peanut butter and jelly sandwich.
14. First make sure you have the necessary ingredients.
15. Finally, wrap the sandwich.
16. Second, assemble the sandwich.
17. Enjoy your lunch and go to a movie with the money you've saved.
18. You can save money and eat better.
19. Today you will learn how to make the perfect peanut butter and jelly sandwich.
20. Are you tired of spending $5 for a greasy hamburger and fries?
21. Making a peanut butter and jelly sandwich involves three basic steps: having the ingredients, assembling the sandwich, and packaging the sandwich.
22. After you have the ingredients, you need to make the sandwich.
23. Unless you are eating it immediately, the sandwich must be wrapped to stay fresh.
24. To review, there are three steps:

NOTES

1. Alan Monroe, *Principles and Types of Speech* (New York: Scott, Foresman, 1935). See also the most recent edition: Bruce E. Gronbeck, Raymie E. McKerrow, Douglas Ehninger, and Alan H. Monroe, *Principles and Types of Speech Communication*, 12th ed. (New York: HarperCollins, 1994).
2. Jay Silverman, Elaine Hughes, and Diana Roberts Wienbroer, *Rules of Thumb: A Guide for Writers* (New York: McGraw-Hill, 1990), 99.
3. Deidra Dukes, "The Right to Breathe," speech delivered at California State University, Chico, 1992.

People with disabilities are a powerful voice against marginalizing language.

Language: Making Verbal Sense of Your Message

 OBJECTIVES

After reading this chapter and reviewing the learning resources on your CD-ROM and at the Online Learning Center, you should be able to:

- Construct examples that illustrate the relationship between language and thought.
- Describe the role language plays in relating to cultural, demographic, and individual diversity.
- Describe the "different voice" that characterizes women's and men's speech.
- Differentiate between denotative and connotative meaning.
- Use rhetorical devices such as metaphor and simile to vary language intensity in your speeches.
- Use concrete language, as well as contrast and action, to reduce uncertainty on the part of your audience.
- Use verbal immediacy and transitional devices in your speeches.
- Avoid marginalizing and totalizing language, using inclusive language instead.
- Avoid sexist and stereotypic language.

How can I tell what I think until I see what I say?
—EDWARD MORGAN FORSTER[1]

 KEY CONCEPTS

competence-enhancing
  language

connotative meaning

denotative meaning

inclusive language

language intensity

linguistic relativity
  hypothesis

marginalizing language

receiver-centric

sexist language

totalizing language

verbal qualifiers

Mary Shapiro and Thomas Donovan have always had a rocky relationship. Shapiro is the former chief of the Commodities Futures Trading Commission, the federal agency that polices the volatile commodities market. Donovan is the former president of the Chicago Board of Trade, which promotes the busiest commodities exchange in the United States. When Shapiro learned that Donovan had told his board members during a closed-door meeting that he wouldn't be "intimidated by some blond, 5-foot 2-inch little girl," their relationship took a turn for the worse.[2]

To suggest that Shapiro was displeased about the content of Donovan's speech would be an understatement. She quickly let the financial press know that she wouldn't be bullied by people "lobbing verbal grenades through the window."[3] For the record, Shapiro added that she was also 5-feet 5-inches tall and, at age 39, no longer a little girl.

This example points to an incontrovertible fact: Language, which is the rule-governed symbol system we use to verbally communicate, is not neutral. The words we choose to express ourselves and to describe others can elicit the full range of human emotions. This chapter is about language and its role in giving meaning and impact to our ideas. It is also about the power of words and how they affect the way we think about ourselves, our experiences, and the people with whom we come into contact.

On one level, our goal in this chapter is to assist you in appreciating the larger role language plays in our lives. On another level, our goal is to show you how you can use your appreciation of language to construct messages that will be appropriate to both your speech's purpose and the audience with whom you share it. We'll explore the relationship between words and the objects they are meant to represent, how language influences experiences, how language relates

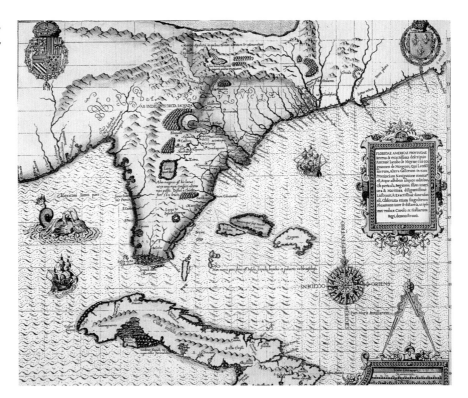

A map represents a territory, but it is not always accurate, as this 16th-century map shows.

Last year, people skied on champagne powder, windblown pack, groomed, corn snow, cold smoke, frozen granular, firm, good crud, bottomless powder, sugar, machine tilled, crust, hero powder, buffed snow, man made, corduroy, ball bearings, velvet, cut up powder, spring snow, ballroom, and acre after acre of virgin powder.

(Eskimos may have more words for snow, but we have more lifts.)

THE ASPENS
SNOWMASS • BUTTERMILK
ASPEN MOUNTAIN

Aspen Central Reservations 1-800-262-7736 Snowmass Central Reservations 1-800-332-3245.
The Aspen Skiing Company Hotels: The Little Nell, The Snowmass Club 1-800-525-6200.

This ad uses connotative terms for snow that are meaningful to skiers and snowboarders. The language is unique to their sports and enhances the images that come to mind when they think about the cold white stuff that is simply *snow* to the rest of us.

to audience diversity, and how you can use language to enhance how you and your speech are perceived by your audience.

WORD POWER

Just as a map is not the territory it represents, a word is not the object it is intended to describe. Words are simply spoken sounds or written characters that symbolize or communicate meaning. People use them to refer to the persons, places, and things with which they come into contact. Their meaning depends on the set of experiences people associate with the words when they use, see, or hear them. As discussed in Chapter 4, words also have two types of meaning: denotative and connotative. Denotative meaning involves the conventional definition of a word found in a dictionary. Connotative meaning, which is not always found in a dictionary, concerns the emotions and images people associate with a word. Connotative meaning can vary tremendously from culture to culture, group to group, and even person to person. For example, snow boarders refer to themselves as "riders." And listeners to Jim Rome's nationwide radio talk show refer to themselves as "clones." People unfamiliar with snowboarding or the Jim Rome show, however, would probably define these words much differently.

Words have a dramatic impact on the process of perception. When we are told something is "good" or "bad" before we see or experience it, we are more likely to rate it the same way. In experiments where subjects have been shown pictures of people described as popular, the subjects rate them as highly attractive. Subjects who are told the same people are unpopular rate them as significantly less attractive. Thus, the words you choose when you speak will influence how your audience perceives your message.

What is true of individual words is even more true of the language you speak. Whether you speak English, French, Spanish, or Russian makes a difference in how you experience the world. Just as perception influences the meaning assigned to words, language influences the meaning people assign to everything they experience. According to the **linguistic relativity hypothesis,** introduced more than 40 years ago by cultural anthropologist Benjamin Whorf, what we perceive is influenced by the language in which we think and speak. Different languages lead to different patterns of thought.[4]

linguistic relativity hypothesis The idea that what people perceive is influenced by the language in which they think and speak.

Whorf formulated this hypothesis while studying the Native American language of the Hopi. He discovered there are no words in their language for the concept of incremental time: no seconds, no minutes, and no hours. Thus, it would never occur to the Hopi that someone could be half an hour early or late for a visit, because they have no words for the concept.

Each language has certain concepts that cannot be easily expressed in other languages. Thus, the expression "something was lost in the translation" doesn't mean part of a statement was literally lost as it was translated from one language to another. It means an identical idea couldn't be found in the second language, so part of the statement's original meaning was diminished. In constructing a speech, the first thing you'll want to do is choose words and sentences that you believe will lead people to perceive and think about your speech as you intend them to.

LANGUAGE AND AUDIENCE DIVERSITY

Having seen that words and language color people's perception and experience, we can now examine the relationship between language and the three types of diversity (cultural, demographic, and individual) introduced in Chapter 5. Understanding the connections between language and diversity is crucial to effective speaking, since today's audience is more diverse than ever.

Because we live in such a diverse world the language we use to communicate is constantly evolving. Words and phrases that may have been acceptable yesterday may not be today or tomorrow. A seemingly innocent word such as *crusade*, for example, is not at all innocent in the eyes of Muslims, as President Bush found out early on in the war on terrorism.

Language and Cultural Diversity

The United States is a multiracial, multiethnic, multicultural nation. With the exception of Native Americans, 98 percent of the population can trace its ancestry to another country.

Recall from Chapter 5 that *cultural diversity* is multidimensional, including audience characteristics such as individualism/collectivism, and masculinity/femininity. Knowing something about the dimensions of culture reflected in your audience is essential to choosing appropriate language for your speech.

One of the authors, for example, had the opportunity to attend an IBM recognition event where former NFL quarterback and ESPN announcer Joe Theismann was one of the keynote speakers. Theismann's audience included many people from IBM operations in the Far East and Latin America, both of which are largely collectivistic in outlook. Although most North Americans in the audience responded positively to Theismann's speech, not everyone did. His remarks were perceived as egotistical and self-aggrandizing by people from such places as Japan, Taiwan, Singapore, Argentina, and Venezuela. As one person from Buenos Aires remarked, "You would have thought American football was an individual sport listening to him [Theismann]—that he won the Super Bowl single-handedly. Does he know a word other than I?"

All too often speakers choose language appropriate to their culture, but not necessarily the cultures of their audience members. Like Theismann, they naively assume that what is good enough for their culture is good enough for everyone's. Of course, this kind of thinking is not only inaccurate, it is arrogant.

Even commonplace language choices, such as what name to call a person, can be influenced by culture. In many cultures, such as those that use the Spanish language, strangers are not addressed informally, and certainly not by their first names. A salesperson, for example, who addresses a potential client by his or her first name may, unintentionally, offend that person. The best advice is to ask people how they prefer to be addressed, rather than automatically assuming that they want to be on a first-name basis.

Although we think all speakers have an obligation to explore the language norms of an audience with whom they will be speaking, we also believe that audience members have an obligation to investigate the degree to which they are **receiver-centric.** People who are receiver-centric assume that the meaning they give to a word or a phrase is its exclusive meaning. Thus, if they take offense to a word or phrase a speaker uses, they may assume the speaker intended to offend them. Meaning in the speech transaction is negotiated between speaker and audience. When either the speaker or an audience member loses sight of this fact, miscommunication and misunderstanding result. As we turn to the topic of demographic diversity, then, remember that speakers and audience members need to be mindful of the fact that each has a responsibility to the other.

receiver-centric A person's assumption that the meaning he or she gives to a word or a phrase is its exclusive meaning.

Language and Demographic Diversity

You will recall from Chapter 5 that *demographic diversity* is reflected in the groups to which people belong and with which they identify. This includes such characteristics as nationality, race and ethnicity, gender, and religion. Demographic diversity also includes social and economic class, the region of the country that people call home, and the generation to which people belong.

Demographic diversity, although always an important consideration of a speaker's audience analysis, has become even more so. Today's college classroom is likely to be populated by people with a variety of different demographic backgrounds. Race and ethnicity, as cases in point, are often an important part of today's audience diversity.

How you refer to a specific racial or ethnic group can have a strong impact on the individual members of that group in your audience. For example, when Anglos speak to a gathering of English-speaking people of Mexican descent, they need to choose the appropriate language in referring to the audience. Scholars

Pola Lopez's graphic powerfully demonstrates how words can alter perceptions.

Mario Garcia and Rodolfo Alvarez suggest that people of Mexican descent in the United States constitute several rather than a single demographic group.[5] Two such reference groups are Mexican Americans and Chicanos/Chicanas. The Mexican American group comprises people who immigrated from Mexico to border states, such as California and Texas, following World War II. According to Garcia and Alvarez, people who consider themselves Mexican Americans are generally older and more conservative than those who identify themselves as Chicanos or Chicanas, who are generally younger and more militant.

Chicanos and Chicanas came of age in the 1960s and gained some attention in the 1970s. They perceived Mexican immigrants who wanted to assimilate with the predominant Anglo culture as sellouts. To distinguish themselves from the Mexican American group, Chicanos and Chicanas adopted specific patterns of behaving, including their own code words. The list of code words included *vendido* (sellout) and *socios* (the old boy network). Today, members of this demographic group sometimes refer to each other as *veteranos* (veterans). Thus, referring to Chicanos/Chicanas as Mexican Americans in a speech would be inappropriate. As a speaker, you need to learn as much as possible about the language preferences of your audiences. Otherwise, you may inadvertently lose at least some of them.

Edward James Olmos's film *My Family, Mi Familia,* did an excellent job of showing how people who share the same culture use language differently depending on their generation.

The varied preferences of Spanish-speaking people apply to many other demographic groups as well. Some African Americans prefer being referred to as Black. And though they may be too polite to tell you so, the Chinese, Hmong, Japanese, Korean, Laotian, Taiwanese, and Vietnamese prefer being referred to by their nationality rather than being categorized as Asian.

As a speaker, you cannot afford to overlook the demography of your audience in choosing language. How you refer to people who identify themselves with specific demographic groups and the words you use in talking about the demographic groups themselves will influence not only how the content of your speech is received but audience perceptions of your credibility as well.

Language and Individual Diversity

Choosing appropriate language for a speech doesn't stop with a consideration of cultural and demographic diversity. You also must consider and evaluate *individual diversity,* which reflects such factors as personal views on the meaning of gender, sexual orientation, and religious beliefs. The fact that someone is Catholic, Jewish, Muslim, Hindu, or Protestant, for example, doesn't tell you much about the diversity of beliefs held by people who consider themselves members of one of these religious groups. Moreover, religious beliefs are only one element of the individual diversity of your audience. Consequently, before choosing the language with which you'll construct your speech, you will also have to explore other individual beliefs, attitudes, and values of the people in your audience.

As a case in point, think about an audience of people who describe themselves as Christians. Such people are extraordinarily diverse in what they believe individually. Some think the Bible is to be taken literally as the word of God; others believe the Bible should be interpreted metaphorically. Knowing this kind of information in advance is essential for speakers who want the language of their speech to be audience appropriate.

Remember, the words and sentences with which you construct your speech will influence the meaning of your speech in the minds of the audience members. You want to control this process as much as possible. Thus, doing your homework about the relationship between language and diversity as it reflects your speech transaction is a matter of common sense.

USING LANGUAGE EFFECTIVELY

Let's assume that you have thoroughly analyzed the speech situation, including how audience diversity should be reflected in your choice of words to construct your speech. You are now ready to begin writing the outline of your speech with language that will enhance your credibility with your audience and create a high degree of mutual understanding. There are a number of guidelines you will want to follow in this process. The first rule concerns choosing language that makes every member of your audience feel included in your message. This is known as inclusive language, as opposed to marginalizing or totalizing language, concepts we will explain shortly. The second rule concerns choosing language that will enhance rather than undermine audience perceptions of your competence as a speaker.[6] The third rule concerns using language to its fullest potential to involve your audience in your speech. The fourth rule focuses on using language that will help you manage your speech, and help your audience understand what you want to communicate.

Use Inclusive Language

inclusive language Language that helps people believe that they not only have a stake in matters of societal importance but also have power in this regard.

The first rule in choosing the words of your speech is to use language that is inclusive. **Inclusive language** helps people believe that they not only have a stake in matters of societal importance, but also have power in this regard. Inclusive language doesn't leave people out of the picture because of their gender, race, ethnicity, age, religion, sexual orientation, or ability. At the same time, however, it avoids defining people exclusively on the basis of such characteristics. Inclusive language also is immediate; it reduces rather than increases the distance that physically separates you and your audience from each other. Remember the example of Joe Theismann? His use of the personal pronoun "I" actually made him seem more distant from members of the audience. Inclusive language emphasizes the fact that a speaker and audience are a collective rather than two separate entities. For example, the late Barbara Jordan not only used immediate language in her distinguished political career, she also spoke eloquently

"We, the People": *Barbara Jordan*

The late Congresswoman and scholar Barbara Jordan was one of the most impressive and eloquent speakers of the second half of the 20th century. Not only did she possess a powerful voice and impeccable diction, she used language in a way that few could match. Many compared her speeches to those of Winston Churchill and Franklin Roosevelt. Here is a brief excerpt of her statements during the debate on the impeachment of President Nixon in 1974:

We, the people. It is a very eloquent beginning. But when that document was completed on the 17th of September in 1787, I was not included in that "We, the people." I felt somehow for many years that George Washington and Alexander Hamilton just left me out by mistake. But through the process of amendment, interpretation and court decision I have finally been included in "We, the people."[1]

Two decades later, Jordan was asked to head the United States Commission on Immigration Reform. Testifying before the very congressional committee of which she was once a member, Jordan echoed her words from long ago:

I would be the last person to claim that our nation is perfect. But we have a kind of perfection in us because our founding principle is universal—that we are all created equal regardless of race, religion or national ancestry. When the Declaration of Independence was written, when the Constitution was adopted, when the Bill of Rights was added to it, they all applied almost exclusively to white men of Anglo-Saxon descent who owned property on the East Coast. They did not apply to me. I am female. I am black. But these self-evident principles apply to me now as they apply to everyone in this room.[2]

[1]"Barbara Jordan: A Passionate Voice," *Sacramento Bee*, 18 January 1996, A16.

[2]Jerelyn Eddings, "The Voice of Eloquent Thunder," *U.S. News and World Report*, 29 January 1996, 16.

about inclusive speech. Both facts are featured in her speech, which is printed in the box "We, the People: Barbara Jordan."

Remember the example with which we opened this chapter? Thomas Donovan, then president of the Chicago Board of Trade, referred to Mary Shapiro, former chief of the Commodities Futures Trading Commission, as a "5-foot 2-inch little girl." Are his words an example of inclusive language? Of course not. His statement illustrates two types of language you'll want to avoid in constructing your speech. The first type is called *marginalizing*. The second type is called *totalizing*.

Marginalizing language diminishes people's importance and makes them appear to be less powerful, less significant, and less worthwhile than they are. Marginalizing language also appeals to biases audience members may hold consciously or subconsciously. When Thomas Donovan called Mary Shapiro a little girl, for example, his language was more than sexist or politically incorrect. He was using language to make Mary Shapiro appear a powerless child incapable of directing powerful adults like himself.

Totalizing language defines people on the basis of a single attribute, such as race, ethnicity, biological sex, or ability. In a speech, the following statements would exemplify totalizing:

marginalizing language
Language that diminishes people's importance and makes them appear to be less powerful, less significant, and less worthwhile than they are.

totalizing language Language that defines people exclusively on the basis of a single attribute, such as race, ethnicity, biological sex, or ability.

TABLE 9.1 How to Say It More Immediately

Less Immediate		More Immediate
I		
Me	}	We
You		Us
Them		
I think		
It's my opinion	}	Wouldn't you agree?
I know		How many of us believe . . . ?
Tell		
Show	}	Share
Explain		Look at
Talk from	}	Talk between

"The disabled in this audience . . ."

"As a woman, you've got to learn to assert yourself."

"As a victim of racism . . ."

"Because you are Latino . . ."

"This is really a guy book."

Each of these statements could be well-meaning and intended to demonstrate the speaker's sensitivity to people with disabilities, women, Latinos, and men. Yet, what each statement does in reality is call attention to a single attribute among audience members and treat the attribute as if it were the only thing about audience members that truly counts. People are more than their disability, women and men are more than their biological sex, and people discriminated against by racists are more than simply victims. Speakers need to use language that acknowledges that people are complex individuals.

TIPS AND TACTICS   *Inclusive Language*

SPEECH COACH

To hear more about these Tips and Tactics go to Audio Tips and Tactics on your CD.

1. Inclusive language avoids defining people on the basis of their gender, sexual orientation, disability, racial, ethnic, or religious identity. Inclusive language uses terms such as *humankind* rather than *mankind*, *athlete* rather than *woman athlete*, and *friend* rather than *Islamic friend*.

2. Inclusive language reflects the self-referents used by the members of a minority group; for example, *gay* or *lesbian* rather than *homosexuals* and *person with a disability* rather than *disabled person*.

3. Inclusive language is immediate. As you can read in Table 9.1, it's about *we* rather than *me* and *us* rather than *you and I*.

Use Competence-Enhancing Language

A number of researchers have documented that there is a difference between "powerful" and "powerless" speech.[7] Powerless speech is characterized by the use of language such as hedges (I *kind of* agree with you), qualifiers (I *could* be wrong), hesitations (uhs and ums), and tag questions (That's right, *isn't it?*). On the other hand, powerful speech is fluent and direct and avoids these types of phrases. Messages containing a significant amount of powerless language produce lower ratings of communicator power, attractiveness, and competence, whereas powerful speech produces higher ratings on these dimensions.

Therefore, the second rule to follow in constructing the text of your speech is to use powerful, **competence-enhancing language,** words that emphasize rather than undermine audience perceptions of your competence. Language that enhances perceptions of competence avoids verbal qualifiers.[8] **Verbal qualifiers** erode the impact of what you say in a speech.

Beginning speakers often use verbal qualifiers without thinking of them as such. They say, for example:

"It's just my opinion, but . . ."

"You'll probably disagree, but . . ."

"This is my belief, but you may think otherwise."

"I'm pretty sure, though I could be wrong in stating . . ."

"Of course, your opinion counts at least as much as mine."

Competence-enhancing language emphasizes the significance of what you say in a speech. Whether giving an informative, persuasive, or testimonial speech, you should be the expert on the subject or person. Not only does this require that you do your homework, it also requires you to choose language that illustrates the fact. Using language such as the following is one way of accomplishing this without appearing to be a "know-it-all" to your audience.

"Ten years of research demonstrates that . . ."

"For the past four summers, I've been involved with . . ."

"Having lived all my life in the United States, . . ."

"Scholars tell us . . ."

Each of these statements begins with a phrase that emphasizes the speaker's competence. They imply that through either research or experience, the speaker knows his or her subject well. You should not exaggerate your claims beyond what you know to be true, but you should take full credit for the facts as you know them.

There are other ways you can use language to increase your audience's perception of your competence. Some of the best are also the most obvious. They include using correct grammar, correct pronunciation, and correct usage of a word. Although you can get away with grammatically incorrect language in conversation, it usually sticks out like a sore thumb when speaking in public.

Grammar   In an otherwise effective speech on educational reform, for example, President Bush asked his audience, " Is your children learning?" He meant to say, "Are your children learning?" Although this was but a single grammatical mistake, it became the most memorable part of the speech in terms of what was written and said about it afterwards.

> **competence-enhancing language** Words that emphasize rather than undermine audience perceptions of a speaker's competence.
>
> **verbal qualifiers** Words and phrases that erode the impact of what a speaker says in a speech.

Some of the most common grammatical mistakes we hear in our own students' speech are double negatives, incorrect subject-verb agreement, and inappropriate slang.

A double negative occurs when someone uses a negative to modify another negative. As in mathematics, a negative times a negative is actually a positive. Thus, "No one never works around here" really means that there is no person who "never works." That suggests people really do work—the opposite of what the speaker intended.

Incorrect subject-verb agreement occurs when a plural subject is matched with a singular verb or vice versa. Thus, you want to avoid such sentences as "We is going to the movies."

Finally, unless they are essential to the speech, certain expressions common in everyday conversation are inappropriate in a speech. Many speech teachers object in particular to the overuse of "you know" and "like." It is irritating to hear, "You know, like, I really mean it."

This is far from a complete list of grammatical pitfalls for the speaker. And a speech is not as formal as written English. Although you are not supposed to end a sentence with a preposition, it is not uncommon to hear someone say, "I know what it's all about." The best advice we can give is that if you are in doubt about any grammatical issues, consult someone who is knowledgeable and ask his or her advice, or check a grammar handbook, such as Diana Hacker's *A Pocket Style Manual*, which you can order from Amazon.com.

Pronunciation   It is easy to mispronounce a word, especially when it is a word you do not routinely use or have heard others use incorrectly. For example, how do you pronounce the word *nuclear?* Many people, including those in positions of authority, pronounce it "nuk-u-lar." The correct pronunciation is "nuk-le-ur." How do you pronounce the word *vehicle?* Many people pronounce it "ve-hick-ul." The correct pronunciation is "ve-ik-ul." Mispronunciation of words may seem a picky point to you. Yet, when speaking before an educated audience mispronunciation is one of the surest ways to risk their perceiving you as incompetent.

Mispronunciation of words can lead to problems other than your competence being undermined. One of the most significant involves meaning. Frequently, for example, people say "assure" when they mean "ensure." Assuring your child that she is safe is not the same as ensuring the safety of your child. *Assure* and *ensure* mean two different things.

Usage   Incorrect usage of a word is the final competence-detracting issue we want to caution you about. We hear many students who confuse the words *except* and *accept*. We also hear students use the terms *irregardless* and *orientated*, when what they really mean is *regardless* and *oriented*. Again, this may strike you as picky on our part. But it's not. When we hear people use words inaccurately, it opens the door for us to question their competence in areas other than language as well.

TIPS AND TACTICS   *Competence-Enhancing Language*

1. Avoid qualifiers such as *I'm pretty sure* or *I'm kind of certain*. Instead, assert yourself with statements such as *I'm convinced, I strongly believe,* or *I am of the firm belief*.

2. Avoid tag questions that make it seem as if you are uncertain. For example, instead of saying, "I think this is a problem but you may not," say, "This is a problem for all of us." Avoid saying, "I believe we have no other course, what do you think?" Instead, say, "Wouldn't you agree that we have no other choice?"

3. Don't be afraid to interject experience or training that gives you expertise or insight to your topic. Personal experience is a powerful form of evidence in the eyes of the audience. Share with your audience the fact that "I've now been rock climbing for over three years"; or "Proper nutrition is not only something I try to practice, it's a subject in which I've taken two courses"; or "This past year marked my tenth year of being smoke free."

4. Use words with which you are familiar. When you do incorporate a word you do not routinely use in your speech, consult a dictionary to find out the word's denotative meaning and phonetically correct pronunciation. Watch out for words that sound alike but mean different things, such as *except* and *accept, access* and *assess,* or *ask* and *ax.* Also watch out for words that are spelled and pronounced alike but may have different meanings depending on usage (homonyms). For example, the word *quail* can be used in reference to a type of bird or in reference to cowering in terror.

Use Language to Its Fullest Potential

The third rule is to use language to its fullest potential in your speeches. There are many ways to do this. The ones we encourage you to use involve:

- using words and phrases that show rather than simply tell an audience something about a topic
- using words and phrases that give your speech a rhythm that facilitates attention and listening
- using words and phrases that vary in language intensity

Show; Don't Simply Tell   Creative writing teachers coach their students to use language that evokes vivid images in the mind's eye of their readers. You can do the same thing in your speeches by using metaphors, similes, and analogies.

Metaphor is one of the most powerful sources of expressive language. A metaphor is a figure of speech in which a word or phrase literally denoting one kind of object or idea is used in place of another to suggest a likeness or an analogy between them. It's one thing, for example, to say that a corporation is "polluting the environment." It's quite another to say that the same corporation is "raping virgin timberland." To say that "freedom is an open window" or that "music unshackles the mind and spirit" would be metaphorical. Metaphors provide an audience with a kind of linguistic break from the expected. Thus, just when audience members may be losing interest in a speech, a phrase or word can grab them by the lapels and help them "see" what you are trying to say.

Metaphors should fit the topic. For example, sports metaphors are often used in the popular media to describe political contests. Thus, a political candidate who does well in a debate "hits a home run," whereas a less successful candidate "strikes out." Sometimes a desperate politician is said to "throw a Hail Mary pass," while the favored candidate is said to "sit on a lead." Be careful, however, not to mix metaphors. It sounds odd to say, "He scored a touchdown while steering the ship of state through troubled waters." Metaphors can add spice and interest to a speech, but they must be used appropriately.

Simile is a form of figurative language that invites a direct comparison between two things that are quite different. A simile usually contains the word *like* or *as*. "Sharp as a tack," "tight as a snare drum," and "pointed as an ice pick" are examples of simile. Similes can also be used effectively to " show" your audience what you are attempting to communicate.

Similes differ from metaphors in that they explicitly state the comparison, whereas metaphors imply it. Similes are useful, therefore, in making a comparison very clear to the audience. For example, a speech on preventing sexually transmitted diseases might use a simile such as "Having unprotected sexual relations is like playing Russian roulette with a 357 Magnum." On a topic such as drunk driving, you might say, " Drunken drivers are like unguided missiles."

Analogies are extended metaphors or similes. Analogies can be effective in helping an audience imagine something you are trying to describe. In an informative speech on writing a basic software program, for example, one of our students used a cooking recipe to help students follow along. In another informative speech, we had a student describe fly-fishing for wild trout as analogous to chasing butterflies with a net.

Your use of metaphor, simile, and analogy in your speeches is limited only by your imagination. What's more, you can get ideas for their effective use from listening to other speakers, and reading both fiction and nonfiction works.

Rhythmic Speech   Rhythm is part of the natural order. We often hear people speak about the "rhythm of life" or the "rhythm of the season." Perhaps this is why we are so easily drawn to beating drums and chanting people. In any case, the best speakers know that a speech needs rhythm every bit as much as does the DJ at a dance club. To create rhythm, speakers commonly use alliteration, parallel structure, and repetition.

Alliteration is the repetition of the same initial sound in a series of words. Jesse Jackson is famous for using alliteration to make his speeches more expressive and memorable. Instead of saying, "People need to be given a purpose," for example, Jackson might say, "Empower people with pride, and purpose is sure to follow."

One of the most famous alliterations of American political history came from former Vice President Spiro Agnew, who called his opponents in the media "nattering nabobs of negativism." The power of alliteration comes from the way it sticks in the audience's minds. The danger is that if the alliteration seems forced, it may be memorable, but ineffective.

Parallel structure is the use of the same structure for each main point of your speech. It provides a way to help your audience remember your key points, and at the same time serves as a verbal cue that you are presenting a main point. For example, when John F. Kennedy ran for president, he used the phrases "I am not satisfied . . . we can do better" to highlight each of his major criticisms of the Republican administration.

In developing your speech outline, look for a consistent refrain or phrase that can serve as the touchstone for the structure of the speech. For example, a speech on gang violence might be built around several main points that each begin, "We can only stop gang violence if we all . . . ." The use of parallel structure helps audiences anticipate the points to come and remember them when the speech is over. However, be careful to use parallel structure that fits the speech. If not, it will seem forced and artificial.

John Madden's use of action words has made him a fixture as a sports announcer.

Repetition is the use of the same words repeatedly in a speech to drive home a point. Unlike parallel structure, in which the same phrase is used only to build each main point, repetition uses a word or phrase repeatedly throughout the speech to emphasize the essential point that the speaker seeks to convey. If you recall the earlier discussed speech by Barbara Jordan in the box on page 225, you will note that the phrase "We, the people" is repeated three times in one short excerpt. The theme of that speech is clearly conveyed by that one phrase, taken from the U.S. Constitution.

Language Intensity   The degree to which words and phrases deviate from neutral affects **language intensity.** The intensity of words varies along a continuum ranging from relatively neutral to highly intense. For example, *savory and delicious* is more intense than *tastes good.* By the same token, the phrase *I find you attractive* is not nearly as intense as *I wanna' rock your world.* Intense language is much more likely to enlist the attention of your audience than neutral language. You can increase language intensity by using action words and humorous language. You can also increase intensity with metaphor and simile, which we have already discussed.

language intensity The degree to which words and phrases deviate from neutral.

Action Words   Try to use words that are exciting and action oriented. For example, which do you find more involving, "The speech was well received" or "The speech was a knockout"? What about "He got mad" versus "He went ballistic"? To hear examples of action words, listen to sportscaster John Madden. His speech is liberally sprinkled with action words such as *whack, annihilate,* and *wham.* Also pay attention to the words used in newspaper headlines and the lead paragraph of individual stories. Newspaper editors know that in order to get you to read a story you must first take note of it.

Humor   In Chapter 8 we talked about using humor to open your speech. The guidelines for using humor we discussed there apply to this discussion as well. Humor should be appropriate to your topic and the occasion, relevant to your topic and/or the occasion, and mindful of the diversity in your audience. Having said that, we also want to emphasize what feminist Gertrude Stein is alleged to have said on her deathbed. When asked if it was hard to die, Stein said, "No . . . dying is easy. Comedy is hard."

While humorous language can increase the intensity of your speech, not all speakers are well suited to using it. Some people really can't tell a joke. If you count yourself in this latter group, don't try being something you are not. On the other hand, if humor is customary to your communication style, use it to your advantage. Poke fun at yourself but not at your audience. Tell a joke you have successfully told before, if appropriate. And share humorous anecdotes you have shared before, assuming that they suit your speech purpose.

Contrast and Action   A final way you can intensify language is to incorporate contrasting phrases and words that suggest action in your speech. In discussing the irrationality that often grips the minds of people when going to war, German philosopher Friedrich Nietzsche wrote, "How good . . . bad music and bad reasons sound when we march against the enemy."[9] Nietzsche's simple contrast between good and bad is much more effective in making war seem illogical than any extended discussion would have been. And this would have been especially true had Nietzsche delivered the line in a speech.

MANAGING LANGUAGE

The final rule for using language effectively involves using language that (1) assists you in managing your speech and (2) helps audience members understand the intended meaning of your message.

Use Concrete Words and Phrases

Speakers do not always use language to enlighten an audience. Sometimes speakers intentionally use language to keep their audience in the dark. Political consultants will tell reporters that a candidate misspoke rather than said something stupid. Military spokespeople will tell an audience that collateral damage occurred rather than candidly admit innocent civilians were injured or killed. And the spokesperson for a company will announce to the general public that it is "right sizing" the work force, when it would be more accurate to say 1,000 employees were losing their jobs.

Do yourself and your audience a favor: Speak in concrete language. Concrete language consists of words and phrases that increase the chance of your audience interpreting the meaning of your message as intended. Put another way, concrete language is void of words and phrases so abstract that each person in your audience can walk away from your speech with a different interpretation of what was said.

The easiest way to make your language concrete is to use words your audience recognizes and routinely uses; for example, *cat* instead of *feline*, *sneaky* rather than *surreptitious*, *book* rather than *tome*, and *abusive* rather than *vituperative language*. You can also make your language more concrete by providing your audience with details that will clarify your intended meaning. For example, instead of saying a person is tall or short, give the person's actual height. Rather than describing someone as a criminal, detail the nature of his or her crime or criminal record as well. And rather than arguing that someone is either conservative or liberal, provide the audience with detailed evidence that you believe supports your claim.

Use Oral Language

We believe the language in your speech should look and sound more like the language of conversation than the language of written discourse. However, we also believe that the language in your speech needs to be a refined version of that used when conversing. Thus, we strongly believe you should strive to use language in your speech that is grammatically sound and clearly enunciated. By the same token, we also think you should feel free to use contractions more liberally in your speech, split all the infinitives you want, and end a thought with a preposition. Spoken thought and written sentences are similar but not identical. It's a good idea to read aloud and even record your speech. You can then listen critically to what you have said, and check to make sure that it sounds like you are conversing with rather than formally talking to your audience.

Keep It Simple

Less is often more in a speech. By that we mean simple words and simple sentences are usually better than polysyllabic words and compound, complex sentences. "Ask not what your country can do for you . . . but what you can do for your country," is much easier to hear and understand than

> "It's important that each of you gives some thought to the kinds of demands that you make on your government, and at the same time begin to think about the meaning of sacrifice, and what you possibly could do to help out your government and elected leaders."

Use Signposts

Still another technique to manage your speech is to make effective use of signposts, which we explained in Chapter 8. We've repeatedly emphasized how important it is to let your audience know where you are going with your speech. You know from your own experience in taking lecture notes that it's much easier to follow an instructor who uses verbal signposts that alert you to changes in direction or clearly link one thought to another. You need to do the same for the members of your audience.

Signposts are transitional words and phrases, such as those discussed in Chapter 8, that tell your audience you are about to make or already have made a shift in direction. Signposts also serve to verbally link your thoughts as you speak. It's always a good idea to let your audience know that there is a sequence to your message—"Let's consider three important issues"—and then to remind your audience where you are in that sequence—"Having covered the first issue, let's now look at the second."

It's also a good idea to let your audience know that your speech is about to end by using transitional words and phrases such as *lastly, to summarize, to conclude,* and *in closing*. Audiences are likely to grow impatient if they think a speech will never end.

Use Visual, Kinesthetic, and Auditory Language

Not all people process information in the same way. Research shows that some people need to see a lesson, others need only to hear it, and still others need to become immersed in the subject matter. These three styles of learning are technically called visual, auditory, and kinesthetic. The obvious way for a speaker to deal with these three is to augment a speech with visual aids, speak audibly and clearly, or involve the audience in demonstrations or other hands-on experiences. Yet, sometimes options one and three are impossible for a speaker.

To get around this fact, author and corporate trainer Loretta Malandro encourages her clients to connect metaphorically with the varied learning styles present in most audiences. Table 9.2 suggests a number of specific visual, auditory, and kinesthetic words that help your audience better process your speech.

Although you may not be able to literally show your audience members prejudice, you can connect with visual learners by

- asking them to envision a world free of hate,
- drawing a picture of racism or sketching out an example for them, or
- making a hazy concept such as affirmative action crystal clear so that they can see the problem.

Although you may not be able to let them literally feel your thoughts, you can connect with audience members who need to experience some things by asking them to imagine

- what racism feels like,
- that a problem is a giant weight pressing down on them, or
- how oppressed people hunger for freedom.

And though you may not be able to literally produce the sound of abused children for your audience members, you can connect to auditory learners by asking them

- whether they hear what you're trying to say,
- to imagine what it's like to live in a world where you cannot speak out for yourself,
- to imagine the mournful sound of children crying.

The point is simple. Not everyone in your audience will respond in a like manner to the words you speak. Thus, to maximize audience members' receptivity to what you say, you must make every effort to use expressive words that reflect their different styles of information processing.

FINAL WORDS OF CAUTION

We conclude this chapter with a discussion of two issues that are not so much a matter of right and wrong but, rather, of rhetorical sensitivity. The use of language appropriate to your rhetorical situation is not just a matter of effectiveness; it is also one of being ethically sensitive to the detrimental effects stereotypic and

TABLE 9.2 Words Linked to Vision, Hearing, and Touch

VISUAL WORDS

Focus	Graphic	Watch	Colorful
Bright	Illustrate	Vision	Glimpse
Show	Color	Brilliant	Look
Pretty	See	Evident	Sight
Envision	Picture	Sketch	Shining
Draw	Hazy	Oversight	Hidden
View	Peek	Clearly	Notice
Clear	Imagine	Perspective	

AUDITORY WORDS

Listen	Ringing	Compliment	Pardon
Hear	Resonate	Loud	Sound
Discuss	Yell	Silent	Request
Declare	Told	Shout	Whispering
Implore	Call	Talk	Quiet
Acclaim	Assert	Noisy	Ask
Harmony	Profess	Orchestrate	
Petition	Noise	Address	

KINESTHETIC WORDS

Feel	Terrified	Hunger	Contact
Pressure	Burdensome	Doubt	Nurture
Hurt	Firm	Shocking	Emotion
Get the point	Tense	Heavy	Graceful
Experience	Touchy	Touch	Sensual
Longing	Pushy	Concrete	Weighty problem
Wait	Shatter	Irritated	

Source: Excerpted from: *Twentieth Century Selling.* © Dr. Loretta Malandro. Taught in her program "Speak With Impact," offered by Malandro Communication Inc., Scottsdale, Arizona.

biased language can have on people. We look at two specific types of problems caused by inappropriate language: first, the use of language that stereotypes people; second, the use of language that stereotypes people on the basis of their biological sex.

Avoid Stereotypes

Do you see anything wrong with the following references?

"John's a victim of cystic fibrosis."

"Don't forget that Susan's wheelchair bound!"

"It's okay, Lupe, there's plenty of disabled seating in the new auditorium."

"The Howards' baby is physically challenged."

According to the Disabled Student Services on our campus, each of these statements is constructed with inappropriate language. If you're surprised, then please know that so were we. We've heard terms like *victim of* and *physically challenged* used by people in all walks of life, including student speakers.

The fact that we think we know what constitutes appropriate language doesn't excuse us from researching the subject. Language is dynamic and in a continuous process of change. What's more, words such as *victim* or terms such as *wheelchair bound* once were acceptable. Today, however, people with disabilities are defining their own terms on their own grounds. Further, in doing so, those with disabilities have said they prefer the following descriptors to the first set we listed for you:

"John has cystic fibrosis."

"Don't forget that Susan's in a wheelchair."

"It's okay, Lupe; there's plenty of seating in the new auditorium for people in wheelchairs."

"The Howards' baby has a disability."

Thus, we want to remind you of the adage "It's better to remain silent and be thought a fool than to open your mouth and prove it." When in doubt about words and their consequences, consult an authority. If that's not possible, then when in doubt about a word, leave it out.

Of course, it is not just people with disabilities who are stereotyped. People in different professions, of different ethnicities, and with different sexual orientations, to name just a few categories, are frequently the subject of stereotypic language. The speaker who is sensitive to language avoids such stereotypes. One particular type of stereotype deserves discussion in its own right, sexist language.

Avoid Sexist Language

sexist language Language, such as *housewife* and *fireman*, that stereotypes gender roles.

Sexist language is language that stereotypes gender roles, for example, *housewife* and *fireman*. Why is sexist language a problem? Because it conveys, intentionally or not, a stereotype of certain roles and functions, based on sex. When the head of an academic department is referred to as a chair*man*, a member of the U.S. House of Representatives is called a Congress*man*, and a flight attendant on an airplane is known as a steward*ess*, it is clear which roles are held to be "male" and which ones "female." A sensitive public speaker needs to avoid sexist language.

One of the easiest ways to unintentionally convey sexism is to use singular pronouns in the masculine form. For years, speakers and writers excluded women from their examples involving a single person, saying such things as

"If a person is strong, he will stand up for himself."

"When someone believes something, he shouldn't be afraid to say so."

"An individual should keep his promise."

If you have no other choice in constructing examples to illustrate your speech, you can do one of two things with regard to singular pronouns. First, you can say "he or she" in conjunction with a singular verb. Second, you can

How Does Language Marginalize People?

A 53-year-old cabdriver is facing vehicular manslaughter charges in the hit-and-run accident that killed a Silicon Valley executive and critically injured his companion, a state trade official, police say.

Arthur Alan Smith of San Francisco, a driver for DeSoto Cab Co., was arrested at the Hall of Justice Thursday after a police inspector investigating the Friday night accident asked him to come in for additional questioning.

"We talked to him at the scene the night of the accident," Inspector Jeff Levin said. "He told us that another car hit the couple and threw them onto the hood of his cab. We have since been able to determine that was not what happened."

Calvin Threadgill II was killed instantly, and his companion, Tina Frank, was seriously injured when they were struck at about 9:30 p.m. last Friday as they crossed the Embarcadero near Mission Street.

Threadgill, 45, of Castro Valley, was recently appointed vice president of marketing for Zapit, a Silicon Valley environmental technology company.

Frank is the director of the Bay Area regional office of the California Trade and Commerce Agency. . . .

Investigators say the pair were walking in a marked crosswalk when they were struck.

Levin said a reconstruction of the accident by Sgt. James Hughes, evidence gathered by the police crime lab and new information from two eyewitnesses had led them to Smith.

Source: John D. O'Connor, "Cops Hold Cabbie in Hit-Run Death," *San Francisco Examiner,* 12 August 1994, A4. Reprinted by permission.

---

use "she" in some cases and "he" in others. Yet both of these alternatives are awkward, and neither is likely to please everyone in your audience. Thus, we suggest a third alternative: Use plural nouns and pronouns when constructing examples to make your speech more vivid, involving, and inclusive. Instead of saying, "If a person is strong, he will stand up for himself," say, "Strong people stand up for themselves." Instead of saying, "When someone believes something, he shouldn't be afraid to say so," try, "When people believe something, they shouldn't be afraid to say so." And instead of saying, "An individual should keep his promise," simply say, "People should keep their promises."

Finally, be on the lookout for the subtle ways the news media can reinforce the use of sexist language in their reporting. As the article reprinted in the box "How Does Language Marginalize People?" illustrates, even journalists can perpetuate the misconception that *executive* is a masculine word and *companion* is a feminine one.

SUMMARY

While words alone can't break your bones, words are powerful symbols and should be treated as such. In recognition of this fact, keep the following in mind as you construct your speeches:

- Language is symbolic and influences the process of perception.
- Language reflects the multiracial, multiethnic, multicultural audience of today.
- Effective language is inclusive rather than marginalizing or totalizing.
- Effective language enhances your audience's perception of your competence.
- Effective language takes advantage of devices such as metaphor, simile, alliteration, parallel structure, and repetition.

 **SPEECH COACH**

To evaluate your understanding of this chapter, see the Quizzes on your CD.

- Effective language connects with the auditory, tactile, and visual styles of processing information present in your audience.
- Effective language avoids unfair stereotypes and the use of words that perpetuate sexism.

CHECK YOUR UNDERSTANDING: EXERCISES AND ACTIVITIES

SPEECH COACH

For a review of key terms in this chapter, see the Key Terms Flashcards on your CD.

1. Rewrite the following paragraph using inclusive language:

   When a speaker begins his speech, the first thing he must do is thank the chairman of the group for the opportunity to speak to his group. As we know, the quality that separates man from the animals is the ability to speak. Regardless of his job, a man must know how to speak clearly. Similarly, a woman must know how to impart language skills to her children. Thus, every speaker is urged to use language to the best of his ability.

2. Write five transitional statements (signposts) without using the following words:

   first (second, third, etc.)

   therefore

   next

   finally

   in conclusion

3. Company X has an internal policies manual that is written in marginalizing language. As an employee of the company, you find the language disturbing and believe the language in the manual should be changed. Write a letter to the head of the documents division explaining why you believe such changes are necessary and why you believe the changes will enhance the image of the company. (Thanks to Dr. Madeline Keaveney for suggesting this exercise.)

4. Exclusive language is marginalizing and biased. Provide an inclusive-language alternative for each of the following, or state under what conditions the term might be appropriately used in a speech. (Adapted from Rosalie Maggio, *The Bias-Free Word Finder: A Dictionary of Nondiscriminatory Language* (Boston: Beacon Press, 1991).)

actress	meter maid
airline stewardess	mother
businessman	majorette
craftsmanship	Mrs. John Doe
doorman	old wives' tale
executrix	waitress
goddess	

NOTES

1. W. H. Auden and L. Kronenberger, *The Viking Book of Aphorisms* (New York: Dorsett Press, 1981), 238.

2. "This Boss Is No Girl, She's Just Stunned," *Sacramento Bee*, 10 October 1995, C2.

3. "This Boss Is No Girl," C2.

4. Benjamin Lee Whorf, *Language, Thought, and Reality* (New York: Wiley, 1956).

5. Earl Shorris, *Latinos: A Biography of the People* (New York: Norton, 1992), 95–100.

6. Julia T. Wood, ed., *Gendered Relationships* (Mountain View, Calif.: Mayfield, 1996), 39–56.

7. See, for example: W. M. O'Barr, *Linguistic Evidence: Language, Power, and Strategy in the Courtroom* (New York: Academic Press, 1982); James J. Bradac and Anthony Mulac, "A Molecular View of Powerful and Powerless Speech Styles: Attributional Consequences of Specific Language Features and Communication Intentions," *Communication Monographs* 51 (1984): 307–319.

8. H. Giles and J. Wiemann, "Language, Social Comparison, and Power," in *Handbook of Communication Science*, ed. C. R. Berger and S. H. Chaffee (Newbury Park, Calif.: Sage, 1987).

9. Auden and Kronenberger, *The Viking Book of Aphorisms*, 359.

How you say something can be as important as what you have to say.

Delivery: Engaging Your Audience

  OBJECTIVES

After reading this chapter and reviewing the learning resources on your CD-ROM and at the Online Learning Center, you should be able to:

- Define nonverbal behavior and distinguish between verbal and nonverbal behavior.
- Describe the relationship between delivery and the seven basic dimensions of the nonverbal system.
- Display nonverbal behaviors characteristic of effective delivery, including control of the speaking environment; proper attire; eye contact and expressive facial cues; vocal variation in pitch, range, rhythm, and tempo; clear and distinct vocal articulation; and gestures and movements that serve as emblems, illustrators, and regulators.
- Control distracting self-adaptive behaviors.
- Use time to enhance your credibility and communicate urgency, drama, humor, and the like during your speech.
- Explain the guidelines for developing a proactive, rather than reactive, delivery.
- Display nonverbal examples of complementing, contradicting, and repeating the message; substituting for a verbal cue; increasing the perception of immediacy; exciting the audience; and delivering a powerful speech.

What people do is frequently more important than what they say.

—EDWARD T. HALL, anthropologist[1]

  KEY CONCEPTS

emblem	impromptu delivery	proactive delivery
environment	manuscript delivery	regulators
extemporaneous delivery	memorized delivery	self-adapting behaviors
illustrators	nonverbal behavior	zone of interaction

Against the advice of the experts, Elizabeth Dole moved among conventioneers as she spoke at the 1996 Republican Convention.

SPEECH COACH

To view examples of different styles of delivery, see segment 10.1 on your CD.

Elizabeth Dole broke with tradition during the 1996 Republican Convention in San Diego, California. Instead of addressing the assembly of delegates from the raised platform from which other speakers had spoken, she actually walked out on the convention floor and moved about the audience as she delivered her message. Dole did so even though Republican consultants had told her that such an approach wouldn't work in the context of a political convention.

Were they ever wrong! Dole's speech not only captivated the convention delegates, but also favorably impressed network news anchors Dan Rather, Tom Brokaw, and Peter Jennings. Having seen nothing like it previously, these news anchors were effusive in their praise of Dole's performance.

This chapter focuses on the delivery of your speech. We want you to recognize from the beginning that there is no single method of effectively delivering your speeches. It depends on you and the style with which you are most comfortable, the occasion, and the context in which you find yourself. Perhaps you like to move in the manner of Elizabeth Dole, or stay firmly planted in close proximity to a lectern in the manner of Secretary of State Colin Powell. Simply put, when it comes to delivery, you have options from which you can choose.

Given this framework, we will first look at the four most common methods of delivery. Next we will discuss how you can use your voice to enhance your delivery. Finally, we will examine the functional role of nonverbal communication in the process of effectively delivering your speeches.

FOCUSING YOUR DELIVERY ON YOUR AUDIENCE

Never forget that public speaking is a transaction between you and your audience. Just as the language you choose for your message should reflect the nature of your audience, so too should your delivery. As a result, we begin our discussion with some audience-related factors you will want to consider while thinking about the delivery of your message. Specifically, we discuss choosing an appropriate method of delivery, adapting to diverse audiences, and adapting delivery to the speech occasion.

 **SPEECH COACH**

To evaluate speech delivery, see the Speech Critique program on your CD.

Choosing an Appropriate Method of Delivery

Recall from Chapter 2 that there is more than one way to deliver a speech. We discussed four different methods of delivery. As you review your analysis of your audience and rhetorical situation, one of your most important decisions will be an appropriate method of speech delivery.

Manuscript Delivery   As you'll recall from Chapter 2, manuscript delivery involves writing out the speech completely and reading it to the audience. This method may be the best choice when your audience requires precise information from you. When you are speaking about highly technical matters before a group of engineers, for example, the precision with which you deliver the information may be extremely important. The same would be true for a plastic surgeon addressing a seminar on advances in rhinoplasty (nose job). Similarly, if you expect your words to be quoted by others, having a manuscript of your speech helps ensure accuracy.

Anytime you use a manuscript, however, the dynamics of delivery are restricted. As we show later in this chapter, eye contact, movement, and gesture are important dimensions of nonverbal behavior that can enhance your delivery. Tying yourself to a manuscript interferes with each of these. Manuscript speaking also impedes spontaneity between you and your audience because the manuscript restricts opportunities to survey and creatively respond to audience feedback. Further, a manuscript demands a lectern, which can stand as a barrier between a speaker and the audience. Finally, this method of delivery can sound stilted and artificial because the language of a written message generally is more formal than spoken language.

If you must utilize a manuscript, therefore, learn it well. Practice repeatedly so that you do not have to look down often. Mark up your manuscript with notes to yourself and underline main ideas. Also, be sure pages are numbered so that they will not get out of order. Use a large typeface and double or even triple spacing. Manuscript speaking is far more difficult than most people realize. Its success depends on practice and skill in converting words on a page into a living speech.

Memorized Delivery   A speaker using memorized delivery writes out the speech and commits it to memory before presenting it to the audience without the use of notes. Most audiences don't expect a memorized speech, unless they are watching a professional speaker who is highly paid, an actor delivering a soliloquy in a play, or a student competing in a speech tournament. In fact, in a typical speech class,

Informal situations such as this one invite a conversational delivery style.

an obviously memorized speech would probably strike most students and the instructor as odd. Although memorization allows you to concentrate on eye contact, movement, and gesture, it does so at a price. You may forget parts of your speech, and it requires a greater investment of time than any other method.

When writing a speech to be memorized, keep the organization simple so that you will not confuse one point with another. A good rule of thumb is to memorize the speech in small chunks. Learn a paragraph, then move on to the next one, and so on. Practice reciting your speech from the beginning through as far as you have it memorized. The repetition of earlier parts will help fix them in your mind. Finally, don't panic if you forget a part of the speech. Try to ad-lib for a bit, and often the next section will come to mind.

Impromptu Delivery   There may be times when you have to give an impromptu delivery—a spontaneous, unrehearsed method of presenting a speech. Usually, these short speeches are given in response to someone who asks you to say a few words, make a toast, or respond to an inquiry. Although an audience is always appreciative of an eloquent impromptu speech, an organized and confidently spoken message is normally enough to fulfill any audience's expectations.

Impromptu speaking eliminates any impediments to using the full range of nonverbal behaviors available to speakers. This can be both good and bad, depending on the comfort level of the speaker. Speakers who are comfortable in an impromptu situation may benefit because their delivery will strike the audience as relaxed and genuine. Uncomfortable speakers, however, are likely to appear rigid, awkward, or distracted.

Impromptu speaking is not nearly as rare as you may think. In business meetings, people are frequently put on the spot and asked to speak on topics relevant to their responsibilities. Students, moreover, are frequently asked to make impromptu remarks. The lesson here is that you should always be prepared to speak on the spur of the moment. To help you in this regard, we offer the following tips. First, be proactive and anticipate situations where you might be asked to speak, for example, in class, at meetings, or social events such as a wedding, Bat Mitzvah, or memorial service. Second, realize that the key to effective impromptu speaking is organization. If you are asked to respond to a question, repeat the question to introduce your answer, specify the number of points you want to make, and try to conclude with a declarative statement. Third, approach your impromptu speech as if you were telling a story that has a beginning, middle, and end. Fourth, consider hitchhiking off the remarks of those who may have preceded you. For instance: "Julie's points are well taken, and I'd like to add to them by first seconding her belief that airport security should not be the responsibility of the airlines." Finally, don't be afraid to assert yourself when you have an informed opinion on the topic about which you've been asked to speak. Don't compound the nervousness you may feel as a result of having been put on the spot by telling yourself you have nothing worthwhile to say. Impromptu speaking is a skill. Like any other skill, it can be honed with experience and practice.

Extemporaneous Delivery   For most students who are still learning to give a speech, extemporaneous speaking remains their best choice of delivery method. Recall from Chapter 2 that extemporaneous delivery combines careful preparation with spontaneous speaking. The speaker generally uses brief notes rather than a manuscript or an outline. Extemporaneous speaking enables you to maintain eye contact, move, gesture, and spontaneously adapt to audience feedback. You may choose not to use a lectern, depending on how extensive your notes are and how comfortable you are moving freely before the audience.

Today's audiences are more likely to expect and appreciate the extemporaneously delivered speech than other methods of delivery. Just as it allows the speaker to remain in contact with the audience, so does it allow the audience to remain connected to the speaker. Audiences not only can give feedback to someone speaking extemporaneously but also can assess the degree to which their feedback registers with the speaker.

This doesn't mean that extemporaneous speaking is without drawbacks. Note cards can restrict the range of gestures used when you refer to them, and they can also be distracting when waved about while you're speaking. Finally, you can get carried away with note cards, writing down so many of your thoughts that the note cards become almost a manuscript.

Delivering Speeches to Diverse Audiences

Both the method and style of delivery should reflect the diversity of your audience. Throughout this chapter we offer numerous specific examples of cases in which a particular nonverbal behavior means one thing to one culture and something entirely different to another. For example, consider how three different audiences might respond to the same speech. As you speak, a North American audience returns your eye contact and nods in agreement with you. A British audience also returns your eye contact, but heads remain motionless. And a West African audience avoids making direct eye contact with you altogether. What should you make of their feedback in each situation? Before you decide, perhaps it would help to know this: When the British agree with a speaker, they sometimes blink rather than nod their head. Further, the more direct the eye contact of West Africans, the less they respect the person to whom it is directed. Knowing the typical patterns of nonverbal behavior in a given culture is essential if you are to accurately interpret the nonverbal behaviors of your audience members.

Another example of differences among culturally diverse audiences concerns your voice. Almost from birth, the norm for the North American culture is "to speak up and let yourself be heard." What is normative here, however, may be loud in Japan or among the upper class in Great Britain. And much as we may want to be heard, we don't want to be perceived as loudmouths.

Adapting Delivery to the Speech Occasion

How you present your speech depends on the specific rhetorical situation you face and the kind of delivery your audience is likely to expect. A speech commemorating or honoring a person calls for a formal and dignified delivery. Other speech situations call for an energetic, dynamic delivery. A motivational speaker, for example, usually dispenses with the lectern and moves about the stage, perhaps even into the audience. A lively style is expected and rewarded. Then there are situations that call for a lighthearted, comic style of delivery. For example, "roasts" honoring someone are often punctuated with good-natured joking at the honoree's expense. Unlike a commemorative speech, a delivery at a roast should be informal and lively. The key is to understand what the audience expects in a given situation and match your delivery style to those expectations.

YOUR VOICE

Before we talk about what makes voices as unique as fingerprints, we want to emphasize the fact that what you say and how you say it are not the same thing. The spoken word has two dimensions. One dimension is content—the words themselves and the way they are configured to form sentences. The other dimension is vocalic—the sound that shapes the meaning the spoken word conveys to the audience. Consider the sentence "I love you." By changing the pitch, volume, and inflection of your voice as you utter the sentence, you can actually alter the meaning the sentence conveys to another person. It can be sensuous or sincere, for example, depending on the tone of voice with which it is spoken.

In a sense, words are like musical notes, and your voice is like an instrument. In the hands of a skilled musician, notes are not simply played but are shaped by the musician. Skilled guitarists playing the same notes can produce quite different sounds, depending on how they bend or agitate the strings with their fingertips. Skilled speakers do much the same thing but do it with the pitch, tempo, and rhythm of their voices.

In the effort to help you gain better control of your voice, you need to know how sound is produced and how it can be manipulated. You also need to appreciate the role articulation plays in the process of shaping this sound so that it is meaningful to your audience. Finally, you need to accept the fact that you are better off speaking in your own voice than trying to imitate the voice of someone else.

Vocal Production

The production of sound in the voice is fairly straightforward. You take in air and expel the air through the trachea across your vocal cords, which are contained in the larynx (voice box), and then across your teeth, tongue, and lips. Variations in the amount of air expelled, the positioning of the vocal cords, or the placement of the teeth and tongue and position of the lips will result in variations in the sounds produced. Shallow breathing and the rapid expulsion of air across the vocal cords, for example, will produce a much different sound than breathing deeply and then slowly expelling the air. In the first case, your voice is likely to be described as feminine and in the second masculine, even though neither is necessarily true. The basic mechanical operation of the voice, however, is not as important to the topic at hand as are the characteristics of the voice. These include volume, pitch, range, rhythm, and tempo.

Volume   How loudly you project your voice is a consequence of both the amount of air you expel when speaking and the force with which you expel it. For example, try to speak loudly without first taking a fairly deep breath. Surprising, isn't it? Some examples of people capable of speaking with great volume are actor/talk show host Oprah Winfrey, broadcaster Rush Limbaugh, actor James Earl Jones (the person you hear saying "CNN"), and the entertainer/rocker Kid Rock. On the other hand, some examples of more soft-spoken public figures include Vice President Dick Cheney, actor Liv Tyler, and singer Sade.

You need not be loud to be heard. What's more, speaking in a consistently loud voice is likely to grate on the ears of your audience. You want to *project* your voice, not break eardrums with it. The key is to vary the volume of your voice depending on the impact you hope to have with your audience. Sometimes lowering the volume of your voice will draw your audience in, whereas a sudden increase in volume may startle your audience. As a public speaker, you need to have enough volume to be heard by your audience. But that can vary tremendously depending on the size of your audience, the room in which you are speaking, and the availability of a microphone. Seasoned speakers prepare differently depending on the preceding factors. That is to say, they vary the volume with which they practice depending on where and with whom they will be speaking. You should do the same thing. Practice your speech as if you were delivering it in the classroom where you will speak, to an audience equivalent in size to your actual class. When you actually do speak to your class, moreover, look for feedback about volume in the faces and posture of audience members. If those in the back of the room are leaning forward or look puzzled, you may need to raise your volume. On the other hand, if people seated in the first row are leaning back in their seats, you may be speaking too loudly.

Pitch   The degree to which your voice is high or low is its pitch. A person who sings bass has a low pitch, whereas a person who sings soprano has a high pitch. The bass knob on your stereo lowers pitch, the treble knob raises it. The pitch of a bass fiddle is lower than that of a violin; the pitch of a ukulele is higher than the pitch of an acoustic guitar. Since pitch is a key to vocal inflection, effective speakers vary their pitch to shape the impact of their words. They may lower pitch to sound more serious or raise it to convey a sense of urgency. Control of pitch depends not only on their skill as a speaker but on the natural range of their voice as well.

Range   The extent of the pitch, from low to high, that lies within your vocal capacity is known as range. Just as a piano has a tremendous range in pitch, some speakers have a great vocal range. On the other hand, some speakers are like an electric bass guitar, which no matter how well played, does not have much range. As a speaker, you need to make the fullest use of your normal conversational vocal range. That means you first need to discover the bottom and top of your own vocal scale.

To get a sense of how pitch and range control the inflection in your voice, you'll need to tape-record yourself. Recite the alphabet beginning in your normal voice. Then raise your pitch with each new letter until your voice cracks. Next do the same thing, but lower your voice as your recite. Play back the recording and note where your voice begins to break as you go up and then breaks as you go down. This will give you an audible idea about the limits of your vocal range, as well as at what pitches your voice sounds relaxed and natural. Then practice varying your pitch within this relaxed and natural range, using the tape recorder to further get in touch with your natural pitch and range.

Rhythm   Think of rhythm as the characteristic pattern of your volume, pitch, and range. Perhaps you have heard someone describe a speaker's voice as "singsong." This means the speaker's voice goes consistently up and then down in pitch, almost as if the person were talking to a small child.

Some speakers use predictable rhythm to great effect. Many Evangelical preachers have a decided rhythm in their sermons. The Reverend Jesse Jackson is an easy target for comedic impersonators because of the predictable rhythm with which he takes his audience up, and then pauses before taking them down. Jackson heightens this effect with his inflection and frequent use of alliteration, which we discussed in Chapter 9.

Tempo   The rate at which you produce sounds, or how quickly or slowly you speak, will influence how you are perceived. Tempo also tends to vary across and even within cultures. In the United States, for example, speech in the South is relatively slow in tempo, while in the East, tempo is accelerated. This is readily apparent if you compare the voices of actress Holly Hunter, who is from the South, and Marisa Tomei, from the East.

Because tempo varies, you have to use good judgment in terms of how quickly or slowly you speak. Doing either to the extreme can turn off your audience. An excessively rapid pace can be perceived as a sign of nervousness. An excessively slow pace may suggest a speaker is not well prepared. Researchers have found that moderate to fast rates of speaking tend to be associated with increased perceptions of a speaker's competence on the part of the audience.[2] Other researchers have noted a ceiling to that effect, however, meaning that too fast a rate of speaking can backfire.[3] In addition, when audiences perceive speech rates as similar to their own, they are more likely to find speakers socially attractive and to comply with their requests.[4] The best advice is to moderately vary your tempo. Not only will this accommodate the different preferences of individuals in your audience, it will also enhance the overall effect of your message.

Your tempo is also affected by pauses. Sometimes a brief moment of silence can convey much to an audience. Pausing just before delivering a crucial word or phrase helps grab the audience's attention. Pausing after you've made an important point gives it time to sink in. Don't be afraid to use pauses when appropriate. It is also better to pause a moment than to fill the air with "ums," "uhs," and "you knows," which are really vocalized pauses.

Articulation   If you expect an audience to understand what you are saying, you need clear articulation, which refers to the distinctness with which you make individual sounds. You may have experienced the frustration of listening to someone who sounds mushy, failing to distinctly vocalize sounds. A common articulation problem comes from either running together differing sounds or dropping parts of a word: *goin'* instead of *going, wanna* instead of *want to,* or *whatcha doin'?* in place of *what are you doing?* A good way to test your articulation is to tape-record your speech and listen critically to yourself. If you find a consistent articulation problem or set of problems, you may want to find out if your college or university offers a course in voice and articulation. Sometimes drama or theatre department courses in voice for performers can also be of assistance. Severe articulation problems are often best treated by a speech pathologist. But for most students in public speaking classes, exercising care, practicing, and slowing down are the keys to being understood by the audience.

In Chapter 9 we emphasized the importance of using words correctly. This is a good place to reemphasize the fact. As you practice articulating words, make sure that you are also pronouncing them correctly. "Nu-ku-lar" is still wrong, no matter how well you articulate it.

In the final analysis, judgments about the relationship between the qualities of your voice and the quality of your delivery will depend on the preceding characteristics operating in concert. Important as pitch or tempo may be on their own, it is their collective impact with range and rhythm that most counts.

Speaking in Your Own Voice

With these qualities of voice in mind, let's now turn to your voice specifically. Are you pleased with the way it sounds and complements your overall delivery? No matter how you answer this question, it is just as important for you to find your own voice as a speaker as it is for authors to find their own voice when they write. We mention this need to find your own voice with good reason. When public speaking students are advised to make better use of their voice in their delivery, all too often they take this to mean they must change their voice to some ideal. The ideal, moreover, is usually thought to be the voice of a television or radio personality.

We don't encourage you to imitate the vocal delivery of someone who hosts a game show, reads the news, or introduces music videos. Instead, we encourage you to experiment with your voice; for example, record your attempts to convey varying emotions in your voice, listen to yourself, and then repeat the process. This kind of exercise will let you hear what your vocal strengths and weaknesses are. In the process, be realistic but not unfairly harsh about how you think you sound. Chances are, what you think you hear is much different from what others hear.

Finally, recognize that important as it is, your voice is but a single component of your overall delivery. Not all good speakers have tremendous "pipes." For example, the *Today Show*'s Katie Couric and Matt Lauer are both engaging, but their voices would hardly be described as rich in timbre. Further, if you were to listen to a number of paid speakers, you would see that this is the case with them as well. All of us tend to underutilize the full potential of our voices. What ultimately counts, then, is whether we're willing to do the hard work necessary to rectify this fact.

TIPS AND TACTICS   *Improving Your Voice*

Like it or not, people will make judgments about you on the basis of the way you sound. Although we want you to be comfortable with your voice, the following tips may help you if you think something about your voice needs to be changed.

- *Relaxation:* More than one problem with voice can be solved by monitoring tension in your vocal apparatus. Nasality, shrillness, or screeching, and excessive rate of speech are often a consequence of tension/stress. The same relaxation techniques discussed in Chapter 3 can be used to alleviate the impact of tension/stress on your voice.

- *Vocal variation:* Tape-record yourself or have someone tape you when you speak. If you find as a result of monitoring your audiotape that greater vocal variation is needed, pick out someone whose vocal characteristics you admire and repeatedly listen to the person. Then try to model the vocal variation in which the person engages. Repeat this process while using a tape recorder.

- *Being heard:* Have a friend monitor your speaking volume. When you speak too softly, tell your friend to raise an index finger within your view. Use this signal to increase the volume of your voice. The goal is to be easily heard, even in the back of the room.

NONVERBAL CHARACTERISTICS OF DELIVERY

nonverbal behavior
A wordless system of communication.

Nonverbal behavior is a wordless system of communicating. What makes a behavior nonverbal as opposed to verbal? Is it the absence of sound? That cannot be the case, because sign language is considered a form of verbal communication, with signs merely substituting for written or spoken language. Although scholars argue about the exact definition of nonverbal behavior, most agree that it is distinct from verbal behavior in at least three ways: It is continuous, uses multiple channels simultaneously, and is spontaneous.

The Continuous Nature of Nonverbal Behavior

Verbal behavior, composed of words, is discrete. This means verbal behavior can be divided into distinct elements, as was the case when you first began to learn about nouns, verbs, and adjectives. These elements of composition are governed by complex rules, dictating how they should be combined in your speech to form phrases, clauses, and sentences. Each word has a denotative meaning that can be found in the dictionary. Words must be arranged in a precise manner to convey the intended meaning. For example, the words *I am happy* must be arranged in that order to convey the intended meaning. To say, "Am I happy" changes the statement to a question. To say, "Happy am I" seems odd to English speakers. When words with agreed-on meaning are used in a specified order, the meaning of the verbal behavior is apparent as in this example. This is not so with nonverbal behavior, which is continuous rather than divisible.[5]

Consider the expression of happiness as you speak. What the audience sees is a complex message that involves the entire face. The muscles of the face contract, affecting the eyebrows, the corners of the mouth, and the corners of the eyes. Unlike verbal behavior, these involuntary movements cannot be broken down into compositional elements. The eyes, for example, do not convey "I," while the eyebrows say "am" and the mouth represents "happy." You cannot rearrange the components to convey a different meaning, as you can with "I," "am," and "happy." There are no rules of grammar to explain the meaning conveyed by these facial expressions. Only the total, continuous combination of these elements can constitute the nonverbal expression of happiness.

The Simultaneous Use of Multiple Channels

Returning to the example of expressing happiness, nonverbal behavior also involves the simultaneous use of multiple channels.[6] For example, try conveying an emotional expression, such as happiness, anger, sorrow, or bewilderment, through a single channel of communication, such as your mouth or eyes or hands. You'll soon see that it is difficult if not impossible. At the same time, you'll recognize that we use these multiple channels simultaneously rather than sequentially. When happy, we express the emotion all over our face, not with our eyes first, mouth second, eyebrows and forehead third and fourth.

The Spontaneous Nature of Nonverbal Behavior

As each of the preceding characteristics might lead you to believe, the final distinguishing characteristic is that nonverbal behavior is spontaneous. With the possible exception of so-called Freudian slips, when people unintentionally say what they really mean, verbal behavior is planned behavior.[7] We consciously think about the words we speak and write, though we do so with such speed it may not occur to us.

Smiles, gestures, and body language occur at a subconscious level. This doesn't mean that people never plan or orchestrate gestures when they speak. Sometimes they do, and their nonverbal behavior is likely to look phony. Most of us learn to distinguish between authentic and phony nonverbal behaviors by the time we reach our teens. Unless nonverbal behavior is rehearsed to the point it becomes habit, planned gestures especially will be recognized as insincere. This is a major reason for people putting so much stock in the meaning they infer from nonverbal behavior.

DELIVERY AND THE NONVERBAL COMMUNICATION SYSTEM

Recall that a system is a collection of interdependent and interrelated components. A change in one component will produce changes in them all. The nonverbal system has as its components several interdependent dimensions of behavior that profoundly affect the delivery of a speech. The specific dimensions we discuss in this section are the environment, appearance, the face and eyes, gestures and movement, posture, touch, and time. As a speaker intent on delivering a message effectively, you need to approach these dimensions systematically. Further, the verbal language with which you construct your speech should take into account what you've learned from your systematic assessment of the nonverbal dimensions.

The Environment

environment The physical surroundings as you speak and the physical distance separating you from your audience.

For our purposes, **environment** refers to the physical surroundings as you speak and the physical distance separating you from your audience. Both surroundings and physical space have an undeniable impact not only on your delivery but also on how the speech is perceived by your audience.

The physical characteristics of the room in which you speak—for example, lighting, temperature, comfort, and aesthetics—will influence both you and your audience physically and psychologically.[8] A bright, aesthetically neutral room, which is neither sterile nor plushly decorated, and in which the temperature is 68 degrees, will have a much different overall impact on the speech transaction than a room that is dimly lit, richly furnished, and 75 degrees. Whereas in the first, both you and your audience are likely to be alert and attentive, the second might prove so comfortable that neither you nor your audience are sufficiently aroused for your transaction. Thus, you would have to plan your delivery accordingly. Whereas your "normal" pattern of delivery probably would be appropriate in the first environment, you likely would need to put extra energy and enthusiasm into the delivery to succeed in the second.

A second environmental consideration is the physical layout of the room. We have been in situations where student presentations were hindered by pillars supporting the roof, by the width and length of the room, and by immovable objects such as tables. Sometimes you have no alternative but to do the best you can in such situations. As a result, you move more than you had planned as you speak, abandon visual aids that would prove impossible for your entire audience to see, or make gestures larger and more exaggerated than is customary for you.

At other times, however, you will have the opportunity to physically arrange the room in which you will speak. This may include the position of a lectern, elevation of a stage, and configuration of an audience. Given this opportunity, experienced speakers will arrange the environment in concert with their style of delivery. Speakers who have a traditional style of delivery may prefer a lectern, perhaps an overhead projector immediately to their side, and an elevated stage from which to speak. Speakers who are much less formal in their style of delivery may want the room to be arranged so that they can move from side to side or even up and down its length.

zone of interaction Area of audience in which speaker and audience members can make eye contact.

Both the traditional and informal styles of delivery can be equally effective. However, the room layout consistent with the traditional style is more restrictive than its counterpart in two ways. The first way concerns the **zone of interaction,** the area in which speakers can easily make eye contact with audience members (Figure 10.1). The second way concerns the amount of space physically separating speakers from their audience.

The zone of interaction is limited to the range of your peripheral vision. The immediate zone of interaction between speakers and their audience dimin-

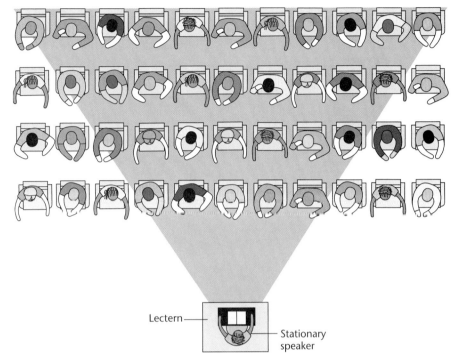

FIGURE 10.1 Zone of Interaction in the Traditional Room Setting Where people are seated in rows and the speaker is stationary, eye contact between speaker and audience is limited to the shaded area. The speaker must turn to make eye contact with those outside the shaded area.

Lectern

Stationary speaker

ishes as a room gets larger. To compensate for this fact, speakers have two choices. Either they can shift the zone of interaction by looking from side to side, or they can physically move from one point to another when they deliver their speeches. This latter choice is illustrated in Figure 10.2. Obviously, in a very large room the traditional style of delivery limits you to looking from side to side in the attempt to shift the zone of interaction. This means that you cannot help but ignore part of your audience part of the time.

The traditional style of delivery allows less flexibility in manipulating the physical distance separating speakers from their audiences. Whereas a speaker who moves about the room can reduce or increase distance physically as well as psychologically, a relatively stationary speaker is restricted to the latter. Thus, for those who prefer this style of delivery, eye contact becomes their primary agent for managing how immediate they are perceived to be by their audience, a point which we discuss shortly.

To summarize: The relationship of the speaking environment to delivery is a significant one. Not only does it influence your style of delivery, it also influences how you are perceived by your audience. Experienced public speakers try to plan the delivery of their speeches accordingly. When faced with a "tough room," for example, they know that the arousal level of their delivery will need to increase if they are to reach their audience. Inexperienced speakers, on the other hand, all too often play "victim" to their speaking environment. Instead of surveying and planning for the environment, they simply deliver their speech as if the environment were of no consequence to them. As a student of public speaking, you know what's good and bad about the layout of the classroom in which you must speak. Thus, you too should plan your delivery accordingly.

FIGURE 10.2 Shifting the Zone of Interaction With Movement Changing positions can increase the perception of inclusiveness as well as add energy to your speech.

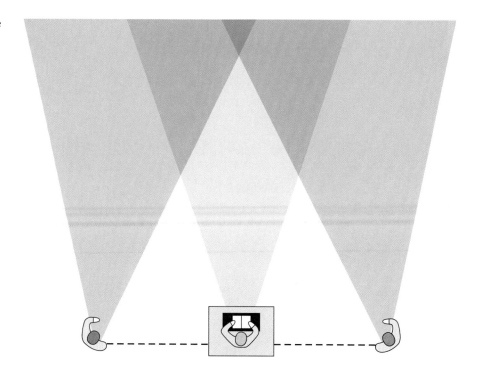

The box "Seating Arrangements" discusses another factor you should consider when planning your delivery.

TIPS AND TACTICS   *The Speaking Environment*

- Check out the room in which you'll speak well in advance. Take note of the seating arrangement, availability of lectern, and availability of equipment necessary to any media you will be using.
- If permissible, consider changing the environment to better reflect your speech purpose and style of delivery.
- Rehearse planned movement, including how you will use any equipment necessary for your presentational media.
- If possible, try to set the room temperature to between 68 and 70 degrees. Check lighting at the same time.

Appearance

Appearance often has a disproportionately significant effect on audience perceptions of a speaker's message and delivery.[9] Speakers never get a second chance to make a first impression with an audience. First impressions are based largely on appearance, including body type and height, skin and hair color, and clothing and accessories.

The significance of appearance to public speaking can be measured in at least two ways. The first involves audience members' first impressions. The sec-

Seating Arrangements

Can the physical seating arrangement have an impact on both your speech and the manner in which it is perceived? A very dramatic one. As a result, you should think about your goals as a speaker and the physical layout of the room in which you speak. Traditional rows will focus attention exclusively on you. A horseshoe arrangement, however, allows audience members to make eye contact with each other. And speaking at the head of a conference table not only narrows the zone of interaction but also puts a physical barrier between you and your audience. Which of these arrangements do you think would most likely encourage audience feedback and participation? Why?

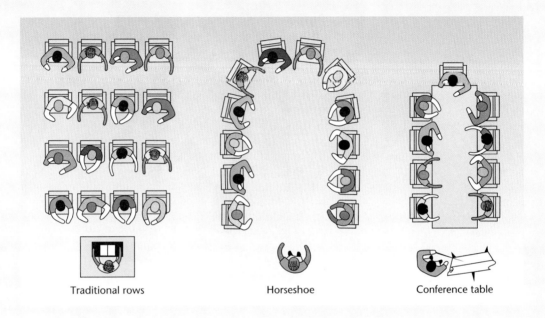

Traditional rows   Horseshoe   Conference table

ond involves how people perceive themselves as a result of their appearance and the impact this perception has on their self-confidence and delivery.

According to communication expert Dale Leathers, "Our visible self functions to communicate a constellation of meanings which define who we are and what we are apt to become in the eyes of others."[10] These "others" are the people with whom we come into contact, including the members of our audiences.

Audience members use appearance initially to make judgments about a speaker's level of attractiveness. The consequences of this judgment are far-reaching for speakers. Research tells us that speakers perceived as attractive by audience members also are perceived as smart, successful, sociable, and self-confident. As a result, speakers who fall into this category enjoy an audience whose initial impression of them is favorable.

Yet appearance influences more than an audience's initial impression of a speaker. Appearance also can have a very real effect on a speaker's self-confidence. Research tells us that speakers who feel they appear attractive report greater self-confidence than those reporting otherwise.[11]

Although some facets of your appearance and their impact on audience perception are outside your control—for example, body type and height—there is one facet you can easily control: your dress. Simply said, your dress should be

What you typically wear to class may not be appropriate for a classroom speech.

appropriate to the situation. Obvious as this advice may seem, it is frequently ignored by students in public speaking classes. All too often they show up to speak dressed as if they had thought little about the appropriateness of their attire. Their attitude, as reflected in their dress, seems to be saying, "It's just a speech class."

Consider an analogy. Good students know what the research suggests about the relationship between the appearance of a term paper and the mark it receives. Frequently, it's the difference between a minus or a plus in their grade. Good students, therefore, go to some length to make sure that their papers not only conform to the requirements but "look" impressive as well.

The same relationship may exist between appearance and the marks students receive on their speeches. Although an Armani suit may not turn a mediocre speech into an outstanding one, it certainly won't cause the speaker to lose points. Inappropriate attire or careless grooming will never add points to a speech; moreover, there is a chance they will unnecessarily detract from such things as the speaker's perceived competence.

The Eyes and Face

The eyes have been called the windows to the soul. Perhaps, then, it is only fitting that many people also believe eye contact is the single most important variable in delivering your speech. The eyes connect the speaker and audience. The eyes also tell the speaker and audience much about each other.

In the North American culture, people use eye contact to make judgments about:

- whether or not a person is competent
- whether or not a person can be trusted
- whether or not a person is approachable

Competence and trustworthiness are two key components of a speaker's credibility, that is, the degree to which a speaker is perceived as believable. Generally, the more a speaker makes eye contact with audience members, the more credible the speaker will be perceived. Since credible speakers are also likely to have more influence with an audience, it only makes good sense for the speaker to maintain as much eye contact as possible with an audience.

Eye contact also has the power to reduce physical distances psychologically. When we make and sustain friendly eye contact with people at a distance, it makes us feel "closer" to each other. It also helps to make people appear attractive and open to dialogue. As was the case with competence and trustworthiness, this is clearly to a speaker's benefit.

But there is yet another reason for maintaining eye contact with an audience. Eye contact is an important source of audience feedback. In North America, for example, an audience will use eye contact to let the speaker know the degree to which it is engaged. Speakers can then use this feedback to make decisions about whether they need to modify their speech to gain the audience's attention.

Having established its importance to delivery, let's talk about how you can optimize the positive effects of eye contact. First, recognize that you cannot fake eye contact! People know you are looking directly at them or looking only at the tops of their heads. Second, some eye contact is better than no eye contact at all. Ideally, however, eye contact works best when you look at individual members of the audience as you speak. This type of eye contact personalizes a public message. All too often, people think eye contact means looking at the audience members as a group, beginning with those in the center seats, and then turning to those seated to your right or left. To the contrary, effective eye contact means making every person in the room feel as if you were speaking only to him or her.

Finally, eye contact also works best when it is complemented with appropriate facial expressions. The face and eyes, for example, can communicate happiness, surprise, fear, anger, disgust, contempt, sadness, and interest. The face and eyes can also modify the intensity of any of these nonverbal expressions of emotion.[12]

Just as you can use metaphor to manipulate language intensity, you can use your face and eyes to intensify your delivery. In most cases, you intensify what you say in this manner with little or no conscious thought. As you grow angry, for example, the muscles in your face tense and your eyes narrow spontaneously. The purveyor of bad news can make things even worse by accentuating it with the face and eyes.

Can you identify the meaning of these different facial expressions?

You can also use your face and eyes to neutralize the message you deliver. Based on an analysis of your situation, you may know that at least some members of the audience will disagree with your views. Suppose you are in a class situation that requires you to deliver a persuasive speech. If your topic is a truly controversial one, you can reasonably predict that not everyone in your audience will agree with everything you say. Although you may not be able to win them over, you also don't want to alienate them. As a result, you may want to use your face and eyes to neutralize some of the more contentious and evocative points you wish to make.

In a sense, what you give an audience in your face and eyes will determine what you can expect to get back from that audience. Thus, an intensely worded argument accompanied by the delivery of an equally intense message in the face and eyes invites the same from those who differ with you. On the other hand, using the face and eyes to neutralize the message improves your chance of a more favorable response from your audience.

To close, keep in mind that what we have suggested here is based on North American norms. In many cultures, the focus and sustained eye contact North Americans expect would be frowned upon. Such eye contact is viewed by members of many Asian cultures, for example, as rude and even hostile. As both a speaker and an audience member, you should keep this in mind. As a speaker, recognize that when international students appear uncomfortable or don't return your attempts to make eye contact, it may be the result of their culture. As an audience member, realize that your expectancies about eye contact may be at odds with the norms of the international student who is speaking.[13]

Using Your Eyes and Face

- Always face your audience when speaking; avoid turning your back to the audience unless absolutely necessary.
- Make eye contact with people before you begin. Maintain eye contact by meeting the gaze of individual audience members in all parts of the room.
- Avoid excessive eye contact with one person, for example, your instructor.
- Don't be afraid to be expressive with your face.

Gestures and Movement

You've heard the expression "different strokes for different folks." Nowhere is it more applicable than to the subject of gestures and movement relative to delivery. Although Ronald Reagan neither moved nor gestured very much when he spoke, he was a consummate public speaker. And though you practically have to nail Elizabeth Dole's feet to the floor to keep her from moving, she too is a public speaker of notable achievement. Thus, before we say a single word about how much or how little you should gesture or move as you speak, we want to say this: Your gestures and your movements as you grow as a public speaker should be a refined reflection of what you do naturally.

As is the case with the face and eyes, gestures and movements also can be used to intensify or lessen the emotional impact of verbal messages. Many gestures, for instance, serve as *affect displays*; that is, they visibly communicate feelings. Placing both hands near the heart at the same time you explain how important a subject is to you is an example. So too are clenched fists, open palms held face up, or lightly slapping the side of the face.

Given the preceding caveat, gesturing and moving can complement your delivery in several ways.[14] These include making your delivery more emblematic, making your delivery more illustrative, and regulating the speech transaction.

Emblems   The speeches of the best public speakers are usually rich in emblems. An **emblem** is a nonverbal behavior that can be directly translated into words and phrases and may replace them.[15] For example, Winston Churchill's "V" was an emblem for victory. Thus, emblems must meet the following criteria:

emblem A nonverbal symbol that can be substituted for a word.

Late-night talk show host Conan O'Brien uses a gesture to add emphasis to his verbal message.

1. The emblem means something specific to the audience members.

2. The emblem is used intentionally by the speaker to stimulate meaning.

3. The emblem can be easily translated into a few words.

Gestures are defined by the culture in which they are learned. As a case in point, when Richard Nixon was Dwight Eisenhower's vice president, he incited an embarrassing protest while deplaning at a South American airport. He greeted the crowd with arms outstretched above his head, the thumb and first finger of each hand joined together in what North Americans take to mean "A-OK." In many South American countries, however, this nonverbal emblem was then synonymous with what we call "giving the finger" or "flipping someone off."

illustrators Nonverbal symbols used to visualize what is being spoken.

Illustrators   Nonverbal behaviors that accompany speech and "show" what is being talked about are called **illustrators.** Although a lot like emblems, they are more general and seldom translate into a few words. The most common way we nonverbally illustrate is with our hands. Verbal directions or descriptions beg for the use of our hands. Try giving someone directions or describing an object—say, a spiral staircase—without using your hands.

Regulators   You use gestures called **regulators** to influence the amount and type of feedback received from the audience. If you hold up your hand when asking audience members whether they've ever felt frustrated waiting in line, for example, you are much more likely to prompt them to raise their hands as well. If you are stationary throughout a speech, your audience will give you much different feedback than if you were to move and periodically change the zone of interaction. Using gestures and movement to regulate feedback requires planning and rehearsal. An unplanned or inappropriate gesture or specific movement may elicit a response from the audience that you don't expect.

    Regulating audience feedback is particularly important when a speaker answers audience questions. Without regulation, such question-and-answer sessions can turn ugly. The box "Handling the Q&A" provides some practical advice on how to handle audience questions.

> **regulators** Nonverbal behaviors that influence the speech transaction.

Posture

This dimension is obviously related to movement, gestures, and your overall appearance. Posture is vital to your delivery and the manner in which it is received. People make all kinds of attributions about speakers on the basis of their posture, ranging from how confident a speaker is to how seriously the speaker takes the topic and the situation. At the least, consequently, you will want to guard against an audience making an incorrect attribution about you because you slouched, folded your arms across your chest, stood with one hand on your hip, or put your hands in your pockets.

    Because the norms governing appropriate posture vary across cultures, there are no hard-and-fast rules for speakers to follow. Still, given what we know generally about the culture of the beginning public speaking class, there are some steps you can follow to achieve a good posture for delivering your speeches. Remember that the more you slouch and shrink posturally, the less powerful you are likely to be perceived. Remember as well that posture influences the mechanics of your voice. Standing with shoulders back stretches the diaphragm and opens the air passages. That's one reason opera singers invariably have good posture. It helps them use their voice to full effect.

Guidelines for Posture While Delivering a Speech   **TIPS AND TACTICS**

- Find your center of balance. Usually this means standing with your feet apart at about shoulder width.
- Pull your shoulders back, sticking your chest out and holding your stomach in.
- Keep your chin up and off your chest.
- Initially let your arms rest at your sides with palms open, which will allow you to gesture easily as you speak.

Touch

Touch, which is by far the most intimate and reinforcing of the nonverbal dimensions, can affect your delivery in at least two ways.[16] The first involves **self-adapting behaviors,** which are distracting touching behaviors that speakers engage in unconsciously.

> **self-adapting behaviors** Nonverbal behaviors used to cope with nervousness; for example, self-touching or grasping sides of lectern with hands.

Handling the Q&A

Frequently after a speech, you will be expected to take questions from the audience. You should not be fearful of this situation, as it is actually an opportunity to gain important feedback from your audience as well as to clarify points that may not have been completely understood. Successfully answering questions, even hostile ones, can add to your credibility as a speaker. The key is to regulate that feedback in a constructive manner. Some basic guidelines for handling the question-and-answer period following a speech are given below.[1]

- *Announce at the outset that you will take questions at the end of your speech.* Under no circumstances take questions during the speech, as it will cause you to lose control of the situation. When audience members know they will have the opportunity to ask questions at the end of the speech, they will be able to think about them as you speak.

- *Overprepare for your speech.* You need to know more than you cover in the speech if you are to take questions. If you expect a hostile audience, it is a good idea to anticipate their toughest questions and prepare answers in advance.

Gestures frequently assist speakers in regulating their transaction with an audience.

- *Restate questions if they cannot be heard by all.* If you are speaking with a microphone, someone asking a question from the audience probably cannot be heard. Restating the question not only allows everyone to hear what was asked, it also allows you time to think of an answer. If a question is wordy, hostile, or imprecise, try to rephrase it in a way that neutralizes some of the problems with the question.

- *Answer questions directly with facts to back up your answers.* This requires you to be fully prepared. However, if you don't know the answer, just say so. You can always promise to obtain the facts and get back to the questioner at a later date. It is better to admit you don't know an answer than to be proved wrong because you tried to bluff your way through an answer.

- *Take questions from different audience members.* Don't let yourself get into a debate or an argument with one audience member. Insist that everyone who has a question gets a chance to ask it before you return to a previous questioner. Choose questioners from different parts of the room as well so that everyone feels they will get their chance.

- *Be brief.* Answer questions as succinctly as possible and move on to the next question. Overly long answers bore the audience and frustrate others who want to ask questions.

- *Announce when you are near the end of the Q&A.* When you sense the audience growing restless, the questions have become repetitive, or you are near the end of your allotted time, simply announce that you can take only one or two more questions.

- *At the end of the Q&A, restate the focus of your speech and summarize its essential points.* This is your chance to get in the last word and remind the audience of the basic theme of your speech. Depending on the situation, you may want to make yourself available for informal discussion after the speech.

[1]Some of these guidelines are based on a pamphlet by Robert Haakensan, *How to Handle the Q&A* (Philadelphia: Smith Kline & French Laboratories, Department of Public Relations, n.d.).

Frequently in arousing situations, people touch their face, hair, or clothes without realizing it. Just as frequently they touch some convenient object. They may squeeze the arm of a chair, roll their fingers on a tabletop, trace the outside edge of a glass with a fingertip, or mistake the top of a lectern for a conga drum. They do these things unconsciously.

Because public speaking is arousing, it too can provoke these self-adaptive forms of touch. Further, they can needlessly detract from your delivery. Tugging at an earlobe, rubbing the outside of your upper arm, or jingling the change in your pocket won't help your delivery. Neither will pounding on the lectern with the palms of your hands or rocking it from side to side.

The second way touch can affect your delivery concerns other people. At some point, it's likely your presentations will involve other people. Corporate trainers spend much of their lives giving informative presentations that involve audience participation. The same can be said for sales managers, teachers, attorneys, and practitioners of public relations. Touch very often comes into play in these scenarios. Sometimes it's as simple but as important as shaking a person's hand. At other times, however, it may involve guiding someone by the hand, patting someone on the back, or even giving a more demonstrative tactile sign of approval. At the same time, you must avoid touch that can be interpreted as inappropriate. For example, there have been several widely reported cases of schoolteachers accused of inappropriately touching students. Unwelcome touching can, in fact, be grounds for accusations of sexual harassment.

Time

The final nonverbal dimension to think about relative to delivery is time. As journalist Michael Ventura writes,

> Time is the medium in which we live. There is inner time—our personal sense of the rhythms of time experienced differently by each of us; and there is imposed time—the regimented time by which society organizes itself, the time of schedules and deadlines, time structured largely by work and commerce.[17]

First, time varies from one individual to the next. Research confirms what you no doubt long ago suspected. The internal body clock each of us has regulates not only when we sleep but also peak performance when we're awake. Some people perform best from early to midmorning, some during the middle of the day, and others late at night. What is true of performance in general, moreover, is true of public speaking specifically. During our time awake, there are periods when our speaking abilities peak, depending on our individual body clock. Most of us know from our own experience that we either are or are not very alert in the early morning or late afternoon. To the extent possible, attempt to schedule a speaking time when you know your mind and body will be alert.

Time affects your delivery in other ways as well. For example, the time limits you face as a speaker can have an impact on your delivery. As a result of attempting to cover too much material, for example, time limits may cause you to hurry your delivery. Conversely, if you find that you're about to finish your speech under the minimum time requirement of an assignment, you may slow down the delivery of your speech in the attempt to meet the time requirement.

The audience's perception of your delivery will also be affected by your "timing," a term frequently used in reference to actors and comics. Just as their timing of a joke or dramatic monologue can spell the difference between success and failure, so too can your timing. Rushing a punch line or dramatic anecdote, for instance, may negate its intended effect. Telling a story too slowly may do likewise.

Because the norms that govern the use of time vary across cultures, how fast or how slowly you deliver your speech may be a consideration. Whereas a relatively speedy style of delivery may be well received in New York City, it may be received as evidence of the "little time" you have for an audience in parts of the South and Southwest. Conversely, a slow rate of speech, which some mistakenly confuse with the speed at which a person thinks, may prove irritating to audience members whose culture is fast paced.

Finally, whether you are "on time" or late, not only for a speech but just in general, affects your credibility in our North American culture. People who are on time are perceived as efficient and courteous, both of which affect perceptions of competence and trustworthiness. People who are routinely late give the impression they are disorganized and not especially considerate of the time needs of an audience. This is very true of both your classmates and your instructor.

THE FUNCTIONS OF NONVERBAL BEHAVIOR IN DELIVERY

The eight dimensions of nonverbal behavior we've been talking about perform a number of important functions in speech delivery.[18] As we've discussed, these dimensions interact to make speeches more emblematic and illustrative. They can also help regulate audience feedback and intensify or lessen the emotional impact of what you say during a speech. Other ways that nonverbal dimensions such as the face, eyes, and voice function to facilitate the delivery of your messages include complementing, contradicting, and repeating the message; substituting for a verbal cue; increasing the perception of immediacy; exciting the audience; and delivering a powerful speech.

Complementing Your Message

A complementary nonverbal cue serves to reinforce what you verbally share with your audience. A genuine smile on your face as you thank your audience for the opportunity to speak, for example, carries more weight than either message standing on its own. There are many ways to complement the delivery of your message nonverbally. Changing the expression on your face, raising the pitch of your voice, or even breaking off eye contact are just a few of them.

Contradicting Your Message

Often, people contradict themselves nonverbally while communicating interpersonally. Forcing a smile and saying, "I had a great time" is a classic example. While the smile may have covered up how they really felt, chances are it only served to contradict what they said but didn't mean.

Usually people try to keep the preceding from happening. In the case of public speaking, however, you can use contradiction to enhance your delivery, for example, by rolling your eyes, shrugging your shoulders, or having a sarcastic expression. Certainly, Shakespeare knew that contradiction could enhance delivery. He frequently wrote speeches for his characters that invited actors to contradict their verbal statements with nonverbal cues. For example, in Marc Antony's eulogy of Julius Caesar, the line "But Brutus was an honorable man" is usually delivered by an actor in a sarcastic voice that says exactly the opposite. Because it is an attention-getting device, this kind of antithesis in a speech can enhance the impact with which the verbal message is delivered.

Repeating Your Message

Repetition is one of the most common ways speakers manipulate their message nonverbally. It's also one of the easiest ways to do this. Raising three fingers as you say you have three points to make doesn't require the oratorical skill of a Colin Powell.

Repetition differs from complementing in a significant way. Whereas a complementary nonverbal cue reinforces the message, a repetitious one serves to make it redundant. The classic example is when *Star Trek*'s Mr. Spock makes the Vulcan V sign while saying, "Live long and prosper." Other examples include nodding your head up and down while communicating agreement and shaking your head from side to side when communicating disagreement.

Substituting for a Verbal Cue

Have you ever seen entertainers and politicians raise their hands and motion in the attempt to stop an audience's continued applause? They are using a nonverbal cue as a substitute for a verbal one. In many circumstances, such a nonverbal cue is both more appropriate and more effective than a verbal one. An icy stare shot in the direction of someone talking as you speak is likely to be less disruptive, for example, than politely asking the person to be quiet. Shrugging your shoulders, reaching out with open palms, and raising your eyebrows, moreover, may more clearly communicate your bewilderment than actually saying you're puzzled by something.

Increasing the Perception of Immediacy

Nonverbal behavior can also increase the perception of immediacy between you and your audience. Immediacy concerns how psychologically close or distant people perceive each other, as well as the degree to which they perceive each other as approachable.[19]

Generally, the perception of immediacy between people is desirable. This is because people who are perceived as immediate are also perceived as friendly and approachable, stimulating, open to dialogue, and interpersonally warm.

Because public speaking normally takes place in a setting that arbitrarily puts physical distance between speakers and their audiences, speakers usually have to reduce this physical distance psychologically. You can do this in at least two ways. The first, which we discussed at length in Chapter 9, involves the use of immediate language. The second is to make your delivery more nonverbally immediate.

The easiest and most effective way to make the delivery more immediate is through nonverbal channels. Eye contact is the perfect case in point. Even when people are separated by substantial physical distance, eye contact enables them to bridge this distance in a psychological sense. The best public speakers, for example, are often the ones who make you feel as if they are speaking to you, and only you, with their eyes as well as their voices.

Eye contact is not the only medium, however, through which you can achieve greater immediacy with your audience. Immediacy can also be achieved with facial expressions such as a smile, with a conversational rather than condescending tone of voice, and by standing beside the lectern instead of appearing to hide behind it.

Exciting the Audience

One way to gauge the effectiveness of a speech is by the degree to which it stimulates the audience. The best speakers make listeners think, provoke them to laugh, or motivate them to act. Generally, an audience's degree of excitement can be traced to the degree of excitement the audience senses in the speaker.

The level of excitement of public speakers is most noticeable in their delivery. This includes rate of speech, volume of speech, and vocal as well as facial expressions. Excited speakers, the research tells us, speak faster and louder than speakers unaroused by their topic or by the transaction between them and their audience. Excited speakers, the research also tells us, reveal more of themselves as they speak, through changes in facial expressions as well as changes in the pitch of their voice.

Does this mean that someone who simply is excited also is a good speaker? Of course not. Too much excitement can be as distracting as too little excitement can be boring. The idea, then, is to moderate your excitement for your topic or audience rather than to inappropriately exaggerate it with your delivery.

Delivering a Powerful Speech

When it comes to public speaking, the power of words depends mightily on the manner in which they are delivered. No doubt many speech writers have suffered as the power of the words they so carefully crafted was wiped out by the person delivering them. This shouldn't and needn't be the case. With care and practice, you can capitalize on the varying dimensions of nonverbal behavior to make the delivery of your speech powerful. Some of the ways you can do this are obvious; others are more subtle.

Posture is an obvious way you can control the power of delivery. Standing tall and self-assured, in and of itself, communicates power. When combined with movement away from the lectern, this is even more the case.

You can also enhance the power of your delivery with your eyes, with your voice, and through movement and gestures. In North America, at least, powerful speakers make eye contact, speak in a controlled and confident tone of voice, reduce the distance between themselves and their audience by moving closer to them, and gesture as a natural extension of their spoken message. In stark contrast, speakers whose delivery lacks power avoid eye contact, fail to speak up, and usually try to tie up their hands by sticking them in their pockets, gripping the side of the lectern, or hiding them behind their back.

TAKING A PROACTIVE APPROACH

proactive delivery Planned and rehearsed presentation.

Knowing something about the nature and functions of nonverbal behavior should assist you in making your speech delivery proactive rather than reactive. To engage in **proactive delivery** means that the speaker takes the initiative and anticipates and controls for as many variables as possible, rather than merely reacting to them. Reactive delivery is like the boxer who only counterpunches. This wait-and-see attitude is rarely the mark of a championship boxer, and it can be disastrous for even the most seasoned public speaker. The guidelines that follow should assist you in making sure that your nonverbal behavior enhances, rather than detracts from, the delivery of your speech.

Guidelines for Proactive Speech Delivery   **TIPS AND TACTICS**

1. *Take control of your appearance.* Dressing appropriately is one of the easiest ways to enhance initial impressions of you as the medium of your message. Think about the possible effects of apparel, such as the baseball cap that seems to be attached to your scalp, the baggy shorts you prefer, or the saying on your favorite T-shirt.

2. *Use natural gestures.* Videotape your practice. Check on your gestures. Do they appear natural and complement your delivery, or do they appear forced and detract from your spoken message?

3. *Time your speech.* Do this more than once and on videotape if you can. Note your timing and the degree to which the rate at which you speak facilitates the mood you want to communicate to your audience. Also, remind yourself that your practice time probably will be longer than when you actually speak before your audience.

4. *Avoid self-adapting behaviors.* During practice, watch out for self-adapting behaviors such as playing with your hair, tugging on a finger, cracking knuckles, licking your lips, and hiding your hands. Self-adapters such as these will call attention to themselves and undermine perceptions of your power and self-confidence.

SUMMARY

You have choices when making decisions about how to best deliver your speech. The bottom line, however, is that the method you decide on should reflect your preferred style of speaking, the environment in which you will speak, and the speech occasion.

 **SPEECH COACH**

To evaluate your understanding of this chapter, see the Quizzes on your CD.

- Effective delivery involves both what you say and how you say it.

- Effective delivery demands skill not only in articulating the words you use to express yourself, but also in using your voice to shape the meaning of what you articulate.

- Nonverbal communication complements the verbal and vocal delivery of your speech. Unlike language, nonverbal communication is continuous, makes use of channels of communication simultaneously, and is spontaneous.

- Specific facets of the nonverbal communication system that influence delivery include the environment, the eyes and face, physical appearance, gestures and movement, posture, time, and touch.

- Gestures frequently take the form of emblems and illustrators, which regulate the speech transaction.

- Important functions of nonverbal communication in the delivery of speeches include complementing the verbal message, contradicting the verbal message, repeating/reinforcing the verbal message, substituting for a verbal cue, increasing immediacy, and increasing excitement and power in the verbal message.

CHECK YOUR UNDERSTANDING: EXERCISES AND ACTIVITIES

SPEECH COACH

For a review of key terms in this chapter, see the Key Terms Flashcards on your CD.

1. Observe a speaker outside of your class. Keep track of the number of times the speaker (a) changes the zone of interaction, (b) moves away from the lectern, and (c) gestures. On a scale of 1 to 10, with 10 being the high end, rate the speaker in each of these areas. Compare and discuss your observation and ratings with those of other students. See if a pattern emerges.

2. Differences in nonverbal norms, as well as differences in communication styles and patterns, are common across cultures. Choose two or three North American norms for nonverbal behavior—for example, eye contact, gesturing, and time. Interview a student or faculty member from a culture other than North American about how these communication behaviors differ in his or her culture. Write a short paper summarizing your findings.

3. Explain why sign language is a *verbal* behavior, whereas vocal variation in pitch, rate, tempo, and the like are *nonverbal* behaviors, even though sign language is not vocalized and vocal variation is.

4. Explain why nonverbal behavior is continuous, uses multiple channels simultaneously, and is spontaneous and how these characteristics distinguish it from the language of your speech.

5. Review the four guidelines for proactive delivery. Before your next speech, develop a plan to use at least three of these guidelines to improve your delivery skills in that speech.

6. Ask a classmate to apply Exercise 1 to your next speech. Talk with the classmate afterward about the relationship between his or her observations and the overall effectiveness of your delivery.

NOTES

1. Edward T. Hall, *The Silent Language* (Greenwich, Conn.: Fawcett Publications, 1959), 15.
2. George B. Ray, "Vocally Cued Personality Prototypes: An Implicit Personality Theory Approach," *Communication Monographs* 53 (1986): 266–276.
3. Richard L. Street and Robert M. Brady, "Evaluative Responses to Communicators as a Function of Evaluative Domain, Listener Speech Rate, and Communication Context," *Communication Monographs* 49 (1982): 290–308.
4. David B. Buller and R. Kelly Aune, "The Effects of Speech Rate Similarity on Compliance: An Application of Communication Accommodation Theory," *Western Journal of Speech Communication* 56 (1992): 37–53.
5. J. Burgoon, D. W. Buller, and W. G. Woodhall, *Nonverbal Communication: The Unspoken Dialogue*, 2nd ed. (New York: Harper & Row, 1989). See also M. Knapp and J. A. Hall, *Nonverbal Communication in Human Interaction*, 3rd ed. (Fort Worth, Tex.: Harcourt, Brace, and Jovanovich, 1992).
6. L. A. Malandro, L. Barker, and D. A. Barker, *Nonverbal Communication*, 2nd ed. (New York: Random House, 1989).

7. V. P. Richmond and J. C. McCroskey, *Nonverbal Behavior in Interpersonal Relationships* (Englewood Cliffs, N.J.: Prentice Hall, 1991).

8. R. Sommer, "Man's Proximate Environment," *Journal of Social Issues* 22 (1966): 60.

9. Ellen Berscheid and Elaine Walster, "Beauty and the Best," *Psychology Today* 5, no. 10 (1972): 42–46.

10. D. Leathers, *Successful Nonverbal Communication: Principles and Practices* (New York: Macmillan, 1986).

11. Malandro, Barker, and Barker, *Nonverbal Communication*.

12. P. Ekman and W. V. Friesen, *Unmasking the Face: A Guide to Recognizing Emotions from Facial Expression* (Englewood Cliffs, N.J.: Prentice Hall, 1975). See also P. Ekman, W. V. Friesen, and S. Ancoli, "Facial Signs of Emotional Expression," *Journal of Personality and Social Psychology* 39 (1980): 1125–1134.

13. P. Ekman, *Telling Lies* (New York: Norton, 1985). See also Bella M. DePaulo, Miron Zuckerman, and Robert Rosenthal, "Humans as Lie Detectors," *Journal of Communication* 30 (1980): 129–139; R. E. Kraut, "Verbal and Nonverbal Cues in the Perception of Lying," *Journal of Personality and Social Psychology* 36 (1978): 380–391.

14. Judee Burgoon, "Nonverbal Communication Research in the 1970s: An Overview," in *Communication Yearbook 4*, ed. D. Nimmo (New Brunswick, N.J.: Transaction Books, 1980), 179–197.

15. Joseph A. Devito, *The Communication Handbook: A Dictionary* (New York: Harper & Row, 1986), 105.

16. Stephen Thayer, "Close Encounters," *Psychology Today* 22, no. 3 (1988): 31–36. See also A. Montague, *Touching: The Significance of the Skin* (New York: Harper & Row, 1971).

17. Michael Ventura, "Trapped in a Time Machine With No Exits," *Sacramento Bee*, 26 February 1995, C1.

18. Burgoon, Buller, and Woodhall, *Nonverbal Communication: The Unspoken Dialogue*; E. T. Hall, "System for the Notation of Proxemic Behavior," *American Anthropologist* 65 (1963): 1003–1026.

19. Malandro, Barker, and Barker, *Nonverbal Communication*.

Visual media must be used carefully, as Microsoft's Bill Gates learned when he presented Windows 98 to the public.

Using Media in Your Speech

CHAPTER

11

 OBJECTIVES

After reading this chapter and reviewing the learning resources on your CD-ROM and at the Online Learning Center, you should be able to:

- Describe presentational media, including objects, models, overheads, flip charts, poster boards, audio and video recordings, CD-ROMS and DVDs, and computer-generated slides.
- List, explain, and avoid common mistakes speakers make when using presentational media.
- Describe and explain how visual media can be used to complement speech, illustrate speech, regulate speech, and be emblematic of speech.
- Describe content that is better depicted visually than described aurally.
- Discuss and appropriately follow rules for the construction and use of presentational media.

 KEY CONCEPTS

audio media	line graph	presentational media
bar chart	organizational chart	visual media
flip chart	overhead transparency	
flow chart	pie chart	

Seeing is believing.

—Anonymous

Computer-assisted presentations can still fall prey to human error. FOXTROT © 1988 Bill Amend. Reprinted with permission of Universal Press Syndicate. All rights reserved.

Murphy's Law states, "Anything that can go wrong will go wrong." No one is immune from Murphy's Law, not even the world's wealthiest person, Microsoft co-founder Bill Gates. Not long ago while introducing a new version of Microsoft Windows to an audience of hundreds of his employees, the PowerPoint presentation he planned on using to support his speech failed to open.

Because Gates is an accomplished and practiced speaker, he was able to continue his speech while an army of support technicians scurried about to fix the problem. Within seconds the problem was found and corrected, and Gates was able to use his PowerPoint slides.

What proved to be a minor inconvenience for Bill Gates would have proved disastrous for most speakers. Lacking Gates's resources, they would have had to find and fix the problem themselves, while their audience waited. Many of them, no doubt, would lose part or most of their audience in the process.

Although we cannot protect you completely from Murphy's Law when you speak, this chapter is designed to help you avoid it as much as possible, whether using presentational media as high tech as Microsoft PowerPoint or as low tech as a flip chart. What follows will help you in (1) avoiding common mistakes speakers make with presentational media, (2) matching the function of a presentational medium with your speech purpose, (3) selecting types of presentational media most suited to your purpose, and (4) learning some helpful rules to follow when you construct and use your presentational media. To find out what your "visual IQ" is, take the test in the accompanying Self-Assessment box.

PRESENTATIONAL MEDIA

If you look up the word *medium*, you'll learn that it is a channel of communication. If you then look up the word *media*, you'll learn that it is the plural of medium and is defined as channels of communication. **Presentational media** are channels of communication that enhance the five natural senses we use routinely to send and receive information: sight, sound, touch, taste, and smell. They also are tools that can be used to effectively supplement our natural means of communicating with voice and body. **Visual media,** for example, use the sense of sight to communicate a message.

Examples of presentational media include objects, models, overheads, flip charts, poster boards, audio and video recordings, CD-ROMS and DVDs, and

presentational media
Channels of communication that extend the five basic senses: touch, sight, sound, taste, and smell.

SPEECH COACH
For an overview of the role of presentational media in public speaking, see segment 11.1 on your CD.

visual media The use of the sense of sight to communicate a message.

Visual IQ Test

Before reading any further, take this simple test to see how much you know about using presentational media. True or false:

1. You should never try to convey more than one idea on a visual medium.
2. The minimum font for an overhead transparency that must be seen clearly from a distance of 30 feet is 18-point type.
3. Always animate a PowerPoint slide.
4. Color enhances the visual impact of an overhead transparency.
5. The colors you choose for a visual medium are a matter of personal preference.
6. When it comes to using presentational media, a good rule of thumb is less is more.
7. Outstanding presentational media are key to an effective speech.
8. Any visual in a speech is better than no visual at all.
9. Some speech content is more suitable to media than others.
10. It's a good idea to limit a visual to no more than six lines of text.

The answers to the questions can be found in this chapter.

computer-generated slides projected onto a screen. These media vary in difficulty of use and construction, as well as technological sophistication. Using actual objects, such as different types of hats to make a point about which provides the best sun protection, may require a collection of hats but no special knowledge or skill. In contrast, using PowerPoint slides in your speech requires knowledge about the software's applications, a computer, a compatible projector, and skill in using them.

AVOIDING COMMON MISTAKES

Of the many possible mistakes we see speakers make with presentational media, here are the most common:

- Overreliance on visual media, sometimes to the point of overkill
- Too much information crammed on a single hard-to-see visual
- The wrong type of presentational media to achieve the purpose

See the box "Murphy's Law Revisited" for some tips on avoiding common mistakes. We'll look at each of these mistakes in greater detail and see how to avoid making them.

Overreliance on Visual Media

Presentational media, no matter how well constructed or technologically sophisticated, are no substitute for the skill of a speaker. Presentational media will not hide a speaker's lack of skill or lack of preparation. In fact, because the effective use of presentational media is a skill in itself, overreliance on presentational media is likely to call attention to, rather than disguise, any weaknesses in other areas. This is especially true in the age of Microsoft's PowerPoint. This

Murphy's Law Revisited

If even Bill Gates is susceptible to this law, then it is important that we all be prepared for it. There is no way to be completely prepared for the unexpected. The best defense is to anticipate problems and prepare alternatives. Here are a few of the things that you need to prepare for. (At one time or another, they have all happened to the authors of this book.)

Problem: The battery in your equipment (tape recorder, microphone, or whatever) is dead.

What to do: Test the equipment the morning of your speech and carry a spare battery.

Problem: There is no overhead projector, even though you reserved one.

What to do: Call to confirm your reservation on the morning of your speech. Physically check out the projector if possible.

Problem: The overhead projector's lightbulb is burned out.

What to do: Most overheads have a spare lightbulb. Make sure you know where it is beforehand.

Problem: The slide projector (film projector, VCR, etc.) does not work.

What to do: Again, check it out in advance if possible. If it unexpectedly fails, you will need to verbally describe what is on your slides. We recall one case where a person simply stood in front of a blank screen, pretended to show slides, and described them in elaborate details as he went along ("As you can clearly see from this slide . . ."). It turned a frustrating situation into a humorous one.

Problem: Your visuals are out of order or upside down, or some are missing.

What to do: An ounce of prevention is worth a pound of cure. Check and double-check them before the speech. If you run into this problem, try not to get flustered. Make a joke while you look for the missing visual; if you can't find it, verbally describe the visual or skip a part of the speech.

Problem: The computer you are using for your PowerPoint presentation fails, or the projector does not work.

What to do: Be sure to prepare backup visuals. For example, we normally have overhead transparencies prepared that duplicate our PowerPoint presentations.

Problem: It takes a lot longer than you thought to demonstrate a process using your visuals.

What to do: First, always practice with your visuals so that you know how long it will take. Second, if you are demonstrating a multistep process, have various steps along the way already prepared.

Remember, nothing can happen to you that hasn't already happened to someone else. Most audiences are sympathetic to speakers who are obviously prepared and yet encounter technical difficulties beyond their control. At the same time, audiences have little sympathy when Murphy's Law strikes someone who is just winging it. And keep in mind, "Murphy was an optimist."

software allows you to prepare basic to complicated slides on your computer, which can then be projected onto a screen. Valuable and functional as PowerPoint can be to a speaker, it is still only a tool. Like any other tool, it is only as good as the level of skill of the person using it. Such skill is measured not only in terms of knowing all there is to know about PowerPoint, but also in terms of exercising constraint in using it.

Consider the PowerPoint slides in Figure 11.1. They were constructed using the stock features available in the PowerPoint software. There are several ways to manipulate slides using the same software. You can animate each of the bulleted points, you can shadow the lettering or italicize the lettering, and you can add a graph, chart, or clip art.

The question is not whether you *can* do any of these things to jazz up the slide; the question is whether you *should* do any of these things. What purpose or function would these manipulations perform to make your speech better? Before you italicize the font of a slide, add a piece of clip art, or animate a point you wish to make, you need to be certain that it will improve your speech and presentation.

FIGURE 11.1 The Options for Visually Manipulating PowerPoint Slides Are Almost Endless.

Thus, to avoid using PowerPoint in the same way a small child uses a hammer—which is to pound anything and everything in sight with it—you must be literate rather than simply knowledgeable about this tool. What's more, you need to exercise the same restraint with less sophisticated presentational media as well. A simple rule to follow in this regard is "When in doubt, leave it out." If you are uncertain about the function of presentational media, or whether they are central to your speech, don't use them.

Too Much Hard-to-See Information

Chances are you have attended a lecture where nearly every word the instructor utters appears on a series of overhead transparencies. Such a common mistake not only defeats the purpose of a transparency, but also produces other unintended and undesirable consequences. First, the overhead causes eyestrain because the writing or print is difficult to see. Second, students are likely to bury their heads in their notebooks as they try to copy the overheads verbatim rather than focusing on their instructor. Thus, students miss many of the nonverbal nuances of the instructor's remarks, which should aid their understanding.

Another simple rule to follow before deciding to use presentational media is "Less is often more." Rather than cramming a visual with every idea or point you plan on making, save your presentational media for those ideas or points you really want to hit home. A good rule of thumb is no more than one idea per visual, no more than six lines to express the idea, and no more than six

All too often people cram their visual media with so much information that it hurts rather than helps their presentation.

words in each of the six lines. This practice forces you to write big enough for people to see what you have written, and it accentuates the fact that the idea is important enough to stand on its own.

Using the Wrong Type of Presentational Aid

You have choices when it comes to the type of presentational medium to select for your speech. Generally, the type of presentational medium should match the function it is meant to perform. Since this is a topic we will address at length later, a couple of points will suffice here. First, before you decide on a specific presentational medium, ask yourself, "What is its purpose—what do I hope to result from its use? Is it meant to provide my audience with an image I cannot achieve with words? Is it an outline both my audience and I can refer to as my speech unfolds? Or is it a representation of an object that is too large to bring into class?"

Next, ask yourself whether using the medium is absolutely necessary. All too often students choose and construct presentational media because they are required, not because they are a logical and functional part of their speech. Simply put, not using presentational media may be better than using media that do not clearly serve the purpose of your speech.

THE NEED FOR EFFECTIVE PRESENTATIONAL MEDIA

Marshall McLuhan was an influential media critic in the 1960s and 1970s. Of the many ideas he advanced, one is especially relevant to our discussion. McLuhan viewed media as an extension of the human faculties. He viewed the wheel as an extension of the foot, the book as an extension of the eye, and electric circuitry as an extension of the central nervous system.[1] We want you to think of presentational media in a similar fashion. Specifically, we want you to think of them as extensions of sight, sound, touch, taste, and smell. We also want you to think of the functions these extensions perform in much the same way as nonverbal communication.

Recall from Chapter 10 that nonverbal communication behaviors add meaning to help us fully understand verbal messages. Also recall that nonverbal communication behaviors have the potential to reinforce what we say, as well as take the place of what we might say. So it is with presentational media. At the very least they can function as (1) a complement to speech, (2) as visual illustrators of speech, (3) as regulators of speech, and (4) as emblematic speech.

A Complement to Speech

One of the chief functions performed by a presentational medium is to visually complement the language used to construct your speeches. One of our international students gave an informative speech on Mexican traditions. In addition to sharing verbal content about these traditions, she visually complemented her speech by wearing traditional folkdress.

Another of our students visually complemented his informative speech on hiking the Appalachian Trail with a large trail map, dry-mounted on tag board, several large colored photos similarly mounted, and the actual backpack he used on his trek over the trail. As he talked about where he trekked, the things he saw, and the gear he took, he used each of these visual media to complement the words he spoke.

A Visual Illustration of the Spoken Word

As mentioned in Chapter 10, nonverbal gestures are often used to illustrate what we are trying to say. Presentational media serve a similar function. Further, when gestures are insufficient in this regard, presentational media can come to the rescue.

As you can see in the accompanying photographs, different types of presentational media can be effective illustrations of the spoken message. Showing a wide-brimmed hat in a speech about the sun and skin cancer is a much better illustrator than using your hands to describe what you mean by wide brimmed. An audience also is much more likely to understand how the rudder and flaps control direction and altitude on a working model of an airplane than if you tried to explain verbally how they work.

As a general rule, the more abstract or unfamiliar something is, the more it begs to be illustrated visually. If you plan to speak on a topic that involves subjects for which the audience has only a vague reference, and gestures alone will not suffice, illustrative media can make these subjects more concrete for the audience.

A Regulator of Speech

Nonverbal behavior is used to regulate everything from the rate at which a conversation unfolds to instilling excitement in an audience. Gestures, movement, and voice are all good channels to change the mood and tone of a

When a speaker is talking about sun protection, a hat makes an excellent visual. Models can be used when it is impractical to use an actual object.

speech. Presentational media can also regulate the mood and tone a speech communicates. PowerPoint software has numerous features that can serve to regulate how your audience responds to what you say. Color and animation are two good examples of such features.

Color affects mood. It also influences the degree to which content is easily seen. Hot colors such as red can cause excitement, whereas cooler colors such as blue can be subduing. Thus, picking the right color for the back- and foreground of a PowerPoint slide shouldn't be left to chance.

Animation similarly regulates presentations. Showing a static slide produces a different effect than an animated one. There is a noticeable difference in how our students respond to our lectures when we animate our PowerPoint slides. Opening with a slide that only reveals the subject of the lecture and then adds individual points one by one, is far more effective than showing them all at once. By revealing points sequentially, students can focus on the point at hand rather than trying to write down points that appear on the slide but are yet to be discussed. This also allows us to pace our lectures. We can slow down and add examples to illustrate a point, or speed up to the next point when student feedback tells us it's time to move on. You can do the same thing in your presentations, thereby regulating the transaction with your audience.

FIGURE 11.2 International road signs substitute words with visual symbols that are widely understood.

Emblematic Speech

A fourth way to boost a presentation's effectiveness is to use an emblem. As explained in Chapter 10, an emblem is a visual representation that has one-to-one correspondence with written or spoken language. The familiar symbols you see in Figure 11.2 need no verbal explanation to be understood. In fact, the highway transportation experts who designed them are counting on the fact that they are instantly recognizable to motorists and pedestrians. Photographs and realistic drawings depicting human emotions can also be emblematic. No one needs to tell us when a person is sad, happy, or angry when these emotions are graphically depicted. Thus, if your intent in a speech is to convey an emotion, it may be easier to show it than to describe it for your audience.

Although presentational media may serve other functions, the ones described here will help you decide which function is most likely to serve your purpose. Keep this in mind as we now turn to the kind of content that is best suited for visual rather than aural delivery in a speech.

Using Presentational Media   **TIPS AND TACTICS**

Before your speech:

• Check the room and your equipment.
• Practice, if possible, with the same equipment in the same room where you will give your speech.
• Double-check your presentational media immediately before the speech. For example, make sure posters, overheads, or slides are in proper order, right-side up, and ready to go.
• Allow ample time for setup and takedown.

During the speech:

• Avoid distractions—cover or remove visuals and turn off projectors when not in use.
• Do not block the audience's view.

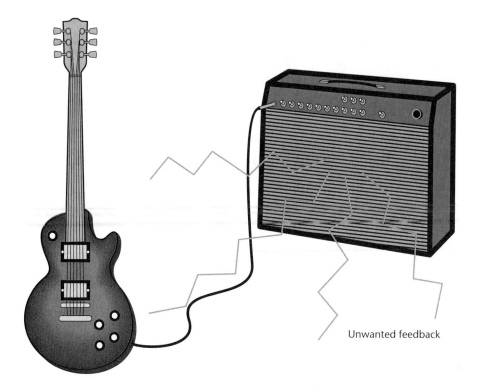

FIGURE 11.3 Sometimes a diagram is worth a thousand words. The concept of electronic feedback is depicted here.

Unwanted feedback

- Allow the audience enough time (at least 10 seconds) to process the information. Then remove the visual.
- Talk to your audience, not to the visual.

CONTENT

Some kinds of information are better suited to visual media than others. Ask yourself, "What is the best possible way to convey what I hope to communicate to my audience?" To answer this question, consider the following kinds of visual information, which are especially well suited to the contemporary presentational media at your disposal.

Diagrams and Illustrations

Sometimes a diagram or drawing will serve your purpose better than a photograph. Diagrams are a good way to represent the parts of an object. For example, a cutaway drawing of a firearm can be used to explain its functional parts, and the diagram—unlike a real gun—is neither illegal nor dangerous. Figure 11.3 illustrates an abstract concept, electrical feedback, through the use of a diagram.

Charts, Graphs, and Maps

Often a speech calls for a particular kind of visual representation of numbers and statistics by way of charts or graphs. Three of the following types of charts and graphs are particularly useful for depicting statistical information: pie charts, line graphs, and bar charts.

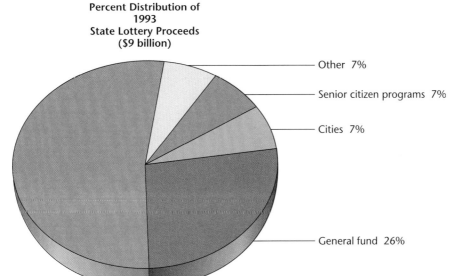

**Percent Distribution of
1993
State Lottery Proceeds
($9 billion)**

Other 7%

Senior citizen programs 7%

Cities 7%

General fund 26%

Education 53%

FIGURE 11.4 Pie charts show the relative proportions of parts of a whole.

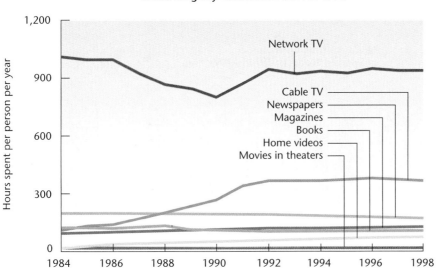

Media Usage by Consumers: 1984 to 1998

Network TV

Cable TV
Newspapers
Magazines
Books
Home videos
Movies in theaters

Hours spent per person per year

FIGURE 11.5 Line graphs show changes over time.

Pie Charts A **pie chart** is a circular chart that divides a whole into several parts, each represented by a slice of the circle proportional to its share of the whole. Figure 11.4 shows a typical pie chart, which represents the percentage distribution of state lottery proceeds in a specific year. The advantage of pie charts is that they simplify and dramatically illustrate the relative proportions of parts of a whole.

pie chart A graphic often used to show proportions of a known quantity.

Line Graphs Whereas pie charts are good for showing proportions, a **line graph** is good for showing numerical data as a series of points connected by a line. Line graphs are convenient for showing changes over time; for example, Figure 11.5 shows changes in media use by consumers over a 15-year period.

line graph A graphic used to show points in time.

FIGURE 11.6 Bar charts show various quantities. You can use them to compare two or more categories.

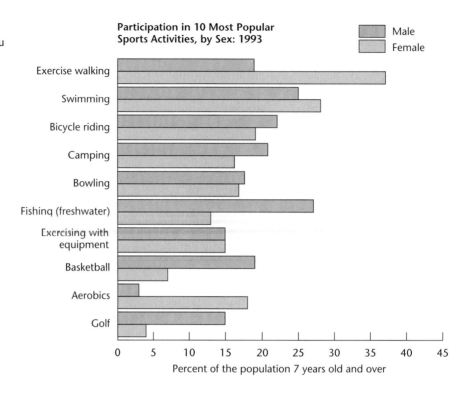

Participation in 10 Most Popular Sports Activities, by Sex: 1993

Percent of the population 7 years old and over

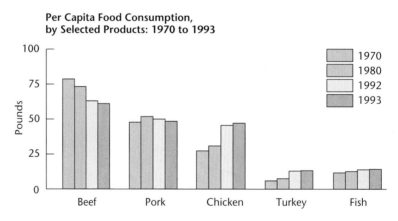

Per Capita Food Consumption, by Selected Products: 1970 to 1993

By using two or more lines with different colors, you can also show how two or more things compare across the same time period. Thus, if you wanted to compare spending on schools with spending on defense over the past 10 years, a line graph with two lines would work well.

bar chart A graphic used for comparing data side by side.

Bar Charts   A **bar chart** uses filled-in vertical or horizontal bars to represent various quantities, as shown in Figure 11.6. By grouping two or more bars or by color-coding them, you can compare two or more categories. For example, the first bar chart in Figure 11.6 compares the participation of men and women in the 10 most popular sports in a given year. The other chart shows how per capita

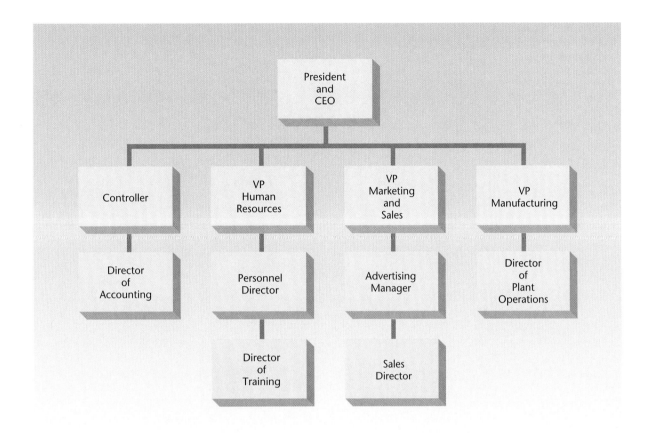

FIGURE 11.7 Organizational Chart

food consumption has changed over the period between 1970 and 1993. You can readily see that consumption of beef has declined, while consumption of chicken and turkey has increased.

Organizational Charts   The structure of an organization, including lines of authority, can be represented in an **organizational chart** like the one shown in Figure 11.7. Such charts are useful in business, industry, or governmental organizations. They might be given to new employees or be part of an annual report to shareholders.

organizational chart A graphic that illustrates hierarchical relationships.

Flow Chart   A **flow chart** uses boxes and arrows to represent the relationship of steps in a process. In other words, a flow chart shows how a process is carried out. For example, you might construct a flow chart like the one in Figure 11.8 to illustrate the steps necessary in preparing a speech.

flow chart A graphic designed to illustrate spatial relationships or the sequence of events in a process.

Text-Only Charts   Sometimes a visual will consist exclusively of text. For example, a speaker might copy textual material, such as the main points of a speech or the steps involved in a process, onto an overhead transparency. Teachers commonly chart their lectures on overheads for students to follow. This textual material clues students to the major topics the teacher plans on covering.

FIGURE 11.8 Flow Chart Showing Speech-Preparation Steps

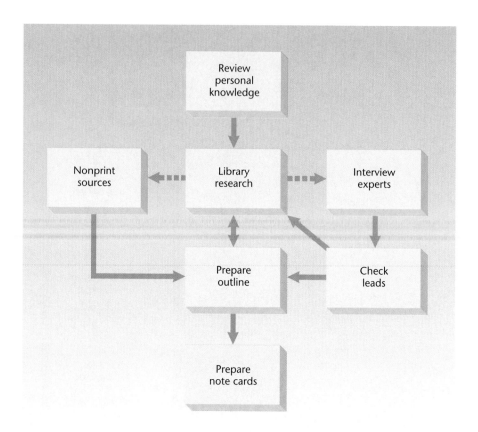

FIGURE 11.8 Flow Chart Showing Speech-Preparation Steps

Maps   You might use a map in a speech describing the spatial layout of an area, whether a dangerous intersection in your hometown or the disputed border between hostile nations. Maps can also be used to describe a dynamic process, such as a battle. At the site of the historic Civil War battle of Gettysburg, for example, numerous maps display various stages of the battle. One large-scale map uses embedded lights to show the daily progress of the battle.

SELECTING THE RIGHT MEDIUM

Once you have determined the content you want to emphasize visually, you need to choose the right medium. The right medium depends on the function you hope to achieve, your knowledge and skill in using the medium, and whether you have access to it. Once you have thought through each of these criteria, you will be able to decide on a presentational medium or combination of media.

Objects

In some cases, the object you are discussing in your speech is perfectly suited to your needs. A speech about the bagpipe might call for you to demonstrate by

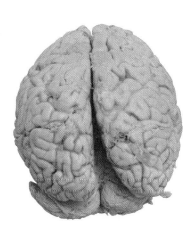

You can add visual impact to your spoken message with an actual object, a three-dimensional model, or an electronic medium such as a DVD.

actually playing the instrument. A demonstration of cooking might require a special pot or pan such as a Chinese wok.

The key things to remember about using objects are to make sure they are easily visible to your audience and that they are appropriate to the situation. Although a speech on auto repair could not use a real car, a worn-out muffler could be used to illustrate how to tell if it needs replacement. The use of inappropriate objects can create problems. For example, almost every semester we have students who wish to do speeches on some aspect of firearms. However, for obvious reasons, firearms are prohibited on our campus (except for those carried by campus police). Wine tasting is another popular topic we must veto, because alcohol is also prohibited on our campus. Thus, before you plan a speech using actual objects, be sure to ask your instructor what is appropriate and permissible on your campus.

Models

Often a three-dimensional model of an object can be used when it is impractical to use the actual object. One of our students spoke on the common American cockroach. Bringing live cockroaches to the classroom would have been disconcerting, to say the least. So instead, she cleverly constructed a large-scale model of a cockroach that she kept hidden in a box until just the right instant, when she revealed the topic of her speech. Not only was her speech informative and entertaining, it was also enhanced by her ability to explain her subject vividly with her model. Another student spoke on fly-fishing. Since tying a fly with actual fish line would have been invisible to the audience, the large-scale model he constructed out of coat hangers and yarn worked perfectly.

Poster Board

Poster board is one of the most common mediums used by students for their speeches. It can also be one of the least effective because poster board requires graphic design skills most students lack. As a result, their posters are usually poorly drawn or lettered.

We recommend students avoid using a poster board unless they either have the skill to make it look professional or have a professional construct it for them. If you must use poster board, draw illustrations, diagrams, or charts on it with colored marking pens. Dry-mount enlarged pictures on poster board rather than using tape or glue. And use rub-on letters or other prepared materials. Finally, use colored poster board only if it contrasts markedly with the lettering you use.

We also recommend using very sturdy poster board, preferably with a foam core. Flimsy posters have a tendency to curl up or fall over at the most inopportune times. It's a good idea to put your posters on an easel that is high enough to be visible to your audience. Finally, remember to cover your posters until you are ready to talk about them, revealing each one as you get to the point it illustrates. Then when you are done with a poster, either move to the next one or cover it up.

Flip Charts

flip chart Large tablet used to preview the outline of a presentation or to record information generated by an audience.

There are two types of **flip charts:** One is basically text; the second is for recording ideas as participants generate them. Flip charts, commonly used in business seminars, are not a good idea for beginning speakers. They are cumbersome to flip and require you to temporarily break off direct contact with your audience. If you must use a flip chart to write or draw on, be sure the paper is thick enough that your writing or drawing will not bleed through to the next page.

PowerPoint

Poster boards and flip charts once were common, not only in student speeches, but also in those given by professional people. Although flip charts are still an essential feature in many of the training seminars professionals attend, poster boards have gone the way of the dinosaur. The photos, diagrams, and charts they were once used to display have been transferred to one of two popular media: the overhead transparency or the PowerPoint slide. Of these two, PowerPoint is potentially the most effective and easy to use. What's more, PowerPoint slides can be transferred to an overhead transparency.

We routinely use PowerPoint slides in our lectures and presentations. We believe they are visually dramatic, easy to read, and help both our audience and us with the organization of our messages. By the same token, we use these slides sparingly and as an extension rather than as a replacement for our everyday speaking skills. See the box "PowerPoint Poisoning" for some pitfalls of PowerPoint use.

Today's public speaking student needs to be skilled in the use of PowerPoint. This is true even if the technology necessary to use it in your class is unavailable. If nothing else, knowledge and skill in the use of PowerPoint will assist you in preparing more effective and attractive overhead transparencies.

The basics of PowerPoint are not that tough to master. The program works essentially the same whether you use a PC Windows operating system or a Mac. First you need to find the Microsoft Office application on your computer. Next find PowerPoint and open the program. Now look for View on your toolbar.

PowerPoint Poisoning

Too much PowerPoint can be like too much of anything else—deadly, at least to your audience. Even in business the heads of some corporations are telling their subordinates to use this technology sparingly.[2] Here are some common pitfalls of PowerPoint use you'll want to avoid:

- **Too many slides.** We've seen PowerPoint presentations where almost every couple of sentences the speaker shifts to a new slide. Trying to keep up with what is being said and what is being shown is impossible.

- **Too much detail on slides.** Use key words, phrases, and visuals, not full sentences. We've seen speakers put virtually every word in their manuscript overhead. It left us wondering, what is the point of having a speaker?

- **Too much razzle-dazzle.** PowerPoint's special effects are "cool," but not necessarily helpful. If you let them take over the show, you will be ignored as a speaker.

- **Too little focus on the speaker.** There have been times when normal delivery skills have been forgotten, as a speaker focuses attention solely on the slides. No matter what visuals you use, ultimately it is you, the speaker, who is responsible for making your presentation engaging.

- **PowerPoint used when it shouldn't be.** Not *every* speech calls for a PowerPoint presentation. Imagine a eulogy, sermon, or tribute speech with PowerPoint. It just doesn't make sense. Make sure if you use PowerPoint that it really is necessary. If not, leave it out!

You'll notice that you can choose from multiple options, including Slide View, Outline View, Slide Sorter, Note Pages, and Slide Show. For a new presentation choose Slide View. Then pick a template and format such as the one shown in Figure 11.9. When choosing a template, remember a dark background works best for showing words. Also, don't lose sight of the fact that you want to call attention to the information on the slide rather than the slide itself. A simple design works best in this regard. Once you've done all of the preceding, you can add content to your slide. The sample shown in Figure 11.10 includes the title of a speech and the three main topics covered. This kind of slide works very well as a previewing device, cueing the audience to the basic organization of the speech. At this point you are ready to insert another slide. To do so, go to Insert on the toolbar and choose New Slide. You'll have to select the format again but not the template. As seen in Figure 11.11, our new slide has the first main point printed in the title space, followed by the supporting points we will make.

Once you've finished with the basics, you can manipulate the slide. If you return to View and select Slide Sorter, for example, you can animate one or all of the slides you've created. Or you can remain in the slide view and modify individual slides with graphs or clip art. (See Figure 11.12.) Once you have your completed set of slides, you'll need to decide on how to best use them. If you have access to a computer and LCD projector, you can use PowerPoint to its best advantage. But even if you don't, you can print your slides, making a hard copy on paper and then using the copy to create an overhead transparency.

Obviously there is much more to PowerPoint than we've provided in the brief discussion here. Further, PowerPoint is best learned from a visual model, so we highly recommend that you check out the PowerPoint Tutorial on your Speech Coach CD.

SPEECH COACH

For help in creating PowerPoint presentations, see the Power-Point Tutorial on your CD.

Overheads

If you have access to PowerPoint but do not have a way to project PowerPoint slides in your class, you can make copies of your slides on paper and then copy the slide onto a plastic overhead sheet. It's best if you can make color copies.

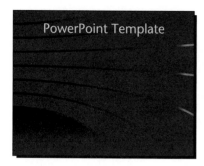

FIGURE 11.9 An Example of a PowerPoint Template

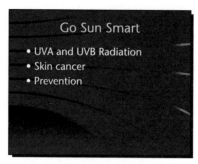

FIGURE 11.10 An Example of PowerPoint Slide with Text

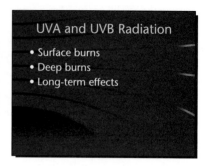

FIGURE 11.11 An Example of a New Slide Using the Same Format

Even if you do not have access to PowerPoint, most word processing programs will enable you to create serviceable overheads. Be sure, however, not to simply type them up as you would a term paper, with 20 lines of text on a page. Rather, follow the basic rule of no more than 6 lines of text and no more than 6 words per line. Use a large font, 18 or 24 point, to ensure that your audience can read the slides from a distance. In fact, a simple test is to hold up the transparency for a friend standing 10 feet away. If your friend can read it without difficulty, then it will be large enough for your audience when it is projected on a screen.

overhead transparency
A graphic that can be projected.

Overhead transparencies are a popular medium in business and classroom presentations. They have the advantage of low cost and ease of preparation, and they can be used without dimming the lights too much. Many classrooms and business conference rooms have overhead projectors, but you should always check in advance to make sure a projector is available. Also be sure to check out the equipment in advance, since machines operate differently.

One easy way to make a transparency is to take a chart or graph from a book or magazine, enlarge it on a photocopier, and then copy the enlarged version onto the transparency. It may take you several tries to get exactly the image you want, so don't try to enlarge directly onto the plastic sheet. Enlarge on plain paper, and then copy your final version onto the transparency. When using a photocopier, be sure to use transparency stock designed for plain-paper copiers; otherwise, the transparency can melt inside the copier!

It is also possible to print text or graphics directly onto a transparency with some computer printers. Again, be sure to use the transparency stock designed for your printer. If you have a color printer, this will help you create colorful overheads, rather than mere black-and-white ones.

Video

Another presentational medium is video, which can be imported from a tape, DVD, or mini-DV. Video is increasingly being used to augment speeches and presentations at corporate gatherings, at political conventions, in courtrooms, and in classrooms. Using video effectively in a speech requires both technological support and technological savvy. Video is not an option unless the context in which you are speaking is designed and equipped to easily show it. Further, unless you are knowledgeable in the use of the equipment or have support personnel who will supply you with video as needed, you should not even consider it.

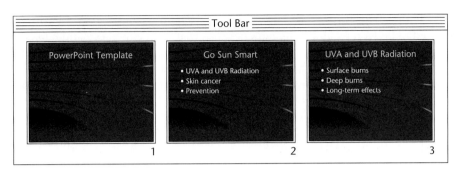

FIGURE 11.12 PowerPoint Slides as Depicted When You Click on Slide Sorter

All too frequently, beginning speakers fail to consider the details of using video in a speech. Simply because they have access to a means of showing video (such as a playback device and monitor), beginning speakers decide to use it without first thinking about:

- Cueing it ahead of time, including monitoring the sound level
- Lighting
- The distance between the means of showing it and its proximity to the audience
- The time it takes to introduce, show, and integrate the video with the remainder of the speech

Simply put, we do not recommend using video in a speech until giving speeches and using less demanding presentational media have become routine.

Audio

Audio media such as a cassette tape or CD reproduce sounds you can incorporate in your speech. One of the laptop computers we use in our own classes includes Apple Itunes. This software allows us to add music to a lecture as well as excerpts from speeches for our students to hear. The decision to use audio media alone in a speech rests on two factors. First, how will it help to make a presentation better? We often talk about how Martin Luther King, Jr., used repetition in his speeches to influence an audience. With the click of a mouse, Itunes allows students to *hear* what we mean.

Of course we are fortunate enough to have at our fingertips both the software and technology to use it. You may not. The second factor that goes into the decision to use audio, then, must be whether you can use it unobtrusively. Otherwise, it has as much chance to hurt as to help you.

audio media Aural channels you can use to augment your speech, such as a recording of a famous speaker.

Slides/Photographs

At one time it was common for speakers to use a 35mm slide projector. Of course, conventional slide projectors require a darkened room, which impedes the audience's view of the speaker. This makes the speaker secondary to the slide show, which is the opposite of what should happen.

We recommend that you import slides and photos to a computer, and then link the computer to a means of projection, rather than try to use the two conventionally. LCD projectors are rapidly displacing conventional 35mm slide projectors. Also, digital cameras, which can be linked to a variety of projection devices, are displacing film.

Photographs have problems of their own. First they must be sufficiently enlarged to be seen by an entire audience, but that is an expensive and cumbersome option. Second, they must be mounted on something, for example, tag board or foam-core board. Third, photographs have to be handled by the speaker so that they are visible when needed. Finally, the speaker has to find some way to discard the photograph once used, or it is likely to distract audience members.

If computer projection is not an option, consider enlarging the photos sufficiently to be transferred to an overhead transparency. At least that does not require completely darkening the room, as do 35mm slides. It is also far less cumbersome than poster-sized photos.

GUIDELINES FOR CREATING AND USING VISUAL MEDIA

SPEECH COACH

To evaluate the use of visual media, see the Speech Critique program on your CD.

Whether your visual media are as high tech as a PowerPoint slide show or as low tech as a poster, there are four basic guidelines you need to keep in mind in their construction: simplicity, size and visibility, layout, and color.[3] Let's consider each of these in turn.

Simplicity

There is a common tendency to put too much information on a single visual. We have seen people simply take a page from a magazine and copy it onto an overhead transparency. Some students try to save a few dollars by putting two or three ideas on one poster. These tendencies undermine the effectiveness of visual media. The best advice we can give you is to keep it simple.

TIPS AND TACTICS   *Using Words and Numbers*

SPEECH COACH

To hear more about these Tips and Tactics, go to Audio Tips and Tactics on your CD.

- Limit yourself to one idea per visual medium.
- Use no more than six words per line.
- Use no more than six lines per visual medium.
- Use short, familiar words and round numbers.
- Keep charts and graphs simple enough to be sketched easily by your audience.

Size and Visibility

If your audience can't see your visuals, instead of listening to you, they will be straining to see or asking a neighbor what's on the screen.

TIPS AND TACTICS   *Increasing Visibility*

- Make your images at least 1 inch high for every 30 feet of viewing distance.
- Make sure you do not block your audience's view of the visual as you show it during the speech. Many PowerPoint projectors, for example, allow you to use a remote device to advance your slides, so you can stand away from the projector.

- Make sure the visual is high enough to be seen by everyone in the audience. This means using a tall easel with posters and photos, and projecting Power-Point slides or overheads high enough on the screen to be visible to everyone.

Layout

An organized, consistent, and uncluttered layout is necessary for an effective visual. One of the great advantages of visual media produced by computer programs, such as PowerPoint, is that the templates are designed for an effective layout depending on the speech purpose.

Laying Out Information   TIPS AND TACTICS

- Place images near the top of your visual to ensure maximum visibility.
- Accentuate key points with bold type, underlining, or contrasting color.
- Make sure text is horizontal, not vertical. Vertical writing is hard to read.
- Leave generous margins, larger on top than bottom, and equal on the sides.
- Present information from left to right and from top to bottom. For example, a chart showing progression over time should have the oldest year on the left and the most recent year on the right, not vice versa. If the information is presented vertically, the oldest should be at the top and the most recent on the bottom.

Color

The proper use of color helps your audience pay attention, comprehend, and remember your visuals.

Using Color   TIPS AND TACTICS

- Use primary colors—red, blue, and yellow—which have been shown to create the strongest impact.
- Use contrasting but complementary colors so that your audience can see clearly. Yellow lettering on a white background, for example, is almost invisible.
- Use colored backgrounds, as long as the color is not so dark that the message is hard to see. Colored backgrounds are more visually soothing.
- Don't use clashing or confusing colors. For example, don't use red to show profits and black to show losses.

SUMMARY

Properly used, presentational media can make the difference between a successful speech and a failure. Improperly used, they can undermine your purpose. Remember:

- Avoid relying too much on presentational media, cramming too much information on a single hard-to-see visual, and using the wrong type of presentational medium to achieve your purpose.

 SPEECH COACH

To evaluate your understanding of this chapter, see the Quizzes on your CD.

- Think of presentational media as extensions of your senses, using them as a complement to speech, as visual illustrators of speech, as regulators of speech, and as emblematic speech.
- Use presentational media appropriately, matching a medium with its best possible purpose.
- Consider all of the possibilities, including actual objects, models, audio, video, and computer-generated slides.
- Match content with the appropriate medium, for example, using visual media such as pie charts and bar graphs to show statistical data.
- Keep presentational media simple, visible, easy to read, and colorful.
- Give the audience at least 10 seconds to process presentational media
- And never forget that presentational media may complement your speech, but they can never take your place or achieve your purpose and goals.

CHECK YOUR UNDERSTANDING: EXERCISES AND ACTIVITIES

SPEECH COACH

For a review of key terms in this chapter, see the Key Terms Flashcards on your CD.

1. Check on your campus or at local copy shops to find out where you can have the following made: black-on-clear overhead transparencies, color overhead transparencies, enlarged photographs.

2. Find out where on campus you can obtain an overhead projector, and find out who can answer questions about its operation. Learn how to turn it on and off, how to focus it, and what to do if the bulb burns out.

3. Find an example of a bar chart, a pie chart, a line graph, and a map in *USA Today* or your local newspaper, and describe whether each one would make a suitable visual for a speech. Evaluate them in terms of simplicity, size and visibility, layout, and color.

4. Contact the computer center at your college or university. What, if any, services are available to help you prepare computer graphics for your speeches? If you own or have access to a computer, go to a computer dealer or consult a software catalog, and find at least three presentation-graphics programs available for your computer.

5. Consider the following speech situations: an informative speech on the impressionist movement in art; an informative speech on a country you have visited; a persuasive speech about health insurance in the United States; a speech to entertain on the topic of traveling by train, plane, or automobile. What types of visual media would be most appropriate for each speech situation, and why?

NOTES

1. Marshall McLuhan and Quentin Fiore, *The Medium Is the Massage* (New York: Bantam Books, 1967), 26–41.
2. Joe Downing and Cecile C. Garmon, "Teaching Students in the Basic Course How to Use Presentational Software," *Communication Education*, 50 (2001): 218–29.
3. Minnesota Western, *Visual Presentation Systems* (Oakland, Calif.: Minnesota Western, 1988–1989).

Contexts for Public Speaking

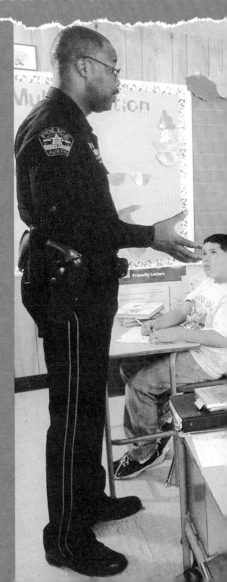

Jaime Escalante motivated his students to achieve through the power of *ganas,* the desire to succeed.

Informative Speaking

CHAPTER 12

 OBJECTIVES

After reading this chapter and reviewing the learning resources on your CD-ROM and at the Online Learning Center, you should be able to:

- Explain how to adapt your informative speech to audiences with diverse learning styles.
- Explain the relationship between informative speaking and learning.
- Prepare an informative speech that is audience involving, audience appropriate, audience accessible, and potentially life enhancing
- Prepare informative speeches that explain, instruct, demonstrate, or describe processes, concepts, and skills.
- Illustrate how informative speaking can be used in your other classes, at work, and in your community.

 KEY CONCEPTS

audience accessible	audience involving	informative speaking
audience appropriate	*ganas*	learning styles

> *Determination plus hard work plus concentration equals success, which equals* ganas.
>
> —JAIME ESCALANTE[1]

ganas Spanish term that loosely translates as the desire to succeed.

Jaime Escalante, whose picture you see in the opening photograph, is not simply a gifted teacher. He is a remarkable person. He immigrated to the United States from Bolivia in 1969, where he had taught mathematics and physics. He spoke not a single word of English. But Escalante had what he called **ganas**— that is, a desire to succeed regardless of the odds against it. Thus, at age 30, he reentered school to work toward his teaching credential, even though it meant subjecting his out-of-shape body to a required course in P.E.

The rest of the story, of course, is probably well known to you. Escalante's life became the subject of the critically acclaimed film *Stand and Deliver.* In the movie, actor Edward James Olmos portrays Escalante, who took East Los Angeles barrio students who could barely do simple math and, in two years of intensive work, prepared them for the Advanced Placement Test in Calculus. His students were so successful that all 18 who attempted the test in 1982 passed, the most from any high school in Southern California. Each year, more students passed; by 1987, 87 of his students passed the exam. Remember, these were students who were not expected to attend college, let alone receive college credit for calculus while still in high school. But as Escalante says, "Students will rise to the level of expectations." When students wanted to quit, Escalante would challenge them by saying, "Do you have the *ganas?* Do you have the desire?"[2]

Although there are many reasons that Escalante was able to overcome odds others would have perceived as insurmountable, we think his success in life as well as in the classroom can be found in that word of his: *ganas*. Not only did Escalante have it when he needed it, but also his life is testimony to the fact that he has instilled it in many of his students. As a result, they too have succeeded.

In a sense, this chapter is about *ganas*. Like Jaime Escalante, the best informative speakers do more than simply pass on information to an audience. With their words and actions, they create a desire in their audience to put the information to constructive use. In the case of Escalante, the desire involved a subject that many students prefer to avoid: mathematics. In yours, it may involve anything from how we treat our environment to the kind of foods we eat.

Teaching can be a form of informative speaking.

Informative speaking is the process by which an audience gains new information or a new perspective on old information from a speaker. Put another way, the goal of informative speaking is audience learning. In order to be an effective informative speaker, you need to master several skills, which we will look at in this chapter. These skills include:

- focusing on your audience and appealing to their various styles of learning;
- understanding the relationship between informative speaking and learning;
- making your message audience involving, audience appropriate, audience accessible, and potentially life enhancing;
- putting theory into practice in speeches that explain, instruct, demonstrate, or describe; and
- understanding the differences and similarities among the forums in which you are likely to give informative presentations, namely, the classroom, the workplace, and the community.

informative speaking The process by which an audience gains new information or a new perspective on old information.

FOCUSING ON YOUR AUDIENCE: ADAPTING TO DIFFERENT STYLES OF LEARNING

Consider the following scenarios. In the first, a high school principal goes before the student body to explain the school board's unpopular decision to restrict students to campus during lunch periods. In the second, a pharmaceutical salesperson demonstrates to a group of physicians how easy it is to use a new skin test for food allergies. In the third, an offensive line coach teaches linemen a new offensive scheme they will use in their next football game. In the fourth, a driving instructor at a high-performance racing school explains the concept of heel-and-toe braking and shifting as a driver prepares to enter a turn on a road course. And in the fifth, a chef at a culinary school explains the difference between blanching and sautéing raw vegetables.

Each of these scenarios can be viewed as a speaking situation. Further, each involves a speaker publicly *informing* an audience. In each case, the speaker must focus on relating the information to the needs and goals of the audience members. Jaime Escalante had to first reach out to and connect with his students before he could really begin to teach them calculus. So too must every informative speaker reach out to and connect with his or her audience before presenting them with information.

Informative Speaking and Styles of Learning

One important consideration in focusing on your audience is recognizing that not everyone has the same style of learning. Not everybody thinks in a linear or "logical" fashion. Some people can simply read a book and absorb the information, whereas others need to hear and see to learn. Still others learn best by doing. Good public speakers recognize these differences and appeal to as many styles as possible. Here is one listing of diverse **learning styles:**[3]

- *Auditory linguistic:* Learning by hearing the spoken word.
- *Visual linguistic:* Learning by seeing the printed word.
- *Auditory numerical:* Learning by hearing numbers.

learning styles Differences in the way people think about and learn new information and skills.

- *Visual numerical:* Learning by seeing numbers.
- *Audio-visual-kinesthetic combination:* Learning by hearing, seeing, and doing in combination.
- *Individual:* Learning when by oneself.
- *Group:* Learning in collaboration with other people.
- *Oral expressive:* Learning by telling others orally.
- *Written expressive:* Learning by writing.

At first, such a long list of diverse learning styles may be intimidating. How in the world can one speech or even a series of speeches adapt to all of these different ways of learning? Of course, you cannot be all things to all people. But teachers confront this variety of learning styles every day. Many teachers use a combination of methods—individual and group work, written and oral assignments, print and visual materials—in an effort to adapt to the variety of learning styles in their classrooms.

Rather than trying to guess which one style of learning is most widespread in an audience and focusing on that, it is better to use multiple channels and modes of learning. That way, you are likely to reach most of your audience members with something that suits their style of learning. In any given audience, there are likely to be individual learners as well as group learners, those who respond best to oral instruction and those who need to read it, and so on. Using PowerPoint slides, for example, is an excellent way to reinforce visually what you say orally. Distributing a handout after a speech can help visual learners retain what was said. Provide your audience with an opportunity to use as many senses as possible to process your message. If parts of your presentation can be seen, heard, and even touched, you will increase the odds that your message will sink in.

One speech we heard, for example, was about using acupressure to relieve stress. By instructing the class to press on certain points on their bodies, the speaker allowed the audience to use their sense of touch to understand what was being said. Other speakers appeal to the sense of taste. We frequently have international students speak about a food unique to their culture and bring samples for the audience to try. We have also seen student speakers involve their audiences in a group exercise to better appreciate the subject on which they are speaking. Specific examples include a speaker asking fellow students to model the simple yoga poses he first demonstrated, and a student who was blind talking in the dark for part of her speech, so that sighted students might better appreciate what she experienced when listening to a lecture.

Informative Speaking, Learning, and Persuasion

Whether your speech is aimed at explaining a process such as photosynthesis, describing the alignment of the planets in our solar system, or demonstrating the uses of the wok in Chinese cooking, informative speaking is basically about learning. As your own experience tells you, exposure to new information or a new perspective doesn't guarantee that you will learn it. No matter how convinced a teacher is of the importance of his or her subject matter, there is no guarantee students will share the teacher's conviction. Jaime Escalante, for example, first had to convince his students that calculus was worth knowing before trying to teach it to them.

So it is with you and your informative speeches. Before you attempt to explain, describe, or demonstrate something to your audience, you must first connect its value with the self-interest of your audience. Then, and only then, will your audience be sufficiently motivated to listen to what you have to say.

Given this framework, you might ask, "How is informative speaking different from persuasive speaking?" There is no simple answer to this question. It is a matter of degree and purpose. The purpose of an informative speech is to provide people with data from which they can potentially benefit. Suggesting to audience members that the information you are sharing can potentially benefit them, however, is not the same as trying to persuade them that their lives will be diminished should they fail to embrace and incorporate this information into their daily routine. For example, informing people about the advantages of carrying a well-stocked emergency kit in their cars is not the same as trying to persuade them that the emergency kit you just happen to be selling for $29.95 is the *best* kit on the market.

MESSAGE KEYS OF EFFECTIVE INFORMATIVE SPEAKING

What makes one speaker's presentation so informative and stimulating that you want to learn more about what you initially thought was a boring topic? And why does another speaker's presentation leave you cold from beginning to end? Is the reason (a) the speaker, (b) the topic, (c) the message, (d) your perceptions, or (e) all of the above? Because the public speaking transaction is an interdependent system, the answer, of course, is (e) all of the above.

However, if an informative speech is seen as personally or professionally relevant, it can be successful in spite of being delivered by a marginally skilled public speaker. The reverse is not always true; that is, we may not find an entertaining speaker personally or professionally informative.

Research over the past two decades suggests that the likelihood of an audience's perceiving information as relevant and conducive to learning depends significantly on the degree to which they find it involving, appropriate, accessible, and potentially life enhancing.[4]

Audience Involvement

Information is worthless unless people pay attention to it. Information needs to be **audience involving.** The history of the world is full of examples of great ideas, practices, and products that failed because no one paid much attention to them. One of the first things you'll want to try to ensure, then, is that your topic and speech get your audience involved with what you have to share.

Novelty is the quality of being new and stimulating. It can be useful in gaining your audience's interest. Just as plants are heliotropic, we human beings are stimulitropic. Whereas plants continuously orient themselves to the sun to activate the process of photosynthesis, we continually orient ourselves to new sources of stimulation.

Although novelty alone is not enough to sustain an informative speech, it certainly can make your speech more effective. Research has time and again documented the fact that the perception of novelty heightens selective exposure,

audience involving Informative topic and speech that succeeds in gaining the audience's attention.

selective attention, and selective retention of information. In other words, people are likely to seek out, pay attention to, and remember novel information. The most obvious way to get the benefit of novelty in an informative speech is to choose a topic that is novel for your audience. You're much more likely to initially captivate the attention of audience members with the unfamiliar than with the mundane. Novelty, however, shouldn't be confused with the obscure. For example, whereas computer software for accountancy probably would be an obscure topic for most audiences, the fact that the software could save you money on your taxes might be a novel topic.

Another way to use novelty to your advantage is in the construction of your message. Even though the rule of thumb is to structure your speech so that the audience can predict what comes next, this is not an unbending rule. Sometimes it is to your advantage to violate the expectancies of an audience. Writers, for example, sometimes begin with a story's end and then backtrack. Similarly, a skilled speaker could start a speech with what normally would be considered its conclusion and build backward.

Finally, novelty in your delivery can work to your advantage when speaking informatively. Audiences, for instance, generally are accustomed to speakers who are relatively stationary. Movement may add needed novelty to your presentation. In addition, if you review some of our suggestions about the nonverbal dynamics of delivery in Chapter 10, you'll find other ways to introduce novelty to your presentation.

Audience Appropriateness

Although novelty can increase the chances of your audience initially paying attention to you, the information you share also needs to be compatible with what audience members believe is appropriate to the occasion. If your topic immediately turns your audience off, the audience also will tune you out.

Early in this book we said that communication is perceptual and that the process of perception is selective. Basically, people perceive what they choose to perceive. **Appropriateness** is the audience's perception that a message is consistent with their belief systems—their attitudes, beliefs, values, and lifestyle. All too often, speakers fail to take appropriateness into account when choosing a topic and then constructing their informative speech.

audience appropriate Informative topic and speech that takes into account the occasion and audience members' belief systems.

For example, we've heard several informative speeches on sexually transmitted diseases (STDs) and their prevention. We've also had students approach us after class and tell us they were offended or made to feel uncomfortable as a consequence of (1) the information in some of these speeches, (2) their perception that these speeches promoted a lifestyle with which they disagreed, and (3) the use of visual aids they didn't perceive to be in good taste. To a large degree, we were surprised by these reactions to a topic we believe needs to be openly discussed. We don't feel that student speakers should altogether avoid sensitive topics such as this one. However, they do need to consider the question of compatibility so that they can soften or qualify the information to make it appropriate for the audience.

Consider how you might approach an informative speech on the constitutional rights of accused felons for two different audiences. The first audience is composed of law school students. The second is a group of veteran police officers. Both audiences need the information you have. Would you give an identi-

Visual media can help make a speech more accessible to an audience.

cal speech to both of them? Probably not. For the police officers, you most likely would have to qualify the information in your speech with such statements as:

> "I realize some of you take exception to the courts' rulings on the rights of the accused."

> "Putting our personal feelings aside, the Constitution is clear . . ."

> "Before I begin, I want you to put the shoe on the other foot; assume that you are the accused."

The point is that information that is potentially incompatible with audience members' world view can be made appropriate if it is presented in a way that acknowledges the audience's point of view.

Audience Accessibility

Simply put, audience members cannot benefit from information that they cannot grasp. An **accessible** informative speech is one that the audience readily understands. Suppose, for example, that you are a biology major and you want to inform an audience about mapping the human genome. Should you use words peculiar to your major? Should you use the same approach with an audience of

audience accessible Content the audience is able to understand, regardless of its complexity.

beginning speech students as you would with a group of seniors in a biochemistry class? Of course not.

Research tells us that one of the quickest ways to turn off an audience is to complicate a topic. You don't have to avoid complex topics for your informative speeches. In fact, they are likely to be both novel for your audience and interesting for you to research. The goal is to make complex topics accessible and compelling.

Jaime Escalante's calculus classes in *Stand and Deliver* are models of the presentation of complex information. He broke the lessons into easy-to-digest bits, what he called "step by step." In fact, he would say to his students, "This is easy." It's not so much the complexity of the topic as the complexity of a speaker's explanation that makes a topic difficult for an audience to understand.

An excellent way to reduce the complexity of a speech is through analogies or comparisons. Explain a complex process, for example, by comparing it with a common process based on the same principle. One speech we heard explained nuclear power plants by using an analogy to the steam produced by heating water in a teakettle.

Visual media can also be helpful in reducing complexity. For example, we recall a speech about a complex carbon molecule in which the speaker used a Tinkertoy model to show what the molecule looked like. The speaker also used an analogy, calling the molecule a "soot ball," to help the audience visualize what it would be like.

 **SPEECH COACH**

To see an excellent example of a complex topic made accessible to an audience, see Lorenmarie Manning's speech on Down syndrome, segment 12.1 on your CD.

Life Enhancement

When we introduced the tools you need to get started on your first speech, we talked about the importance of connecting with your audience. If they are to learn, audience members need to know explicitly why it is in their interest to listen to what you have to say.

When we connect with our audience, we are in effect saying, "My topic and message are potentially life enhancing." Life enhancement can take the form of a more informed view on some topic or an improved way of behaving. Don't think that just because you have a good idea, people will necessarily see the advantage in adopting it. History is replete with good ideas, the proverbial better mousetrap, that are collecting dust for want of the public's attention. Consider two examples from Everett M. Rogers's classic work, *The Diffusion of Innovations*.[5]

If you have studied the history of science, you may recall that the disease scurvy, caused by a deficiency of vitamin C, was a serious problem for sailors on long voyages. As early as 1601, it was found that sources of vitamin C effectively inhibited scurvy. Yet it took almost 200 years for the British navy to put this finding to use on its ships, and almost 75 years more for sources of vitamin C to be made available on commercial ships.

The second example concerns the arrangement of the keyboard on typewriters and personal computers. If you have ever thought the keys were illogically arranged, you are not alone. A far better method of arrangement of keys has been available since 1932. The Dvorak method is more efficient than the system almost everybody uses and is more easily mastered. So why weren't you taught the Dvorak method in the beginning? Because the one you use was invented in 1873 and has been designed into almost all keyboards ever since.

One of the reasons for staying with the less logical keyboard was that the metal keys of early typewriters stuck when the typist worked too quickly. Thus, the keyboard we use today on computers and electric typewriters was originally invented to *slow down* typists on mechanical typewriters.

All too often, speakers assume that audience members will recognize they have something to gain personally or professionally from a speech. What may be perfectly obvious to the speaker, however, may be just the opposite for the audience. Consider a case with which you already have some experience—college classes. Regardless of the subject matter of their classes, most college professors believe that the information they have to share is absolutely essential to every student's intellectual well-being. So secure are they in this belief, in fact, some seldom spend any time convincing students that there are "good reasons" for their being in the professor's class.

Occasionally, this oversight doesn't much matter—for example, when students are taking a course in their major. Students listen because they know they "have to learn" what is being taught, regardless of how well it's being taught. This is seldom the case, though, when they find themselves in a required course outside their major. "Why do I need a course in art history?" complains the computer science major, while the chemistry major asks, "Why do I need a class in public speaking?" To motivate students in math classes, Jaime Escalante put together a video called *Who Needs Math?* starring people like Bill Cosby.

Just as teachers have an obligation to connect their course to the professional aspirations of students, so do speakers have the same kind of obligation to their audiences. It's not enough that their information is perceived as involving or appropriate by their audience. Their information—their speech—must also be readily perceived as something that will enhance audience members' lives.

PUTTING THEORY INTO PRACTICE

Now that you know some of the principles related to conveying information to an audience, it's time to plan your own informative speech. This section offers some practical suggestions for how to give an informative speech. We discuss four ways to inform an audience: explanation, instruction, demonstration, and description. Informative speeches may employ more than one of these modes of informing. And the list is not exhaustive. Nevertheless, these four categories should be a useful way of thinking about how to translate the principles of informative speaking into an actual speech.

 **SPEECH COACH**

To evaluate informative speeches, see the Speech Critique program on your CD.

Speeches That Explain a Process

One of the primary functions you may wish to accomplish in an informative speech is to explain a process. Technically, a *process* is a continuous phenomenon without an obvious beginning or end. Examples of processes are plentiful in science and include photosynthesis, erosion, and osmosis. Because true processes are complex and often hidden from our ordinary senses, their explanation requires genuine creativity from a speaker. At a minimum, the speaker must break down the process into increments that the audience can readily comprehend. If the process involves a specialized vocabulary, the speaker also needs to define terms for the audience. Because the process also may be invisible, the speaker may have to create visuals that approximate the process.

The key to explaining a process is to find the right complement of language and visual media for your audience. This involves finding the best analogies, metaphors, and similes to start. You can then complement these elements of language with static visual media such as overheads or dynamic visual media such as videotape or CD-ROM.

Speeches That Explain a Concept

Although not as difficult to explain as a process, a concept demands care on the part of the speaker who chooses to explain it. A *concept* is a symbolic abstraction that pulls together a class of objects that share common attributes. The word *ball*, for example, is also a concept that can be applied to baseballs, basketballs, footballs, golf balls, racketballs, squash balls, and volleyballs. Although different in size and purpose, these types of balls share at least one common attribute: They are round.

The key to explaining a concept is to describe the criterial attributes that distinguish it from other concepts. How is a democracy different from a republic? The United States is a republic, yet most people refer to it as a democracy. A good informative speech would not only explain why this is the case, but also point out the specific attributes that distinguish a republic from a democracy.

In selecting a topic for a speech that explains a process or a concept, keep in mind that the topic should be relevant to the audience, something they are capable of understanding, and something you can explain in the time allotted. Although the theory of relativity is highly relevant, explaining it in a 5- to 10-minute speech is a tall order.

The message attribute of accessibility is particularly important in speeches that explain. Recall that one way to reduce complexity for an audience is to use an analogy. Consider the use of analogy in this excerpt from a speech by Jonathan Studebaker explaining a process, namely, the progressive disease he has:

> Like I said, I'm a nice person. I'm cheerful, I'm energetic. Okay, so I have a disability. I was born with osteogenesis imperfecta, a disease which causes my bones to be fragile. Have you ever accidentally dropped a glass on the floor? What happens? It breaks. Well, my bones kinda break like glass, which is why I tell people, when you carry me, treat me like your best crystal.[6]

The use of a simple analogy of bones to glass helps the audience understand a disease most of us cannot even pronounce. For Jonathan's purposes, which are to introduce himself and explain his disability, that is the extent of the technical information his audience needs to know.

A second factor that is important in speeches that explain a process or a concept is to make it observable with visuals. They can make an abstract concept concrete and thus easier to understand.

During your college career, you will undoubtedly be called on to explain something to an audience, if not in your public speaking class, then in another setting. Similarly, in the professional world, it is common for people to be called on to explain everything from a new product idea to why the last quarter's sales were so bad. Using the principle of accessibility can help you enhance your explanations. You can review the outline of this type of speech in the box "Sample Informative Speech Outline: Down Syndrome by Lorenmarie Manning."

Speeches That Instruct

Informative speaking can also be used to instruct an audience. The key to instruction is to provide new information the audience can put to use, or a new perspective on old information. Modern educational theory emphasizes observable behavioral objectives; that is, after receiving instruction, students should be able to show that they have mastered the subject, either by answering questions or by engaging in some activity.

Making your speech audience involving is important to speeches that provide instruction. Unless the information in your speech presents *new* information or a *fresh perspective* to your audience, all you have done is bore them with what they already know. For example, speeches on how to ride a bike or how to pack your suitcase are unlikely to provide anything new to an audience. However, even new topics can be perceived as irrelevant by large portions of an audience. For example, a speech on how to wax your skis is old news to experienced skiers, but irrelevant to nonskiers in the class.

So, the key to speeches that instruct is to provide new yet relevant information to your audience, or at least a new perspective on such information. That means using the novelty of your topic to involve people while pointing out how learning the information can be life enhancing.

Speeches That Demonstrate How to Do Something

Speeches that demonstrate how to do something are closely related to those that provide instruction, but the speaker actually shows the audience how to do something. Further, a good demonstration allows the audience to try out what is being demonstrated, if not during the speech itself, then later on their own. A good example of speeches that demonstrate are the late-night infomercials you see on TV. From food dehydrators to onion slicers, the product is demonstrated for the audience. Viewers at home and in the studio can clearly see how to use the product. Audience members are often given a chance to try the product. Viewers are urged to order the product and try it at home, with a no-risk, money-back guarantee. The combination of demonstration and allowing customers to try the product without risk has made infomercials highly successful.

Whatever a speaker is demonstrating, he or she needs to provide audience members with enough information to do the activity on their own, or with information on where to obtain further instruction, so that they can try out the activity. For example, although no one can master karate from just listening to a single speech, or even a series of speeches, a demonstration of karate moves can spur an audience member to seek out individual instruction in the martial arts. In fact, many martial arts studios make a practice of giving demonstrations in schools and at public events as a way of recruiting new students.

Topics for speeches that demonstrate need to be chosen with care. A complex, difficult task cannot be adequately demonstrated in a few minutes. There can even be the danger of making people think they know how to do something based on a speech when in fact they do not. Few of us could do CPR, for example, based on simply watching a speaker demonstrate the activity. We need the opportunity to try

SPEECH COACH
To get a better handle on an informative speech explaining a concept, watch Lorenmarie Manning's speech on Down syndrome, segment 12.1 on your CD.

Sample Informative Speech Outline

DOWN SYNDROME
by Lorenmarie Manning

Introduction

Notice how speaker incorporates her personal experience into opening.

I. **Open With Impact:** Is there anything more beautiful than a baby's face? My last semester of my senior year I worked in a place where the answer is definitely no, even if that child has Down syndrome.

II. **Thesis Statement:** Today I will inform you about the chromosomal anomaly that is Down syndrome.

Speaker connects to audience members, whether they know someone with Down syndrome or not.

III. If you've ever known someone who has Down syndrome, you know that they are special people. And even if you haven't, today is your chance to find out what makes them special scientifically.

Preview of speech clearly identifies her three points.

IV. **Preview:** First I will tell you the history of D.S.; second, I'll explain chromosomes and why they divide; and lastly, I'll discuss the three different types of Down syndrome.

Body

First main point shows audience the history and extent of the disease.

I. **Main Point:** First let's talk about how Down syndrome came to be discovered and named.

A. Down syndrome was first discovered by John Langdon Down in 1866 (Leshin, 1997).

1. He published an essay as superintendent of an asylum for mentally retarded children.
2. He called the children "mongoloids" due to his perceived likeness to the Mongolian people.
3. The condition was renamed in the 1960s to be politically correct.
4. Jerome Lejeune and Patricia Jacobs were the first to discover that it was a chromosomal problem.

B. Currently D.S. is diagnosed in 1.3 out of 1,000 births (Bristol Branch of Down Syndrome Association, 2001).

(**Signpost:** Now that you know the history of D.S., I will move on to explaining what chromosomes are and how they divide.)

Second main point explains the complex process by which chromosomes divide.

II. **Main Point:** When talking about D.S. it is important to understand what a chromosome is and how it divides in cells.

A. Chromosomes are threadlike structures that carry DNA. They are found in every cell of the body (Leshin, 1997).

B. Normal human cells contain 46 chromosomes that can be divided into 23 even pairs. There are 47 chromosomes in a D.S. cell.

C. Meiosis is cell division that occurs due to fertilization. This is the stage in the life of the cell where a problem resulting in D.S. occurs.

it out (perhaps on a life-size doll) before we can know whether we can do it. On the other hand, another lifesaving technique, the Heimlich maneuver, is often the subject of demonstration and can be learned in a reasonably short time.

The key to making your demonstration effective is careful planning. For example, if you have ever watched the show *Home Improvement*, you know that

(**Signpost:** Since we now understand chromosomes I will explain the types of D.S.)

III. **Main Point:** There are three different types of Down syndrome that are diagnosed (Pueschel, 2001).

    A. The first and most common type is called Trisomy 21.

        1. This means that each cell has 47 instead of the usual 46 chromosomes, and it accounts for 95% of all cases.

    B. The second type is known as Translocation.

        1. This means that the extra 21 chromosome or parts of it attached to other chromosomes. It is responsible for 3–4%, and it is important to note that this is the only type of D.S. that can be genetically passed down

    C. The final and rarest type is called Mosaicism.

        1. This type accounts for only 1% of all cases and is defined by some cells having 46 chromosomes and some having 47.

        2. Even though the conditions vary, all three types are defined by an extra 47th chromosome.

Third main point explains the three different types of Down syndrome. By using visual aids, speaker makes the process visible to her audience.

Conclusion

  I. **Summarize:** Today I have talked about the history of D.S., the way chromosomes divide, and the three different types of D.S.

 II. **Close With Impact:** I hope this information will be of help to you since more than 1,600 babies a year are born in the United States alone with D.S. (Mattheis, 2001.) If your life has not already been touched by someone who has it, then it probably will be in the future.

Conclusion first summarizes the speech, then closes with impact by pointing out how likely it is that audience members may be touched by Down syndrome in their lives.

References

Bristol Branch of Down Syndrome Association. (2001, May 22.) *What is Down syndrome?* Retrieved October 12, 2001 from http://www.dsa-bristol.org.uk/

Leshin, L. (1997). *Trisonomy 21: The story of Down syndrome.* Retrieved October 12, 2001 from http://www.ds-health.com/trisomy.htm

Mattheis, P. (1997–2000). Down Syndrome. *Microsoft® Encarta® Online Encyclopedia 2001,* Microsoft Corporation. Retrieved October 13, 2001 from http://encarta.msn.com

National Down Syndrome Society. (2001). Retrieved October 13, 2001 from http://www.ndss.org/main.html

Pueschel, S. M. (2001, April 10). *Down syndrome.* Retrieved October 13, 2001 from http://www.thearc.org/faqs/down.html

Richards, G. (2001, August 28). *Growth charts for children with Down syndrome.* Retrieved October 15, 2001 from http://www.growthcharts.com/

Thios, S. J., ed. (2000). *Denison Down syndrome quarterly.* Ohio: Denison University.

References are listed using APA style.

Tim (The Tool Man) Taylor rarely has practiced what he is doing. If you plan to demonstrate a process in your speech, rehearse it carefully. Also, it is sometimes useful to prepare various steps of the process in advance. Watch any cooking show demonstration on TV. The onions are already chopped, the flour is already sifted and measured, and an example of the finished product is near at

Failure to properly prepare for a demonstration is the hallmark of Tim Allen's comedy on *Home Improvement,* but it can lead to disaster in an informative speech.

hand. You don't want the audience drifting off as you measure ingredients or sift the flour. Providing a written recipe in a handout or as a visual will save you a lot of time and let the audience focus on watching your demonstration. In short, a demonstration requires extra preparation.

In addition, be sure that the demonstration is an accurate re-creation. If you misinform an audience, you have done more harm than good. Depending on what you are demonstrating, you might even be inviting injury to the audience members or someone else. Make certain, therefore, that you can accurately demonstrate the process in the time allowed.

Finally, make sure the demonstration is visible to the audience. A demonstration speech on making sushi, or small origami paper figures, may initially seem like a good idea. Unless you had a way to magnify the demonstration so that all your audience could see what you were doing with your hands, making sushi or origami figures isn't a very good idea. Fencing, on the other hand, is a dramatic and highly visible topic. (See the box "Sample Informative Speech Outline: Fencing by Evan N. Mironov.")

 **SPEECH COACH**

To gain a clearer understanding of an informative speech demonstrating a speaker's topic, watch Evan Mironov's speech on fencing, segment 12.2 on your CD.

Speeches That Describe

Another function of informative speeches is description. Using visuals can enhance a descriptive speech. Not only can visuals be useful; you may also want to provide a word picture of your subject. Consider the following description of a familiar character, Mickey Mouse, provided by student speaker Jennie Rees:

> They designed him using a circle for his head and oblong circles for his nose and snout. They also drew circles for his ears and drew them in such a way that they appeared to look the same any way Mickey turned his head. They gave him a pear-shaped body with pipe-stem legs, and stuffed them in big, oversized shoes, making him look like a little kid wearing his father's shoes.[7]

Can't you almost picture Mickey from that description? Visual language is key to effective description.

Description can be used not only for physical objects but also for scenes or events. Consider the briefings given by General Norman Schwarzkopf during the 1991 Persian Gulf War. He used a variety of maps and charts to explain every move. He used terms from football and other sports, calling the American troop movements a "Hail Mary pass." Further, rather than merely telling the audience about the success of U.S. smart bombs, he used a video to show the accuracy with which targets were destroyed. In one memorable incident, he pointed to a vehicle passing through the crosshairs of the bomber just before the target was hit. He called the driver "the luckiest man in Iraq."

Tips and Tactics for Informative Speaking   TIPS AND TACTICS

When putting your informative speech together, remember to:

- Use words that appeal to the different learning styles of audience members.
- Use techniques that make your speech involving, appropriate, accessible, and potentially life enhancing.
- Establish in your own mind whether your speech purpose is to explain a concept or a process, demonstrate or instruct.
- Maximize observability through the use of appropriate presentational media.

FORUMS FOR INFORMATIVE SPEAKING

Informative speaking is probably the form of public speaking you're most likely to be called on to do at some point in your life. One of the chief reasons is that informative speaking is used in so many settings, including the classroom, the workplace, and the community.

Informative Speaking in the Classroom

Two time-honored traditions in the college classroom are the term paper and oral report. Although most students have at least passing familiarity with the elements of a good term paper, many students don't make the connection between the elements of a good oral report and the process of informative speaking.

Undergraduate speech majors are usually pleased to see that an oral report is required in a course outside their major. They know that an oral report basically is an informative speech. Thus, by putting to use what they know about

Sample Informative Speech Outline

FENCING
by Evan N. Mironov

Outline states the speaker's specific purpose.

Specific Purpose: To tell people about fencing.

Introduction

Speech opens with impact as the speaker turns and draws sword, yelling, "On-guard!"

I. **Open With Impact:** On-guard!, your opponent yells as he draws his sword.
   A. Take a deep breath and exhale slowly.
   B. He lunges wildly at you.
   C. The first point is good, as you watch your opponent's eyes fill with horror.

II. **Focus on Thesis Statement:** Fencing has evolved over time.

Connects with audience by referring to common dreams.

III. **Connect With the Audience:** Everyone has had dreams of damsels in distress and musketeers.

Note speech has four main points.

IV. **Preview:** Today I will tell you where fencing has come from and how it evolved into the different disciplines that are around today, as well as the modern equipment necessary to keep you safe. And finally the rules of the strip, so if you ever see a match, you will understand what is occurring.

Body

I. **Main Point:** Fencing has been around as early as 1190 B.C. (Lancaster University Fencing Club, 2000).
   A. The rapier was created in Italy and became the basis for modern fencing weapons (Fencing.net, 2000).
   B. Where did the rapier come from?
   C. How the rapier led to the foil.

Signposts are provided as transitions between points.

(**Signpost:** This leads me to the three different styles of fencing that are practiced today.)

II. **Main Point:** The three disciplines of fencing are foil, epee, and saber (US Fencing Online, n.d.).

informative speaking, they are usually able to give oral reports that are both substantively and stylistically more effective than those of their classmates.

Viewing the oral report as an opportunity to speak informatively has several advantages. First, it provides you with an organizational framework for constructing your report. Second, it reminds you that you have an audience for your report whose background and perceptual reality must be taken into account. Finally, it forces you to think about how relevant the information in your report is to both your instructor and student colleagues.

Informative Speaking in the Workplace

All the people we have profiled in this book realize now what they didn't necessarily realize as undergraduates: Regardless of major or career, the ability to stand up and speak publicly is a skill both admired and rewarded in the real world.

A. Foil is the basic practice dueling weapon.
B. Epee is more like a traditional dueling style because whole body is target area.
C. Saber came from swords cavalry use.

(**Signpost:** Now that you know a little about the weapons, I'll talk about safety.)

III. **Main Point:** Since we no longer believe in hurting people, we use protection.
A. The mask and its importance.
B. The glove and how it protects the hand.
C. The jacket and chest protector and what they prevent from happening.
D. The knickers and what they protect.

(**Signpost:** You now know about the weapons, as well as the armor that a modern fencer must use; now I will tell you about the fencing strip and basic moves.)

Main Point: The rules of fencing are difficult to fully comprehend.
A. The fencing strip is 2 meters wide by 14 meters long.
B. What is the concept of right of way.
C. The basic movements.

Conclusion

Summarize: Recap each topic and say a little about it.
Close With Impact: I leave you with the ending of a bout, a salute.

Could the speaker have provided more detail in his conclusion?

References

Fencing.net. (2000, May 22). *History of fencing—Where did it start?* Retrieved on October 7, 2001 from http://www.fencing.net/intro2.html
Lancaster University Fencing Club. (2000, August 6). *A brief history of fencing.* Retrieved on October 7, 2001 from http://www.lancs.ac.uk/socs/fencing/fenbri.htm
US Fencing Online. (n.d.) *What is fencing?* Retrieved on October 7, 2001 from http://www.usfencing.org/welcome/whatisfencing.asp

References are listed using APA style.

No matter what you plan on doing to make a living, the odds are great that you will need to make informative presentations. Although you won't necessarily have to speak informatively to large numbers of people, you can reasonably expect to speak informatively to your immediate co-workers, perhaps your entire department, or in a meeting with people to whom you're subordinate. It is common in the workplace to make informative presentations before groups. For some presentations you will have to stand and speak; other presentations may be delivered from your seat.

Although the different situations require adjustments in your style of delivery, the substantive elements of your informative presentation are the same. You will still need to follow a cohesive organizational sequence, analyze your audience carefully, and consider the message attributes described earlier in this chapter.

All too often, speakers get trapped into thinking that the smaller their audience, the more informal their delivery and content can be. Instead, they need to make the relational features of the message more interpersonal without sacrificing the content of the message. They can increase nonverbal immediacy, for example, while protecting the formal structure of the speech.

Informative Speaking in the Community

You can reasonably expect to speak informatively with members of your community in at least one of two capacities: as a representative of your employer or as a concerned citizen. Private, as well as public, enterprises are justifiably concerned about their image within their local community. Opinion poll after opinion poll shows that the public is increasingly suspicious of the motives of private enterprise and increasingly dissatisfied with the performance of public agencies in particular. It's not uncommon, therefore, for these organizations to make themselves available to service groups, such as Rotary International, the general public, or a citizens' group organized around a specific cause.

Some businesses have a person whose job is company spokesperson; large corporations may even have whole departments dedicated to public relations. Many organizations, however, have come to expect anyone in management to serve as an informative speaker to the community. In fact, private corporations, such as IBM, and public agencies, such as the police or fire department, may actually write such community service into their managers' job descriptions. Thus, just because you currently perceive your intended career as low profile, that doesn't necessarily make it so.

Finally, remote as the possibility may seem to you now, you may one day want or need to speak informatively as a private citizen. If you live in a community where cable television is available, your city council meetings probably are televised on your community access channel. If you tune in, you will see ordinary citizens making informative presentations at these meetings. Topics can range from the environmental impact of a new housing development to excessive noise from student housing. If you watch several of these presentations, you will probably conclude that very few of the speakers have much training in public speaking; people who do have training are easy to spot.

Your days as a public speaker will not be over once you've completed this class. Given what we've said here, in fact, you should now realize they are just beginning.

SUMMARY

 **SPEECH COACH**

To evaluate your understanding of this chapter, see the Quizzes on your CD.

Informative speaking is the process by which an audience gains new information or a new perspective on old information from a speaker.

- Learning is frequently the goal of informative speaking.
- It's important therefore that the individual learning styles of audience members be reflected in the verbal and nonverbal content of informative speeches.
- Successful informative speeches are audience involving, audience appropriate, audience accessible, and potentially life enhancing.
- Informative speeches can be used to explain, instruct, demonstrate, or describe processes, concepts, and skills.
- Informative speeches are common in the classroom, the workplace, and the community.

CHECK YOUR UNDERSTANDING: EXERCISES AND ACTIVITIES

1. Develop an outline for a one- to two-minute speech in which you inform an audience about a topic with which you are personally very familiar. Then show how you would adapt that speech to at least three different learning styles: auditory linguistic, visual linguistic, and audio-visual-kinesthetic.

2. Come up with at least two possible topics each for speeches that explain, instruct, demonstrate, and describe. Do some topics seem to fall naturally into one category? Are there other topics that might be used for more than one type of speech?

SPEECH COACH

For a review of key terms in this chapter, see the Key Terms Flashcards on your CD.

NOTES

1. Jay Mathews, *Escalante: The Best Teacher in America* (New York: Henry Holt, 1988), 191.
2. *Stand and Deliver,* director Tom Menendez, with Edward James Olmos, Lou Diamond Phillips, Rosana De Soto, and Andy Garcia, An American Playhouse Theatrical Film, A Menendez/Musca & Olmos Production, Warner Bros., 1988.
3. P. Friedman and R. Alley, "Learning/Teaching Styles: Applying the Principles," *Theory Into Practice,* 23 (1984): 77–81. Based on R. Dunn and K. Dunn, *Teaching Students Through Their Individual Learning Styles: A Practical Approach* (Reston, Va.: Reston Publishing, 1978).
4. Michael D. Scott and Scott Elliot, "Innovation in the Classroom: Toward a Reconceptualization of Instructional Communication" (paper presented at the annual meeting of the International Communication Association, Dallas, Texas, 1983).
5. Everett M. Rogers, *Diffusion of Innovations* (New York: Free Press, 1983).
6. Jonathan Studebaker, "Speech of Self-Introduction: Who Am I?" The full text appears in Appendix A.
7. Jennie Rees, "Informative Speech: Mickey: A Changing Image," California State University, Chico, 1992.

Mayor Rudy Giuliani's calm after the terrorist attacks of September 11, 2001, helped persuade New Yorkers to return to their normal lives.

Persuasive Speaking

 OBJECTIVES

After reading this chapter and reviewing the learning resources on your CD-ROM and at the Online Learning Center, you should be able to:

- Describe how your assessment of the audience and situation is important to persuasive speaking.
- Describe the four goals persuasive speeches are designed to achieve.
- Analyze the audience of a persuasive message in terms of cultural, demographic, and individual diversity.
- Define ethos, logos, and pathos.
- Achieve persuasiveness through the use of speaker credibility.
- Describe the process of elaborated thinking in relation to persuasion.
- Demonstrate how to use first-, second-, and third-order data as evidence in a persuasive speech.
- Explain the rationale for presenting a two-sided persuasive message, and construct a two-sided persuasive message.
- Demonstrate how certain types of persuasive appeals are linked to audience members' emotions and primitive beliefs.

 KEY CONCEPTS

behavioral intention	first-, second-, and third-order data	persuasion
elaboration likelihood model	logos	source credibility
ethos	pathos	

> *Character may almost be called the most effective means of persuasion.*
>
> —ARISTOTLE[1]

Shortly after the terrorist attacks that destroyed the World Trade Center in New York City, Mayor Rudy Giuliani spoke to the people of New York and of the nation. He urged them to come to New York, to return to their everyday lives and not be cowed by terrorists. He even suggested that it might be possible to get tickets to the hottest show on Broadway, *The Producers*. This persuasive effort went a long way toward bringing New York back to life and returning the city to a sense of normalcy. It also helped to make Mayor Giuliani one of the most admired leaders in America. While mere words could not erase the events of that day, the mayor was able to persuade his constituents and the nation that New York City would not live in fear. With that in mind, this chapter is about **persuasion,** the process by which a speaker influences what audience members think or do. The topics covered in this chapter include:

persuasion The process by which a speaker influences what audience members think or do.

- the relationship between persuasive speaking and the situation you face;
- factors to take into account in your attempts to reinforce what an audience believes, inoculate an audience against counterpersuasive speeches, change audience attitudes, and prompt an audience to act;
- how you can use your own credibility, your message, and your understanding of your audience to craft and deliver an effective persuasive speech.

FOCUSING ON YOUR AUDIENCE AND ASSESSING THE SITUATION

Audience-focused persuasive speaking begins with an assessment of the audience and the situation you face. You need a clear understanding of your goals as a speaker, knowledge about your audience, and an assessment of the constraints facing you, including the ethical boundaries you must respect.

Schoolchildren are often subjected to antidrug persuasive speakers, but do these messages really help prevent later drug use?

Does Drug Education Really Work?

Remember elementary school and the "just say no" campaign to discourage drug use? It is just one part of a massive drug education campaign, ranging from Drug Abuse Resistance and Education (DARE) to Red Ribbon Weeks, designed to inoculate youngsters against being persuaded to try drugs. Billions of taxpayer dollars are spent nationally on such programs, and the State of California alone spends about $400 million annually on drug education. To determine if the programs were worth the cost, the California Department of Education commissioned educational research consultants at the University of California at Berkeley to study the state's drug education programs. The results of the three-year study, completed in 1995, were so controversial that the Department of Education refused to release them. They were finally published two years later, in 1997, in the academic journal *Education Evaluation and Policy Analysis*. The results were shocking to drug educators. Only 15 percent of students found drug education persuasive. Nearly 70 percent of the 5,000 students surveyed were either neutral or even negative toward the programs.

According to the study's lead author, Joel Brown, "Not only are the programs ineffective, but for many youth they have an effect counter to what is intended." Among the comments from students about such programs, a typical one was "I don't think handing someone a ribbon saying 'Drug Free Is for Me' is going to make someone stop using drugs." In contrast, many students praised presentations by people suffering from AIDS as something that "really gets to you."

Brown's study has not been without its critics, however, including the California Department of Education, which rejected the findings as "significantly flawed." Nevertheless, the facts are that drug use among teens has risen in the past five years, despite the expenditures of billions on drug education programs.

If you experienced drug education programs such as these during your elementary and secondary education, what did you think about their effectiveness? As attempts to inoculate youth against the temptation of drugs, were these efforts persuasive to you and your peers? If not, how could they have been made more persuasive?

Source: Peter Hecht, "School Anti-Drug Programs Bashed," *Sacramento Bee*, 19 March 1997, A1, A12.

The Four Goals of Persuasive Speaking

There are four common, and sometimes interdependent, goals that can be achieved through persuasive speaking. The first is to *reinforce* the attitudes, beliefs, and values an audience already holds. Keynote speeches at national political conventions, for example, are usually designed to bolster the common core of beliefs, attitudes, and values to which members of a political party subscribe. Much of the rhetoric after the terrorist attacks of September 11, 2001, was designed to reinforce and bolster basic American values. For example, despite the nationalities of the known hijackers, President Bush spoke out frequently against judging Muslims or Arab Americans as a monolithic group, reinforcing the core American values of tolerance and fairness.

The second goal of persuasive speaking is to *inoculate* an audience against counterpersuasion, that is, persuasive messages opposed to the speaker's views.[2] Although it is possible to bolster audience members' attitudes, beliefs, and values through straight reinforcement, it takes more to make them truly resistant to counterpersuasion. Anti–drug use messages aimed at children, for instance, are most effective when they give sound reasons not to use drugs, rather than telling kids to "just say no." (See the box "Does Drug Education Really Work?") Children can then use these reasons to defend their anti–drug use behavior when confronted with peer pressure to experiment with illegal substances.

The third goal of persuasive speaking is to *change attitudes*. This is a difficult task, because the audience is often one that disagrees with or is even hostile to your position. A speaker calling for the complete legalization of marijuana needs

317

to realize that many audiences do not share that point of view. Changing people's attitudes requires incremental change over time. Thus, taking small steps, such as first convincing an audience that marijuana should be legalized for medical purposes, is more likely to achieve success than trying to change people from total opposition to total support in a short time.

Attitude change may also occur with an audience that is apathetic or disinterested in your topic. To convince an audience that they should care about a problem, rather than be unconcerned, is itself a change of attitude. Thus, many campaigns for political offices or ballot initiatives are targeted toward undecided voters, those sometimes least interested in the political process. The initiatives passed recently in several states to legalize medicinal marijuana focused on motivating undecided voters by stressing the need to relieve the suffering of cancer and AIDS patients, among others—an argument that many undecided voters found persuasive.

The fourth goal of persuasive speaking is to *prompt an audience to act*. This is the most difficult goal to achieve. People are seldom moved to act as a result of a single persuasive speech. A foundation must first be laid that will make the audience likely to act. That takes time and repetition of the message. When it appears that people are responding to a single message, the persuasive speech is usually the most recent in a long line of catalysts that have been building momentum for action. Consider the efforts of President Bush to get people to travel after the attacks on the World Trade Center and Pentagon. It took a number of efforts to restore a sense of security for the traveling public, including an airline safety bill, which the president signed, and an advertising campaign in which he appeared. People did not simply resume their old travel habits overnight.

Which of these four goals you will pursue in a given speech depends largely on the audience you are addressing. If they already share your attitudes and values, then a speech of reinforcement is warranted. On the other hand, if they are likely to be the subjects of counterpersuasion or if their commitment to your point of view is shaky, then inoculation is likely to be your goal. If you face an audience opposed to your views, you will need to attempt to change their attitudes, usually a time-consuming, incremental process. Finally, if the audience is primed by prior persuasive messages to behave in accordance with your goals, then prompting them to action may be your best approach. Although these goals are related, any given persuasive speech is likely to focus primarily on one outcome.

Adapting to Your Audience

The realization of any of these four persuasive speaking goals begins with a thorough analysis of your audience. Audience analysis starts with an assessment of the relationship between the audience and the goal you hope to achieve. Not all audiences are capable of acting to help you achieve your goals, even if they want to do so. For example, people who are not U.S. citizens or who are under age 18 cannot vote in elections. The candidate who directs a persuasive campaign toward either of these groups is wasting time and money. Preparing and delivering a persuasive speech intended to induce a specific group to act makes sense only if that group is capable of acting.

Once you are sure your goal makes sense in relation to your audience, the next step is to analyze audience diversity. Review the discussion in Chapter 5 of the three levels of audience diversity you'll need to consider: cultural, demographic, and individual.

Simply put, the more you know about your audience, the better you will be able to predict how the audience is likely to respond to issues and the people associated with those issues, as well as the kind of message likely to prove resonant with the audience. A persuasive speech about product safety delivered to the National Association of Manufacturers, for example, would be quite different from one delivered to a group of personal-injury attorneys. In either case, you would have to construct your persuasive message on the basis of what you knew about each demographic group.

Audience Attitudes Toward Your Topic   In addition to a general analysis of your audience, in a persuasive situation, you need to determine their specific attitudes toward your topic. For example, speaking to a group of your classmates about avoiding binge drinking, it's important to know whether they consider themselves to be heavy drinkers. If they do not acknowledge that there is a problem in their own behavior, they may agree with your speech, but see no relationship to their own lives. Thus, you may want to focus on defining binge drinking and showing them that their behavior may fit this category, something they previously would not have realized. On the other hand, if you were speaking to a group of acknowledged heavy drinkers, such as a meeting of Alcoholics Anonymous, you would not need to convince them of the problem. Rather, you might focus on providing coping mechanisms to avoid the temptation to drink in social situations.

Audience Attitudes Toward You   You also need to know how the audience perceives you as a speaker. For example, some speakers come to their audiences with a high degree of perceived trust and expertise. As we will discuss in this chapter, speakers with such high credibility have an easier time persuading listeners than do speakers who are either unknown or even disparaged by their audiences. Speakers in the latter group must first provide the audience with evidence of their expertise and trustworthiness; otherwise, the audience is predisposed to dismiss the positions advocated by the speaker. Knowing where you are on the credibility continuum is important in assessing how difficult your persuasive task will be.

Behavioral Intentions Toward the Topic   A **behavioral intention** is a person's subjective belief that he or she will engage in a specific behavior.[3] The more you can predict your audience's initial intentions toward your topic, the better you can adapt your message. Behavioral intentions sometimes can be inferred from a person's beliefs, values, and attitudes. In other instances, you may want to survey your audience in advance or even ask for a show of hands. In a speech that was opposed to the unrestricted use of cell phones, one of our students began by asking how many of her classmates used cell phones while driving. When most people's hands shot up, she knew that persuading them not to use their phones at all was probably an impossible task. Thus, she limited her goal in the speech to encouraging the use of hands-free cell phones while driving.

As a speaker, it is not enough simply to obtain a statement of behavioral intentions from an audience; ideally, you want to empower your audience to behave in accordance with their stated intentions. Although this is not always

behavioral intention A person's subjective belief that he or she will engage in a specific behavior.

easy, one technique for doing so involves having audience members make public commitments. For example, automobile salespeople long ago learned that they should do everything they can to discourage customers from leaving the lot before committing to a purchase. They recognize what research repeatedly demonstrates: Commitments made in the presence of others are more difficult to break than private ones. Thus, the more speakers encourage audience members to publicly commit to a certain behavior, the more likely their goals will be achieved.

Involvement in the Topic   Two persons may hold roughly the same beliefs, attitudes, and values regarding a topic and yet be quite different in how easily they are influenced. Consider the issue of drug use. While most people have a position on the issue, their involvement in the topic is another story. Suppose a close friend or relative of yours had cancer and wanted to be able to use medicinal marijuana to relieve the suffering. You would probably have a position on this topic that you felt very strongly about. On the other hand, suppose a close friend of yours, who used marijuana in combination with more dangerous drugs, had died from a drug overdose. You probably would also have a strong position on drug use, opposing any relaxation of the laws. It is not just a matter of what attitude people express on a topic, but how strongly they hold the opinion. Knowing that one person favored medicinal marijuana while another opposed any relaxation in drug laws is only part of the story. The likelihood of changing the minds of those personally touched by the drug issue is very slim. In contrast, an audience composed of people with no personal stake in the issue might be far more persuadable.

You also need to assess how involved your audience members are with the topic. Research shows the more involved people are with a topic, the more likely they are to interpret messages that even mildly disagree with their own position as highly discrepant from their own. This is known as a *contrast effect*. Consider the person who lost a close friend to a drug overdose. He or she might interpret a speaker advocating legalization of marijuana for medicinal use as the first step toward full legalization. On the other hand, people also *assimilate*. This happens when people perceive messages that are reasonably close to their own as more similar than they actually are. In this case, a person favoring total drug legalization might also misperceive the medical marijuana message as favoring a broader form of legalization. Thus, highly involved persons tend to polarize views: You are either with them or against them. Attempts to change the views of highly involved people even a little are likely to be rejected out of hand.[4]

Related to the concept of involvement is the idea of latitudes of acceptance, rejection, and noncommitment. Highly involved persons normally have a very narrow latitude of acceptance of positions different from their own, and they have wide latitudes of rejection. In fact, they often perceive positions different from their own as more extreme than they really are. Conversely, persons with low levels of involvement have large latitudes of noncommitment and small latitudes of rejection. These people are much more likely to listen to opposing views than their highly involved counterparts. In Figure 13.1, person A tends to have very little room for noncommitment and probably is highly involved in the topic. Person B, on the other hand, while holding the same most-preferred position as A, has a much bigger latitude of noncommitment and is

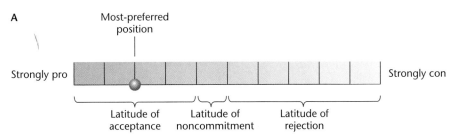

A

Most-preferred
position

Strongly pro   Strongly con

Latitude of   Latitude of   Latitude of
acceptance   noncommitment   rejection

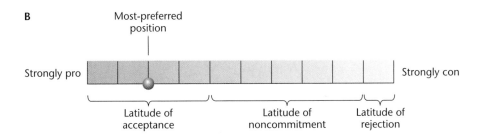

B

Most-preferred
position

Strongly pro   Strongly con

Latitude of   Latitude of   Latitude of
acceptance   noncommitment   rejection

FIGURE 13.1 Latitudes of Acceptance, Rejection, and Noncommitment

thus more open to different ideas on this topic. This is the group of people that politicians, marketers, and advertising professionals target. They recognize that whereas they have little or no chance to gain the favor of people already involved and committed, those less involved will not reject their persuasion out of hand.

Often speakers need to make uninvolved audiences feel more involved in their topic. This is especially true if their goal is inoculation. By using real or even hypothetical examples, such as personal experiences, speakers can bring life to an abstract subject. Whatever the audience's initial level of involvement, successful persuaders need to make the topic come alive and seem directly relevant to their audience.

Ethical Constraints

Achieving your persuasive goals shouldn't come at the expense of your audience. Audience-focused persuasive speaking is bound by ethical constraints. Selling worthless swampland may help the speaker achieve the goal of making money, but only at the expense of gullible audience members who may lose their life savings. The end you hope to achieve must reflect not only your interests but also those of your audience. Along the same lines, you need to think through the persuasive means you plan on using to achieve your goal. Noble ends do not justify ignoble means. As a case in point, we happen to believe that the remaining stands of giant sequoias should be protected from logging. We also would be happy to assist someone in preparing and delivering a speech that suggests reasonable means to achieve this end. This doesn't mean, however, that we would help someone who, as a part of his or her persuasive message, plans to advocate tree spiking (placing metal spikes in trees to keep them from being cut down). Such activity can lead to serious injury or even the death of loggers.

Speaking on behalf of his uncle, George P. Bush used his similarity to Latino and Hispanic voters to help persuade them to vote for George W. Bush for president.

SPEAKING WITH CREDIBILITY

We want you to think of yourself as the speaker as we begin our discussion of how to effectively present a persuasive message. Two thousand years' worth of theory and research suggest that whether an audience is likely to be persuaded by a speaker depends on two interdependent dimensions of perception. The first dimension involves the degree to which the audience perceives the speaker as similar to them. The second, and most important, involves the speaker's ethos, that is, the degree to which the audience perceives the speaker as credible.

Similarity

To begin with, people are suspicious of people they perceive as dissimilar to themselves. How can an outsider, for example, understand their needs? As a speaker, it is wise to stress the factors that tie you to your audience. For example, President George W. Bush spoke in Spanish in many of his television ads targeted at Latino and Hispanic voters. He also called on his nephew, George P. Bush, whose mother is from Mexico, to speak for him in ads and at the GOP convention. The message being sent by these actions was that George W. Bush understood and cared enough about Latino and Hispanic voters to learn their language.

By the same token, however, people are not likely to follow the advice of those they perceive to be their clones. What can they learn, after all, from

How Similar or Dissimilar Are You and Your Audience?

Fill out this form prior to your first persuasive speech. Compare your appearance to that of your audience. In what ways are you similar and in what ways dissimilar? Do the same for your cultural, demographic, and individual factors. In what ways can you use your similarities to build your credibility? How can you overcome or even positively utilize your dissimilarities?

Factors to Assess Prior to Persuasive Speech	Similar to Audience	Dissimilar to Audience
Appearance _____	_____	_____
Cultural Factors _____	_____	_____
Demographic Factors _____	_____	_____
Age _____	_____	_____
Socioeconomic status _____	_____	_____
Geographic origin _____	_____	_____
Ethnicity _____	_____	_____
Gender _____	_____	_____
Religion _____	_____	_____
Language _____	_____	_____
Factors Relating to Your Speech Topic		
Attitudes [toward it] _____	_____	_____
Beliefs [about it] _____	_____	_____
Values [regarding it] _____	_____	_____
Behavioral intentions [toward it] _____	_____	_____
Other Factors _____	_____	_____

someone whose background, education, and experience is nearly identical to their own? The key, then, is to be perceived by an audience as a member of the community who is similar in terms of background and values, but who is also uniquely qualified to shape opinions about relevant matters. This is where credibility comes into the picture. The box "How Similar or Dissimilar Are You and Your Audience?" lets you test this relationship before you speak.

Credibility

Any discussion of the concept of credibility begins with Aristotle's concept of ethos. Aristotle defined rhetoric as "the faculty of observing in any given case the available means of persuasion."[5] Aristotle identified three primary means of persuasion—ethos, logos, and pathos. Aristotle believed that to be persuasive a speaker must be not only competent but also a person of substantial character, a combination he called **ethos.** He believed that ethos was a personal attribute

ethos The degree to which an audience perceives a speaker as credible.

and was essential to a speaker's chances of persuading an audience. In fact, as the opening quotation in this chapter suggests, he viewed ethos as the most important aspect of a speaker's persuasiveness.

Modern communication researchers have substantiated Artistotle's thinking about the importance of ethos. Today's scholars use the term **source credibility,** which is the audience's perception of the believability of the speaker.[6] It is a quality your audience gives to you rather than one with which you are born. Thus, a speaker might be truly competent in a particular subject matter, but if the audience does not know this, the speaker's expertise will not increase his or her credibility. Similarly, a speaker may be of good character, but if the audience does not believe it, the speaker will suffer low credibility.

source credibility The audience's perception of the believability of the speaker.

Components of Credibility   Credibility is rooted in audience perceptions of believability. Researchers have shown that credibility consists of two primary components. Although researchers label these differently, the two perceptions that lead audiences to confer credibility on a speaker are competence and character.[7] Both are necessary to sustain the perception of ethos. To perceive you as credible, your audience must believe that you are not only competent and knowledgeable about your topic but also a person of character who can be trusted.

Competence   If you are largely unknown to your audience, how your audience perceives you as a speaker in terms of knowledge, intelligence, and expertise on the topic of your speech is critical to your success. If you have special expertise or firsthand experience, by all means let your audience know. If you have done extensive research on your topic, this will help your audience appreciate your newly acquired competence on the subject. Use facts, statistics, and quotations from experts to help your audience know that you are well informed on the subject.

Character   Even an expert can lack credibility with an audience if he or she is perceived as untrustworthy. For example, attorneys frequently call on expert witnesses to bolster their cases. Scientists testify about DNA evidence, forensic pathologists testify to matters such as time and cause of death, and accident investigators testify about such things as driver negligence. The trouble with such experts is that they are usually paid handsomely for their testimony. This calls their character into question in the minds of many, including jurors. This can and often does undermine perceptions of their overall credibility.

Enhancing Audience Perceptions of Credibility   There are three times when a speaker can help to enhance audience perceptions of his or her credibility—the time before the speech; during the speech; and perhaps one you didn't expect, after the speech. Because it is a perception, credibility is dynamic and changeable. The fact that a speaker is perceived as credible going into a persuasive speech doesn't guarantee that he or she will still be perceived as credible afterward. Similarly, the speaker who begins with little credibility can build the perception in the process of speaking. One of your goals is to build and maintain your credibility as you speak. You want it to be at least as high—and preferably higher—when you conclude as it was when you began. This is one reason why careful audience analysis is essential. You need to know how your audience perceives your credibility before you speak in order to determine whether you need to enhance it, and if so, how.

Credibility Before the Speech   Often, speakers' reputations precede them; in fact, reputation may be what prompts the audience to attend, especially when the speaker is famous, is an expert, or has new or unusual information about the topic. For example, a recent speech on our campus by actor Edward James Olmos was so well attended that there was standing room only. His fame as an actor and reputation as a powerful speaker and crusader against gang violence had ensured a degree of credibility with his audience before he spoke a single word.

Of course, most of us are not experts and may not even be known to our audience. One way to build your credibility before you speak is to have someone introduce you to the audience. In Chapter 15, we will talk about how to present a speech of introduction that will enhance an audience's perception of the speaker's credibility. If you are not introduced, you will have to establish your own credibility by what you say in your speech and how you say it.

Credibility During the Speech   Under most but not all conditions, the speaker's level of credibility at the outset of the speech is insufficient to sustain the audience's perception of believability. Credibility by way of reputation can be negated as a result of the speaker's appearance, message, and delivery. Audience members can quickly become disenchanted and may even turn against speakers whom they feel are just going through the motions or resting too much on their laurels.

On the other hand, even speakers with little initial credibility can build perceptions of competence and character during their speech. As a case in point, students in an introductory public speaking course may have little initial credibility with each other because they don't know each other and don't know each other's qualifications to speak on various topics. Practically speaking, then, these students begin to build their credibility with their first speeches. Their appearance, the care with which they have prepared their message, and their delivery can begin to establish their competence and character with their fellow students and instructor.

To make certain you are perceived as a credible speaker in a persuasive transaction, though, you'll need to provide your audience with proof of your credibility through the reasoning and evidence in your message. The reasoning and evidence you present in your persuasive speech should not only support the arguments you make but also support the audience's perception that you are competent and a person of high character. Also, if you have special expertise or credentials that are relevant to your topic, you'll want to share the fact with your audience.

Credibility After the Speech   Speakers whose persuasive message bolsters their credibility with an audience cannot rest on their laurels. Just as initial credibility can suffer from a poor speech, the credibility you establish during your speech can be negated as well. No one knows this better than former President Clinton. After denying for seven months that he had an improper sexual relationship with intern Monica Lewinsky, he was forced to recant his denials before a grand jury and the public at large. His forceful denial initially quelled the public outcry. However, when it was later learned that he had not been fully truthful, his presidency suffered as a result, and he became only the second American president in history to be impeached. Never lose sight of the fact that perceived credibility is dynamic. Once gained, credibility needs continued nourishment. The following list provides some reminders and tips for maintaining credibility.

TIPS AND TACTICS   *Speaker Credibility*

- Ask yourself about the degree to which your audience already perceives you as credible. Also ask yourself whether your classroom behavior could have lowered your credibility in the eyes of the other students. For example, coming to class late and interrupting a speaker, not being ready to speak when it is your turn, or delivering speeches that are hastily put together tell other students about your competence and character. If this is the case, you'll need to work harder to establish your credibility.

- Dress appropriately for the occasion. Persuasion is serious business and should be approached seriously.

- Incorporate any special expertise or experience you have with your topic into the body of your speech. This information will enhance the audience's perception of your competence.

- Use evidence to support the claims you make. The facts and logical arguments you provide will help enhance your ethos.

- Engage your audience nonverbally, using the characteristics of effective delivery described in Chapter 10.

- Use powerful language (which research suggests is linked to persuasive effects), as described in Chapter 9.

- Use inclusive language, discussed in Chapter 9, to make certain all audience members believe they have a stake in the topic of your persuasive speech.

CONSTRUCTING A PERSUASIVE MESSAGE

logos The proof a speaker offers to an audience through the words of his or her message.

Although you cannot always choose your audience and you cannot always ensure that they will have a favorable image of your credibility, there is one element of the persuasive process that you can control—your message. Aristotle recognized the power of words (*logos* is Greek for "word") in the process of persuasion. As a result, he spent considerable time theorizing about both the nature of words and the manner in which they are arranged to form a message. **Logos** is the proof a speaker offers to an audience through the words of his or her message. Aristotle believed speakers should use logical proof. Understanding the options you have for constructing a persuasive message is the first step to crafting an effective appeal. The first thing to realize is that some audiences and situations call for a sophisticated, carefully reasoned speech, while others call for a less sophisticated message. In an effort to understand how audiences come to process persuasive messages, consider a model of persuasion known as elaboration likelihood.

The Elaboration Likelihood Model

In some persuasive transactions, the audience engages actively in thinking critically about a complex topic. In other situations, the audience responds almost without thinking. Social psychologists Richard Petty and John Cacioppo offer the **elaboration likelihood model** of persuasion to explain why audience members will use an elaborated thinking process in some situations and not in others.[8]

Consider a speech about doctor-assisted suicide. One possibility is that an audience is deeply concerned about the topic; perhaps members of the audience know someone who is terminally ill. They want a thorough and detailed discussion of the pros and cons of changing the laws to permit doctors to assist terminally ill patients in ending their lives. Another possibility is that audience members have no direct experience with the topic and simply prefer not to think about such difficult issues. Some ways of presenting the speech might invite the audience to engage in what Petty and Cacioppo call "central route processing," or elaboration. On the other hand, some messages on this topic might be designed to avoid elaborated thinking. Petty and Cacioppo call this "peripheral route processing."

The questions for a public speaker are (1) what factors are likely to lead an audience to engage in either central or peripheral message processing, and (2) which of these processes is most likely to lead to the achievement of speaker goals?

The second question is the easier to answer. In most situations, the speaker wants the audience to use the elaborated, or central, processing route. The reason is that if the argument presented by the speaker is accepted by audience members, they are more likely to undergo long-term attitude change. For example, if you are concerned that doctor-assisted suicide might lead to the patient's family members hastening their relative's death in order to collect on life insurance, you might want to cite examples from nations with such laws. Or you might want to discuss the moral issues involved in terminating a life, no matter how ill the patient. After all, one of the greatest minds of our time is Stephen Hawking, who suffers from ALS (Lou Gehrig's disease). In many cases, people with ALS would probably be considered prime candidates for doctor-assisted suicide by some of its advocates. On the other hand, if you are simply interested in a short-term goal, for example, getting voters to vote no on an upcoming initiative to allow doctor-assisted suicide in your state, you might simply want to say, "Killing is wrong, period. No ifs, ands, or buts about it. Vote no!"

To reiterate, then, the first question speakers should ask is "What factors in this situation will increase or decrease the likelihood of elaboration on the part of an audience member?" If audience members are motivated and able to understand a message, they are more likely to engage in elaborated thinking. On the other hand, if they find a message irrelevant or are unwilling or unable to understand the message, they are more likely to follow the peripheral route. Some factors are beyond the speaker's control. For example, individual listeners differ in their "need for cognition," that is, their need to process information centrally.[9] There is not much a speaker can do to make people who don't like to think about messages do so. On the other hand, a speaker can take steps to make the topic relevant to the audience and to provide understandable and strong arguments that will be persuasive to those who are motivated to process the message centrally.

Let's walk through the elaboration likelihood model depicted in Figure 13.2 to further explain the process. On the far left we have the persuasive speech. Next we see the audience. There are two possibilities—that they are motivated and able to understand the message or that they are unmotivated or unwilling or unable to understand it. If the first condition applies, the process follows the boxes along the top of the model. It is likely that the audience will engage in

elaboration likelihood model A model of persuasion designed to explain why audience members will use an elaborated thinking process in some situations and not in others.

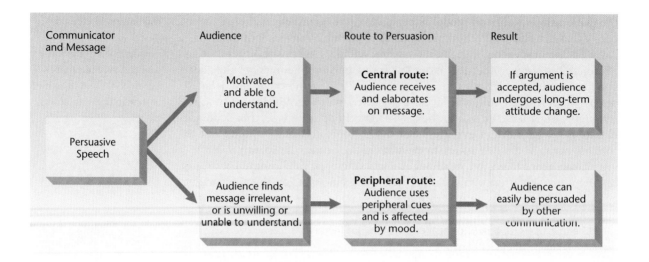

FIGURE 13.2 Two Routes to Persuasion in the Elaboration Likelihood Model

central route processing. Two factors make this route more likely. First, if the message is perceived as *relevant*, the audience is more likely to pay attention. Second, the message needs to be *understandable*. An audience member may find a speech on nuclear terrorism relevant but be lost in the technical jargon and thus unable to process the message. Even when messages are understandable and relevant, there is no guarantee that the audience will accept them. If a message is perceived as incompatible with what audience members already know or believe in, it is likely to be rejected. For example, a speech on nuclear terrorism that misstated well-known facts or proposed violating basic civil liberties, would likely be unacceptable to many audience members, even if they understood it and saw its relevance.

If an audience member engages in central route processing, then the quality of the message, in terms of evidence and reasoning, is the paramount basis for either accepting or rejecting the message. If the message is poorly constructed or presented, then even though the audience member engages in elaboration, the result may be contrary to the speaker's intent. Many times we have heard students speak on important, relevant, and significant topics, only to discover that their research was shoddy and their reasoning flawed. Rather than being persuaded, we are in fact more likely to reject the message because we have thought critically about it. So, if you choose a message that is designed for central route processing, you must be sure to make a strong case for your position. If you do, the audience will be more likely to undergo long-term attitude change and be resistant to subsequent persuasion to the contrary.

The boxes along the bottom of the model in Figure 13.2 illustrate the peripheral route process. In this case, the audience either finds the message irrelevant or difficult to understand, or simply is uninterested in dealing with its complexities. Yet there is still the possibility of at least short-term persuasion taking place. Suppose you are having a busy day and suddenly the doorbell rings. At your door is a young girl in a scout uniform with a box of cookies for sale. It isn't likely you want to take the time to learn about the details of the Girl Scouts. Perhaps you aren't a parent and never participated in scouts yourself.

Audience members who are motivated and see the relevance of a persuasive speech are more likely to engage in an elaborated thinking process.

So the message is largely irrelevant. Nevertheless, you might be hungry and the cookies aren't very expensive. The girl is an appealing person, and she seems sincere. What the heck, you think, I'll take a box, no, make that two boxes. In this example, you haven't engaged in an elaborated process of critical thinking. Rather, you have just made a snap decision based on peripheral cues. The likelihood of being persuaded by the peripheral route usually depends on such things as your mood (hunger), emotional cues (such as the appealing salesperson), and perhaps the apparent credibility of the source (you know she's a Girl Scout by the uniform). The problem with peripheral route processing is that it does not lead to stable attitude change. You might not be hungry the next time the girl comes by to sell the cookies. But if, as a speaker, you are simply interested in short-term persuasive effect, a peripheral route may be sufficient. And if your audience is uninterested or unwilling to engage in central route processing, it may be your only alternative. But, beware; persuasion that occurs as a result of the peripheral route is easily reversed. While this isn't a problem for the girl going door to door selling cookies, imagine the effect on the tobacco education program if it turns out that most public service announcements on TV only stimulate peripheral route processing in youth. Do we really want a tobacco education program that doesn't involve long-term attitude change that is also resistant to subsequent change?

To summarize: Elaboration likelihood clearly suggests an active role on the part of the audience you hope to persuade. This active role includes (1) seeing your topic as relevant to their needs, (2) understanding and comprehending your message, and (3) centrally processing the nature and quality of the information you offer in terms of their preexisting knowledge and beliefs.

Evidence and Persuasion

Assuming you are seeking long-term attitude change through central route processing, it is likely that you'll be seeking credible evidence to support your message. For many years, social scientific research on the value of evidence in persuasion was thought to be conflicting and inconsistent. In 1988, however, communication scholar John Reinard published a thorough analysis of 50 years of research on the persuasive effects of evidence.[10] Unlike many previous researchers, Reinard did not rely solely on the conclusions of other studies; he went back to the original works and reinterpreted the data using comparable definitions. He found that the research was surprisingly consistent. Further, he found that evidence, under most conditions, did in fact enhance the likelihood of persuasive effects. As Reinard writes: "After fifty years of research on the persuasive effects of evidence, the claims for the persuasiveness of evidence emerge as quite strong."[11] Some of his most important findings follow.[12]

Testimonial assertions (the judgment and opinions of people other than the persuader) are most effective when the sources are identified and their qualifications explained to receivers. Mere "name-dropping" has not been found to be persuasive.

Reports (a type of factual information that describes events as seen by either participants or observers) are persuasive, especially when they are believable, specific, and the receivers are intelligent. It is also important that the reporter's qualifications be explained for receivers.

Statistics, somewhat surprisingly, tend not to be very persuasive in the short term, although results are better in the long term. To be most effective, statistics should be preceded by a specific example, which is then shown to be representative through the use of statistics. To be persuasive, it is also important to explain how statistics were gathered. Research has demonstrated that when examples and personal anecdotes conflict with statistics, people are more likely to be persuaded by the examples.

Source credibility—that is, the believability of the person delivering a persuasive message—has an important impact on the persuasiveness of evidence. Using evidence tends to build a persuader's credibility. However, a source that is already highly credible is not likely to become more persuasive through the use of evidence in the short term (although long-term persuasiveness is enhanced). This is because of a *ceiling effect,* which means the persuader has already reached the maximum persuasive potential through his or her source credibility. With or without evidence, the persuader cannot become more persuasive.

Although the mode of presentation (video, tape, live, etc.) doesn't seem to make any difference, a poorly delivered presentation will not be persuasive no matter how good the evidence.

One very consistent research finding is that the most persuasive evidence comes from highly credible sources, found to be believable by receivers. The overall finding of the body of research is that high-quality evidence is more persuasive than low-quality evidence, especially for receivers who have a personal stake in the issue, who are trained in reasoning, who find the topic novel, who are not biased about the issue, and who have attended college.

Reinard's analysis supports the view that it is important to use credible, high-quality evidence in seeking to persuade others. Furthermore, he provides specific guidance as to the best evidence in specific situations. One of his most interesting findings is that statistics alone are not likely to be very persuasive. Persuaders need to bring the statistics to life by first presenting a vivid example. Statistics then serve to bolster the specific case, rather than replace it.

Technically, there are three types of evidence. They are called first-, second-, and third-order data.[13] **First-order data** is evidence based on personal

first-order data
Evidence based on personal experience.

Culture and Persuasion

As a society, we value a reasoning process that is more likely to produce true than false beliefs, likely to produce a large number of truthful arguments and statements, and likely to do so with a fair amount of speed. Through our collective experience we learn that certain types of reasoning work well. We internalize these and use them as templates for evaluating communicators and their messages.

Some cultures value reasoning more than others. Western culture tends to value rational argument and view anything labeled fallacious with suspicion. As Rodney A. Reynolds and Michael Burgoon point out, "Logical explanations are typically rewarded and contradictions or ab-

surdities punished as children develop."[1] Another culture, such as that of Japan, may place greater emphasis on tradition and appeal to authority than does the North American culture. Thus, operating in a system that values rationality requires a persuader to at least appeal to reason and evidence in order to be successful.[2]

[1]Rodney A. Reynolds and Michael Burgoon, "Belief Processing, Reasoning, and Evidence," in *Communication Yearbook 7*, ed. Robert N. Bostrom (Beverly Hills, Calif.: Sage, 1983), 88.

[2]John C. Reinard, *Foundations of Argument: Effective Communication for Critical Thinking* (Dubuque, Iowa: W. C. Brown, 1991), 171.

experience. When a person whose life was almost destroyed by drugs speaks to a high school audience about the dangers of drugs, this is first-order data. It not only carries with it logical force, but also helps enhance the credibility of the speaker. **Second-order data** is evidence based on expert testimony. When those who debate the efficacy of drug laws cite professors, public officials, and other experts on the wisdom or folly of the current policy, they are presenting the audience with second-order data. **Third-order data** is evidence based on facts and statistics. The number of drug arrests each year and the percentage of teenagers experimenting with drugs are examples of third-order data.

Of course, the importance of evidence and reasoning can vary from culture to culture. As the box "Culture and Persuasion" points out, Western culture puts a premium on rationality.

second-order data
Evidence based on expert testimony.

third-order data Evidence based on facts and statistics.

Using Evidence   **TIPS AND TACTICS**

- If you want your audience to engage in central route processing, use credible evidence to support your position.
- Be sure to tell your audience who your sources are and what makes them qualified to speak on the topic.
- Statistics are most effective when preceded by specific vivid examples.
- Visuals help your audience to process statistics.
- If you are not perceived as highly credible by an audience, the use of high-quality evidence can enhance their perception of your credibility.
- Personal experience on the topic can be a credible form of evidence if you clearly establish that you have direct experience.

The Importance of a Two-Sided Message

To be most effective, you also need to carefully order the arguments in your persuasive message and include an acknowledgment of the other side of the issue. Whereas the research once was not consistent in this regard, it now shows that

331

whenever possible, you'll want to make sure your persuasive speech is two-sided rather than one-sided.[14]

Whereas a one-sided persuasive speech only offers evidence in support of your claim, a two-sided persuasive speech makes use of a brief statement of the other side of the issue and your response to it. Let's say, for example, that you want to persuade your audience to support the claim that the war on drugs is a failure. In a standard, one-sided persuasive speech, you would only present evidence and appeals you believe will prove effective with your audience. In a two-sided speech, you would do all of this and more. After making the argument, you would indicate what the other side might have to say, as well as present your answer to those arguments. Of course, this does not mean you abandon your point of view. Rather, this means you acknowledge counterarguments to it. You would then go on in your speech to point out the weaknesses in the other side's point of view. You simply tell the audience that there are reasonable people who don't support your position and then give the audience an example of the kind of evidence these reasonable people have given for not supporting your side. You then refute this example with a further argument or show that in spite of their argument, your overall claim is more credible.

Not only is a two-sided message more persuasive than a one-sided message, but research suggests at least two other benefits from its use. First, a two-sided message enhances the audience's perceptions of the speaker's credibility. Second, it makes audience members more resistant to counterpersuasion because it gives them a rebuttal to common arguments associated with the opposing view.

PERIPHERAL CUES TO PERSUASION

In spite of his emphasis on rationality, even Aristotle recognized the role of emotions in the process of persuasion. He reasoned what modern researchers have demonstrated again and again: People are persuaded not simply by cold logic but also by emotional appeals. **Pathos** refers to the emotional states in an audience that a speaker can arouse and use to achieve persuasive goals. These methods are not inherently unethical, but they can be abused by unscrupulous persuaders. Emotional appeals do not necessarily lead to peripheral route processing, but many do. On the one hand, it is perfectly rational to be fearful of cancer and therefore to get regular checkups and eat a diet high in the proper nutrients. On the other hand, expensive early detection procedures on people with no reason to think they have the disease may be taking advantage of these fears. When emotional appeals are used to bypass central route processing, they become peripheral cues to persuasion.

Aristotle catalogued the many emotions a speaker can evoke in the attempt to persuade people. Specific emotions he mentions in his writings about persuasion include anger, fear, kindness, shame, pity, and envy.[15] Sometimes the speaker may choose to appeal to the audience members' emotions or primitive beliefs. Because of social conditioning from the earliest years of childhood, people respond to some messages in specific, predictable ways. Whereas logical proofs are designed to induce elaborated thinking on the part of the audience, emotional appeals are designed to provoke audience members to respond without elaborated thought. These appeals are linked to emotions such as anger,

pathos The emotional states in an audience that a speaker can arouse and use to achieve persuasive goals.

Animal-rights groups often base their persuasive messages on strong appeals to their audience's emotions.

fear, kindness, calmness, confidence, unkindness, friendship, shame, pity, enmity, shamelessness, and envy.[16] To illustrate the way appeals to the emotions operate, we will review one of the most researched: fear.

Motivating Through Fear

Common sense tells us that we sometimes do things as a result of fear; for example, we obey the law because we are afraid of the penalties we could suffer should we break it. Yet the research suggests that when it comes to persuasive speaking, fear has its limits. Whether your goal is to encourage the use of shoulder and lap belts while driving, demonstrate how flossing your teeth can prevent gum disease, or convince people everyone needs a gun for self-protection, the research is clear: Persuasive messages that arouse moderate levels of fear in audience members are more effective than those that generate high levels of fear. This fact is especially true, moreover, when the speaker gives audience members a set of clear-cut steps they can take to reduce the fear the speaker has aroused.[17]

As you can see in Figure 13.3, the relationship between fear and persuasive effects is like the relationship between speech anxiety and performance, explained

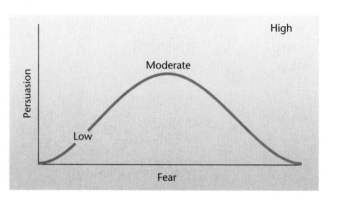

FIGURE 13.3 The Relationship Between Fear Appeals and Persuasion. As the level of fear aroused in an audience begins to increase, so do persuasive effects. Too much fear, however, diminishes persuasive effects.

in Chapter 3. As the level of fear aroused in an audience begins to increase, so do persuasive effects. Too much fear, however, diminishes persuasive effects because it tends to elicit denial from audience members. In a sense, audience members respond to the high level of fear the speaker has aroused in them by thinking, "That could never happen to me." If employed in moderation, however, fear can be effective. Many public service campaigns use moderate levels of fear to encourage positive behaviors such as not smoking, practicing safe sex, and taking advantage of medications that control high blood pressure. The slogan "If not for yourself, then do it for the ones you love" is a good example. Produced by the American Heart Association, this persuasive message tells people with high blood pressure that they need to think about the feelings of the people they would leave behind if they failed to control their blood pressure. This message involves a mild but effective level of fear. Fear isn't an inherently unethical form of persuasion. Used moderately to achieve an ethical end, it is but one of the choices you have in deciding how to appeal to your audience.

Appealing to Primitive Beliefs

Appeals to emotions such as fear are frequently combined with appeals to primitive beliefs. Primitive beliefs are instilled from childhood. Research shows that the use of appeals that connect with primitive beliefs about reciprocity, liking, authority, social support, scarcity, and commitment is both widespread and effective in persuasive communication.[18]

Reciprocity   The saying "You scratch my back, and I'll scratch yours" illustrates reciprocity. A reciprocity-based appeal can work in one of two ways in a persuasive speech. Candidates for political office often promise to give something in return for a person's vote. They may promise to reciprocate by proposing legislation, supporting a specific bill, or voicing a concern of their constituency.

Another common way reciprocity is used in a persuasive speech is when the speaker calls on the audience to reciprocate. During homecoming week, as a case in point, the school president may appeal to alumni for financial support. The appeal is usually couched in terms of "giving something back to the institution that gave you so much."

Reciprocity appeals are effective because people are conditioned from an early age to return favors, gifts, and services. Reciprocity is a norm. Thus, when

Celebrities such as Tiger Woods are effective in promoting products because they are well liked by the public.

people receive a promise or are asked to return something received, the conditioned response is to reciprocate in kind.

Liking   Appeals to primitive beliefs about liking are commonly used in persuasive campaigns. Politicians, for instance, enlist stars from film and music to speak persuasively on their behalf. The assumption is that if a star is well liked, the feeling may be generalized to the candidate endorsed by the star. Liking is a staple of advertisers, who employ well-known people as spokespersons for a product. It's not that the celebrities are experts on the product, but they are well liked by the public. Thus, if well-liked figures Tiger Woods and Michael Jordan wear Nikes, the hope is that the public will also like the product.

Authority   Research shows that some people are predisposed to comply with the requests of individuals and institutions perceived as authoritative. Examples of these authoritative sources range from members of law enforcement and the clergy to federal agencies such as the military. Thus, a speaker attempting to encourage a group of Catholics to voice their opposition to stem cell research might use the words of the pope as an appeal. Similarly, a politician speaking to veterans might rely on an endorsement received from a military hero to win the audience's vote in the election.

Social Support An appeal based on social support is nothing more than an appeal based on numbers. There's a tendency among people to think that if enough folks say something is so, then it must be so. Thus, product advertisers tout their product as "the number-one seller in its class" in an effort to convince consumers that their product must be the best. Research shows that when people are confronted with an appeal supported by large numbers, they are much more likely to be persuaded by the appeal—to jump on the bandwagon, so to speak. In a sense, they accept social support as a form of grounds for the argument.

Scarcity The appeal to scarcity is based on the law of supply and demand. It is a maxim in economics that when demand exceeds supply, the value of the commodity increases. Thus, an appeal based on scarcity is also one based on relative value. As is the case with reciprocity, authority, and social support, people are conditioned to believe that something that is scarce is valuable enough to demand their attention. Persuasive speeches about the environment frequently use scarcity as the basis of appeal. For instance, the ecological benefit of the rain forests is made even more valuable when the speaker tells the audience that the world's rain forests are disappearing at an alarming rate.

Commitment One of the most powerful methods of persuasion is the appeal to commitment. In the aftermath of September 11, 2001, millions of Americans made the commitment to donate blood. Even when the blood banks were overwhelmed with more donors than they could take, people were encouraged to pledge that they would come back at a later date when blood supplies needed replenishment. When people make even small commitments as a result of a persuasive message, the principle of psychological consistency comes into play. This principle tells us that we all feel pressure to keep our attitudes, beliefs, and values consistent with our commitments. Thus, if an appeal to commitment leads a person to write a letter, or to volunteer to serve, or to sign a petition, it increases the chances that the person's attitudes, beliefs, and values will reflect the commitment. Thus, in some cases action may actually precede changes in attitude, reversing the normal order of persuasive goals.

To reiterate, the appeals you make in your persuasive message should reflect your goal and your audience. Not all audiences jump aboard after hearing an authority-based appeal. There are those who steadfastly refuse to get on a bandwagon, no matter how many other people have already done so. Choosing the right appeals to flesh out your persuasive message, therefore, is part science and part art. The box "Sample Persuasive Speech Outline: Condemnation to Compassion" features a persuasive speech by Josette Parker in which she uses a wide variety of appeals to make her case.

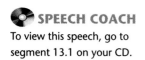 **SPEECH COACH**
To view this speech, go to segment 13.1 on your CD.

PERSUASIVE SPEAKING IN PRACTICE

The last topic to discuss is, knowing what you now know, how do you actually prepare your persuasive speech? We recommend three steps: (1) Adapt your goals to your audience, (2) organize your speech effectively, and (3) balance the means of persuasion.

Adapt Your Goals to Your Audience

Speeches to reinforce or inoculate an audience presume that your audience members are either already supportive of your point of view or uninformed about the topic. These are friendly or neutral audiences. In such cases, you can expect your views to receive a fair hearing. You will want to build a strong case, of course, but you need not fear that your audience will reject you and your message out of hand.

A speech to change attitudes, by definition, means your audience disagrees with you. This is termed a hostile audience. Although they may not be overtly hostile (booing and hissing), they are unlikely to be open to your point of view without a lot of work on your part. Such a speech requires you to begin with a common ground on which you and your audience can agree. After doing so, it is realistic only to try to move them slightly toward your position on the topic. Speaking to a group of SUV owners about the need for conserving fuel is a difficult task. You might begin by indicating you agree with their right to drive any car they wish. But you might point out that the United States now imports more than half its oil, which makes us vulnerable to instability in the oil-producing nations of the world, many of which also harbor terrorists. If the cost of gas becomes prohibitive, their SUV may become very expensive to operate. Perhaps rather than abandoning their SUV, they could look to fuel-saving measures, such as keeping tires properly inflated, the engine in tune, and so on. And even SUV owners might also want to use public transportation, where it's available, for in-town trips. While you might not get these SUV owners to trade in their vehicles for a gasoline-electric hybrid (which gets over 50 miles to a gallon), you might at least get them to make some changes in their driving habits to save fuel. In any case, you would not expect a massive conversion from this type of audience.

Finally, speeches that seek to prompt people to act presume that your audience is prepared by prior messages to take action or that your topic is not inherently controversial. For example, prompting people to donate blood is not a topic that people are hostile to, though they may be fearful of doing so. Such a speech needs to focus on reducing irrational fears, such as the transmission of blood-borne diseases, which cannot occur for the donor. In the case of an audience already primed by previous messages, your main task is to motivate them to act. People have heard for years about the benefits of wearing seat belts, yet a significant number still fail to do so. Rehashing arguments they have already heard is of little use with such people. You need to tell them something new that will get them to act. A dramatic story, for example, about how your own life was saved by wearing a seat belt might be the key ingredient in such a speech.

Organize Your Persuasive Speech

In Chapter 8 we introduced a number of ways to organize a speech. Three organizational patterns described there are particularly suited to your persuasive speeches. The first is the problem–solution pattern, the second is called stock issues, and the third is Monroe's motivated sequence.

The first pattern of organization analyzes a problem in terms of harm, significance, and cause and proposes a solution that is described, feasible, and advantageous. Many persuasive topics are about problems we face individually or as a society. By beginning with a discussion of the problem, the speaker heightens

SPEECH COACH

To evaluate persuasive speeches, see the Speech Critique program on your CD.

Sample Persuasive Speech Outline

Title of speech.

CONDEMNATION TO COMPASSION
by Josette Parker

Specific purpose is to change audience attitudes about welfare recipients.

Specific Purpose: To persuade the audience that many factors contribute to poverty, and we should learn to treat the poor with respect and dignity.

Introduction

Speaker begins with a story of her own experience as a welfare recipient, enhancing her credibility.

I. **Open With Impact:** In April 1993 I lost my job when the company I worked for went bankrupt, had our car break down, and had no health insurance and a baby on the way.
   A. I was forced to take unemployment, WIC [Women, Infants and Children], and food stamps.
   B. I have never been treated with such disrespect.
   C. Are the poor not worthy of respect and dignity?

Thesis statement is clearly labeled.

II. **Focus on Thesis Statement:** We should consider all factors that contribute to poverty before we pass a harsh judgment on the poor.

Speaker shows the audience that they could find themselves in the same situation, citing one of her professors.

III. **Connect With the Audience:** Dr. George Wright of California State University–Chico states that all of us in the middle class are about two paychecks away from poverty or homelessness (personal communication, 1998).

Preview of main points is clear.

IV. **Preview:** Today I want to show you how the media propagate myths about welfare recipients, how we are not all given the same opportunities to succeed financially, and finally, how accepting the differences in our life circumstances can lead us to have compassion and understanding for the poor.

Body

Body of speech is labeled.

Speaker refutes stereotype of welfare recipients.

I. **Main Point:** The media show the average welfare queen as a Black, single woman with many children, who is too lazy to work.
   A. These are the facts (Chideya, 1995; Ellingson & Ferrini, 1997):

Speaker shows the facts don't fit the myths.

     1. Most welfare recipients work for a living.
     2. The majority are White and live in the suburbs.
     3. Seventy percent have two children or less, the same as the national average.
     4. Seventy percent leave the rolls within 2 years.
     5. The average AFDC payment is less than half the poverty level.
   B. So the average welfare recipient isn't who I thought it was.

(**Signpost:** But don't we live in the land of opportunity?)

II. **Main Point:** Our country has an enormous disparity in income (Naiman & Zepezauer, 1996).
   A. The top 1 percent owns 80 percent of our nation's wealth.

Notice how the speaker personalizes the figures on disparity in wealth.

     1. Unless you are making $2.3 million a year, you aren't in this group.
     2. That means 99 percent must share 20 percent of the wealth.
   B. We have a large disparity, but what about tax dollars going to welfare?
     1. Welfare is only 1 percent of the federal budget (Naiman & Zepezauer, 1996).

2. We spend billions on subsidies and tax breaks for the rich.
3. The military budget is $265 billion, larger than the next six largest military budgets in the world combined.

C. What about fraud?
1. Any public system is susceptible to fraud.
2. Millions are lost to tax fraud by the middle and upper class.

(**Signpost:** So, the average welfare recipient is not who I thought and there is great disparity, but you're thinking, I've overcome the odds and so can you!)

III. **Main Point:** The problem with this is that we are not all born with the same life chances.
A. We form templates of our lives built on foundations of family, morality, and education.
B. We impose our templates on those without foundations.
C. We think: If I can do it, so can you.
D. A child born in poverty does not have the same chance to succeed.

(**Signpost:** The more accepting we are of others' different life situations, the more compassion we can have; if we fail to see the whole picture, we can make blanket statements.)

Notice that this is a two-sided presentation, in which the speaker states and then answers the common arguments that are offered against welfare.

Conclusion

Conclusion labeled.

I. **Summarize:** Our country was founded on the principles of life, liberty, and the pursuit of happiness.
A. The system does not work and today's reform is punitive.
B. The poor have always been with us and probably always will be; what will we do?
C. Buddhists, Muslims, Christians, and Jews, all believe we should serve the poor.

Does this really summarize the points of the speech or make yet another point?

II. **Close With Impact:** Reform begins in here, the heart, our attitudes and beliefs about each other.
A. We must sift through the myths, see the disparity, and accept the differences in life chances if we have compassion.
B. I am not asking to bring in the homeless, or to volunteer 20 hours at the local homeless shelter, although that would be great.
C. The next time you see your neighbor in need, speak to him or her with respect and dignity.
1. This may be the only time someone treats that person with dignity.
2. Let it come from you.

How effectively does the speech conclude? Does the conclusion have the same impact as the opening?

References

Chideya, F. (1995). *Don't believe the hype*. New York: Plume.
Ellingson, L., & Ferrini, A. (1997). *Women's health issues*. Dubuque, IA: Kendall-Hunt.
Naiman, A., & Zepezauer, M. (1996). *Take the rich off welfare*. Tucson, AZ: Odonian Press.

Note that the references do not include the personal communication from Dr. Wright. This is the correct format for APA style, where personal communications are cited only in the text itself.

the audience's interest but avoids turning off a hostile audience with a solution they might initially reject. A speech on trying juveniles as adults that begins with a discussion of the growing gang problem is far more likely to receive a hearing from a parent's group than a speech that begins by calling for locking up 14-year-olds as if they were 18.

The second pattern uses the stock issues of *ill, blame, cure,* and *cost* to encourage people to make changes in either governmental policies or in their own lives. For example, a speech about cellular phones might identify an ill in terms of the greater risk of an auto accident when driving while using a cell phone. The blame might be due to the driver's divided attention, not just the use of one hand on the phone. Thus the cure wouldn't simply be hands-free phones, but rather a law that banned use of phones while driving (such as passed in New York). The costs of this proposal might be higher law enforcement costs and some inconvenience to the drivers, but the lives saved would be well worth it.

SPEECH COACH

To evaluate speeches that use the motivated sequence, see the Speech Critique program on your CD.

The third pattern useful for persuasive speaking is Monroe's motivated sequence, a five-step organizational scheme including attention, need, satisfaction, visualization, and action. Because the final step is action, this pattern is particularly well suited to speeches calling for your audience to act. As should all good speeches, this type begins by capturing the audience's attention. Like the problem–solution pattern, this speech focuses on a problem (called a need) before proposing its solution (satisfaction). But this pattern goes further by asking the audience to visualize the satisfaction of the need and then calling on them to act.

Regardless of the organizational pattern you choose, there are some principles of organization you should follow. First, always put your best arguments and support either early or late in the speech. Do not hide them in the middle. Over the years, research has shown that in some cases people best remember what they hear first, whereas in other cases, what comes last is most memorable. Either way, the middle of the speech is not the place for your best material.

Second, with hostile or indifferent audiences, it is particularly important to have some of your best material early in the speech. Otherwise, they will tune you out before you get to the critical points you want to make.

Balance the Means of Persuasion

Finally, although it might seem as if we have treated source credibility, evidence, and emotional appeals as separate means of persuasion, this is not really the case in practice. Your credibility will affect how your audience perceives the substance of your speech. If you have high credibility, the audience is more likely to accept your arguments. Similarly, if you have strong evidence and arguments in your speech, your credibility will grow in the audience's mind. And unless you touch the audience's emotions, it is unlikely that they will be motivated to act or believe in what they have heard. Mayor Giuliani was not only viewed as a credible figure as a result of his actions in the wake of September 11, 2001; he also used strong emotional appeals to get people back to some degree of normalcy, and reasoning and evidence to calm people's fears of visiting New York City. In short, a good persuasive speech relies on using all the available means of persuasion for its success.

SUMMARY

Four common goals of a persuasive speech are to:

- reinforce existing beliefs and attitudes,
- inoculate against counterpersuasion,
- change attitudes, and
- prompt the audience to act.

Source credibility (ethos) is composed of competence and character. The elaboration likelihood model reflects two potential paths an audience can take in response to a persuasive message:

- Central route processing involves elaborated and critical thinking.
- Peripheral route processing relies on cues, such as emotional appeals.

Evidence can greatly enhance a persuasive presentation. Three types of evidence are:

- first-order data: personal experience
- second-order data: expert testimony
- third-order data: facts and statistics

Two-sided messages are generally more effective than one-sided speeches:

- Two-sided messages confer greater credibility.
- Two-sided messages help inoculate an audience against counterpersuasion.

Peripheral cues include emotions such as fear and primitive beliefs about:

- reciprocity
- liking
- authority
- social support
- scarcity
- commitment

Persuasive patterns of organization include:

- problem–solution
- stock issues
- Monroe's motivated sequence

CHECK YOUR UNDERSTANDING: EXERCISES AND ACTIVITIES

1. Suppose you are giving a speech on the topic of civil liberties versus national security. How would you change your persuasive message to achieve each of the four persuasive goals: reinforcement, inoculation, attitude change, and action? How would these goals differ depending on possible audiences for this topic and the constraints you would face in each situation?

SPEECH COACH

To evaluate your understanding of this chapter, see the Quizzes on your CD.

SPEECH COACH

For a review of key terms in this chapter, see the Key Terms Flashcards on your CD.

2. On a topic of your choosing, construct examples of appeals based on the six primitive beliefs discussed in the chapter (reciprocity, liking, etc.).

3. Consider the following list of topics: (1) preventing AIDS, (2) preventing tooth decay, and (3) the importance of wearing seat belts. Construct a brief message based on a moderate-level "fear" appeal for each of these topics. At what level—low, moderate, or high—do you think your fear appeal would diminish the persuasive effects, causing audience members to reject your message? At what point do you think arguments based on fear on these topics would become unethical?

4. Follow up on the list of tips we gave for assessing and enhancing perceptions of your credibility. List the specific factors you believe make you credible about the topic of your persuasive speech. Then describe how you plan on using these specific factors so that they will sustain the perception of credibility as you deliver your speech.

5. Newspaper editorials constitute a persuasive message. To improve your ability in recognizing the types of appeals being used, select a recent column from a nationally syndicated writer such as George Will, William Safire, Molly Ivins, or Ellen Goodman. Mark what you consider to be appeals the columnist is using. Note whether these appeals are intended to affect your emotions or your primitive beliefs. Finally, label the emotion or belief that the appeal is targeted at arousing.

NOTES

1. Aristotle, *Rhetoric*, trans. W. Rhys Roberts (New York: Modern Library, 1954), 25.

2. William J. McGuire, "Inducing Resistance to Persuasion: Some Contemporary Approaches," in *Advances in Experimental and Social Psychology*, ed. L. Berkowitz (New York: Academic Press, 1964), 191–229.

3. M. Fishbein and I. Ajzen, *Belief, Attitude, Intention, and Behavior* (Reading, Mass.: Addison-Wesley, 1975), 12–13.

4. M. Sherif and C. I. Hovland, *Social Judgment: Assimilation and Contrast Effects in Communication and Attitude Change* (New Haven: Yale University Press, 1961).

5. Aristotle, *Rhetoric*, 25.

6. Sarah Trenholm, *Persuasion and Social Influence* (Englewood Cliffs, N.J.: Prentice Hall, 1989).

7. Carl I. Hovland, Irving L. Janis, and Harold H. Kelly, *Communication and Persuasion* (New Haven: Yale University Press, 1953); James C. McCroskey, *An Introduction to Rhetorical Communication*, 5th ed. (Englewood Cliffs, N.J.: Prentice Hall, 1986); David K. Berlo, James B. Lemert, and Robert J. Mertz, "Dimensions for Evaluating the Acceptability of Message Sources," *Public Opinion Quarterly*, 33 (Winter 1969–1970): 562–76; Kenneth E. Anderson, *Persuasion: Theory and Practice* (Boston: Allyn & Bacon, 1971). For a useful chart comparing various researchers' terms for these key components of credibility, see John R. Wenburg and William W. Wilmont, *The Personal Communication Process* (New York: Wiley, 1973), 145–47.

8. Richard E. Petty and John T. Cacioppo, *Communication and Persuasion: Central and Peripheral Routes to Attitude Changes* (New York: Springer-Verlag, 1986).

9. Irvin A. Horowitz and Kenneth S. Bordens, *Social Psychology* (Mountain View, Calif.: Mayfield, 1995), 287–88.

10. John C. Reinard, "The Empirical Study of the Persuasive Effects of Evidence: The Status After Fifty Years of Research," *Human Communication Research*, 15 (Fall 1988): 3–59.

11. Reinard, "The Empirical Study," 46.

12. This summary of findings is abstracted from Reinard's excellent book, *Foundations of Argument: Effective Communication for Critical Thinking* (Dubuque, Iowa: W. C. Brown, 1991), 125–27.

13. James C. McCroskey, *An Introduction to Rhetorical Communication*, 7th ed. (Needham Heights, Mass.: Allyn & Bacon, 1997).

14. Mike Allen, "Meta-Analysis Comparing the Persuasiveness of One-Sided and Two-Sided Messages," *Western Journal of Communication*, 55 (1991): 390–404.

15. Aristotle, *Rhetoric*.

16. Aristotle, *Rhetoric*.

17. Irving Janis, "Effects of Fear-Arousal on Attitude Change: Recent Developments in Theory and Experimental Research," in *Advances in Experimental and Social Psychology*, vol. 3, ed. L. Berkowitz (New York: Academic Press, 1967), 166–224.

18. Robert Cialdini, *Influence: Science and Practice*, 2nd ed. (New York: HarperCollins, 1988).

Republican Mary
Matalin and
Democrat James
Carville prove that
people can argue
about ideas and yet
respect each
other's opinions.

Thinking and Speaking Critically

 OBJECTIVES

After reading this chapter and reviewing the learning resources on your CD-ROM and at the Online Learning Center, you should be able to:

- Explain the difference between argumentativeness and verbal aggressiveness.
- Analyze, construct, and evaluate arguments using the Toulmin model of reasoning.
- Differentiate among patterns of reasoning.
- Identify and refute common fallacies of argument.

It is better to debate a question without settling it than to settle a question without debating it.

—JOSEPH JOUBERT

  KEY CONCEPTS

argumentativeness	critical thinking	qualifier
authority warrant	fallacy	rebuttal
backing	generalization warrant	sign warrant
causal warrant	grounds	verbal aggressiveness
claim	inference	warrant
comparison (analogy) warrant	pseudoreasoning	

What do you think? Is smoking marijuana any more harmful to your health than drinking alcohol? Does the recreational use of cocaine or ecstasy inevitably lead to a life of ruin? Should drug addicts be punished as criminals, or should they receive medical treatment for their addiction?

What do you believe about the war on drugs? Do you think it has reduced drug use in our country—for example, kept drugs out of the workplace or minimized their use among young people? Or do you think that the billions of dollars committed by government to the war on drugs could have been better spent elsewhere?

And what do you think about drug testing? Would you mind being routinely tested in order to keep your job? Or if you are an athlete, do you think collegiate associations should demand that football and volleyball players, or swimmers and divers, submit to drug testing before each competition?

These kinds of questions are not easily answered. Illegal drugs and their widespread use continue to be topics of heated discussions in the halls of Congress, during the meetings of school boards, and over the dinner table in many homes. What's more, they have even been the centerpieces of blockbuster films such as *Traffic*, which won four Academy Awards and was nominated for best picture, and *Blow*, which starred Penelope Cruz and Johnny Depp.

Recently, two of our students took opposite positions in their persuasive speeches. One took the position that mandatory drug testing in the workplace should be the law of the land. See excerpts in the box "Sample Persuasive Message: Mandatory Drug Testing." The other emphatically declared that the war on drugs has been an abysmal failure. Excerpts of this speech are shown in the box "Sample Persuasive Message: The War on Drugs." Both speeches made some good points; but more than that, each tested the audience's ability to think critically about a topic that is anything but black and white. You will find both speeches in their entirety on your CD. Decide for yourself who presents the stronger case.

This chapter takes up the subject of critical thinking. Recall from Chapter 13 that when a speaker wants the audience to have a lasting attitude change, it is important to engage them in the elaborated thinking process. And if a speaker motivates the audience and presents the material in an interesting and understandable way, the likelihood that the speaker's ideas will prevail depends directly on the strength of the evidence and reasoning the audience hears. In this chapter we want to give you the tools as a speaker to present quality arguments and evidence that audiences are likely to find persuasive. Further, we want you as audience members to engage in the critical thinking process so that you will be persuaded only when the arguments are strong and the evidence reliable. To rationally answer questions like these on the drug issue, both speakers and listeners need to think carefully about the topic.

SPEECH COACH
To view Miranda Welsh's full speech, "Mandatory Drug Testing," see segment 14.1 on your CD.

SPEECH COACH
To view David Sanders' full speech, "The War on Drugs," see segment 14.2 on your CD.

CRITICAL THINKING AND PUBLIC SPEAKING

critical thinking The process of making sound inferences based on accurate evidence and valid reasoning.

Critical thinking is the process of making sound inferences based on accurate evidence and valid reasoning. Understanding how to think critically about arguments is the first step to constructing and communicating those arguments to an audience. As noted in Chapter 13, logical proof should be an ethical part of

Sample Persuasive Message

MANDATORY DRUG TESTING
by Miranda Welsh

This is an excerpt from the speech by Miranda Welsh. The full speech can be found in segment 14.1 on your CD.

Why should we be concerned about drug use? Who other than the user is it affecting? There are some specific problems with student drug abusers. Often student drug abusers tend to drift from school, which is their number one job. They tend to drift from their family; they tend to get below average grades, and they tend not to be physically active. Or if they are, they often use their drugs to keep them that way.

There are also some specific problems with employee drug abusers. According to the drug testing website, employees who are on drugs are 3.6 times more likely than nonusers to injure themselves or others [in an] on-the-job accident. They are 5 times more likely than nonusers to file a workman's compensation claim, 2.5 times as likely as nonusers to have absences of 8 or more days; they are consistently tardy; they only work two-thirds as effectively as nonusers; and to the business, drug abusers increase insurance cost, increase employee theft and decrease productivity.

But, what about the drug problem in the United States as a whole? . . . According to the Department of Health and Human Services, American drug use is on the rise. It peaked in 1979 and has declined since but is back on the increase. If we don't start implementing drug testing now, we are allowing the problem in the United States to continue. . . .

There have been some unfortunate circumstances that have occurred due directly to drug use and could have been stopped by drug testing. In April of 1987, a bus driver drove his bus directly into a bridge in Virginia, killed one, injured thirty. Only after the accident was he drug tested positive for cocaine, valium and marijuana. In January of 1988, a pilot crashed his plane into rural Colorado. The crash was solely attributed to the pilot, which killed 30 people. Again, only after the accident was he drug tested positive for cocaine. And some years back, the federal railroad administration drug tested 759 of their railroad employees only after 125 different accidents had occurred. At that time 29 of their current employees drug tested positive for one or more illegal drugs. All of these stories are according to the Drug Testing book by David Newton.

Now, I wouldn't be much of a person if I stood up here and told you who the drug testing problem is harming and who we have to blame if I didn't give you a cure. Simply put, a cure for a large part of our nation's drug problem is drug testing. There are a few legal and constitutional ways to go about this, such as urinalysis, through other bodily fluids, by the human hair, and through a blood test. And, the government does see a need for a cure to the increasing drug problem. They have passed some laws that are still in effect today. For example, in 1981 President Reagan mandated that all military personnel be drug tested on a regular basis. In 1986 he extended that to all law enforcement, national security and public health and safety personnel. However, there is still more to be done. Not a single state in this nation mandates that all of their students and all of their employees be drug tested. It is apparent that something needs to be done. The CQ Researcher on American teens states that studies prove that drug testing deters drug use. So, my point is simple. Why not drug test all employees and all students?

What will drug testing specifically do for our nation? If we can identify all of the employees on drugs we will have caught three-fourths of the nation's illicit drug users. That means that 75% of our nation's drug users are employed. In the workplace drug testing will specifically reduce workplace accidents, increase productivity, support the goals of a drug-free nation, improve corporate morale, and reduce drug use in our society. And in schools, drug testing will specifically deter students from drug use. . . .

I would like to share with you some of my arguments to some common anti–drug testing viewpoints. Tests invade my right to privacy according to the 4th Amendment. Actually, if you read the 4th Amendment carefully, you would see that it only protects you from unreasonable searches done by the federal government . . . not by private organizations. People take [legal] drugs from prescriptions, and those can show up positive on tests. Yes, they can, but every employee application and every school application must ask about any prescriptions that you are currently taking. And before any drug test is administered, you must be questioned about your prescriptions. Some tests are wrong. Well some [in]accuracy is inevitable, but technology is working day by day to decrease that inaccuracy. Costs more than it helps. Actually, each urinalysis only costs one dollar per person per test and if that's done on a random basis in your school or your workplace, your name's only on the average going to be called up once every 2 years. You do the math. Why should we waste time on testing, there's work to be done. Not much work can be done if there isn't anybody alive to do it and that's what drug use does to our society. Any of the testing methods take 3 to 5 minutes. And if that's done on a random basis, your name's only going to be called out 3 to 5 minutes once every 2 years. 3 to 5 minutes is very worth it.

Sample Persuasive Message

THE WAR ON DRUGS
by David Sanders

This is an excerpt from the speech by David Sanders. The full speech can be found in segment 14.2 on your CD.

The war on drugs was founded during the Nixon presidency. Not of a need to cure a great social ill in America, but simply out of politics. Richard Miller in his book The Case for Legalizing Drugs *quotes Nixon's domestic policy chief, John Ehrlichman, as saying that "'Narcotics repression is a sexy political issue. Parents are worried about their kids using heroin, and parents are voters.' That is why the Nixon White House got involved."*

Now, every president since then has used the war on drugs to gain political mileage. . . . No president used the war on drugs more effectively than Ronald Reagan. In his book, Rhetoric in the War on Drugs, *William Elwood quotes Reagan's famous drug war speech. ". . . now we're in another war for our freedom, and it's time for all of us to pull together. . . . It's time, as Nancy said, for America to 'Just Say No' to drugs. When we all come together, united, striving for this cause, then those who are killing America and terrorizing it with slow but sure chemical destruction, will see that they are up against the mightiest force for the good that we know. They will have no dark alleyways to hide in."*

They didn't need them because they were hiding in the White House. Former Drug Enforcement Agent and author of the book The Big White Lie, *Michael Levine points out that the CIA and other federal agencies were deeply involved in the drug trade as part of the Iran-Contra scandal.*

Now our law enforcement and legal system are in equally precarious positions. Because of the nature of the politically motivated justice system it does not target all social groups equally. In her book, Power, Ideology, and the War on Drugs, *Christina Johns points out that "law enforcement tactics primarily target lower class individuals even within the drug using and trafficking communities." Another big legal problem is assets forfeiture. And this is really really important. Asset forfeiture is a program where if law enforcement individuals believe that you have gained some of your property by selling drugs and being involved in the drug trade, they can seize that property. They can take your house, your boat, your car, whatever it is that you've gained, they just seize it. They do not have to charge you with a crime, nor do they have to prove in any way that you actually gained it from selling drugs. If you want your property back and you feel you're innocent, you have to go to court and you have to prove that you are innocent. Big difference from our normal criminal laws. . . .*

Now with all that money flowing around, there are bound to be casualties in this war. So let's look at who the physical and emotional casualties are in the war on drugs. Now as in any war, it's not the generals on both sides that get killed and injured, but it's the soldiers and civilians in the field. In this particular war we can divide it into two groups—the good guys and the bad guys. Let's talk about the good guys. Unfortunately, hundreds of officers are killed and injured in the line of duty in the war on drugs every year. . . .

Now, unfortunately, the good guys are not always good. In the book America's Longest War: Rethinking Our Tragic Crusade Against Drugs, *Yale Law School Professor Steve Duke points out that "Only one time before in our history was corruption of law enforcement officials a more serious problem. And that was during our efforts to enforce alcohol prohibition. The corruption during prohibition may have been greater than it is now, but there are reasons to fear that it will eventually exceed that level if we continue on our present course."*

Now the bad guys. We pretty much all know who the bad guys are. But unfortunately hundreds and thousands of America's youth are being killed and injured on our streets every year. And it's not just the druggies or the dealers that are getting injured but it's innocent civilians who just happen to get in the way. Now society is the one that ultimately pays for this war. Not just the $75 billion [that is spent on the war] . . . , but another $70 billion is passed on to us as consumers every year by businesses to pay for things like insurance, the crime that's inflicted on them, and things like drug tests to make sure the person at Kmart who's serving you isn't a druggie. . . .

Who would lose if we stopped this war on drugs? The people who would lose are primarily the people that gain now. The prison system would have to build and staff about half the number of prisons that we're doing right now. And prisons is the biggest growth industry in America today. The other group that would lose, obviously, are the dealers. Drugs would be available from sources that were clean, safe, such as federal drug stores at a significantly reduced cost. In fact in the case of cocaine, the National Review points out it would be available at between 5,000 and 20,000 percent less cost.

Who would win? I think, we would all win if we were to end the war on drugs. The police and court systems would have been freed up to deal with the real problems that are effecting society and real crimes. We would have vast amounts of money to spend to get people off drugs and to keep them off drugs and to deal with other social problems that are in a way connected to this war, like AIDS.

BEWARE OF SPEAKERS BEARING GIFTS...

any persuasive message. To successfully persuade others of your side of a controversial issue, it is important to have well-constructed, sound arguments for your side. As the elaboration likelihood model introduced in the preceding chapter shows, you are more likely to induce a permanent change in attitude if you use sound evidence and reasoning.

Pseudoreasoning and Fallacies

As pointed out in Chapter 4, we spend more of our time listening to others than actually speaking. Understanding critical thinking is essential to differentiating messages that are logical from those that are not. Frequently, something sounds good on first hearing but proves to be illogical. **Pseudoreasoning** refers to an argument that appears sound at first glance but contains a fallacy of reasoning that renders it unsound. A **fallacy** is "an argument in which the reasons advanced for a claim fail to warrant acceptance of that claim."[1] Thus, one of the goals of this chapter is to help you recognize fallacies that are a sign of pseudoreasoning. Even if you agree with the conclusion of a speaker, you ought to do so based on sound logic, not just because he or she sounds good.

It is important to distinguish here between intentional and unintentional fallacies. Certainly not everyone who makes an error in reasoning is intending to deceive. On the other hand, someone who is seeking to "pull the wool over an audience's eyes" may indeed use fallacies intentionally. Either way, it is the consumer of communication—the audience—who must remain vigilant to avoid being misled, whether by accident or design, by pseudoreasoning.

pseudoreasoning An argument that appears sound at first glance but contains a fallacy of reasoning that renders it unsound.

fallacy An argument in which the reasons advanced for a claim fail to warrant acceptance of that claim.

Verbally aggressive people can destroy relationships by engaging in personal attacks.

Argumentativeness and Verbal Aggressiveness

argumentativeness The trait of arguing for and against the positions taken on controversial claims.

verbal aggressiveness The trait of attacking the self-concept of those with whom a person disagrees about controversial claims.

In Chapter 6, we maintained that when listeners detect fallacious reasoning, they are ethically obligated to bring it to light. Simply remaining silent allows the speaker to mislead those who are not well trained in critical thinking. However, there is an important distinction between being argumentative and being verbally aggressive. In his book *Arguing Constructively,* Dominic A. Infante makes the distinction between these two personality traits.[2] **Argumentativeness** is the trait of arguing for and against the *positions* taken on controversial claims. For example, an argumentative person might say, "The idea of a flat tax sounds good, but it would lead to massive increases in the federal debt." **Verbal aggressiveness,** on the other hand, is the trait of attacking the *self-concept* of those with whom a person disagrees about controversial claims. A verbally aggressive person might say, "Only a drug-crazed maniac would favor legalizing drugs." Argumentativeness is not only socially beneficial, it is the only way to take the process of critical thinking into the public arena. Verbal aggressiveness, on the other hand, is a destructive and hostile trait that destroys personal relationships. Constructive argumentativeness is the best approach for the public speaker. Being able to disagree without being disagreeable fosters a positive communication transaction.

The authors were recently witnesses to the possibility that people can disagree without being disagreeable. Mary Matalin, current advisor to Vice Presi-

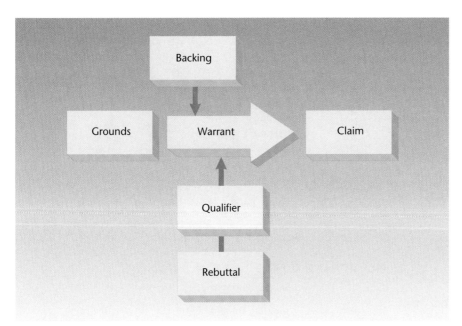

FIGURE 14.1 The Toulmin Model of Argument

dent Dick Cheney and former conservative talk show host, "debated" her husband, James Carville, who managed the 1992 presidential campaign of Bill Clinton and served as one of his chief defenders during the Lewinsky scandal. Despite their obvious political differences, they treated each other with good-humored respect. The audience, which was apparently deeply divided on partisan lines, nevertheless cheered both speakers and even gave them a standing ovation at the end of the evening. Learning to disagree about issues, while respecting the other side's right to believe as they do, is the hallmark of civility in argument. You can be argumentative without being verbally aggressive.

THE TOULMIN MODEL OF ARGUMENT

One way to become a better critical thinker and speaker is to use philosopher Stephen Toulmin's model of argument, depicted in Figure 14.1. Toulmin's model makes an excellent template to use in constructing and evaluating arguments. According to Toulmin, a sound argument involves *at least* a claim, grounds for making the claim, and a warrant that connects grounds and claim.[3]

A **claim** is a conclusion that a persuasive speaker wants an audience to reach as a result of a speech. Speakers can make claims about the facts as they see them, about basic human values, and about public policies. As you might imagine, it's not uncommon for a speaker to make claims about each of these during the course of a speech. The differences between these types of claims are discussed later in this chapter.

Just because someone asserts a claim, that doesn't constitute an argument for its truth. An argument also requires **grounds,** which are the evidence a speaker offers in support of a claim. This evidence can be based on personal experience, expert testimony, established fact, or statistics or other data.

claim A conclusion that persuasive speakers want their audience to reach as a result of their speech.

grounds The evidence a speaker offers in support of a claim.

FIGURE 14.2 Analysis of an Argument Using Toulmin's Model

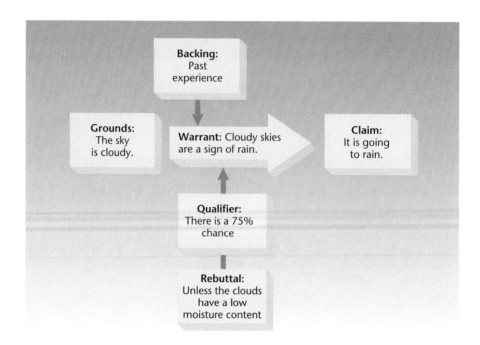

Good speakers also connect the grounds they offer as evidence in support of their claims. Such a connection between grounds and claim is called a **warrant.** Although warrants can be implied, we think these connections between grounds and claim are best stated by the speaker.

This is not the complete model, however. Toulmin indicates that three additional parts of an argument *may* be present. In some cases, for example, the warrant may be one that is not obvious to audience members. In that case, a fourth element of Toulmin's model, backing, comes into play. **Backing** is support for the warrant. If an audience does not already believe in the warrant, the speaker will need to build additional argument and evidence to support it before attempting to convince the audience of the soundness of the whole argument. Knowing which warrants an audience will accept and which require additional backing is essential to effective speaking.

An additional component is the **rebuttal,** which represents an exception to or a refutation of the argument. It is usually preceded by the word *unless,* indicating that the claim is true except when conditions stated in the rebuttal are present. As we discussed in Chapter 13, it is important in presenting a two-sided message to let the audience know they may encounter exceptions to or refutations of your argument. Finally, unless an argument is 100 percent certain, it will need to have a **qualifier,** which is an indication of the level of probability of the claim.[4] Qualifiers may be a single word, such as *probably*; a brief phrase, such as *very likely*; or even a probability expressed as a percentage. In human affairs, it is rare to deal with absolute certainty. Acknowledging to an audience your degree of certainty helps you avoid appearing to take an extreme or unreasonable position.

How does this model of argument apply in actual practice? Let's begin with a simple case. Suppose you glance out the window and the sky is filled with

warrant The connection between grounds and claim.

backing Support for a warrant.

rebuttal An exception to or a refutation of an argument.

qualifier An indication of the level of probability of a claim.

clouds. You think to yourself, "It's going to rain," and you grab your umbrella. Although you may not realize it, your reasoning can be analyzed as an argument using Toulmin's model. Figure 14.2 shows how this analysis would look. Based on the *grounds* of a cloudy sky, you reason using the *warrant*, cloudy skies are a sign of rain, which is based on the *backing* of your past experience, that there is a 75 percent chance (*qualifier*) of the truth of the *claim* that it is going to rain, unless (*rebuttal*) the clouds have a low moisture content.

Now that you understand this basic version of Toulmin's model, let's look at the relationships among claims, grounds, and warrants in a more complicated situation. As the speeches of our students illustrate, both sides of the drug-war argument can cite evidence and reasoning to support their position.

In the spirit of constructive argumentation, therefore, we will consider how to test arguments for their soundness. Using the Toulmin model, we will suggest appropriate tests for the grounds, claims, warrants, backing, qualifiers, and rebuttals of various types of arguments. Further, we will show how the failure to meet these tests can result in fallacies, turning what could be sound arguments into pseudoarguments.

FALLACIES ASSOCIATED WITH GROUNDS

All arguments are built on the grounds, or evidence, which the arguer points to in supporting the claim. If the grounds are either absent or defective, then the argument cannot be sound. In Chapter 7, we discussed various types of supporting material that might form the grounds of an argument, including examples, facts, statistics, expert opinion, explanations, descriptions, and narratives.

When you are examining the grounds of an argument, be sure that the examples are relevant, of sufficient quantity, and typical. Facts should come from a reliable source and be verifiable, recent, and consistent with other known facts. Statistics should be taken from a reliable and unbiased source, based on fair questions, and accurately collected. You should be told how the sample was selected to ensure that it was random and representative. Any differences should be greater than the margin of error, and the base of any percentages should be stated. Expert opinion depends on the source's expertise, reliability, and lack of bias. Explanations should be clear and accurate. Descriptions should be accurate and vivid. Narratives must have probability (coherence) and fidelity to the real world.

Grounds that fail one or more of these tests are likely to constitute a fallacy. In particular, there are four fallacies associated with grounds: unsupported assertion, distorted evidence, isolated examples, and misused statistics.

Unsupported Assertion

There are a number of ways in which the grounds, or evidence, in support of an argument can be defective. The most egregious case is the absence of any grounds to support a claim. The **unsupported assertion** is really the absence of any argument at all. Fans of the sitcom *Cheers* probably recognize this tendency in Cliff Claven, who is always spouting the most absurd facts as if they were gospel. An argument without grounds is no argument at all.

In her argument for mandatory drug testing, Miranda Welsh answers the complaint that some tests are wrong by asserting that "technology is working day by day to decrease that inaccuracy." Where does she find the proof of that statement? No source is given and no specific technologies are mentioned. The claim is made with no grounds to support it. That is not to say that her statement isn't true. In fact, we suspect it probably is. But there are no grounds to support it in her speech.

Distorted Evidence

Less easily discovered is the argument that relies on distorted evidence to support its claim. **Distorted evidence** is significant omissions or changes in the grounds of an argument that alter its original intent.

A good example of distorted evidence is found on the movie advertisement page of your local newspaper. Frequently, a movie will tout itself as "daring," "enthralling," or "thumbs up" when a reading of the full review will reveal that these words were used in a different context. Perhaps the reviewers really said, "This movie was a daring attempt that missed the mark. The only thing that was enthralling about this movie was the credits that signaled it was ending. In deciding whether to rate this movie thumbs up or down, it took only about 10 minutes to see that this was thumbs way down!"

Isolated Examples

Another problem with grounds lies in the use of **isolated examples,** nontypical or nonrepresentative examples, to prove a general claim. Recall that to reason from examples requires that the instances be representative of the larger class—in a word, typical. It is almost always possible to find an isolated example to illustrate just about any claim. For example, we often hear about cases of welfare abuse. One radio commentator recently told the story of a man who reported to the police that his food stamps had been stolen from his car—a Mercedes. Of course, most people on welfare don't drive a Mercedes. Yet the image of welfare recipients living it up at the taxpayers' expense has been a staple of popular mythology for decades. The reality is that most people on welfare are children living in poverty. Isolated examples do not prove that everyone on welfare is lazy or abusing the system.

Misused Statistics

Statistics are often very helpful in giving us a general picture of a topic, something not provided by examples. However, to be useful, grounds must meet the basic tests outlined in Chapter 7. Let's now look at four of the most frequent cases of **misused statistics.**

Poor Sampling   Statistics based on self-selected or nonrandom samples are worse than useless—they're misleading. For instance, many television stations and newspapers now have call-in polls whereby you can express your opinion on the issues of the day by dialing one of two numbers, each representing one side of the issue. Of course, there is no guarantee that the station's audience represents the public at large or that members of the audience will call in proportion to their number in the general population.

Lack of Significant Differences   Often the difference between two candidates in a preference poll is less than the poll's margin of error. Thus, if candidate A leads B by three points, but the poll has a five-point margin of error, there is no statistical significance to that difference, a fact often ignored by political pundits.

Misuse of "Average"   People frequently cite the "average," or mean, to support a claim. They say such things as, "The average salary for college graduates is X." The intent is for the audience to infer that most college graduates make the salary mentioned. However, the average (or mean) is only one of three numbers that can be used to describe a collection of numbers like the salaries paid to college graduates. The other two are the median and the mode. Further, the average is frequently misleading because it is so easily distorted by extreme numbers.

As an example, consider the differences between the mean, the median, and the mode of houses selling at a range of prices:

$100,000

$100,000

$150,000

$250,000

$1,000,000

Mean = $320,000

Median = $150,000

Mode = $100,000

The *mean* is simply the arithmetic average: Add all the selling prices, and divide the total by the number of houses sold. The *median* is the midpoint in a series of numbers. Half of the houses sold for more and half for less than the median. Finally, the *mode* is simply the most frequently occurring number or value. In most cases, the median is more accurate than the mean. Certainly that is the case here because the mean would lead you to believe that most houses in the area described are more expensive than they are in actuality. The single home selling for $1 million not only inflates the "average" but misleads your thinking in the process.

Misuse of Percentages   Percentages are meaningful only if you know the base on which they are computed. Consider the confusion often present in political and commercial advertising. For example, although it is true that while Bill Clinton was governor, Arkansas led the nation in job creation in the year prior to his election as president, it is also true that Arkansas had one of the lowest job bases to begin with. If you start out at a very low level, even large percentage increases may not be very large in real terms.

FALLACIES ASSOCIATED WITH CLAIMS

There are three types of claims a person can make. A *claim of fact* is one that can in principle be verified by objective means. For example, Miranda Welsh argues that "According to the drug testing website, employees who are on drugs are 3.6 times more likely than nonusers to injure themselves or others [in an] on-the-job accident." This claim is easily verified by looking up the Web site. Even if a claim of fact is not currently known to be true or false, as long as it is theoretically verifiable, it is still a factual claim. We don't know for sure if there is life on other planets, but theoretically the question could be answered empirically, if we had the means to directly observe radio signals from deep space, for example.

A *claim of value* makes judgments about good and bad, right and wrong. When David Sanders talks about the "good guys" and the "bad guys," he has gone beyond mere fact to make a value judgment. He is denoting one side as good and another as evil. And when President George W. Bush referred to the terrorists who attacked the United States on September 11, 2001, as "evil," he left no doubt about his values.

A *claim of policy* offers a solution to some problem. Miranda Welsh believes the solution to the problem of drug abuse in the United States is more drug testing. David Sanders takes a very different position, arguing for an end to the policy of conducting a war on drugs. To convincingly prove a claim of policy, you must prove the stock issues of *ill, blame, cure,* and *cost,* which we discussed in Chapters 8 and 13. Both of our student speakers address these stock issues. David believes that the drug war is destroying America and blames politicians for the problem. He proposes a cure of legalizing drugs and argues that the cost of his program will be less than that of the present system. Miranda believes the abuse of drugs is harming innocent people who work alongside drug abusers. She blames the situation on the failure to test for drugs in schools and the workplace. Her cure is to institute mandatory testing. She argues that it will not be very costly and that it can be done without violating the Constitution.

Red Herring

Claims may be fallacious if they are irrelevant, the so-called red herring. Sometimes called a **smoke screen,** a **red herring** is an irrelevant issue introduced into a controversy to divert attention from the real controversy. Debates over public issues are well known for the use of red herrings to divert attention from the issues that concern most people. For example, suppose a speaker arguing for drug testing were to say, "The people who oppose drug testing are the same ones who were against fighting terrorism when America was attacked." Of course, drug testing and terrorism have nothing in common. Bringing up the discussion of terrorism would be an attempt to divert attention from the issue at hand. Fortunately, neither of our student speakers on the drug issue engaged in such spurious reasoning.

Arguing in a Circle

Another common fallacy is the use of a claim to prove its own truth, called arguing in a circle. **Arguing in a circle,** sometimes called **begging the question,** occurs when the argument actually proves nothing because the claim to be proved is used as the grounds or warrant for the argument. For example, consider the door-to-door evangelist who insists that you must believe in his or her version of the Bible. Why? you ask. The person immediately opens a Bible and quotes you scripture to support the claim. Basically the argument looks something like this:

Claim: My version of the Bible is the truth.

Grounds: Quotation from scripture.

Warrant: My version of the Bible is the truth.

In other words, the claim is also the warrant.

Of course, such clear-cut expressions of question-begging are rare. But many arguments, when distilled to their essence, do in fact beg the question.

FALLACIES ASSOCIATED WITH WARRANTS AND BACKING

Grounds do not directly prove a claim. There is a connection between the grounds and the claim, whether stated or unstated. You may recall that Toulmin calls this link the warrant. The warrant is the license that authorizes an arguer to move from grounds to a claim. Thus, if you were to argue, as in our earlier example, that it's going to rain because it is cloudy, the observation about clouds only proves it will rain given the warrant that clouds are a sign of rain. The process of moving from grounds, via a warrant, to a claim is called an **inference.**

Sometimes people confuse observed grounds with claims based on inference. To see how well you can distinguish between inferences and observations, try reading the story and answering the questions in the box "Uncritical Inference Test" on the next page. This test was devised by William V. Haney, a former business professor who now heads his own consulting firm.

To his basic model of grounds-warrant-claim, recall that Toulmin adds backing, which is support for the warrant. In some cases a warrant is readily believed by an audience. In others, the warrant needs additional backing in the form of evidence before the audience will believe it is true. For example, suppose someone in your audience believes the Constitution prohibits mandatory drug testing by private companies. You've said that it is permissible under the Constitution. You would have to present backing for your warrant, just as Miranda Welsh did when she said, "Actually, if you read the 4th Amendment carefully, you would see that it only protects you from unreasonable searches done by the federal government . . . not by private organizations." Backing is required, therefore, when a warrant either is not known to the audience or is contrary to what they already believe.

Different types of warrants provide different ways of moving from grounds to claim and are associated with different patterns of reasoning. We introduce here the five most common types of warrants: generalization, comparison, causal, sign, and authority. In examining any argument, it is important to determine whether the warrant and its accompanying backing are sound. We look at each type of warrant and suggest some of the common fallacies peculiar to each type of argument.

Generalization Warrants

A **generalization warrant** is a statement that either establishes a general rule or principle or applies an established rule or principle to a specific case. Warrants involving generalizations are used in two ways. Some warrants take specific instances and use them to establish generalizations. For example, suppose we want to generalize about college students. Based on our experience with the students in our public speaking class, we might generalize that "most college students are politically

> **inference** The process of moving from a ground, via a warrant, to a claim.

> **generalization warrant** A statement that either establishes a general rule or principle or applies an established rule or principle to a specific case.

SELF-ASSESSMENT

Uncritical Inference Test

INSTRUCTIONS

Read the following story. Assume that all the information presented in it is definitely accurate and true. Read it carefully because it has ambiguous parts designed to lead you astray. No need to memorize it, though. You can refer to it whenever you wish.

Next read the statements about the story and indicate whether you consider each statement true, false, or "?". "T" means that the statement is *definitely true* on the basis of the information presented in the story. "F" means that it is *definitely false*. "?" means that it may be either true or false and that you cannot be certain which on the basis of the information presented in the story. If any part of a statement is doubtful, make it "?". *Answer each statement in turn, and do not go back to change any answer later, and don't reread any statements after you have answered them. This will distort your score.*

To start with, here is a sample story with correct answers.

SAMPLE STORY

You arrive home late one evening and see that the lights are on in your living room. There is only one car parked in front of your house, and the words "Harold R. Jones, M.D." are spelled in small gold letters across one of the car's doors.

Statements About Sample Story

1. The car parked in front of your house has lettering on one of its doors. (T) F ?
   (This is a "definitely true" statement because it is directly corroborated by the story.)
2. Someone in your family is sick. T F (?)
   (This could be true, and then again it might not be. Perhaps Dr. Jones is paying a social call at your home, or perhaps he has gone to the house next door or across the street, or maybe someone else is using the car.)
3. No car is parked in front of your house. T (F) ?
   (A "definitely false" statement because the story directly contradicts it.)
4. The car parked in front of your house belongs to a woman named Johnson.
   T F (?)
   (May seem very likely false, but can you be sure? Perhaps the car has just been sold.)

So much for the sample. It should warn you of some of the kinds of traps to look for. Now begin the actual test. Remember, mark each statement *in order*—don't skip around or change answers later.

uninvolved." Other warrants take already existing generalizations and apply them to specific instances. For example, suppose we know from a previously established generalization that all college students must be high school graduates. Thus, we can conclude that any specific student in a college class is a high school graduate.

The relationship between a generalization-establishing warrant and a generalization-applying warrant is illustrated by the diagram in Figure 14.3.

Establishing Generalizations   A warrant that establishes a generalization uses specific instances, as represented in examples, statistics, narratives, and the like, to reach general conclusions. Consider Miranda Welsh's argument. She

THE STORY[1]

A businessman had just turned off the lights in the store when a man appeared and demanded money. The owner opened a cash register. The contents of the cash register were scooped up, and the man sped away. A member of the police force was notified promptly.

Statements About the Story

1. A man appeared after the owner had turned off his store lights.   T   F   ?
2. The robber was a *man*.   T   F   ?
3. The man who appeared did not demand money.   T   F   ?
4. The man who opened the cash register was the owner.   T   F   ?
5. The store owner scooped up the contents of the cash register and ran away.   T   F   ?
6. Someone opened a cash register.   T   F   ?
7. After the man who demanded the money scooped up the contents of the cash register, he ran away.   T   F   ?
8. While the cash register contained money, the story does *not* state *how much*.   T   F   ?
9. The robber demanded money of the owner.   T   F   ?
10. A businessman had just turned off the lights when a man appeared in the store.   T   F   ?
11. It was broad daylight when the man appeared.   T   F   ?
12. The man who appeared opened the cash register.   T   F   ?
13. No one demanded money.   T   F   ?
14. The story concerns a series of events in which only three persons are referred to: the owner of the store, a man who demanded money, and a member of the police force.   T   F   ?
15. The following events occurred: someone demanded money; a cash register was opened; its contents were scooped up; and a man dashed out of the store.   T   F   ?

Answers appear following the chapter notes, on page 379.

Source: Excerpted with special permission from William V. Haney, *Communication and Interpersonal Relations*, 6th ed. (Homewood, IL: R. D. Irwin, Inc., 1992), 231–233, 241.

[1]The story and statements are a portion of the "Uncritical Inference Test," copyrighted 1955 and 1983 by William V. Haney.

uses specific examples and statistics to support her generalization that drug use on the job can be dangerous. During her speech she cites specific examples of deaths due to drug use: "In April of 1987, a bus driver drove his bus directly into a bridge in Virginia, killed one, injured thirty. Only after the accident was he drug tested positive for cocaine, valium and marijuana. In January of 1988, a pilot crashed his plane into rural Colorado. The crash was solely attributed to the pilot, which killed 30 people." She also cites overall statistics on the higher costs to employers of employees who are drug abusers. Warrants establishing generalizations are subject to tests of relevance, quantity, typicality, precision, and negative example. These tests can be expressed in the questions listed below.

FIGURE 14.3 Relationship Between Generalization-Establishing and Generalization-Applying Warrants. Generalizations are established based on a number of specific instances. Once accepted, generalizations are then applied to further specific instances.

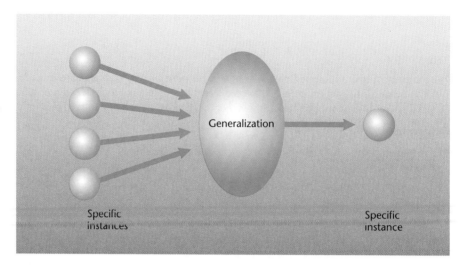

Specific instances

Generalization

Specific instance

TIPS AND TACTICS   *Questions to Ask When Evaluating a Generalization*

- Are the grounds relevant to the claim?
- Is there a sufficient quantity of grounds to establish the claim?
- Are the grounds typical of the larger population?
- Is overgeneralization avoided?
- Are there significant negative examples?

Let's apply these tests to Miranda's generalization that mandatory drug testing is needed. Clearly her examples are relevant. Is there a sufficient quantity of grounds to support the claim? She cites two specific cases of deaths from drug abusers, one of a bus driver and the other of a pilot. While these examples are troubling, are the grounds typical? Her argument is further bolstered by the statistics on the railroads. "And some years back, the federal railroad administration drug tested 759 of their railroad employees only after 125 different accidents had occurred. At that time 29 of their current employees drug tested positive for one or more illegal drugs." Still, her argument would be stronger if she had overall national statistics on the numbers of deaths from workplace-related drug use. Is overgeneralization avoided? She is calling for testing in all workplaces and schools. But, as David Sanders points out in his speech, there's a big difference between the Kmart checker using drugs and a pilot or bus driver. At most, the examples of busses, planes, and trains justify drug testing when lives are at stake. Ask yourself if her examples are as applicable to other occupations as well. Finally, are there negative examples? Are there cases where using drugs might have saved lives? That's difficult to imagine, and even Sanders, in his speech against the drug war, admits using drugs is a bad idea. The complete argument might look like the model in Figure 14.4.

Hasty Generalization   The most common fallacy associated with warrants that generalize from specific instances to a general conclusion is known as **hasty generalization.** This occurs when there are too few instances to support a gen-

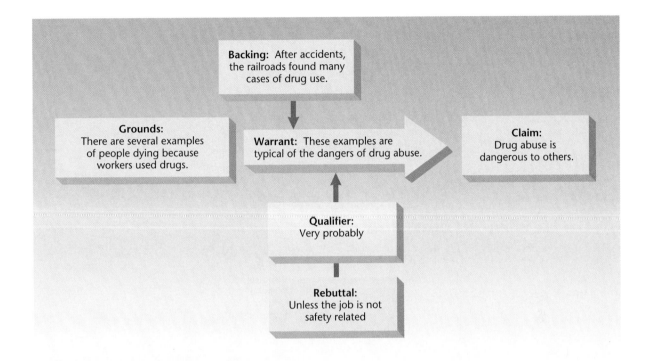

FIGURE 14.4 Argument Establishing a Generalization

eralization or the instances are unrepresentative of the generalization. The key here is to limit generalizations to the extent justified by the grounds. For example, suppose you once purchased an American car. It gave you nothing but trouble. You decide American cars are unreliable and vow to purchase only foreign automobiles. You have engaged in hasty generalization. Maybe Fords are more reliable than Dodges. Perhaps American manufacturers have improved their product. To reach a generalization from one or even a handful of instances is to form a hasty generalization.

Applying Generalizations   On the other hand, if we know a generalization is true, we can apply it to a specific instance and reach some valid conclusions about that specific instance. For example, we know that anyone born in the United States is, by definition, a U.S. citizen. Thus, if you show us your birth certificate, and it says you were born in Alaska, we know you are a U.S. citizen. Warrants applying generalizations are subject to tests of applicability to all cases, exceptions, backing, and classification.

Questions to Ask When Evaluating Applications of a Generalization   **TIPS AND TACTICS**

- Does the generalization apply to all possible cases?
- Are there exceptions to the generalization? If so, does the specific case fall within one of the exceptions?

FIGURE 14.5 Argument Applying a Generalization

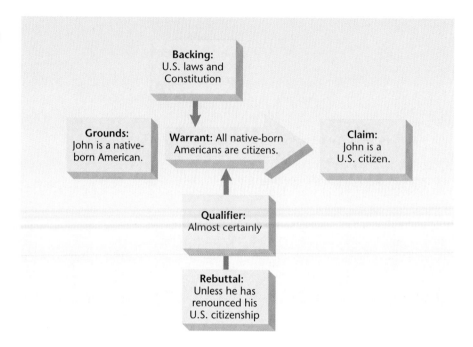

- Is the generalization well backed?
- Does the specific instance fall clearly within the category specified by the generalization?

Figure 14.5 illustrates an argument that applies a generalization. In this case, we know that the generalization *warrant*, all native-born Americans are citizens, is true because of the *backing* found in the U.S. laws and Constitution. Given the *grounds* that John is a native-born American, we can be almost certain (*qualifier*) that the *claim*, John is a U.S. citizen, is true. There is a possible *rebuttal*, however; the claim is true unless he has renounced his citizenship.

Stereotyping   The most common fallacy associated with warrants that apply established generalizations to specific instances is known as **stereotyping.** This fallacy assumes that what is considered to be true of a larger class is necessarily true of particular members of that class. Thus, although it may be true that professional basketball players are generally tall, you would be wrong to assume that 5-foot-3-inch Mugsy Bogues is tall just because he played in the NBA. When you hear people talk about all people of any given race or group being the same, you can be fairly sure that the speakers are guilty of the stereotyping fallacy. "Everybody on welfare is lazy," "All college students are liberals," and "All politicians are crooks" are examples of stereotyping.

Always be cautious about applying generalizations. One of the authors recalls a lecture in which he was discussing the impact of proposed tuition increases on minority students. He argued that such students would be disproportionately hurt by the increased fees. After the class, he was approached by an African American student who pointed out that not all minority students

Not all NBA players fit the stereotype of being tall, as Mugsy Bogues proved when he played for teams like the Golden State Warriors, Charlotte Hornets, and Toronto Raptors.

are from poor families and not all poor students are from minority groups. Indeed, the student was right. In dealing with generalizations, there is always a danger of stereotyping a whole group when there are notable exceptions to such generalizations.

False Dilemma   Another common fallacy associated with applying generalizations is the **false dilemma,** a generalization that implies there are only two choices when there are more than two. "America, love it or leave it," was a common false dilemma during the protests of the 1960s. Those who responded, "America, change it or lose it," were probably just as guilty of either-or thinking. Thus, a true dilemma requires proof that there really are only two choices. Consider the following telephone call to a newspaper:

They should fight child abuse
I'd like to talk to the pro-lifers about abortion. They want to stop abortion so bad and they take their time to do it. Why don't they take the same painstaking time to help fight children being killed by dads and moms when they get a very light sentence?[5]

Of course, someone can be both pro-life (or anti-abortion) and against children being killed by their parents. The key to a real dilemma is that there are in fact only two choices and that they are mutually exclusive. In this case, someone could support both of these values without contradiction, and thus no real dilemma exists.

comparison (analogy) warrant A statement that two cases that are similar in some known respects are also similar in some unknown respects.

Comparison (Analogy) Warrants

An argument based on a **comparison (analogy) warrant** claims that two cases that are similar in some known respects are also similar in some unknown respects. These arguments are called comparisons or, more commonly, analogies. They are subject to tests of literalness versus figurativeness, similarity, and relevance.

TIPS AND TACTICS   *Questions to Ask When Evaluating Comparisons or Analogies*

- Are only literal analogies used for proof?
- Do the similarities outweigh the differences?
- Are the similarities more relevant than the differences to the claim being made?

Let's begin with the difference between literal and figurative analogies. A *literal analogy* claims that two different instances are really similar. For example, prior to the 1991 war in the Persian Gulf, many proponents of using military force compared Saddam Hussein to Adolf Hitler. They argued that if Saddam's occupation of Kuwait was allowed to stand, he would continue to conquer his neighbors and expand his territory, just as Hitler had done in Europe. Opponents of military involvement, on the other hand, often argued that the Gulf War could become another Vietnam War, with the United States bogged down in a faraway foreign land, in a war that would be both unpopular at home and costly in terms of lives and money. Both sides were attempting to provide literal analogies to other wars in order to support their claims that the United States either should or should not fight in the Persian Gulf.

A *figurative analogy,* on the other hand, is a device of language that is used to enhance the persuasiveness of a speech. While a figurative analogy clearly seeks to establish some similarity between the two items being compared, no one could reasonably argue that they are really alike. For example, some people made the comparison of Saddam to a schoolyard bully. If the United States didn't stand up to him, he would be encouraged to become a bigger bully. No one believed, however, that Saddam was just a big bully using his fists to beat up little kids and steal their lunch money. A schoolyard bully might cost you a black eye and your lunch money. Saddam cost human lives and billions of dollars.

Although there is nothing wrong with figurative analogies as a persuasive device, if you rely on them to provide proof for a claim, you are on shaky ground. There is no logical force to such arguments.

Next, in a good analogy or comparison, the similarities should outweigh the differences. If they do not, the analogy will not be very powerful. For example, when comparing Adolf Hitler and Saddam Hussein, there are clearly many similarities. Both were dictators, both engaged in atrocities against their neighbors and their own people, and both invaded neighboring nations. There are

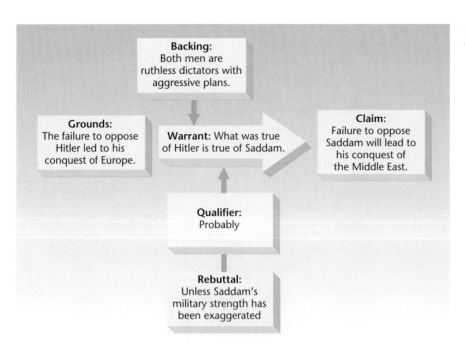

FIGURE 14.6 Argument by Comparison

also important differences. For example, Hitler commanded one of the most powerful military machines in history, whereas Saddam's army proved to be technologically backward. Further, initially there was no united front against Hitler; in fact, the Soviet Union had signed a pact with him. With very few exceptions, there was an array of nations opposing Saddam that was almost unparalleled up to that point in history.

Finally, the similarities, rather than the differences, should be most relevant to the claim being made. In the comparison of Saddam and Hitler, whereas Hitler and his allies had the military might to make war on the world, Saddam was unable to launch a meaningful attack on even his closest enemy, Israel.

Figure 14.6 shows how the complete argument by comparison might evolve on this topic. Based on *grounds* that the failure to oppose Hitler led to his conquest of Europe, and using the *warrant* that what was true of Hitler is true of Saddam, probably (*qualifier*) the *claim* that the failure to oppose Saddam will lead to his conquest of the Middle East is true. *Backing* for the warrant comes from the common traits that both men are ruthless dictators with aggressive plans. The claim is true unless (*rebuttal*) Saddam's military strength has been exaggerated.

False Analogy   The most common fallacy associated with comparison warrants is the **false analogy.** This occurs when two things that are not really comparable are compared as if they were essentially the same. For example, we recall a letter written to a newspaper by a reader angered with newly enacted laws requiring motorcyclists to wear helmets. This reader complained that the legislature had become another Saddam Hussein, acting like a dictator in passing a mandatory helmet law.

Of course, the differences in these two situations are dramatic. The legislature is an elected body. The law was passed based on safety concerns and is not unlike laws requiring motorists to wear seat belts. The key to the analogy is whether the

FIGURE 14.7 Reasoning From Cause to Effect

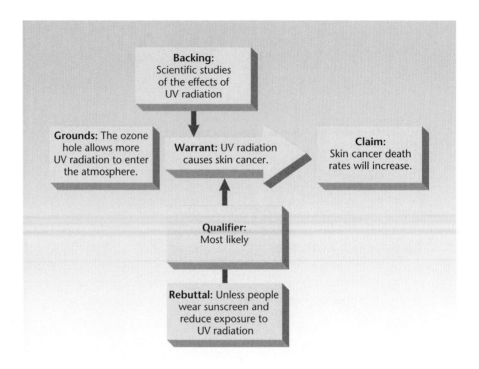

legislature and Saddam are both dictators. In the case of Iraq, the people have no way, short of a coup or revolution, to remove the offending person, whereas the voters have an opportunity every two years to "throw the bums out."

Causal Warrants

causal warrant An argument that claims a cause will produce or has produced an effect.

Frequently people seek to determine either what has caused something or what effect a particular action will have. An argument based on a **causal warrant** claims that a cause will produce or has produced an effect. You can reason either from cause to effect or from effect to cause.

Reasoning from *cause to effect* involves predicting what will happen if some action is taken. For example, in recent years the ozone layer that protects the earth has developed "holes," or thin spots. Based on this fact, some experts predict that there will be many more deaths from skin cancer than if the ozone layer had not developed holes. Clearly this reasoning process moves from a cause (depletion of the ozone layer) to a predicted effect (skin cancer deaths) (Figure 14.7). Based on the *grounds* that the ozone hole allows more UV radiation to enter the atmosphere and using the *warrant*, UV radiation causes skin cancer, which has *backing* from scientific studies, most likely (*qualifier*) the *claim* is true that skin cancer death rates will increase, unless (*rebuttal*) people wear sunscreen and reduce their exposure to UV radiation.

On the other hand, you might ask why the ozone layer has been depleted. According to some experts, chlorine-containing chemicals, called CFCs (chlorofluorocarbons), are the principal culprit in destroying the ozone. These chemicals were found in auto air conditioners, refrigerators, and the like. In this

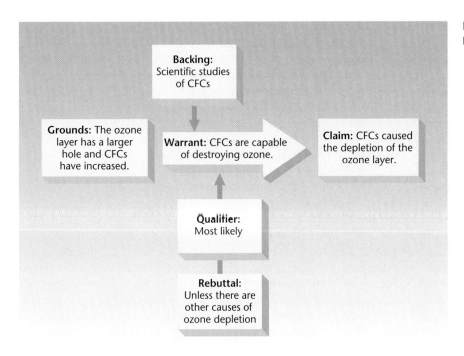

FIGURE 14.8 Reasoning From Effect to Cause

instance, the reasoning is from *effect* (depletion of the ozone layer) *to cause* (CFCs) (Figure 14.8). This argument shows that based on the *grounds* that the ozone layer has a larger hole and CFCs have increased, using the *warrant* that CFCs are capable of destroying ozone, which has *backing* from scientific studies, most likely (*qualifier*) the *claim* is true that CFCs caused the depletion of the ozone layer, unless (*rebuttal*) there are other causes of ozone depletion.

Causal warrants are subject to tests of relatedness, other causes, other effects, and mistaking order in time for causality.

Questions to Ask When Evaluating Causal Reasoning	**TIPS AND TACTICS**

- Is the cause related to the alleged effect?
- Are there other causes of the effect?
- Are there other effects from the same cause?
- Has time sequence been mistaken for cause (post hoc fallacy)?

Let's apply these tests to the argument about CFCs and the depletion of the ozone layer. First, is the depletion *related* to CFCs? Based on a considerable body of scientific study, this connection seems well established. Further, is the ozone depletion *related* to the increase in skin cancer? Again, scientific studies have established that ultraviolet radiation is a cause of skin cancer and that the ozone layer screens out ultraviolet radiation from the sun.

Are there *other causes* of the effect? Although CFCs cause ozone depletion, there are other causes as well. For example, the exhaust from shuttle rockets contributes to the breakdown of the ozone layer. Although this may not be the major cause of the problem, it means that eliminating CFCs alone may not be enough to end the problem.

How about *other effects* from the same cause? If CFCs are banned immediately, we may lose many of their benefits, such as air conditioning in older vehicles. Although some substitutes have been developed, they may not work in existing refrigeration units. So, although banning CFCs might seem like a simple solution, we need to consider other effects such a ban would cause.

Finally, you must be careful not to assume a causal relationship just because two events occur one after the other in *time*. We recall a letter to a local newspaper that attributed the end of the California drought to the prayers of particular ministers in a small foothill community. Although it is true that the ministers prayed and the rains came, that does not mean one event caused the other. Similarly, although skin cancer death rates are rising as the ozone is decreasing, that does not prove, in and of itself, that the ozone depletion is causing the death rates from skin cancer to rise. It might be the case, for example, that people are spending more time in the sun than they once did. You should always be particularly suspicious of claims of cause and effect based solely on time sequence.

Although the preceding discussion may suggest that causal arguments are difficult to make, they can, nevertheless, be successfully and persuasively made. For example, there is considerable scientific evidence to support the effects of tobacco on health, and few independent scientists dispute the harmfulness of the product. A speaker relying on such experts and scientific studies would be on solid ground. Often a speaker is best advised to make causal arguments when they can be buttressed by expert testimony and scientific studies, and clearly meet tests of relatedness, other causes and effects, and time sequence as outlined in this chapter.

Post Hoc   Warrants dealing with effect-to-cause reasoning frequently commit the fallacy of assuming that because one event preceded another, the first event must be the cause of the second event. Technically, this is known as the **post hoc, ergo propter hoc** fallacy ("after the fact, therefore because of the fact"). Shortly after President George W. Bush was inaugurated on January 20, 2001, the first signs of economic recession began to appear. By March 2001, the economy had moved into negative economic growth. After six months of such negative growth, the country was officially declared to be in a recession. Some of Bush's political opponents attempted to blame him for the recession. We recall seeing letters to the editor and hearing callers to radio talk shows lamenting that Bush had destroyed the prosperity of the 1990s. Of course, as most people realized, the seeds of recession were sown before Bush was even elected, let alone took office. After the longest peacetime expansion in history, it was clear the country was headed for at least a slowdown, if not an outright recession. Just because one event, Bush's inauguration, was followed by a recession, does not mean that Bush caused the economy to falter. As much as we like to blame or credit presidents for our economy, the reality is that there are far more complex causes for economic growth or recession. To automatically blame or praise the new president for the economy is a classic example of post hoc reasoning.

Slippery Slope   Warrants that reason from cause to effect are susceptible to the **slippery slope fallacy.** This fallacy involves assuming that just because one event occurs, it will automatically lead to a series of undesirable events, like a row of dominoes falling down automatically once you knock over the first one. In common language, this fallacy is sometimes expressed, "If you give them an inch, they'll take a mile."

How many times have you heard someone argue that allowing abortions will lead to infanticide? Or perhaps you've been told that if you don't get a college degree, you will end up homeless and broke. The slippery slope fallacy occurs when you assume that a series of events will result from one action without there being a relationship between the action and the projected events. Nevertheless, it is not necessarily a slippery slope to argue that one action will follow another if the relationship can be clearly demonstrated. For example, it can be mathematically demonstrated that to continue to charge items on a credit card without paying any more than the minimum monthly payment will lead to deeper and deeper debt. And, of course, the judicial system relies heavily on the role of precedents in making decisions. Much of the debate surrounding the use of military tribunals to try suspected terrorists relied on the precedents set in the Civil War and World Wars I and II. So future effects are important, if they can be clearly shown by sound reasoning.

Sign Warrants

Perhaps you've heard someone say, "It's going to rain. I can feel it in my bones." Or you've read a newspaper article stating that the economy is in a recession, because the latest "leading economic indicators" are pointing downward. These are examples of reasoning from sign. A **sign warrant** is reasoning in which the presence of an observed phenomenon is used to indicate the presence of an unobserved phenomenon.

In sign reasoning, the warrant asserts that the grounds provide a reliable sign that the claim is true. Some signs are infallible; most are merely probable. The absence of brain waves is considered legally as an infallible sign of death. On the other hand, no one would claim that the rise or fall of stock prices is even close to an infallible sign of the state of the economy. Sign warrants are subject to tests of reliability and conflicting signs.

> **sign warrant** Reasoning in which the presence of an observed phenomenon is used to indicate the presence of an unobserved phenomenon.

TIPS AND TACTICS

Questions to Ask When Evaluating Sign Reasoning

- Are the signs reliable indicators of the claim?
- Are there conflicting signs?

A detective examines a crime scene for signs of forced entry, struggle, and the like. Anyone who is a fan of Sherlock Holmes will recall that he often made a case based on the most obscure signs. One small sign would point him to the guilty subject every time.

Unfortunately, in real life, such reliable signs are harder to find. In testing sign reasoning, ask how reliable such signs have been in the past. For example, economists often make predictions about the future of the economy based on figures for unemployment, housing starts, and so on. A careful examination of their track record in making such predictions will suggest just how much confidence you should have in their reasoning.

FIGURE 14.9
Sign Reasoning

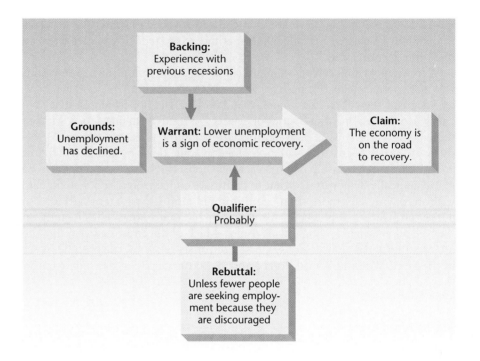

The second test is to look for conflicting signs. Whereas one economist may point to decreased unemployment as a sign of economic upturn, another may conclude that there are fewer unemployed because the economy is so bad many workers have given up seeking jobs.

Unless a sign is infallible, most sign reasoning at best indicates the probability that a claim is true. For example, Figure 14.9 represents the argument about lower unemployment and the future of the economy. Based on the *grounds* that unemployment has declined, using the *warrant* that lower unemployment is a sign of economic recovery, based on the *backing* of experience with previous recessions, probably (*qualifier*) the *claim* is true that the economy is on the road to recovery, unless (*rebuttal*) fewer people are seeking employment because they are discouraged.

Mistaking Correlation for Cause   The most common fallacy associated with sign reasoning is **mistaking correlation for cause.** A correlation simply means two things occur in conjunction with each other, without regard to their cause. How often have you heard someone claim that one event caused another, just because they occurred in tandem? Historically, when the stock market was on the rise, so were women's hemlines. Although one may be a "sign" of the other, it is ludicrous to assume the stock market caused the hemlines to go up or vice versa. Just because one event signifies another does not mean they are causally related. For example, a recent news report noted that there is a higher-than-normal incidence of heart disease among bald men. However, this does not prove that baldness causes heart disease or that wearing a toupee will reduce the risk of heart attack. Although the two factors are correlated, the most likely explanation is that common underlying factors cause both baldness and heart disease.

Authority Warrants

Sometimes the link between grounds and claim comes from the authoritativeness of the source of the grounds. An **authority warrant** is used in reasoning in which the claim is believed because of the authority of the source. Recall from Chapter 13 that many people respond almost unthinkingly to authority figures. This is not reasoning, but an unthinking response. Just because Barry Bonds endorses Wheaties, for example, does not mean that every Wheaties eater is a potential home run hitter. On the other hand, when an argument relies on the expertise of a respected authority, that can be a valid reason for acting. For example, if your doctor tells you that you need to lose weight, you are likely to trust her judgment and at least *try* to shed the unwanted pounds. The key to an authoritative argument is that the person is truly an expert in the area of concern. Further, it is important that the authority is relying on correct information. If your doctor is given the wrong test results, no matter how knowledgeable or reliable she is, her conclusions are suspect.

Authority warrants are subject to tests of whether the authority is truly an expert and whether the authority has accurate information.

> **authority warrant** Reasoning in which the claim is believed because of the authority of the source.

Questions to Ask When Evaluating Authority Warrants   **TIPS AND TACTICS**

- Is the authority truly an expert in the area under discussion?
- Is the authority acting on reliable information?

An example of an argument from an authority warrant is found in Figure 14.10. Based on the *grounds* that your doctor tells you to lose weight, using the *warrant* that you have confidence in the doctor's expertise, based on the *backing* of training in medical school and years of experience, almost certainly (*qualifier*) the *claim* is true that you should lose weight, unless (*rebuttal*) you can't afford a weight-loss plan and you are unable to lose weight on your own.

Halo Effect   One common fallacy associated with reasoning based on an authority warrant is called the **halo effect.** Just because you like or respect a person, you tend to believe whatever he or she says. Millions of people, for example, listen to radio talk show host Rush Limbaugh. However, Limbaugh has apparently misstated a number of "facts," according to a recent report by the media watchdog group FAIR (Fairness and Accuracy in Reporting). For example, Limbaugh claimed that "if 4,000 votes . . . had gone the other way in Chicago—Richard Nixon would have been elected in 1960."[6] Yet FAIR points out that Kennedy won by a greater margin than all of Illinois's electoral votes, and thus the results in Chicago could not have changed the outcome of the election. And FAIR cites Limbaugh as ignoring the overwhelming medical evidence to the contrary when he stated, "It has not been proven that nicotine is addictive."[7]

Ad Hominem   The reverse of the halo effect is called argument **ad hominem,** meaning an argument "against the person." This fallacy says a claim must be false because the person who said it is not credible, regardless of the argument itself. This should be distinguished from legitimate questions about the truthfulness or character of a source of evidence. Clearly, an admitted perjurer is not

FIGURE 14.10 Argument Using an Authority Warrant

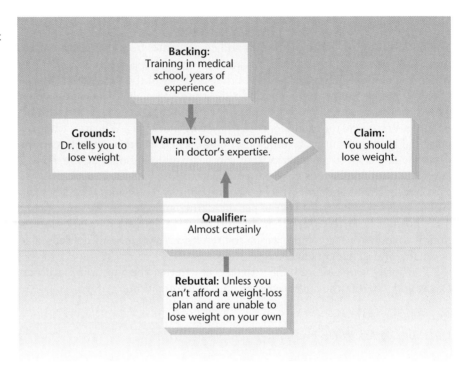

a reliable source of evidence in a civil or criminal trial. The ad hominem fallacy applies when the attack on character is not directly related to legitimate concerns about a person's reliability as a source of evidence, but is substituted for a rational consideration of the person's argument.

Ad hominem is often associated with name-calling. Name-calling occurs when a person or group of people are characterized by a term that is loaded with negative connotations. When a political candidate is characterized as a "bozo," "womanizer," or "wimp," these terms raise emotional feelings without providing rational grounds for rejecting the candidate. The use of negative terms for ethnic, religious, racial, and sexual groups is also a type of name-calling. Consider, for example, the use of terms such as "chick," "hottie," or "bimbo" to characterize a woman or terms such as "jock," "stud," or "hunk" to refer to a man. Sexist, racist, and bigoted language is an insidious form of name-calling that degrades entire groups of people. Just because you do not like someone, or someone is called a derogatory name, does not mean their arguments should be rejected out of hand. It is just as bad to reject everything Rush Limbaugh says as false, as it is to assume everything he says is gospel.

FALLACIES ASSOCIATED WITH QUALIFIERS

Toulmin believes that arguers should qualify their claims. As we pointed out earlier in this chapter, a qualifier is an indication of the level of probability of a claim. Some arguments are virtually certain to be true, whereas others have a much lower degree of certainty. Depending on the nature of the argument, a

Loaded language is a fallacy because it inflames passions rather than appealing to reasoning.

qualifier can make a big difference. For example, in a criminal trial, the claim that the defendant is guilty must be true "beyond a reasonable doubt," a phrase that acts as the qualifier of the argument for guilt. Thus, a very high degree of certainty is required before a jury can convict someone of a criminal offense. On the other hand, in a civil case, the standard is "a preponderance of evidence." Thus, if it is more likely than not that the defendant wronged the plaintiff, the judgment should go to the plaintiff. That is why someone found not guilty in a criminal trial can still be sued in civil court. The level of proof that is required is different.

So, too, in your argumentation, you need to know what level of proof your audience will expect. Thus, as with virtually every other aspect of public speaking, the success of your reasoning depends on careful analysis of your audience. As a listener, you should also be clear about what level of proof you need before accepting a claim. Many of the fallacies of reasoning associated with qualifiers are a result of overstating or distorting the degree of certainty with which the arguer has supported his or her claim. Two such common fallacies are the use of loaded language and hyperbole.

Loaded Language

Language that has strong emotional connotations is termed **loaded language.** Depending on the specific characteristics of your audience, what you might consider neutral language may in fact carry strong emotional connotations. During his tenure in office, Bill Clinton was characterized by just about every loaded term in the book. Even after he left office, we recall hearing the former president being called everything from a communist to a fascist. And Senator Hillary Rodham Clinton continues to be a lightning rod for loaded language from her opponents. Such language may create a lot of heat, but it doesn't shed much light on the real issues of the day.

Of course, effective persuasion often requires vivid, intense, and expressive language, as we discussed in Chapter 9. There is a fine but important line between language that is necessarily vivid and language that is so "loaded" that it distorts the reasoning being presented. There is no hard-and-fast rule that can be applied here. Speakers and listeners need to exercise their judgment in evaluating the use of language.

Hyperbole

Hyperbole is an exaggeration of a claim. Rather than properly qualifying or limiting the impact of a statement, the person engaged in hyperbole exaggerates the claim in question. When boxer Mohammed Ali declared himself to be "the greatest," it may have been an effective way to build interest in his fights, but it was certainly an exaggeration of his prowess, especially since he didn't limit his claim to the boxing ring. Other examples of hyperbole include the use of such terms as "superstar," "greatest ever," and "mega-hit." It often seems as if it is not enough any more to be a star, to be great, or to have a mere hit. Hyperbole ends up cheapening the currency of language, inflating claims and devaluing more moderate language.

FALLACIES ASSOCIATED WITH REBUTTALS

The rebuttal to an argument is an exception to or refutation of an argument. It too can be flawed. Fallacies of rebuttal can occur when a speaker misanalyzes an opponent's argument or sidesteps the other side of the issue completely.

Straw Person

The **straw person** fallacy occurs when someone attempts to refute a claim by misstating the argument being refuted. Rather than refuting the real argument, the other side constructs a person of straw, which is easy to knock down.

In Chapter 7 we told you about the San Francisco radio talk show host, Ronn Owens, who was accused of saying on the air that we should bomb Afghanistan into the Stone Age. Owens was attacked for that position, and he was forced to explain both on the air and on his Web site that he had never made such a statement. It's easy to argue against something when it isn't the real position of your opponent. No responsible person advocated indiscriminate bombing of innocent civilians to retaliate for terrorist attacks on the United States. Owens, along with millions of Americans, believed we needed to take military action to respond to the attacks, not simply kill everyone we could. If a person was opposed to that viewpoint, he or she had every right to disagree. But to misstate what Owens said was to attack a straw person, not engage the real issue.

Be wary of rebuttals that seem too easy. It may be that the other side of the argument has been misstated just to make it easy to refute.

Ignoring the Issue

The fallacy of **ignoring the issue** occurs when the claim made by one side in an argument is ignored by the other. For example, imagine that you are speaking before a group about the effects of the depletion of the ozone layer on the environment. Skin cancer death rates will increase, you argue. We need to change over to safer refrigerants in our cars. Suppose someone attempts to rebut your argument by saying that environmental extremists have killed loggers by spiking trees. This rebuttal is simply not responsive to the argument you have posed. In short, the issue you have presented has been ignored, and the rebuttalist has shifted ground to another issue entirely.

THE NON SEQUITUR: AN ARGUMENT THAT DOES NOT FOLLOW

Up until now, we've looked at each component of an argument as a separate source of fallacies. Of course, you also have to look at the argument as a whole. Even if the grounds are true, the warrant believable, and so on, if the argument doesn't hang together logically, it is still fallacious. Thus, the final fallacy of reasoning we examine is the non sequitur.

A **non sequitur** is an argument that does not follow from its premises. In Toulmin's terms, there is no logical connection between the claim and the grounds and warrant used to support the claim. Consider the example of a person who called in this opinion to a local newspaper:

> **No wonder welfare is so popular**
> I'd like to thank the person who dropped the two little black lab-mix puppies off at the golf course some time in the week of Jan. 28. What irresponsible person caused others to try to find homes for these dogs? It's amazing people don't take responsibility for their actions and cause other people to. No wonder everybody's on welfare.[8]

Aside from stereotyping people on welfare as irresponsible and hyperbolizing in claiming that "everybody's on welfare," this argument has absolutely no link between its grounds—the two dogs abandoned at the golf course—and its claim—that this irresponsibility is symptomatic of people on welfare.

We have discussed numerous fallacies in this chapter. To review them, see the box "Defects of Reasoning: The Fallacies."

Defects of Reasoning: The Fallacies

FALLACIES ASSOCIATED WITH GROUNDS

unsupported assertion: The absence of any argument at all.

distorted evidence: Significant omissions or changes in the grounds of an argument that alter its original intent.

isolated examples: Nontypical or nonrepresentative examples that are used to prove a general claim.

misused statistics: Statistics that involve errors such as poor sampling, lack of significant differences, misuse of average, or misuse of percentages.

FALLACIES ASSOCIATED WITH CLAIMS

red herring (smoke screen): An irrelevant issue introduced into a controversy to divert attention from the real controversy.

arguing in a circle (begging the question): An argument that proves nothing because the claim to be proved is used as the grounds or warrant for the argument.

FALLACIES ASSOCIATED WITH GENERALIZATION WARRANTS

hasty generalization: An argument that occurs when there are too few instances to support a generalization or the instances are unrepresentative of the generalization.

stereotyping: The assumption that what is considered to be true of a larger class is necessarily true of particular members of that class.

false dilemma: A generalization that implies there are only two choices when there are more than two.

FALLACY ASSOCIATED WITH COMPARISON (ANALOGY) WARRANTS

false analogy: The comparison of two different things that are not really comparable.

FALLACIES ASSOCIATED WITH CAUSAL WARRANTS

post hoc, ergo propter hoc ("after the fact, therefore because of the fact"): The assumption that because one event preceded another, the first event must be the cause of the second event.

slippery slope: The assumption that just because one event occurs, it will automatically lead to a series of undesirable events even though there is no relationship between the action and the projected events.

FALLACY ASSOCIATED WITH SIGN WARRANTS

mistaking correlation for cause: The assumption that because one thing is the sign of another, they are causally related.

FALLACIES ASSOCIATED WITH AUTHORITY WARRANTS

halo effect: The assumption that just because you like or respect a person, whatever he or she says must be true.

ad hominem: The claim that something must be false because the person who said it is not credible, regardless of the argument itself.

FALLACIES ASSOCIATED WITH QUALIFIERS

loaded language: Language that has strong emotional connotations.

hyperbole: An exaggeration of a claim.

FALLACIES ASSOCIATED WITH REBUTTALS

straw person: An argument made in refutation that misstates the argument being refuted. Rather than refuting the real argument, the other side constructs a person of straw, which is easy to knock down.

ignoring the issue: An argument made in refutation that ignores the claim made by the other side.

ADDITIONAL FALLACY

non sequitur: An argument that does not follow from its premises.

SUMMARY

 **SPEECH COACH**

To evaluate your understanding of this chapter, see the Quizzes on your CD.

Reasoning and critical thinking are important both in constructing good arguments and in listening to the arguments of others.

Pseudoreasoning involves arguments that may appear sound at first glance but ultimately contain a fallacy of reasoning.

Argumentativeness is the trait of arguing for and against the positions taken on controversial claims.

Verbal aggressiveness is the trait of attacking the self-concept of those with whom a person disagrees about controversial claims.

Grounds for an argument consist of evidence supporting a claim, such as:

- examples
- facts
- statistics
- expert opinion
- explanation
- description
- narratives

Fallacies associated with defective grounds are:

- unsupported assertions
- distorted evidence
- isolated examples
- misused statistics

Claims of fact, value, or policy may contain the following fallacies:

- the red herring
- arguing in a circle

Warrants link grounds and claims by means of:

- generalization
- comparison
- cause
- sign
- authority

Backing is support for the warrant and is especially important in cases in which the audience is either unfamiliar with the warrant or unconvinced of its truth.

Fallacies associated with generalization warrants include:

- hasty generalization
- stereotyping
- false dilemmas

The fallacy associated with comparison warrants is:

- the false analogy

Fallacies associated with causation warrants are:

- post hoc, ergo propter hoc
- slippery slope

The fallacy associated with sign warrants is:

- mistaking correlation for cause

Fallacies associated with authority warrants are:

- the halo effect
- ad hominem

Qualifiers are an indication of the level of probability of the claim. Fallacies associated with qualifiers are:

- loaded language
- hyperbole

A rebuttal is an exception to or refutation of an argument. Fallacies associated with rebuttals are:

- straw person
- ignoring the issue

The non sequitur is a fallacy that occurs when an argument does not follow from its premises.

CHECK YOUR UNDERSTANDING: EXERCISES AND ACTIVITIES

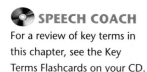 **SPEECH COACH**

For a review of key terms in this chapter, see the Key Terms Flashcards on your CD.

1. Find a published argument, such as a letter to the editor, an advertisement, an editorial, or a political ad. Identify the claim being made and the grounds on which the claim is based. Is the warrant explicitly stated? If not, determine the implied warrant. What backing, if any, is offered for the warrant? Is the argument adequately qualified? Are there possible rebuttals to the argument?

2. Find an example of each of the following types of arguments in a publication: cause to effect, effect to cause, sign, comparison, establishing a generalization, applying a generalization, authority. Which of these arguments is the strongest, logically, and which is the weakest? Explain your answer in terms of the tests of reasoning outlined in this chapter.

3. Pick an advertisement from any print medium—for example, magazines, newspapers, or direct mail. In a brief paper, identify at least three fallacies used in the advertisement. Define each fallacy in your own words. Cite the specific example of each fallacy from the ad, and explain why the example meets the definition. Finally, highlight the fallacies on a copy of the ad and attach the copy to your paper.

4. Analyze the arguments for and against drug testing and the drug war as presented by Miranda Welsh and David Sanders in this chapter. Which argument is logically the stronger? Which contains more fallacies? Which do you find more persuasive?

NOTES

1. Brooke Noel Moore and Richard Parker, *Critical Thinking,* 5th ed. (Mountain View, Calif.: Mayfield, 1998), 476.
2. Dominic A. Infante, *Arguing Constructively* (Prospect Heights, Ill.: Waveland Press, 1988).

3. Stephen Toulmin, Richard Rieke, and Allan Janik, *An Introduction to Reasoning*, 2nd ed. (New York: Macmillan, 1984).

4. Toulmin originally termed this the *qualifier* but added the term *modality* in his later works. We prefer the simpler term, *qualifier*, which is what we will use in this book.

5. "Tell It to the ER," *Chico Enterprise Record*, 13 March 1992, 2A. Reprinted by permission.

6. "Facts and Fantasy," *Newsweek*, 11 July 1994, 6.

7. "Facts and Fantasy," 6.

8. "Tell It to the ER," *Chico Enterprise Record*, 16 February 1992, 2A. Reprinted by permission.

ANSWERS TO "SELF-ASSESSMENT: UNCRITICAL INFERENCE TEST"

1. ?   Do you know that the "businessman" and the "owner" are one and the same?
2. ?   Was there necessarily a robbery involved here? Perhaps the man was the rent collector—or the owner's son. Either might demand money.
3. F   An easy one to keep up the test-taker's morale.
4. ?   Was the owner a man?
5. ?   May seem unlikely, but the story does not definitely preclude it.
6. T   The story says that the owner opened the cash register.
7. ?   We don't know who scooped up the contents of the cash register or that the man necessarily ran away.
8. ?   The dependent clause is doubtful—the cash register may or may not have contained money.
9. ?   Again, a robber?
10. ?   Could the man merely have appeared at a door or a window without actually entering the store?
11. ?   Stores generally keep lights on during the day.
12. ?   Could not the man who appeared have been the owner?
13. F   The story says that the man who appeared demanded money.
14. ?   Are the businessman and the owner one and the same—or two different people? The same goes for the owner and the man who appeared.
15. ?   "Dashed"? Could he not have "sped away" on roller skates or in a car? And do we know that he actually left the store? We don't even know that he entered it.

A wedding toast is a common public speaking event that almost everyone faces at some time.

CHAPTER 15

Speaking Across the Life Span

OBJECTIVES

After reading this chapter and reviewing the learning resources on your CD-ROM and at the Online Learning Center, you should be able to:

- Make an effective impromptu presentation.
- Lead or participate in a small group and a panel discussion.
- Present a speech of introduction.
- Present or accept an award.
- Make a speech of commemoration.
- Make a speech to entertain.
- Be interviewed on television.

You've been giving your attention to a turkey stuffed with sage; you are now about to consider a sage stuffed with turkey.

—WILLIAM MAXWELL EVARTS (1818–1901), American statesman, speaking after a Thanksgiving dinner[1]

KEY CONCEPTS

agenda	reframing	speech of introduction
eulogy	speech of acceptance	speech of recognition
group	speech of	speech to entertain
panel discussion	commemoration	

In Chapter 3 we mentioned that approximately 40 percent of all adults report that their greatest fear is giving a public speech. Perhaps it is not too surprising to learn, then, that fully 97 percent of Americans fear presenting a wedding toast! The reasons offered by the people surveyed include but are not limited to: (1) forgetting what to say, (2) being too emotional, (3) being boring, and (4) unintentionally saying something that is perceived as offensive. In response to this survey, Korbel Champagne Cellars, a California winery, established a hotline for people to call to learn tips about the do's and don'ts of wedding toasting (see the box "The Wedding Toast"). In its first three years of operation the hotline received 22,000 calls.[2] It became so popular, in fact, Korbel had to abandon it. The hotline was taking too much time away from more pressing business.

This chapter focuses on both the predictable and occasionally special situations in which you will be required to speak over the course of your life. These situations include impromptu speaking, sometimes leading group discussions, participating in informative panel discussions, saying thank you when you've been singled out for recognition, introducing someone who is being honored or who is the principal speaker of the occasion, and speaking to commemorate an occasion of celebration or solemnity. We begin by talking about reframing your perspective about speaking in situations both everyday and special.

REFRAMING: SPEAKING AS STORYTELLING

The late Senator Robert F. Kennedy was fond of paraphrasing Irish playwright George Bernard Shaw by saying, "Some people see things as they are and say: why? I dream things that never were and say: why not?"[3] This familiar quotation eloquently alludes to the importance of perspective in analyzing and responding to circumstance. This kind of behavior can be thought of in terms of **reframing**—revising your view of a situation or an event. Recall that the degree to which you are anxious about a speaking transaction depends on how you view it. As we said early on in this book, looking at a speech as a performance is likely to make you more anxious than looking at a speech as a natural but refined extension of your everyday communication skills.

reframing Revising your view of a situation or an event, usually in a positive direction.

One effective way to reframe your point of view about the kind of speaking this chapter describes is to think of it as a form of storytelling. Although you probably gave few "speeches" prior to taking this class, chances are good that you told innumerable stories. Good stories share a similar organizational sequence with good speeches. An involving story hooks an audience with its introduction, builds to a climax either humorous or dramatic, and concludes with a memorable resolution to the climax.

Rhetorical scholar Walter R. Fisher argues that storytelling is not only an effective way to involve an audience but also an effective way to share a message.[4] Former President Ronald Reagan frequently conveyed the point he was attempting to make through storytelling. Many pundits in the media, moreover, attribute much of his reputation as an effective communicator to his ability to weave an involving and convincing story.[5]

Storytelling needn't be long-winded nor overly complicated. To the contrary, many of the best stories are short and to the point. Effective stories or narratives share two common elements, as we first discussed in Chapter 7: *probability* and *fidelity*.

The Wedding Toast

Here are some tips offered by the Korbel Wedding Toast Hotline for nervous toasters:

1. Remember why you are being asked to give the toast.
2. Make sure your toast is something everyone can relate to.
3. Jokes, humor, and anecdotes are great ways to enliven a toast.
4. Try to know your material well enough so that you do not need your note cards.
5. Speak loudly enough so everyone can hear you.
6. Make your toast with your own personal style.
7. Remember, people will not be judging you as they might if you were giving a business presentation.
8. Toasts should be kept short and sweet.
9. When preparing your toast, sometimes it helps to look through old photographs or letters.
10. When delivering a wedding toast, make sure to stand and indicate the couple you are toasting.

Source: Adapted from Korbel Wedding Toast Hotline Web site, http://korbel.com/trade.html#source

Probability

The property of storytelling termed probability is straightforward. Narrative probability is the internal coherence of the story. Coherence concerns the degree to which the structure of the story holds up in the eyes of an audience. Does the story make sense as told? Do the parts of the story hang together? Effective stories are logically consistent in structure, even if the content of the story requires that we suspend disbelief, as is the case with fairy tales and some science fiction. Did you know that Mark Twain, for example, was a gifted public speaker as well as writer? He could tell even the most improbable story in such a way that what he was suggesting seemed completely plausible. What's more, this was true whether he was talking about the exaggerated athleticism of a jumping frog in the gold fields of California or transporting a Connecticut man back into the time of King Arthur's court.

Fidelity

The second property of effective storytelling—fidelity—concerns truthfulness. We are predisposed to believe stories whose messages ring true with our own experience. Depending on the occasion, you probably share a lot in common with your audience, from being friends of the bride and groom at a wedding to sharing the sorrow of family members when giving a eulogy. You can draw on these commonalities to increase the narrative fidelity of your stories, whether they grow out of your individual experience or experiences with which most of your audience can relate.

It can be helpful to approach a speech task such as thanking people or making an introduction as a form of storytelling. Audiences relate well to recognition speeches and the like when they are told as a story. Remember, though, that to be effective your speech and the story it tells must meet the tests of probability and fidelity. This framework sets the stage for preparing to meet head-on the predictable situations in which you will be expected to speak both now and in your future. Because these situations vary tremendously in the degree to which you'll be able to prepare, let's look first at the type of speaking where you'll have little or no time to gather your thoughts and supporting material.

IMPROMPTU SPEECHES: SPEAKING WITHOUT ADVANCE NOTICE

There will be times in your life when you will be asked to speak without specific, advance notice. Recall from Chapter 2 that such unrehearsed speeches are called impromptu. You may be asked to make an unanticipated toast or say a few words at a wedding, bar or bat mitzvah, or christening. Or you may be asked to defend or argue against the position of a colleague at work. Finally, you simply may be asked to explain yourself to a superior or agency to which you are accountable.

First Things First: Anticipate the Occasion

If you read Stephen J. Covey's book *The Seven Habits of Highly Effective People*, you'll learn that being unprepared isn't one of them.[6] Frankly, there are situations where the probability of your being asked to speak ranges from low to high. No one knows better than you the chances that you'll be asked to say a few words at a social occasion or in a professional setting. Forewarned is forearmed. Thus, if there is even the slightest chance you'll be asked to speak, you should prepare in advance. Does this mean that you should write out a speech? Not really. What we are talking about here is anticipating what you might be asked to say based on the context in which you'll find yourself. This will, at the very least, enable you to mentally and visually rehearse your response. Should you not be asked to speak as you'd anticipated, you'll only be better prepared for the next time one of these occasions to speak pops up.

Tips for Impromptu Speaking

If you were to participate in impromptu speaking at a collegiate speech tournament, this is what would typically happen. You would be handed a slip of paper with three topics on it. The topics might be general and abstract, such as the quotation we cited from Robert F. Kennedy, or an issue widely reported in the media. You would be given two minutes to prepare and five minutes to speak on the one topic you selected.

If this sounds frightening, then consider this: There may be times during your life when you don't even get two minutes to prepare, much less choose your topic from a choice of three. To assist you in adapting to such truly impromptu situations, we offer the following guidelines.

Get Organized The thing that impresses people the most about people who speak effectively off-the-cuff is the appearance of organization. Whether you are responding to the query of an instructor or speaking to an issue being debated at work, the first thing you want to do is get organized. One of the easiest and most effective patterns for organizing an impromptu speech is to (1) introduce the point(s) you want to make, (2) expand on the point(s) you make, and (3) conclude with a statement that summarizes the point(s) made. This harks back to the "tell 'em what you're going to tell 'em, tell 'em, and then tell 'em what you told 'em" sequence introduced in Chapter 8. Consider a classroom example, in which the instructor asks, "What's your take on the effects of rap lyrics on violence?" One student responds: "I have two points to make . . . about the effects of rap. First, the effects are exaggerated. Second, most people who think rap affects violence are clueless about modern music. So what I'm saying is they're making a mountain out of another molehill." Notice in this example that the first sentence not only previews the points being made but also restates in modified form the question asked. The two points are made and then summarized in the final sentence. Compare this response with another hypothetical but not atypical one from a student: "I don't know . . . I guess I disagree. It's just a bunch of people who are out of it coming down on alternative music. Get a life, you know?" This second response is both disorganized and equivocal, bringing us to our second guideline.

Take a Position   Few of us are favorably impressed with people who fail to take a stand, who equivocate even as they're trying to build a response to a query. When someone asks a speaker, "What's your opinion or your position?" we think the speaker is obligated to give it. On the other hand, if a speaker has not yet formulated a clear-cut opinion, an audience would much rather hear the person say "I'm ambivalent" or "I'll need more information than I've been given" than hem and haw in response to such a query.

Use Powerful Language   Powerful language goes hand in hand with the first two guidelines. Organization is key to appearing powerful. We expect powerful people not to equivocate, to take a stand even if it is clearly one of neutrality. For example, sometimes a person may say simply, "That is really none of my business. It is for the people directly affected to decide for themselves." Recall that powerful language avoids the use of unnecessary qualifiers and long questions. Powerful people say such things as "My opinion is firm" or "My experience leads me to the unequivocal belief. . . ." Powerful people do not say, "I could be wrong but I think . . ." or "I believe it's okay, do you?" Impromptu speaking is tough enough without undermining your authority with powerless language.

Hitchhike   It's sometimes effective to begin an impromptu message with what others have already said on the matter. This hitchhiking technique shows that you have been actively listening. It also acknowledges the contributions of others, even if you disagree with what they've said. For example, "Bill's point that this situation demands caution is well taken, but I must respectfully disagree for a couple of reasons." You also might say, "Let me summarize what's been said thus far, and then I'll add my two cents worth." Again, this kind of bridge tells your audience you are tuned in *and* organized.

Use Stories and Anecdotes   If you know a story or an anecdote that contains a lesson that is both relevant and straightforward, by all means use it as a basis for your impromptu speech. History is full of examples of stories and anecdotes about the famous and notorious. Organizational culture, moreover, often gives rise to stories about people and events that can be used to make one or more points in an impromptu speech. Some stories and anecdotes are so general they can be applied to almost any point you choose to make. The real power of Aesop's fables, for instance, is that each contains multiple lessons you can apply to life.

Invest in Reference Works   Impromptu speaking is a matter of when, not if. Thus, we recommend you purchase for your personal and permanent library at least two kinds of reference books, in addition to a standard book of quotations such as *Bartlett's*. First, look for one composed of contemporary quotes from well-known and widely recognized people. At the same time, invest in a book of anecdotes compiled from the lives of the famous and notorious. Then find and commit to memory quotes and anecdotes that can be applied generally to topics and issues you may be asked to speak about. Although these tips are meant to help you most with impromptu speaking situations, they can be easily generalized to everyday situations where you know for certain that you will be speaking, and situations where there is a high probability that you will be speaking.

LEADING AND PARTICIPATING IN SMALL GROUPS

group Three or more individuals who are aware of each other's presence, share a mutually interdependent purpose, engage in communication transactions with one another, and identify with the group.

Besides impromptu speaking, you will probably speak in numerous group discussions in both your educational and professional careers. A **group** consists of three or more individuals who are aware of each other's presence, share a mutually interdependent purpose, engage in communication transactions with one another, and identify with the group. As a leader of a group, you are also the chief spokesperson. As such, there are several important functions you will be asked to perform. Although we cannot introduce you to all of these functions here, we want to alert you to those most relevant to the main topic and scope of this book.

Leadership Functions

As you attempt to lead a group, there are a number of functions that you need to perform yourself or delegate to someone in the group: These include but are not limited to developing an agenda, keeping the discussion on track, asking questions to promote discussion, summarizing and transitioning to other points, and setting the agenda for the next meeting.

agenda Something that defines the purpose and direction a group takes, the topics to be covered, and the goals to be achieved.

Developing an Agenda   A group without an agenda is one that will likely flounder. The **agenda** defines the purpose and direction the group takes, the topics to be covered, and the goals to be achieved. A sound agenda is every bit as important to a group's success as sound organization is to a speech's success. For example, suppose you are dealing with the problem of crime on your campus. Each person in the group can be assigned to gather some information prior to the meeting. Then, you might meet with an agenda such as the following:

I.   What is the crime rate on our campus? What specific crimes occur and how often?

II.   What percentage of crime in our city is committed by college students? What types of crimes are committed against college students?

III.   What steps have been taken on campus to reduce crime?

IV.   How do our campus crime rates compare with national statistics?

V.   What conclusions can we draw? Is crime "under control" on our campus? Do we need to make changes to reduce crime?

VI.   Set agenda for next meeting.

To be effective, small groups need leadership and active participation by all members.

Keeping the Discussion on Track   Although "off-topic" discussions can sometimes be productive, more often than not they are a diversion from the real issues at hand. Particularly disruptive are "ain't it awful" tangents, where everybody in the group shares their complaints—about the task, the boss, or whatever. These complaints may have their place, but they are unlikely to help the group get the job done. Most group members are reluctant to criticize their peers as being off the subject, and it is usually the leader who has to bring the group back on track. A tactful suggestion that "maybe we're straying from the topic" or a question that refocuses the group on the subject is usually enough to get things back on task. Even a little humorous reminder that the group has wandered can do wonders.

Asking Questions to Promote Discussion   There are many types of questions a designated leader (or any member, for that matter) can ask. Four of the most important types of questions are questions asking for information, those asking for interpretation, those asking for suggestions, and questions about procedure. A *question of information*, for example, might be to ask, "What is the average crime rate for colleges our size?" Such a question requires a factually based response. A *question of interpretation* might be, "Do students really feel safe on our campus?" This question is not one that can be answered simply by reading off statistics. It calls for group members to form conclusions based on the information they've gathered, as well as to add their own subjective interpretation of the information. The third type of question, *asking for suggestions*, might be, "What can we do to reduce crime on this campus?" This question calls for ideas from group members aimed at solving a problem the group has identified. Finally, a *procedural question* might be asked of the group, "Do we want to brainstorm possible solutions?" This question asks the group if they want to follow a certain procedure. All four types of questions are important if a group is to achieve its goals.

Summarizing and Transitioning to Other Points As we pointed out regarding your speeches, summaries and transitional devices such as signposts are highly functional. At some point it will become apparent that the group is moving in some direction. Although not everyone may agree on every point, as the leader you can try to summarize those points on which everyone agrees, thus defining which issues need further exploration. For example, you might say: "It seems that we all agree that there's a serious crime problem on our campus. Furthermore, it looks like assault and theft are the biggest problems. What we need to figure out is why these problems are getting worse and if there's anything we can do about them. Any ideas?"

Setting the Agenda for the Next Meeting Assuming the group's task has not been completed, the next action is to agree on time and place and agenda items for the next meeting. Particularly important is making sure members know what their individual responsibilities are prior to the next meeting. One of the great advantages of groups is that tasks can be subdivided. But that works only if everyone does what is agreed upon.

Panel Discussions

panel discussion An extemporaneous group discussion held for the benefit of an audience.

A **panel discussion** is an extemporaneous group discussion held for the benefit of an audience. In a panel discussion, as in a speech, it is important that the group have a clear outline of the topics to be covered, and that members are adequately prepared. The advantage of a panel discussion is that it is a blend of preparation and spontaneity. Members should feel free to comment on one another's points, ask questions, and openly discuss points throughout the presentation.

A panel discussion requires a leader to act as the *moderator* of the presentation. The moderator calls on members and keeps the discussion on track. Members who want to comment on another member's statement should wait to be recognized by the moderator. A panel discussion is more formal than a normal private group discussion.

Most panel discussions also provide an opportunity for audience members to ask questions. This can occur as the group moves through its outline or can be held as a *forum* period at the end of the panel presentation.

The outline for a panel discussion is similar to that of a speech; however, some modifications need to be made. The following would be an example of a panel discussion outline on the topic of secondhand smoke:

I. Introduction of topic and group members.

II. Is secondhand tobacco smoke harmful?

III. What is being done to limit exposure to secondhand smoke?

IV. What is causing these efforts to fall short?

V. Recommendations for new regulations on smoking in public places.

Ideally, each member should be able to offer comments on each of these topics, rather than having one member prepared on each topic. A panel discussion should be a true discussion, not a series of individual presentations.

Emma Thompson's brief but eloquent thanks for her best actress Oscar is a model for a gracious speech of acceptance.

SPEAKING ON SPECIAL OCCASIONS

Speaking at special occasions may be less common than speaking in groups, but it is still likely during the course of your life. At such times your job will be to emphasize the special nature of the occasion in thought, word, and deed. Most of the time, you will be able to prepare and practice in advance of such situations. Other times, you may be asked, in impromptu fashion, to "say a few words." The special occasions you can anticipate speaking at over the course of your life include: expressing thanks; introducing a speaker or an honored guest; speaking in recognition of a person, group, or organization; making a commemorative speech; and speaking to entertain people.

Speech of Acceptance

A **speech of acceptance** is a speech expressing thanks for an award or honor. Consider Emma Thompson's speech of acceptance at the 1993 Academy Awards ceremony. She said: "Ladies and gentlemen, I really don't know how to thank the Academy for this [holding the Oscar], but also for this view. It's overwhelming to see so many faces of people who have entertained me all my life. It takes my breath away."[7]

In connecting with her audience, Thompson combines the principles of reciprocity and liking to create a favorable impression. Not only does she thank

speech of acceptance A speech expressing thanks for an award or honor.

the Academy for the award, but for her view as well. In the process she tells members of the audience they have been giving something to her she can't repay: a life's worth of entertainment. Research shows that we have a tough time not liking people who like us—for example, people who sincerely flatter us. Thompson's thank-you speech, then, is a model you may want to follow in patterning your own. In the span of three sentences it shows that a good speech of acceptance (1) is brief, (2) is genuine, (3) reciprocates for the award or praise given, and (4) attempts to engender liking. This is not to say that all speeches of acceptance must be as brief as this speech. Thompson's thank you at the Golden Globe Awards ceremony the same year was much longer, yet it did not exceed the audience's patience.

Speech of Introduction

speech of introduction A speech that briefly sets the stage for an upcoming speaker.

A **speech of introduction** is a speech that briefly sets the stage for an upcoming speaker. Speeches of introduction are designed to meet two objectives. The first is to enlist the audience's attention and interest. The second objective is to reinforce or induce audience perceptions of credibility. Perhaps the most unusual speech of introduction we have heard recently was in 1998 when James Carville and Mary Matalin, a married couple who represent the liberal and conservative ends of the political spectrum, debated each other at our university. They were supposed to be introduced by a graduate of our university, political consultant Ed Rollins. However, he was unable to attend. So Carville, in what appeared to be an impromptu speech, introduced his own wife and adversary for the evening, praising her as "my best friend, and the best wife any man could have."[8] His introduction set the stage for a spirited and entertaining debate between the oddest of couples in contemporary American politics.

Although you may never introduce your own opponent in a debate, it is likely that at some time you will be called on to introduce a speaker to an audience. Usually, the audience is favorably disposed toward the speaker or they wouldn't be there. However, sometimes a speaker is not well known and needs a buildup of credibility before the speech. In any case, a good way to look at a speech of introduction is to remember the three basic principles of introducing any speech: Open with impact, connect with the audience, and focus on the upcoming presentation.

Open With Impact   Your first task as an introducer is to build enthusiasm for the main speaker. A lukewarm or trite introduction is worse than none at all. Thus, look for a way to capture the audience's attention immediately. Sometimes humor, a brief anecdote, or a moving story will fill the bill.

Connect With the Audience   Why should the audience listen to the speaker? What's in it for them? Just as you must connect with the audience in your own speeches, the same is true in a speech of introduction. What special qualifications does the speaker have? Why is the topic of special concern to the audience? Answer these questions in terms the audience can relate to if you want them to be motivated to listen. Focus on the speaker's competence and character. Even if a speaker's credibility is established, you should reinforce the perception by mentioning one or two examples that clearly emphasize competence and character. If the speaker's credibility has yet to be established, mention at least one thing that addresses the speaker's competence on the topic and one that addresses the speaker's good character.

Focus on the Upcoming Presentation   Finally, it is the introducer's task to focus the audience's attention on the upcoming presentation. Make sure you know the speaker's topic, and coordinate your introduction with his or her speech. Nothing is worse than preparing an audience to hear a speech on one topic only to have the speaker announce that the topic has been changed. There are also some general guidelines that you should follow for a speech of introduction.

Guidelines for a Speech of Introduction   **TIPS AND TACTICS**

- *Be brief.* The audience came to hear the speaker, not the introducer. A one- or two-minute introduction is sufficient for most speech situations. For a particularly lengthy or formal speech situation, the introduction might be longer, but in no case should it exceed about 10 percent of the speaker's time (six minutes out of an hour, for example).
- *Don't steal the speaker's thunder.* Although you want to prepare the audience for what is to come by focusing their attention on the topic, you should not discuss the substance of the speech topic. Again, the audience wants to hear the speaker's views on the topic, not yours. Your job is to create an appetite for the upcoming main course, not fill up the audience with hors d'oeuvres.
- *Be prepared: Work with the speaker in advance.* It is best to talk to the speaker or a representative about your role as introducer. Are there specific points to be stressed? Is there anything the speaker wants to avoid? Some speakers may even want to preview your introductory remarks or may provide written suggestions for you.

Speech of Recognition

The elements of a good speech of introduction also apply to speeches of recognition. A **speech of recognition** is a speech presenting an award or honor to an individual. Open your recognition speech by discussing the importance of the occasion, the award being made, or the special contribution made by the honoree. Provide examples or testimony from those who know the honoree to illustrate his or her merit. Also, consider couching your speech in the form of a story about the person.

speech of recognition A speech presenting an award or honor to an individual.

Connect with your audience. Give them a personal glimpse, either from your own experience or from testimony of those who know the honoree. It is important for your audience to feel that the award is, in a sense, coming from them.

Unless the name of the honoree is known in advance, it should be saved until the end of the recognition speech. Not only will this build suspense, audience members will start to guess at the honoree with each new bit of information you provide. As you conclude, focus on the honoree by name. Usually a recognition speech ends with something like this, "And so it is my great pleasure to announce the winner of the lifetime achievement award, our own Taylor Smith!"

Earl Spencer's moving eulogy for his sister, Diana, Princess of Wales, was seen throughout the world.

Speech of Commemoration

speech of commemoration
A speech that calls attention to the stature of the person or people being honored, or emphasizes the significance of an occasion.

A **speech of commemoration** is a speech that calls attention to the stature of the person or people being honored, or emphasizes the significance of an occasion. There are several kinds of commemorative speeches. Some of these speeches focus on cause for celebration, for example, a national holiday or a 50th wedding anniversary. Remember, it is the occasion or people who have given cause for celebration that should be the focus of your speech.

Another type of speech of commemoration is one given to memorialize a specific person (Martin Luther King, Jr.) or the people we associate with a special and solemn occasion (members of the armed forces on Memorial Day). Finally, a **eulogy** is a kind of commemorative speech about someone who has died that is usually given shortly after his or her death. For example, when Earl Spencer eulogized his sister, Diana, Princess of Wales, he spoke lovingly of her as "the very essence of compassion, of duty, of style, of beauty. All over the world she was a symbol of selfless humanity, a standard-bearer for the rights of the downtrodden, a very British girl who transcended nationality, someone with a natural nobility who was classless, who proved in the last year that she needed no royal title to continue to generate her particular brand of magic."[9]

eulogy A kind of commemorative speech about someone who has died that is usually given shortly after his or her death.

In many ways, a speech of commemoration is like an extended recognition speech. With the obvious exception of a eulogy, the honoree may even be present and be asked to say a few words after the commemoration. Sometimes these speeches take a humorous form, such as a "roast." Although jokes and embarrassing incidents are recited, they are done in good fun and ultimately the honoree is praised for his or her accomplishments.

A speech of commemoration should, like any other speech, open with impact. Begin by calling attention to the stature of the person being honored or the occasion that necessitates the memorial.

As with any speech, it is important to connect with the audience. What ties the audience and the person, people, and occasion together? A eulogy often recounts the deceased's common ties to the audience. Family and friends are usually present, and recounting memorable events from the life of the deceased helps everyone cope with their loss.

For the honoree, focus on the best that person has accomplished. For a retiree, it might be his or her accomplishments in the workforce. For a public figure, it might be what he or she stood for. For a fallen hero, the heroic deeds that cost a life are a source of meaning.

The substance of a speech of commemoration is usually less structured than that of other speeches. Nevertheless, there should be a theme or an essential point that you want to share with the audience. For example, in Jeraline Singh's high school graduation speech (see the box "America!"), she emphasizes throughout her belief that living in the United States is a gift and should be viewed as such. Speaking as someone who immigrated from Fiji, she shares her experiences in a way that uplifted her classmates.

Finally, a speech of commemoration should close with impact, leaving a lasting impression. A verse of scripture might provide just the right note to close a eulogy. Jeraline Singh used an anonymous quote to close her graduation speech.

Speeches to Entertain[10]

Sometimes known as after-dinner speaking because it's frequently given following a meal, a speech to entertain is more than just a string of jokes or a comedy monologue. A **speech to entertain** is a speech that makes its point through the use of humor. Like all speeches, a speech to entertain should have a clear focus. Of course, many speeches contain humor as an element. What makes the speech to entertain different is that its primary purpose is to bring laughter to the audience, not to persuade or inform them, though that may occur along the way. A speech meant to entertain is ideally suited to the storytelling format of speaking. This type of speech also is every bit as taxing as persuasive or informative speaking.

speech to entertain A speech that makes its point through the use of humor.

Selecting a Topic   The first task is to select a topic for your speech to entertain. The best place to begin is with yourself. Have you had experiences that, at least looking back, were funny? A good topic needs to have the potential to develop into a full-blown speech, not just one or two good punch lines. It needs to be something your audience can relate to. Many of the funniest speeches are about the frustrations of everyday life. Avoid the temptation to adopt the latest *Saturday Night Live* routine. Work from your own experiences and from experiences shared by those in your audience.

Consider your audience's expectations for the speech. You probably don't want to repeat stories you know your audience has heard before. If you are speaking to a group of lawyers, you probably can count on their having heard every lawyer joke known to humankind. Pick something that can connect

America! *by Jeraline Singh*

If you know anything about me, you would know that February 14, 1987, was a very special day for me. If you do not know why it is special, that's fine. It was the day that I came to America. And it will always be the greatest day of my life.

On my first day as a freshman, the one thing that I told everyone was how proud I am to be an American, and to this day, I am still saying it with the same passion if not more. I am hoping that all those hours I spent preaching sunk into some of you and today you sit in your chairs and are proud to be in America.

I have spent the majority of my life in America, but unlike many of you out there, I have spent some years away from America. Because of these experiences I truly can say that America is the greatest nation in the world. I know that I can give you all the reasons to be proud of being an American, but your mind is set. The teachers in this school learned the hard way; changing a teenager's mind is like changing the beginning of the world. So, I will not waste my time (or yours) telling you something that you already know—but will not admit because it is not popular belief.

For those of you out there who love America, but will not say so because you are afraid of being an outcast, let me tell you something. I have lived my life as an outcast, and I would rather live that way than not be able to express my true feelings for the greatest nation in the world. I want you to remember that the next time a war breaks in the Middle East or Bosnia, the next time a person comes into office when the people did not vote him in, or the next time you walk down the street and make it back home safe with all your limbs, that you are free in America.

So, you ask, what does being an American have to do with the rest of your lives? Whether it be in a four-year university, junior college, the armed forces, or the workforce, you will always be an American and because of that you are one of the few in the world who got to choose the path you take in life.

Prepare well for the rest of your life. Be confident enough for yourself so that you may someday help another get the confidence you have. I was lucky in high school because SIFE (Students in Free Enterprise) and Butte College Connection gave me that confidence I needed this past year. For the past three years, Upward Bound helped me as well (so that I knew what I wanted in life and helped me realize that the simple things in life are the ones worth fighting for the most). I remember that I learned who I really am by talking to Mr. Steve Ladrech. I know that all of us out there thank the teachers who got us interested in computers: My teacher would be Mr. Michael Bertsch and the teachers of Chico High West. I recommend to all of you, if you have someone special who changed your life, tell them before it is too late.

Next year, when most of our support bonds will be gone, what can we do so that we move up instead of down in life? I would recommend you do something for someone else. Mentor a child in your college town, or help an organization like the American Red Cross or do something as simple as donating blood. Remember the younger generation will follow in our footsteps.

The transition that we had from our first day at Chico High School to our last day was a very hard one for our class. We lost idols, heroes, and a princess along with classmates who we adored and admired, went through major floods and El Niño, and we had our last laugh with Seinfeld and the gang. But through strong ties with Chico High we made it through, and we thank all the Gods for that, along with ourselves.

Class of 1998, be proud of Chico High, be proud of leaving Chico High with a diploma in your hand, and above all be very very proud of being an American because no doubt you are living in the greatest nation in the world. I leave you with an anonymous quote: "Life's battles don't always go to the stronger or faster man, but soon or late the man who wins is the man who thinks he can." Class of '98: Good luck in your future endeavors.

Bill Maher almost had his program *Politically Incorrect* canceled when he made a statement viewers found offensive in a time of national grieving.

you, assuming you are not a lawyer, to them. For example, there are few people today, including lawyers, who have not shared the frustrations of dealing with computers that seem to know just when to crash and make your life miserable.

You must, of course, be sensitive to an audience's diversity and state of mind in developing and delivering a speech to entertain. We live in an era in which a racial or ethnic joke that would have been accepted a few years ago can end a career or lead to the demise of a relationship. And as *Politically Incorrect*'s host Bill Maher learned, suggesting that Americans were cowardly and hijackers were courageous in a time of national grief almost ended his show.

In developing the content of your speech to entertain, brainstorming is a useful technique. Recall from Chapter 2 that brainstorming involves a group of people getting together and rapidly firing off ideas. Someone keeps a list. No criticism or evaluation of the ideas is permitted—that comes later. The key to brainstorming is to hitchhike one idea on another. The wilder and crazier the ideas, at this point, the better. You can always tone them down later.

Once you have a list of ideas, write each one on a card or slip of paper. The next step is to sort them out and organize them into a speech.

Organization   A speech to entertain should resemble any other good speech in organization: Open with impact, connect with your audience, and provide a clear focus in your introduction. It is very important to capture your audience's attention almost immediately. Unless you are already a highly skilled and entertaining speaker, this is not the time for a three-minute story leading to one punch line. So, try to get a laugh in the first sentence or two. Sometimes just an outrageous statement will do this. When Mary Matalin spoke of her husband, James Carville, for example, she began by pointing out that he had served his country as a Marine, reaching the rank of corporal. This, she noted, "makes him the highest ranking military officer in the current administration." Even liberals in the audience saw the humor in her backhanded compliment to her husband, which simultaneously reminded everyone of President Clinton's lack of military experience.

Another example of an attention-getting opening came when Russ Woody, who is an Emmy- and Golden Globe–winning comedy writer, spoke at our university commencement. He began by stating:

> Look . . . I write sitcoms for a living, so don't expect much. Which means . . . basically, I'm gonna tell a few jokes. Hit a few well-worn platitudes. And try to sell you a Dodge minivan.

Russ's helpful hints for writing humorous introductions are found in Chapter 8, on page 202.

Although it is important to focus your audience's attention on the topic of your speech, a preview of points is rare in a speech to entertain. Part of humor is surprise, and telegraphing your jokes in a preview will undermine the audience's surprise.

The body of your speech can be organized in a number of ways. A simple chronological or narrative form works well when telling a story or describing a series of events. A topical arrangement allows you to organize your speech around major topics.

In concluding a speech to entertain, you normally would not summarize your points. You would, however, want to close with impact or, as the old adage goes, "Leave 'em laughing."

Sources of Humor   What are some sources of humor? We hesitate to try to define what is funny. After all, everyone's sense of humor is different, and what is funny to one person will leave another completely stone-faced. Some people love David Letterman and hate Jay Leno, others the reverse, and some people enjoy them both.

Nevertheless, a few traditional sources of humor deserve mention:

- *Exaggeration*. Exaggeration is a well-tested source of humor. Wits from Mark Twain to the present day have relied on exaggeration to make their point. Russ Woody, mentioned earlier, used exaggeration to describe his own graduation experience:

  > I will be brief . . . because I remember my own graduation . . . though not *too* clearly. We were over in Laxson Auditorium, and it was a comfy 105 degrees out . . . and just slightly less than double that in the auditorium.
  >
  > Anyway, the man who gave the commencement speech talked for close to 15 hours. He said we were all sailing ships out on the ocean of life, and we were the beating hearts of an upwardly mobile nation, and we had a bunch of mountaintops to climb . . . And the only thing I *really* came away with, besides hathair, was something about a new technology in ventilation systems that was greatly improving the output of poultry in tested areas of Missouri.

- *Incongruity*. Something that doesn't fit in seems funny. Woody Allen once wore tennis shoes with a tuxedo (semiformal attire?). We frequently poke fun at politicians whose words and deeds don't match. When the State of

California was sending out IOUs instead of checks, Jay Leno commented that the latest Southern California earthquake wasn't really an earthquake, just the governor bouncing more checks.

- *Attacking authority.* The attack on authority has been a staple of humor since anyone can remember. Will Rogers made fun of Congress, Jay Leno makes fun of politicians, and Chris Rock makes fun of everybody, himself included!

- *Puns.* Use at your own risk!

- *Sarcasm.* Used with care, sarcasm can be a good source of humor (particularly when directed against sources of authority). But be careful you don't create sympathy for your victim. Sarcasm that is too edgy or biting can seem mean-spirited and bitter rather than funny. One of Mary Matalin's charms is that she is able to poke fun at her husband and his Democratic friends and yet still appear a loving wife.

- *Irony.* Sometimes a powerful source of humor, irony can also make a serious point. The fact that Microsoft founder and billionaire Bill Gates had his presentation of Windows 98 marred by a computer failure was a source of material for late-night comedians for several days.

- *The rule of three.* Milton Berle once claimed that he could make an audience laugh at anything, if he preceded it with two funny jokes. Try it. Once you have people laughing, they often will continue to laugh even at a line that isn't funny.

- *Self-deprecating humor.* Often the safest humor is that directed at yourself. Not only do you avoid alienating anyone, you show that you are a regular person. When Hall-of-Fame quarterback Terry Bradshaw spoke at a "speechathon" along with such luminaries as former president Gerald Ford, former congressman Jack Kemp, and former senator Bill Bradley, he wondered out loud why he was there. Gazing out at an audience of prominent business leaders, he admitted: "I made my living, unlike you, by putting my hands under another man's butt."[11]

- *Delivery.* Humor depends on direct contact and immediacy with your audience. Thus, use of a manuscript or conspicuous notes will destroy the spontaneity of the experience. Even if you have memorized your speech, however, it is important that it sound fresh and spontaneous.

   Use a lively and animated manner in presenting your speech. Timing in comedy is everything. Knowing when to pause, what word to punch, and the right tone of voice to use are not things you can learn from reading a book. Only by trying out your speech with friends and experimenting with different ways of delivering the same line can you tell what delivery is best.

Not everyone is comfortable with speaking to entertain. But done well and tastefully, it can be an enjoyable experience for both the speaker and the audience.

SPEAKING ON TELEVISION

Although you might not plan on being a television newscaster or celebrity, many people in ordinary life find themselves confronted with a television interview at some time or another. Not just business executives need to be able to

One of the authors, Michael Scott, is shown here interviewing Al Roker on CNBC television.

handle a television interview; so do supervisors and line personnel who may be on the scene of a breaking news event. Unless you expect to be on television and have been given a list of questions you will be asked in advance, speaking on TV is a lot like impromptu speaking. You want to appear organized, come across as firm rather than indecisive, and use powerful language. Speaking on TV also demands nonverbal immediacy behaviors, so you'll want to look back at Chapter 10 for a discussion of effective delivery tips.

One question that always arises when being interviewed on television is where to look. Do you look at the camera or at the interviewer or from one to the other? One suggestion comes from Dorothy Sarnoff, who provides communication training to corporate executives. She suggests: "Focus on the left eye of the interviewer, then the right eye—and back to the left. Not a windshield-wiper effect, but slowly so your own eyes don't look dead."[12] Some other suggestions for talking on television are included in the box "Chatting It Up on TV: Paul Burnham Finney."

Chatting It Up on TV: Paul Burnham Finney

Many executives turn into TV regulars and routinely go out on cross-country tours to promote a new product or service. But few of the veterans take their camera assignments casually.

"Steal the show," says Mariana Field Hoppin, president of MFH Travel Marketing Ltd. and a longtime spokeswoman for Avis Europe. "When you walk into the studio, win over the camera crew and interviewer, and you've got them in the palm of your hands."

It's important to do that. "The public is taking the lazy way out—getting their information on the tube," as one corporate communications director puts it.

"Smart executives have to be prepared for surprises on the road," he goes on to say. When the Tylenol-tampering scare struck Johnson & Johnson, C.E.O. James E. Burke signed up for a crash course at the Executive Television Workshop [ETW] before facing the public.

Screen test: Among the tips ETW feeds its corporate students:

- Get a good fix on the questions you'll be asked by contacting the TV or radio station. (Ask around if the direct approach doesn't work.)
- Tell your story, or somebody else will—and not always correctly.
- Memorize the basic points you want to make, and keep them uppermost in your mind.
- Stick to solid colors in dress—no loud patterns allowed. And wear contacts rather than glasses, if possible.
- Women: don't show up in a short skirt that rides above the knees.

- Park yourself in the front third of the chair. You'll look more alert and interested that way.
- Glance at 3-by-5 card notes during commercials or station breaks—never when on camera.
- Say it all in 45 seconds when answering an interviewer. "Short, clear answers," as TV commentator David Brinkley advises.
- Use anecdotes and "sparklers" to brighten your delivery.
- Don't repeat a negative statement—it only lends credence to it.

Digestible bits: "We stress the importance of establishing a conversational tone," says Executive Television Workshop marketing director Carol Heimann. "Executives get very techy in the way they talk. A reporter is only a conduit to the public. Break your explanations into digestible bits. Try to act as though you're in a living room, chatting with someone."

Ultimately, the impression you leave with your audience counts more than your words. Some 90% of what they remember is your "voice" and "nonverbal communications," according to studies. In short, body language matters as much as your thoughts.

"One of your biggest assets," says Heimann, "is a smile. It can change a million opinions. You can disarm your audience. If you're relaxed, you'll relax the people who are watching."

Source: Article appeared first in *Newsweek*'s 1990 Special Ad Section, "Management Digest." Reprinted by permission.

In conclusion, the best advice we can give is to be prepared and stick to your theme. Interviews are frequently videotaped and then edited for a sound bite. You want to make sure that whatever is left on the cutting-room floor, your essential message will reach the viewers.

SUMMARY

Approach most special speaking occasions as storytelling. Good stories are:

- organized
- probable
- have fidelity and ring true for the audience

 **SPEECH COACH**

To evaluate your understanding of this chapter, see the Quizzes on your CD.

Effective impromptu speeches should:

- be clearly organized
- take a stand
- use powerful language

Other types of speeches that can benefit from storytelling include:

- speeches of acceptance
- speeches of introduction
- speeches of recognition
- speeches of commemoration, such as eulogies
- speeches to entertain an audience

Advice for TV interviews includes:

- be well prepared
- look at the interviewer, not the camera
- dress appropriately
- keep answers brief
- use anecdotes and sparklers
- appear relaxed

CHECK YOUR UNDERSTANDING: EXERCISES AND ACTIVITIES

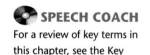
SPEECH COACH

For a review of key terms in this chapter, see the Key Terms Flashcards on your CD.

1. Your best friend is getting married, and you will be asked to say a few words at the wedding. Prepare your toast. Do the same thing for a wedding anniversary, a baptism, and a bar or bat mitzvah.

2. Think of a special award for one of your classmates. Write a speech of recognition for presenting the award.

3. Track down several quotations and anecdotes that are general enough to be used as an opening or a closing for a speech of acceptance or a speech of recognition. Three sources to which you can turn are:

   Clifton Fadiman, ed., *The Little Brown Book of Anecdotes* (Boston: Little, Brown, 1985).

   Edmund Fuller, ed., *2,500 Anecdotes for All Occasions* (New York: Avenel Books, 1980).

   James B. Simpson, ed., *Simpson's Contemporary Quotations: The Most Notable Quotes Since 1950* (Boston: Houghton Mifflin, 1988).

4. A speech of nomination can either make or break the nominee's chances for being elected to office. Speeches of nomination are more common than you may think. Social clubs such as fraternities and sororities, business and professional associations such as the Soroptimists, Rotary, or local Bar are all examples. On a separate sheet of paper, list and explain what you think are the essential characteristics of a speech of nomination. Then see if you can find a published example of a speech of nomination that conforms to

your criteria. Note conforming examples on a copy of the speech with a highlighter and share your analysis with classmates.

NOTES

1. Edmund Fuller, ed., *2,500 Anecdotes for All Occasions* (New York: Avenel Books, 1980), 135.
2. *News from Korbel* [http://korbel.com/trade, 28 September 1998].
3. Theodore H. White, *The Making of the President 1968* (New York: Atheneum, 1969), 171. Shaw's original lines appear in his play *Back to Methuselah,* Part I, Act I. The Serpent in the Garden of Eden says to Eve, "You see things; and you say 'Why?' But I dream things that never were; and I say 'Why not?'" See George Bernard Shaw, *The Complete Plays of Bernard Shaw* (London: Odhams Press Limited, 1934), 857.
4. Walter R. Fisher, *Human Communication as Narration* (Columbia: University of South Carolina Press, 1987).
5. Peggy Noonan, *What I Saw at the Revolution: A Political Life in the Reagan Era* (New York: Random House, 1990).
6. Stephen J. Covey, *The Seven Habits of Highly Effective People* (New York: Fireside Books/Simon & Schuster, 1989).
7. Anita Creamer, "One More Word on the Oscars," *Sacramento Bee,* 3 April 1993, Scene, 1.
8. Kevin Jeys, "Irreconcilable Differences," *Chico News and Review,* 8 October 1998, 29.
9. "I Stand Before You . . . ," *Newsweek,* 15 September 1997, 24.
10. Adapted from Jack Perella and Steven R. Brydon, "Speaking to Entertain," in *Intercollegiate Forensics: A Participant's Handbook,* ed. T. C. Winebrenner, 42–46. © 1992 Northern California Forensics Association.
11. Sam Stanton, "Clinton Remains Topic A at Cal Expo Speechathon," *Sacramento Bee,* 10 October 1998, A23.
12. Article appeared first in *Newsweek's* 1990 Special Ad Section, "Management Digest," Paul Burnham Finney, "The Business of Communicating," 16.

APPENDIX A

Speech of Introduction

This speech was transcribed from videotape. Because speaking extemporaneously often leads to unintended errors or misspoken words, we have edited and corrected the transcript for you to read.

Speech of Self-Introduction: Who Am I? *by Jonathan Studebaker*

This speech was delivered by Jonathan Studebaker, who is profiled in Chapter 1. In reading this speech, try to answer the following questions:

- How well does Jonathan open, focus, and connect with his audience?
- How does this speech of introduction differ from a more formal speech in terms of structure and use of supporting materials, such as evidence?
- Comment on Jonathan's use of rhetorical questions throughout his speech.
- What do you think is Jonathan's purpose in presenting this speech? In what ways is Jonathan using this opportunity to speak as a credible expert on the issue of how we perceive persons with disabilities?
- Look at the speech on your *Speech Coach* CD, segment 1.2. Compare the experience of seeing and hearing Jonathan with reading his speech.

Good morning!

Who am I? Why am I here? Seems like I've heard that before. For myself, I've been asked these and other questions. Two of them I'd like to answer for you today.

I've been asked: "Are you a midget?" "What do you have?" "What's your disability?" "Why are you small?" But I'd really like people to ask me: "What do you like to do?" "What's your favorite color?" So what I'll try to do is answer both of these today.

I'm a nice guy. Don't worry, I won't bite. I like to do many things, except water ski. I've gone to school. I've gone to elementary school, high school, and I graduated from Cal State Chico.

A lot of people ask, "So why are you here?" Well, I'm here because I want to educate others. I've coached football at Chico State University. I was the kicking coach for three years. And out of those three years I had two kickers make first team all-conference. So how do you coach football? You do it by simply telling people what to do. Well, how do you do that? You do it by doing a lot of the things that we all do—by studying, by reading, by listening to others. And that's what I've done throughout my life, and that is what made me who I am.

Like I said, I'm a nice person. I'm cheerful, I'm energetic. Okay, so I have a disability. I was born with osteogenesis imperfecta, a disease which causes my bones to be fragile. Have you ever accidentally dropped a glass on the floor? What happens? It breaks. Well, my bones kind of break like glass, which is why I tell people, when you carry me, treat me like your best crystal.

I'm happy about being who I am. I wouldn't change a thing. I've done a lot of things in my life. Like I said, I've coached football, I graduated from college, things that people wouldn't think a person with my condition would do.

So who am I? Well, I'm Jonathan Studebaker, Jonathan Peter Charles Studebaker. Why such a long name? Well, my middle name is Charles, which came later. And Charles is kind of a symbol of a lot of things. My dad used to call me chicken when I was younger. And then it evolved to chicken Charles, and now Charles. Now, some of you might be offended by being called chicken. But, you know what, it doesn't matter to me. I like being who I am. I've been put here to educate others, not by teaching others, but by just being myself.

Thank you.

Public Speeches

Remarks Before the 1992 Republican National Convention, *by Mary Fisher*

This speech was delivered by Mary Fisher at the 1992 Republican National Convention in Houston, Texas, on Wednesday, August 19. As founder of the Family AIDS Network and a person who is HIV-positive, Fisher addressed a convention that was largely socially conservative about issues such as AIDS. As you read this speech, attempt to answer these questions:

- How well did Mary Fisher adapt to the situation she faced as a speaker at the Republican National Convention?
- To what audience or audiences was this speech addressed?
- What do you see as Fisher's purpose or purposes in presenting this speech?
- How do you feel about the issue of AIDS after reading this speech? Have you changed your beliefs, attitudes, values, or behavioral intentions?

Thank you. Thank you.

Less than three months ago at Platform Hearings in Salt Lake City, I asked the Republican Party to lift the shroud of silence which has been draped over the issue of HIV and AIDS. I have come tonight to bring our silence to an end. I bear a message of challenge, not self-congratulation. I want your attention, not your applause.

I would never have asked to be HIV-positive, but I believe that in all things there is a purpose; and I stand before you and before this nation gladly. The reality of AIDS is brutally clear. Two hundred thousand Americans are dead or dying. A million more are affected. Worldwide, 40 million, 60 million, or 100 million infections will be counted in the coming few years. But despite science and research, White House meetings, and congressional hearings; despite good intentions and bold initiatives, campaign slogans, and hopeful promises, it is—despite it all—the epidemic which is winning tonight.

In the context of an election year, I ask you, here in this great hall, or listening in the quiet of your home, to recognize that the AIDS virus is not a political creature. It does not care whether you are Democratic or Republican; it does not ask whether you are black or white, male or female, gay or straight, young or old. Tonight, I represent an AIDS community whose members have been reluctantly drafted from every segment of American society.

Though I am white and a mother, I am one with a black infant struggling with tubes in a Philadelphia hospital.

Though I am female and contracted this disease in marriage and enjoy the warm support of my family, I am one with the lonely gay man sheltering a flickering candle from the cold wind of his family's rejection.

This is not a distant threat. It is a present danger. The rate of infection is increasing fastest among women and children. Largely unknown a decade ago, AIDS is the third leading killer of young adult Americans today. But it won't be third for long, because unlike other diseases, this one travels. Adolescents don't give each other cancer or heart disease because they believe they are in love, but HIV is different; and we have helped it along. We have killed each other with our ignorance, our prejudice, and our silence.

We may take refuge in our stereotypes, but we cannot hide there long, because HIV asks only one thing of those it attacks. Are you human? And this is the right question. Are you human? Because people with HIV have not entered some alien state of being. They are human. They have not earned cruelty, and they do not deserve meanness. They don't benefit from being isolated or treated as outcasts. Each of them is exactly what God made—a person, not evil, deserving of our judgment; not victims, longing for our pity—people, ready for support and worthy of compassion. (Applause.)

My call to you, my Party, is to take a public stand, no less compassionate than that of the President and Mrs. Bush. They have embraced me and my family in memorable ways. In the place of judgment, they have shown affection. In difficult moments, they have raised our spirits. In the darkest hours, I have seen them reaching out not only to me, but also to my parents, armed with that stunning grief and special grace that comes only to parents who have themselves leaned too long over the bedside of a dying child.

With the president's leadership, much good has been done. Much of the good has gone unheralded, and as the president has insisted, much remains to be done. But we do the president's cause no good if we praise the American family but ignore a virus that destroys it. (Applause.)

We must be consistent if we are to be believed. We cannot love justice and ignore prejudice, love our children and fear to teach them. Whatever our role as parent or policymaker, we must act as eloquently as we speak—else we have no integrity.

My call to the nation is a plea for awareness. If you believe you are safe, you are in danger. Because I was not hemophiliac, I was not at risk. Because I was not gay, I was not at risk. Because I did not inject drugs, I was not at risk.

My father has devoted much of his lifetime to guarding against another holocaust. He is part of the generation who heard Pastor Nemoeller come out of the Nazi death camps to say, "They came after the Jews and I was not a Jew, so, I did not protest. They came after the trade unionists, and I was not a trade unionist, so, I did not protest. Then they came after the Roman Catholics, and I was not a Roman Catholic, so, I did not protest. Then they came after me, and there was no one left to protest." (Applause.)

The lesson history teaches is this: If you believe you are safe, you are at risk. If you do not see this killer stalking your children, look again. There is no family or community, no race or religion, no place left in America that is safe. Until we genuinely embrace this message, we are a nation at risk. Tonight, HIV marches resolutely to AIDS in more than a million American homes. Littering its pathway with the bodies of the young men, young women, young parents, and young children. One of those families is mine. If it is true that HIV inevitably turns to AIDS, then my children will inevitably turn to orphans.

My family has been a rock of support. My 84-year-old father, who has pursued the healing of nations, will not accept the premise that he cannot heal his daughter. My mother refuses to be broken. She still calls at midnight to tell wonderful jokes that make me laugh. Sisters and friends, and my brother Phillip, whose birthday is today, all have helped carry me over the hardest places. I am blessed, richly and deeply blessed, to have such a family. (Applause.)

But not all of you have been so blessed. You are HIV-positive, but dare not say it. You have lost loved ones, but you dare not whisper the word AIDS—you weep silently. You grieve alone. I have a message for you. It is not you who should feel shame. It is we, we who tolerate ignorance and practice prejudice, we who have taught you to fear. We must lift our shroud of silence, making it safe for you to reach out for compassion. It is our task to seek safety for our children, not in quiet denial but in effective action.

Some day our children will be grown. My son Max, now 4, will take the measure of his mother; my son Zachary, now 2, will sort through his memories. I may not be here to hear their judgments, but I know already what I hope they are. I want my children to know that their mother was not a victim. She was a messenger. I do not want them to think, as I once did, that courage is the absence of fear. I want them to know that courage is the strength to act wisely when we are most afraid. I want them to have the courage to step forward when called by their nation or their party and give leadership, no matter what the personal cost. I ask no more of you than I ask of myself or my children. To the millions of you who are grieving, who are frightened, who have suffered the ravages of AIDS firsthand—have courage and you will find support. To the millions who are strong, I issue the plea—set aside prejudice and politics to make room for compassion and sound policy. (Applause.)

To my children, I make this pledge: "I will not give in, Zachary, because I draw my courage from you. Your silly giggle gives me hope; your gentle prayers give me strength; and you, my child, give me reason to say to America, 'You are at risk.' And I will not rest, Max, until I have done all I can to make your world safe. I will seek a place where intimacy is not the prelude to suffering. I will not hurry to leave you, my children, but when I go, I pray that you will not suffer shame on my account." To all within the sound of my voice, I appeal: "Learn with me the lessons of history and of grace, so my children will not be afraid to say the word AIDS when I am gone. Then, their children and yours may not need to whisper it at all." God bless the children, God bless us all, and good night.

Source: This text is from the Official Report of the Proceedings of the Thirty-Fifth Republican National Convention, published by the Republican National Committee.

Remarks Before the 1996 Democratic National Convention, *by Carolyn McCarthy*[1]

This speech was delivered by Carolyn McCarthy at the 1996 Democratic National Convention in Chicago. As the wife and mother of two victims of the Long Island train massacre, McCarthy had become a spokesperson for the victims of that crime and other violent crimes. When rebuffed by her Republican congressman, she registered as a Democrat and ran against him, defeating him and becoming a member of Congress herself. As you read this speech, ask yourself:

- How well did Carolyn McCarthy adapt to the situation she faced as a speaker at the Democratic National Convention?
- To what audience or audiences was this speech addressed?
- What do you see as McCarthy's purpose or purposes in presenting this speech?
- How do you feel about the issue of gun control after reading this speech? Have you changed your beliefs, attitudes, values, or behavioral intentions?

December 7th, 1993—that was the day of the Long Island Railroad massacre. My life and the lives of many others changed forever. A man with a semi-automatic weapon boarded the train that my husband and my son took to work every day. He killed 6 people and wounded 19. My husband, Dennis, was one of those killed. My son, Kevin, was left partially paralyzed. Kevin has had a courageous recovery. He's back at work. But he still spends many hours a day with rehabilitation. It's every mother's dream to be able to stand up on national TV and say she's proud of her son. Kevin, I'm very proud of you.

On that day I started a journey, a journey against gun violence in this nation. Today I am here as a nurse, as a mother, as a person who isn't afraid to speak up on what is going on in this country.

Gun violence adds millions of dollars in hospital costs every year, and threatens families with a mountain of bills, and so much pain. Until our government listens to ordinary people speaking out against gun violence instead of listening to special interest groups like the NRA leadership, we are not going to have safety in our streets!

I was not planning on speaking here tonight, but this is where my journey has taken me—to the Democratic Party, the party that believes in including ordinary citizens. That's why I'm here. I am here as a woman with common sense and determination, and I am going to make a difference.

I will fight to keep the assault weapons ban the law of the land. I—Yeah, I will. I will work for the day when President Clinton's Victims Rights Amendment is in the Constitution. And those of us who are concerned about gun violence will not tolerate being ignored, as I was by my congressman, who voted to repeal the assault weapons bill.

We have all been ignored by the Gingrich congress. They have not listened to us on education, on the environment, or on making our streets safe. We will not be ignored. We will make them listen.

[1]Reprinted by permission of the author.

The journey I began in 1993 wasn't one that I had planned. Getting involved in politics wasn't anything I ever wanted to do. But this journey will make a difference when our neighborhoods pull together, when government listens to us again. When all of us, Democrats and Republicans, come together to solve our problems, not just fight about them. We have a responsibility to our children to speak up about what we know is right and to do what is right. I ask you to join me and my son, Kevin, on that journey. Thank you so very much.

Address to a Joint Session of Congress and the American People[2]
United States Capitol, Washington, D.C.
September 20, 2001
President George W. Bush

This speech was delivered before a Joint Session of Congress by President George W. Bush nine days after terrorists attacked the United States in New York City, Washington, D.C., and Pennsylvania. As you read this speech, ask yourself the following questions:

- What are the multiple audiences for this speech? It is obviously to Congress and the American people, but are there other audiences throughout the world to whom the speech is addressed?

- How does the president seek to reassure the American people and encourage them to go on with their lives, while also emphasizing the difficulties the nation faces in rooting out terrorism?

- How does the president use examples of individual heroes in his speech?

- How does the president make his case about the responsibility for the terrorist attacks?

- If you saw the speech when it was delivered or have an opportunity to view it on videotape, ask yourself how the experience of seeing it compares with reading it.

THE PRESIDENT: Mr. Speaker, Mr. President Pro Tempore, members of Congress, and fellow Americans:

In the normal course of events, presidents come to this chamber to report on the state of the Union. Tonight, no such report is needed. It has already been delivered by the American people.

We have seen it in the courage of passengers, who rushed terrorists to save others on the ground—passengers like an exceptional man named Todd Beamer. And would you please help me to welcome his wife, Lisa Beamer, here tonight. (Applause.)

We have seen the state of our Union in the endurance of rescuers, working past exhaustion. We have seen the unfurling of flags, the lighting of candles, the giving of blood, the saying of prayers—in English, Hebrew, and Arabic. We have seen the decency of a loving and giving people who have made the grief of strangers their own.

[2]The White House, Office of the Press Secretary, September 20, 2002, http://www.whitehouse.go/news/releases/2001/09/20010920-8.html

My fellow citizens, for the last nine days, the entire world has seen for itself the state of our Union—and it is strong. (Applause.)

Tonight we are a country awakened to danger and called to defend freedom. Our grief has turned to anger, and anger to resolution. Whether we bring our enemies to justice, or bring justice to our enemies, justice will be done. (Applause.)

I thank the Congress for its leadership at such an important time. All of America was touched on the evening of the tragedy to see Republicans and Democrats joined together on the steps of this Capitol, singing "God Bless America." And you did more than sing; you acted, by delivering $40 billion to rebuild our communities and meet the needs of our military.

Speaker Hastert, Minority Leader Gephardt, Majority Leader Daschle, and Senator Lott, I thank you for your friendship, for your leadership and for your service to our country. (Applause.)

And on behalf of the American people, I thank the world for its outpouring of support. America will never forget the sounds of our national anthem playing at Buckingham Palace, on the streets of Paris, and at Berlin's Brandenburg Gate.

We will not forget South Korean children gathering to pray outside our embassy in Seoul, or the prayers of sympathy offered at a mosque in Cairo. We will not forget moments of silence and days of mourning in Australia and Africa and Latin America.

Nor will we forget the citizens of 80 other nations who died with our own: dozens of Pakistanis; more than 130 Israelis; more than 250 citizens of India; men and women from El Salvador, Iran, Mexico, and Japan; and hundreds of British citizens. America has no truer friend than Great Britain. (Applause.) Once again, we are joined together in a great cause—so honored the British Prime Minister has crossed an ocean to show his unity of purpose with America. Thank you for coming, friend. (Applause.)

On September the 11th, enemies of freedom committed an act of war against our country. Americans have known wars—but for the past 136 years, they have been wars on foreign soil, except for one Sunday in 1941. Americans have known the casualties of war, but not at the center of a great city on a peaceful morning. Americans have known surprise attacks, but never before on thousands of civilians. All of this was brought upon us in a single day, and night fell on a different world, a world where freedom itself is under attack.

Americans have many questions tonight. Americans are asking: Who attacked our country? The evidence we have gathered all points to a collection of loosely affiliated terrorist organizations known as al Qaeda. They are the same murderers indicted for bombing American embassies in Tanzania and Kenya, and responsible for bombing the USS Cole.

Al Qaeda is to terror what the mafia is to crime. But its goal is not making money; its goal is remaking the world and imposing its radical beliefs on people everywhere.

The terrorists practice a fringe form of Islamic extremism that has been rejected by Muslim scholars and the vast majority of Muslim clerics—a fringe movement that perverts the peaceful teachings of Islam. The terrorists' directive commands them to kill Christians and Jews, to kill all Americans, and make no distinction among military and civilians, including women and children.

This group and its leader—a person named Osama bin Laden—are linked to many other organizations in different countries, including the Egyptian

Islamic Jihad and the Islamic Movement of Uzbekistan. There are thousands of these terrorists in more than 60 countries. They are recruited from their own nations and neighborhoods and brought to camps in places like Afghanistan, where they are trained in the tactics of terror. They are sent back to their homes or sent to hide in countries around the world to plot evil and destruction.

The leadership of al Qaeda has great influence in Afghanistan and supports the Taliban regime in controlling most of the country. In Afghanistan, we see al Qaeda's vision for the world.

Afghanistan's people have been brutalized—many are starving and many have fled. Women are not allowed to attend school. You can be jailed for owning a television. Religion can be practiced only as their leaders dictate. A man can be jailed in Afghanistan if his beard is not long enough.

The United States respects the people of Afghanistan—after all, we are currently its largest source of humanitarian aid—but we condemn the Taliban regime. (Applause.) It is not only repressing its own people, it is threatening people everywhere by sponsoring and sheltering and supplying terrorists. By aiding and abetting murder, the Taliban regime is committing murder.

And tonight, the United States of America makes the following demands on the Taliban: Deliver to United States authorities all the leaders of al Qaeda who hide in your land. (Applause.) Release all foreign nationals, including American citizens, you have unjustly imprisoned. Protect foreign journalists, diplomats, and aid workers in your country. Close immediately and permanently every terrorist training camp in Afghanistan, and hand over every terrorist, and every person in their support structure, to appropriate authorities. (Applause.) Give the United States full access to terrorist training camps, so we can make sure they are no longer operating.

These demands are not open to negotiation or discussion. (Applause.) The Taliban must act, and act immediately. They will hand over the terrorists, or they will share in their fate.

I also want to speak tonight directly to Muslims throughout the world. We respect your faith. It's practiced freely by many millions of Americans, and by millions more in countries that America counts as friends. Its teachings are good and peaceful, and those who commit evil in the name of Allah blaspheme the name of Allah. (Applause.) The terrorists are traitors to their own faith, trying, in effect, to hijack Islam itself. The enemy of America is not our many Muslim friends; it is not our many Arab friends. Our enemy is a radical network of terrorists, and every government that supports them. (Applause.)

Our war on terror begins with al Qaeda, but it does not end there. It will not end until every terrorist group of global reach has been found, stopped, and defeated. (Applause.)

Americans are asking, why do they hate us? They hate what we see right here in this chamber—a democratically elected government. Their leaders are self-appointed. They hate our freedoms—our freedom of religion, our freedom of speech, our freedom to vote and assemble and disagree with each other.

They want to overthrow existing governments in many Muslim countries, such as Egypt, Saudi Arabia, and Jordan. They want to drive Israel out of the Middle East. They want to drive Christians and Jews out of vast regions of Asia and Africa.

These terrorists kill not merely to end lives, but to disrupt and end a way of life. With every atrocity, they hope that America grows fearful, retreating from the world and forsaking our friends. They stand against us, because we stand in their way.

We are not deceived by their pretenses to piety. We have seen their kind before. They are heirs of all the murderous ideologies of the 20th century. By sacrificing human life to serve their radical visions—by abandoning every value except the will to power—they follow in the path of fascism, and Nazism, and totalitarianism. And they will follow that path all the way, to where it ends: in history's unmarked grave of discarded lies. (Applause.)

Americans are asking: How will we fight and win this war? We will direct every resource at our command—every means of diplomacy, every tool of intelligence, every instrument of law enforcement, every financial influence, and every necessary weapon of war—to the disruption and to the defeat of the global terror network.

This war will not be like the war against Iraq a decade ago, with a decisive liberation of territory and a swift conclusion. It will not look like the air war above Kosovo two years ago, where no ground troops were used and not a single American was lost in combat.

Our response involves far more than instant retaliation and isolated strikes. Americans should not expect one battle, but a lengthy campaign, unlike any other we have ever seen. It may include dramatic strikes, visible on TV, and covert operations, secret even in success. We will starve terrorists of funding, turn them one against another, drive them from place to place, until there is no refuge or no rest. And we will pursue nations that provide aid or safe haven to terrorism. Every nation, in every region, now has a decision to make. Either you are with us, or you are with the terrorists. (Applause.) From this day forward, any nation that continues to harbor or support terrorism will be regarded by the United States as a hostile regime.

Our nation has been put on notice. We are not immune from attack. We will take defensive measures against terrorism to protect Americans. Today, dozens of federal departments and agencies, as well as state and local governments, have responsibilities affecting homeland security. These efforts must be coordinated at the highest level. So tonight I announce the creation of a cabinet-level position reporting directly to me—the Office of Homeland Security.

And tonight I also announce a distinguished American to lead this effort, to strengthen American security: a military veteran, an effective governor, a true patriot, a trusted friend—Pennsylvania's Tom Ridge. (Applause.) He will lead, oversee, and coordinate a comprehensive national strategy to safeguard our country against terrorism, and respond to any attack that may come.

These measures are essential. But the only way to defeat terrorism as a threat to our way of life is to stop, eliminate it, and destroy it where it grows. (Applause.)

Many will be involved in this effort, from FBI agents to intelligence operatives to the reservists we have called to active duty. All deserve our thanks, and all have our prayers. And tonight, a few miles from the damaged Pentagon, I have a message for our military: Be ready. I've called the Armed Forces to alert, and there is a reason. The hour is coming when America will act, and you will make us proud. (Applause.)

This is not, however, just America's fight. And what is at stake is not just America's freedom. This is the world's fight. This is civilization's fight. This is the fight of all who believe in progress and pluralism, tolerance, and freedom.

We ask every nation to join. We will ask, and we will need, the help of police forces, intelligence services, and banking systems around the world. The United States is grateful that many nations and many international organizations have already responded—with sympathy and with support. Nations from Latin America, to Asia, to Africa, to Europe, to the Islamic world. Perhaps the NATO Charter reflects best the attitude of the world: An attack on one is an attack on all.

The civilized world is rallying to America's side. They understand that if this terror goes unpunished, their own cities, their own citizens may be next. Terror, unanswered, can not only bring down buildings, it can threaten the stability of legitimate governments. And you know what—we're not going to allow it. (Applause.)

Americans are asking: What is expected of us? I ask you to live your lives, and hug your children. I know many citizens have fears tonight, and I ask you to be calm and resolute, even in the face of a continuing threat.

I ask you to uphold the values of America, and remember why so many have come here. We are in a fight for our principles, and our first responsibility is to live by them. No one should be singled out for unfair treatment or unkind words because of their ethnic background or religious faith. (Applause.)

I ask you to continue to support the victims of this tragedy with your contributions. Those who want to give can go to a central source of information, libertyunites.org, to find the names of groups providing direct help in New York, Pennsylvania, and Virginia.

The thousands of FBI agents who are now at work in this investigation may need your cooperation, and I ask you to give it.

I ask for your patience, with the delays and inconveniences that may accompany tighter security; and for your patience in what will be a long struggle.

I ask your continued participation and confidence in the American economy. Terrorists attacked a symbol of American prosperity. They did not touch its source. America is successful because of the hard work, and creativity, and enterprise of our people. These were the true strengths of our economy before September 11th, and they are our strengths today. (Applause.)

And, finally, please continue praying for the victims of terror and their families, for those in uniform, and for our great country. Prayer has comforted us in sorrow, and will help strengthen us for the journey ahead.

Tonight I thank my fellow Americans for what you have already done and for what you will do. And ladies and gentlemen of Congress, I thank you, their representatives, for what you have already done and for what we will do together.

Tonight, we face new and sudden national challenges. We will come together to improve air safety, to dramatically expand the number of air marshals on domestic flights, and take new measures to prevent hijacking. We will come together to promote stability and keep our airlines flying, with direct assistance during this emergency. (Applause.)

We will come together to give law enforcement the additional tools it needs to track down terror here at home. (Applause.) We will come together to strengthen our intelligence capabilities to know the plans of terrorists before they act, and find them before they strike. (Applause.)

We will come together to take active steps that strengthen America's economy, and put our people back to work.

Tonight we welcome two leaders who embody the extraordinary spirit of all New Yorkers: Governor George Pataki, and Mayor Rudolph Giuliani. (Applause.) As a symbol of America's resolve, my administration will work with Congress, and these two leaders, to show the world that we will rebuild New York City. (Applause.)

After all that has just passed—all the lives taken, and all the possibilities and hopes that died with them—it is natural to wonder if America's future is one of fear. Some speak of an age of terror. I know there are struggles ahead, and dangers to face. But this country will define our times, not be defined by them. As long as the United States of America is determined and strong, this will not be an age of terror; this will be an age of liberty, here and across the world. (Applause.)

Great harm has been done to us. We have suffered great loss. And in our grief and anger we have found our mission and our moment. Freedom and fear are at war. The advance of human freedom—the great achievement of our time, and the great hope of every time—now depends on us. Our nation—this generation—will lift a dark threat of violence from our people and our future. We will rally the world to this cause by our efforts, by our courage. We will not tire, we will not falter, and we will not fail. (Applause.)

It is my hope that in the months and years ahead, life will return almost to normal. We'll go back to our lives and routines, and that is good. Even grief recedes with time and grace. But our resolve must not pass. Each of us will remember what happened that day, and to whom it happened. We'll remember the moment the news came—where we were and what we were doing. Some will remember an image of a fire, or a story of rescue. Some will carry memories of a face and a voice gone forever.

And I will carry this: It is the police shield of a man named George Howard, who died at the World Trade Center trying to save others. It was given to me by his mom, Arlene, as a proud memorial to her son. This is my reminder of lives that ended, and a task that does not end. (Applause.)

I will not forget this wound to our country or those who inflicted it. I will not yield; I will not rest; I will not relent in waging this struggle for freedom and security for the American people.

The course of this conflict is not known, yet its outcome is certain. Freedom and fear, justice and cruelty, have always been at war, and we know that God is not neutral between them. (Applause.)

Fellow citizens, we'll meet violence with patient justice—assured of the rightness of our cause, and confident of the victories to come. In all that lies before us, may God grant us wisdom, and may He watch over the United States of America.

Thank you. (Applause.)

Glossary

abstract A summary of an article or a report.

active listening Listening that involves conscious and responsive participation in the communication transaction.

active mindfulness The degree to which speakers and audiences are consciously aware of the transactions between them.

ad hominem The claim that something must be false because the person who said it is not credible, regardless of the argument itself.

agenda Something that defines the purpose and direction a group takes, the topics to be covered, and the goals to be achieved.

appreciative listening Listening that involves obtaining sensory stimulation or enjoyment from others.

arguing in a circle (begging the question) An argument that proves nothing because the claim to be proved is used as the grounds or warrant for the argument.

argumentativeness The trait of arguing for and against the positions taken on controversial claims.

attitude A learned predisposition to respond in a consistently favorable or unfavorable manner with respect to a given object.

audience The individuals who share and listen to a public speech.

audience accessible Content the audience is able to understand, regardless of its complexity.

audience appropriate Informative topic and speech that takes into account the occasion and audience members' belief systems.

audience diversity The cultural, demographic, and individual characteristics that vary among audience members.

audience involving Informative topic and speech that succeeds in gaining the audience's attention.

audio media Aural channels you can use to augment your speech, such as a recording of a famous speaker.

authority warrant Reasoning in which the claim is believed because of the authority of the source.

backing Support for a warrant.

bar chart A graphic used for comparing data side by side.

behavioral intention A person's subjective belief that he or she will engage in a specific behavior.

belief An assertion about the properties or characteristics of an object.

Boolean operators Terms, such as *and, or,* and *not,* used to narrow or broaden a computerized search of two or more related terms.

brainstorming A creative process used for generating a large number of ideas.

call and response pattern A pattern of organization in which a call by the speaker is followed by a response from the audience.

categorical imperative Immanuel Kant's ethical principle that we should act only in a way that we would will to be a universal law.

categorical pattern A pattern of organization based on natural divisions in the subject matter.

causal pattern A pattern of organization that moves from cause to effect or from effect to cause.

causal warrant An argument that claims a cause will produce or has produced an effect.

central beliefs Beliefs based directly or indirectly on authority.

channel The physical medium through which communication occurs.

claim A conclusion that persuasive speakers want their audience to reach as a result of their speech.

communication apprehension Fear about communicating interpersonally and in groups, not just in public.

comparison (analogy) warrant A statement that two cases that are similar in some known respects are also similar in some unknown respects.

competence-enhancing language Words that emphasize rather than undermine audience perceptions of a speaker's competence.

comprehension The act of understanding what has been communicated.

connotation The secondary meaning of a word, often with a strong emotional, personal, and subjective component.

constraint A limitation on choices in a speech situation.

constructive self-talk The use of positive coping statements instead of negative self-talk.

content (of messages) The essential meaning of what a speaker wants to convey.

context Information that surrounds an event and contributes to the meaning of that event.

coping skills Mental and physical techniques used to control arousal and anxiety in the course of speaking in public.

credibility The degree to which an audience trusts and believes in a speaker.

critical listening Listening for the purpose of making reasoned judgments about speakers and the credibility of their messages.

critical thinking The process of making sound inferences based on accurate evidence and valid reasoning.

cross cue–checking Gauging what a person says verbally against the nonverbal behaviors that make up metacommunication.

cultural diversity Differences among people in terms of beliefs, customs, and values—in a sense, their world view.

cultural relativism The notion that the criteria for ethical behavior in one culture should not necessarily be applied to other cultures.

culture A learned system of beliefs, customs, and values with which people identify.

decoding The process by which a code is translated back into ideas.

deficiency needs Basic human needs, which must be satisfied before higher-order needs can be met. They include needs for food, water, air, physical safety, belongingness and love, and self-esteem and social esteem.

demographic diversity Variations among people in terms of such attributes as socioeconomic background and level of education.

demographics Basic and vital data regarding any population.

denotation The generally agreed upon meaning of a word, usually found in the dictionary.

elaboration likelihood model A model of persuasion designed to explain why audience members will use an elaborated thinking process in some situations and not in others.

distorted evidence Significant omissions or changes in the grounds of an argument that alter its original intent.

emblem A nonverbal symbol that can be substituted for a word.

encoding The process by which ideas are translated into a code that can be understood by the receiver.

environment The physical surroundings as you speak and the physical distance separating you from your audience.

ethical relativism A philosophy based on the belief that there are no universal ethical principles.

ethics A system of principles of right and wrong that govern human conduct.

ethos The degree to which an audience perceives a speaker as credible.

eulogy A kind of commemorative speech about someone who has died that is usually given shortly after his or her death.

expert opinion A quotation from someone with special credentials in the subject matter.

extemporaneous delivery A mode of presentation that combines careful preparation with spontaneous speaking. The speaker generally uses brief notes rather than a full manuscript or an outline.

extended narrative A pattern of organization in which the entire body of the speech is the telling of a story.

fact Something that is verifiable as true.

fallacy An argument in which the reasons advanced for a claim fail to warrant acceptance of that claim.

false analogy The comparison of two different things that are not really comparable.

false dilemma A generalization that implies there are only two choices when there are more than two.

feedback Audience member responses, both verbal and nonverbal, to a speaker.

first-order data Evidence based on personal experience.

flip chart Large tablet used to preview the outline of a presentation or to record information generated by an audience.

flow chart A graphic designed to illustrate spatial relationships or the sequence of events in a process.

formal outline A detailed outline used in speech preparation, but not, in most cases, in the actual presentation.

ganas Spanish term that loosely translates as the desire to succeed.

general purpose The primary function of a speech. The three commonly agreed upon general purposes are to inform, to persuade, and to entertain.

generalization warrant A statement that either establishes a general rule or principle or applies an established rule or principle to a specific case.

good reasons Statements, based on moral principles, offered in support of propositions concerning what we should believe or how we should act.

goodwill The perception by the audience that a speaker cares about their needs and concerns.

grounds The evidence a speaker offers in support of a claim.

group Three or more individuals who are aware of each other's presence, share a mutually interdependent purpose, engage in communication transactions with one another, and identify with the group.

growth needs Higher-order human needs, which can be satisfied only after deficiency needs have been met. They include self-actualization (the process of fully realizing one's potential), knowledge and understanding, and aesthetic needs.

halo effect The assumption that just because you like or respect a person, whatever he or she says must be true.

hasty generalization An argument that occurs when there are too few instances to support a generalization or the instances are unresponsive of the generalization.

hyperbole An exaggeration of a claim.

illustrators Nonverbal symbols used to visualize what is being spoken.

impromptu delivery A spontaneous, unrehearsed mode of presenting a speech.

inclusive language Language that helps people believe that they not only have a stake in matters of societal importance but also have power in this regard.

index A listing of sources of information, usually in newspapers, journals, and magazines, alphabetically by topic.

individual diversity How individuals in an audience differ in terms of knowledge, beliefs, attitudes, values, motives, and expectations.

inference The process of moving from a ground, via a warrant, to a claim.

informative speaking The process by which an audience gains new information or a new perspective on old information.

interdependence A relationship in which things have a reciprocal influence on each other.

invention The creative process by which the substance of a speech is generated.

isolated examples Nontypical or nonrepresentative examples that are used to prove a general claim.

language intensity The degree to which words and phrases deviate from neutral.

learning styles Differences in the way people think about and learn new information and skills.

line graph A graphic used to show points in time.

linguistic relativity hypothesis The idea that what people perceive is influenced by the language in which they think and speak.

listening The process of receiving, attending to, and assigning meaning to aural as well as visual and tactile stimuli.

loaded language Language that has strong emotional connotations.

logos The proof a speaker offers to an audience through the words of his or her message.

long-term goals Those ends that we can hope to achieve only over an extended period of time.

main points The key ideas that support the thesis statement of a speech.

manuscript delivery A mode of presentation that involves writing out a speech completely and reading it to the audience.

marginalizing language Language that diminishes people's importance and makes them appear to be less powerful, less significant, and less worthwhile than they are.

memorized delivery A mode of presentation in which a speech is written out and committed to memory before being presented to the audience without the use of notes.

message The meaning produced by communicators.

metacommunication The message about the message; generally conveyed nonverbally.

mistaking correlation for cause The assumption that because one thing is the sign of another, they are causally related.

misused statistics Statistics that involve errors such as poor sampling, lack of significant differences, misuse of average, or misuse of percentages.

Monroe's motivated sequence A five-step organizational scheme, developed by speech professor Alan Monroe, including (1) attention, (2) need, (3) satisfaction, (4) visualization, and (5) action.

narrative An extended story that is fully developed, with characters, scene, action, and plot.

narrative fidelity The degree to which a narrative rings true to real-life experience.

narrative probability The internal coherence or believability of a narrative.

negative self-talk A self-defeating pattern of intrapersonal communication, including self-criticizing, self-pressuring, and catastrophizing statements.

non sequitur An argument that does not follow from its premises.

nonverbal behavior A wordless system of communication.

online catalog A computerized listing of library holdings.

organizational chart A graphic that illustrates hierarchical relationships.

overhead transparency A graphic that can be projected.

panel discussion An extemporaneous group discussion held for the benefit of an audience.

pathos The emotional states in an audience that a speaker can arouse and use to achieve persuasive goals.

perception The process by which we give meaning to our experiences.

peripheral beliefs The least central type of beliefs, the easiest to change.

persuasion The process by which a speaker influences what audience members think or do.

physiological arousal The physical changes that occur when a person is aroused, such as increased pulse, greater alertness, and more energy.

pie chart A graphic often used to show proportions of a known quantity.

pinpoint concentration Listening that focuses on specific details rather than patterns in a message.

plagiarism Stealing the ideas of others and presenting them as your own.

post hoc, ergo propter hoc ("after the fact, therefore because of the fact"): The assumption that because one event preceded another, the first event must be the cause of the second event.

presentational media Channels of communication that extend the five basic senses: touch, sight, sound, taste, and smell.

preview A forecast of the main points of a speech.

primary sources Original sources of information.

primitive beliefs (also known as type A beliefs) Those beliefs learned by direct contact with the object of belief and reinforced by unanimous social consensus.

proactive delivery Planned and rehearsed presentation.

problem–solution pattern A pattern of organization that analyzes a problem in terms of (1) harm, (2) significance, and (3) cause, and proposes a solution that is (1) described, (2) feasible, and (3) advantageous.

pseudoreasoning An argument that appears sound at first glance but contains a fallacy of reasoning that renders it unsound.

qualifier An indication of the level of probability of a claim.

rebuttal An exception to or a refutation of an argument.

receiver-centric A person's assumption that the meaning he or she gives to a word or a phrase is its exclusive meaning.

red herring (smoke screen) An irrelevant issue introduced into a controversy to divert from the real controversy.

reframing Revising your view of a situation or an event, usually in a positive direction.

refutational pattern A pattern of organization that involves (1) stating the argument to be refuted, (2) stating the objection to the argument, (3) proving the objection to the argument, and (4) presenting the impact of the refutation.

regulators Nonverbal behaviors that influence the speech transaction.

relational component (of messages) The collective impact of the verbal and nonverbal components of a message as it is conveyed.

research The process of gathering supporting materials for a speech.

retention The act of storing what was communicated in either short- or long-term memory.

rhetorical question A question that the audience isn't expected to answer out loud.

rhetorical situation A natural context of persons, events, objects, relations, and an exigence (goal) which strongly invites utterance.

search term A word or phrase used in library catalogs and indexes to identify a subject.

secondary sources Information sources that rely on other (primary) sources rather than gathering information firsthand.

second-order data Evidence based on expert testimony.

selective attention Making a conscious choice to focus on some people and some messages, rather than others.

self-adapting behaviors Nonverbal behaviors used to cope with nervousness; for example, self-touching or grasping sides of lectern with hands.

self-talk (sometimes referred to as intrapersonal communication) Communicating silently with oneself.

sensorial involvement A process that involves listening with all the senses, not simply the sense of hearing.

sexist language Language, such as *housewife* and *fireman*, that stereotypes gender roles.

short-term goals Those ends that we can reasonably expect to achieve in the near term.

sign warrant Reasoning in which the presence of an observed phenomenon is used to indicate the presence of an unobserved phenomenon.

signposts Transitional statements that bridge main points.

situational ethics The philosophy that there are overriding ethical maxims, but that sometimes it is necessary to set them aside in particular situations to fulfill a higher law or principle.

slippery slope The assumption that just because one event occurs, it will automatically lead to a series of undesirable events even though there is no relationship between the action and the projected events.

socioeconomic status Social grouping and economic class to which people belong.

source credibility The audience's perception of the believability of the speaker.

spatial pattern A pattern of organization based on physical space or geography.

speaker's notes Brief notes with key words, usually written on cards, used by a speaker when presenting a speech.

specific purpose The goal or objective a speaker hopes to achieve in speaking to a particular audience.

speech anxiety Feelings of discomfort that people experience before, during, and after speaking in public.

speech of acceptance A speech expressing thanks for an award or honor.

speech of commemoration A speech that calls attention to the stature of the person or people being honored, or emphasizes the significance of an occasion.

speech of introduction A speech that briefly sets the stage for an upcoming speaker.

speech of recognition A speech presenting an award or honor to an individual.

speech to entertain A speech that makes its point through the use of humor.

spiral pattern A pattern of organization that employs repetition of points, with the points growing in intensity as the speech builds to its conclusion.

star pattern A pattern of organization in which all of the points are of equal importance and can be presented in any order to support the common theme.

statistics Numerical summaries of data, such as percentages, ratios, and averages, that are classified in a meaningful way. Age, height, and weight are not statistics, although they are commonly mistaken as such.

stereotyping The assumption that what is considered to be true of a larger class is necessarily true of particular members of that class.

stock issues pattern A four-point pattern of organization that is based on (1) ill, (2) blame, (3) cure, and (4) cost.

straw person An argument made in refutation that misstates the argument being refuted. Rather than refuting the real argument, the other side constructs a person of straw, which is easy to knock down.

subpoint An idea that supports a main point.

supporting point An idea that supports a subpoint.

symbol Something that stands for or suggests something else by reason of relationship or association.

system A collection of interdependent parts arranged so that a change in one produces corresponding changes in the remaining parts.

thesis statement A single declarative sentence that focuses the audience's attention on the central point of a speech.

third-order data Evidence based on facts and statistics.

time pattern A pattern of organization based on chronology or a sequence of events.

totalizing language Language that defines people exclusively on the basis of a single attribute, such as race, ethnicity, biological sex, or ability.

transaction A simultaneous exchange of verbal and nonverbal messages between two or more people.

trustworthiness The perception by the audience that they can rely on a speaker's word.

universalism The philosophy that there are ethical standards that apply to all situations regardless of the individual, group, or culture.

unsupported assertion The absence of any argument at all.

utilitarianism The philosophy based on the principle that the aim of any action should be to provide the greatest amount of happiness for the greatest number of people.

values Our most enduring beliefs about right and wrong.

verbal aggressiveness The trait of attacking the self-concept of those with whom a person disagrees about controversial claims.

verbal qualifiers Words and phrases that erode the impact of what a speaker says in a speech.

visual imagery The process of mentally seeing (imagining) oneself confidently and successfully performing an action or a series of actions.

visual media Channels that augment the sense of sight to communicate a message.

warrant The connection between grounds and claim.

wave pattern A pattern of organization in which the basic theme, often represented by a phrase, is repeated again and again, much like a wave cresting, receding, and then cresting again.

wide-band concentration Listening that focuses on patterns rather than details.

zone of interaction Area of audience in which speaker and audience members can make eye contact.

Credits

Index